The Portuguese
and the
Straits of Melaka,
1575–1619

Power, Trade and Diplomacy

The Portuguese
and the
Straits of Melaka,
1575–1619

Power, Trade and Diplomacy

Paulo Jorge de Sousa Pinto
Translated by Roopanjali Roy

NUS PRESS
SINGAPORE

THE MALAYSIAN BRANCH OF
THE ROYAL ASIATIC SOCIETY

Published by:

NUS Press
National University of Singapore
AS3-01-02, 3 Arts Link
Singapore 117569

Fax: (65) 6774-0652
E-mail: nusbooks@nus.edu.sg
Website: http://www.nus.edu.sg/nuspress

ISBN 978-9971-69-570-5 (Paper)

and

Malaysian Branch of the Royal Asiatic Society
4B (2nd Floor) Jalan Kemuja, off Jalan Bangsar
59000 Kuala Lumpur
Malaysia
Tel: 603-2283-5345
Fax: 603-2282-2458

ISBN 978-967-9948-51-6 (Paper)

Financial support for the English translation was provided by the Fundação Oriente.

Fundação Oriente
Rua do Salitre, 66
1269-065 Lisbon
Portugal

Fax: 21 352 70 42
E-mail: info@foriente.pt
Website: http://www.foriente.pt

Cataloguing-in-Publication Data for the book is available from the National Library, Singapore and Perpustakaan Negara Malaysia.

Cover: Luís Monteiro Coutinho Fighting the Acehnese
(Manuel Godinho de Erédia, *História de Serviços com Martírio de Luís Monteiro Coutinho*, Biblioteca Nacional, Lisbon, Cod. 414.)

Typeset by: International Typesetters Pte Ltd
Printed by: Mainland Press Pte Ltd

CONTENTS

5.   The City of Melaka   171
      The Structure of the City: Population and Society
      The Centres of Power: Captain, Bishop and Casados
      Security: Fortifications, Material and Human Resources

LIST OF MAPS

LIST OF ILLUSTRATIONS

(between pp. 122 and 123)

PREFACE

As the age of imperialism and the painful process of decolonization fade into a more distant horizon, the study of European presence in Asia is experiencing something of a renaissance. Students and researchers are subjecting source materials to fresh scrutiny, shaping a fresh image of the colonial era and capturing experiences across different strata of society. Attention is now being paid to a spectrum of social processes such as acculturation, assimilation, social insertion, hybridity, marginalisation, cooperation, and globalisation.

Over the past decades, attention has been placed on the early motives, means, mechanisms and epochs of European expansion together with the social, economic, technological, religious and political factors that enabled these processes. Many older exposés upheld the three "G's" — God, gold and glory — and celebrated conquest as the triumph of a superior Europe over the other peoples around the globe. These admittedly over-simplistic paradigms of historical analysis, it would appear, have finally been fortunately relegated to the dustbin of discarded research methodologies.

Arguably, in no historical subfield have the underlying paradigms of analysis shifted more than for the early modern period. It was the 15th and 16th century that witnessed the establishment of the first European colonial settlements. Stimulus for deeper research on the latter Middle Ages and the early modern world almost certainly stemmed from a relatively recent plethora of "quincentennial celebrations" — from the "discovery" of the Cape of Good Hope (1488–1988), the Portuguese circumnavigation of the African continent (1498–1998) and the Portuguese conquest of the Melaka Sultanate to the Portuguese (1511–2011) to the Spanish "discovery" of the Americas (1492–1992) and soon also of the Pacific

Ocean (1513–2013). At an official level, these commemorations of the European reconnaissance are now being matched, and to an extent also intentionally juxtaposed, by earlier Asian — specifically Chinese — feats of maritime navigation: the great voyages of the Chinese Admiral Zheng He of the early 15th century. It can hardly escape attention that Europe's aggressive, military and expansionist programme is sharply contrasted by the (supposedly) peaceful, cultural and commercial intentions of Zheng He, that Imperial Eunuch of the Ming Dynasty whose voyages — rightly or wrongly — are celebrated in Asia as missions of "friendship" and "intercultural exchange".

Thanks to considerable research funds generously made available in recent times from both private and public sponsors, the topic of European presence in Asia from the late 1400s to the late 1700s is experiencing a revival. The now classic works of Boxer, Chaudhuri, Furber, Lach, MacGregor, Meilink-Roelofsz, Reid, Schrieke, Thomaz, or Van Leur — just to select a handful of examples — are now supplemented by a growing pool of historical studies that revisit known source materials, and sometimes also draw on rare prints or recently (re-) discovered manuscripts. With respect to 16th- and 17th-century Southeast Asia, Portuguese and Dutch sources certainly retain their pre-eminent position in scholarly circles. But recent studies are making more extensive use of documents, reports and cartographical materials written in European languages including Danish, English, French, German, Italian, Latin, Portuguese and Spanish.

Under the editorship of Armando Cortesão, the Hakluyt Society in London published the *Suma Oriental* of Tomé Pires with English translation in two volumes. With the benefit of hindsight, this bi-lingual edition marked a major breakthrough for the study of early modern Southeast Asia generally speaking. It has proven especially important to historians of Asia examining the dynamics of regional and long-distance inter-Asian trade and it has proven to be an invaluable source for understanding of that important period of transition between the Melaka Sultanate and Portuguese colonial port settlement. In this context one invariably thinks of the landmark studies by Luís Filipe R. Thomaz, Professor of History at the Universidade Católica in Lisbon, who has so meticulously combed the histories, documents and chronicles of Portuguese expansion. From the information he has gleaned from this pool of sparsely studied materials, he has cogently reconstructed an image of early colonial Melaka that was embedded in a patchwork of interlocked and overlapping commercial networks and found itself surrounded by competing, sometimes expanding polities that sustained a fragile but ever-shifting balance of power in Malaya, the Indonesian Archipelago and naturally also further afield. There can be little doubt that Thomaz has left for himself an enduring place in the history writing of the Malay world, and arguably Southeast Asia at large.

The present study *The Portuguese and the Straits of Melaka, 1575–1619: Power, Trade and Diplomacy* by Paulo Pinto fruitfully draws on new historiographical trends and builds carefully on the accomplishments of Thomaz as well as other internationally recognized scholars from Europe, Asia and beyond. The work was originally completed as a *mestrado* thesis for the Universidade Nova in Lisbon in 1994 and was first published in a revised Portuguese language edition in 1997. The period Pinto has chosen is a relatively narrow one — 1573/5 to 1619 — that spans an exciting yet highly problematic period for the Portuguese *Estado da Índia*. Geographically and thematically the author's attention is focused on the inter-dependent, triangular relationship between Portuguese Melaka, Johor and Aceh and is limited in time from the Acehnese attacks on Melaka (1573/5) to the establishment of Dutch Batavia under Jan Pieterszoon Coen (1619). In contrast to the earlier decades of the 16th century, the period between 1573 and ca. 1605 is far less familiar to present-day students and researchers. Several reasons stand behind Pinto's choice of this period. With the end of the Melaka sultanate in 1511, regional power constellations were to change dramatically. By the second half of the 16th century two "successor polities" of the fallen Melaka sultanate, namely Johor and Aceh, rapidly emerged as formidable agents of trade, diplomacy and war. Portuguese presence in the region also affected the regional balance of power, but the end of the 1500s sees the *Estado da Índia* grappling with a range of institutional, financial and security problems. Its interests are seriously threatened by armed competition from Northern European traders and the East India Companies: the English, French, Danes, and especially the Dutch. Some of the East India Companies, notably the Dutch VOC, entered into alliances with Asian princes with the aim of wresting colonial strongholds from Portuguese control. These attacks initially scored a mixed success. The attack on the Moluccas proved successful in the early 1600s, but Melaka, that celebrated city of spices and commerce, was plucked from Lusitanian control only in 1641 after several failed attacks on that colony.

The late 1500s and early 1600s remain a period when Portuguese business intelligence, familiarity with the region, cartography, technical know-how and diplomatic savvy were important. The period of transition between the late 1500s and early 1600s saw a veritable explosion in Europe of documenting the produce, marketplaces, peoples and customs of Southeast Asia. The majority of these reports were written in Portuguese, but increasingly also in other European languages including Dutch, French, German, Italian, Latin, and Spanish. These later European accounts doubtlessly processed or based their insights on earlier Portuguese accounts. Jan Huyghen van Linschoten's *Reysgeschrift* (1595) and *Itinerario* (1596) can be taken as classic examples of how earlier Portuguese materials were collated, translated, and published.

Without doubt, at the heart of Pinto's work stands the city, port and Portuguese colony of Melaka. He underscores that Portuguese-language documentation dating from the second half of the 16th century appears to be beset with puzzling assessments and sometimes outright contradictions that require careful reading and evaluation. To appreciate this body of documentation more fully it is imperative to place problematic statements or accounts within their proper social, political, economic, diplomatic and geo-strategic context. Pinto displays a special interest in ascertaining diverging forces that nudged toward social and institutional assimilation in Portuguese Melaka on the one hand, and written instructions received from superiors in Goa or Lisbon on the other. Although Melaka was located at the crossroads of principal, converging networks of trade from the South China Sea, the Indonesian Archipelago and the Gulf of Bengal, the Portuguese colony found itself relatively removed and detached from the political centre of the *Estado da Índia* in Goa, and even more so from the colonial metropolis Lisbon. As a result, some higher ranking officers of Melaka, those men-on-the-spot, enjoyed considerable leeway for independent action and decision-making. In order to appreciate more fully the forces broadly underlying these specifically locational contradictions, as well as the perceived symptoms of institutional decay and corruption, Pinto sees it appropriate to first delve into a more comprehensive examination and evaluation of the regional economic, political, diplomatic, military, and social context. This multi-faceted approach gradually narrows toward the city through what Pinto calls "concentric circles". This enables not only a deeper appreciation of Portuguese Melaka in the late 1500s and early 1600s, but through his perusal of Portuguese primary materials makes a noteworthy contribution toward reconstructing the internal histories of the Johor and Aceh sultanates in the late 16th and early 17th century.

To researchers interested in early colonial Melaka who are proficient in the Portuguese language, Paulo Pinto's study is of course already well known. It is a work that has already impacted the field, even if it may have been supplemented since the completion of this study during the early 1990s by a growing body of historical studies focusing on the Luso-Dutch conflict in Southeast Asia at the dawn of the 17th century. Nevertheless, this work remains a seminal and arguably unsurpassed study covering Johor-Melaka-Aceh relations during the final quarter of the 16th century. The present English translation now makes this interesting and useful study accessible to a far wider, non-Lusophone audience, and readers will find the present edition doubly useful for its documentary appendices. In this sense, Pinto's work also serves as a handy reference volume that contains valuable primary sources. Given his extensive archival research and deep familiarity with surviving Portuguese-language documentary materials as well as more recent secondary studies, this study retains its usefulness to the historians of the Malay Peninsula and of Sumatra at the close of the 16th century.

Peter Borschberg

ACKNOWLEDGEMENTS

This book is a revised and updated version of the original Portuguese edition, published under the title *Portugueses e Malaios: Malaca e os Sultanatos de Johor e Achém, 1575–1619* in 1997 by the Sociedade Histórica da Independência de Portugal in Lisbon. It is based upon a Masters thesis presented at the Faculdade de Ciências Sociais e Humanas of the Universidade Nova de Lisboa. I would like to express my thanks to some of the people who, throughout this process, contributed towards this work.

I am indebted in the first place to Luís Filipe Thomaz for the scientific guidance and friendly support he has always given me, and I would like to express my foremost and most profound thanks to him. Secondly, my thanks to my colleagues in the Masters course, who helped this study in many ways, from providing advice, research clues or bibliographic indications, especially to Manuel Lobato, with whom I discussed at length many of the questions contained herein and to whom I am indebted for important pointers and suggestions.

Most of the research work during the preparation of the Masters thesis was facilitated by the financial support of the Fundação Oriente, without which this work would not have been possible. I am grateful to this institution, as well as to the Instituto (now Centro) de História de Além-Mar of the Universidade Nova for the support provided for the bibliographic and archival research abroad.

The original Portuguese edition of this work was published due to the generosity of the Sociedade Histórica da Independência de Portugal and the efforts of the then Vice-President of this institution, João Paulo Oliveira e Costa, to whom I would like to reiterate my thanks.

I am indebted to NUS Press in Singapore and the Malaysian Branch of the Royal Asiatic Society, more precisely to Peter Borschberg, Paul Kratoska and Peter Schoppert, for publishing the English version of this work, as also, once more, to the Fundação Oriente for the financial support extended to this edition. My most sincere thanks to all of them.

Abbreviations

Libraries and Archives/*Collections*

AGI   Archivo General de Indias (Seville)
AGS   Archivo General de Simancas
           Secr. Prov. – Secretarias Provinciales
AHU   Arquivo Histórico Ultramarino (Lisbon)
           Cons. Ultr. – Conselho Ultramarino
AN/TT   Arquivos Nacionais / Torre do Tombo (Lisbon)
           ColVic. – Colecção de S. Vicente
           CorCron. – Corpo Cronológico
           MiscMssCGL – Miscelâneas Manuscritas do Convento da Graça de Lisboa
           MssLiv. – Manuscritos da Livraria
           NuclAnt. – Núcleo Antigo
BA   Biblioteca da Ajuda (Lisbon)
BM   British Museum (London)
           Add. – Additional Manuscripts
BN   Biblioteca Nacional (Lisbon)
           Res. – Reservados
BNM   Biblioteca Nacional de Madrid
HAG   Historical Archives of Goa (Panaji-Goa)
           MonçReino – Monções do Reino

Document Collections

AC   *Arquivo das Colónias*
ACE   *Assentos do Conselho de Estado* (ed. P. S. S. Pissurlencar)

ACF	*Assentos do Conselho da Fazenda* (ed. V. T. Gune)
AIA	*Archivo Ibero-Americano*
APO	*Archivo Portuguez Oriental* (ed. J. H. da Cunha Rivara)
BAHC	*Boletim do Arquivo Histórico Colonial*
BOGEI	*Boletim Oficial do Governo do Estado da Índia*
CAA	*Cartas de Afonso de Albuquerque* (ed. A. R. de Bulhão Pato)
DHMPPO	*Documentação para a História do Padroado Português do Oriente* (ed. A. Silva Rego/ A. Basílio de Sá)
DI	*Documenta Indica* (ed. J. Wicki)
DM	*Documenta Malucensia* (ed. H. Jacobs)
DRI	*Documentos Remet(t)idos da Índia* (ed. A. R. de Bulhão Pato *et al.*)
DUP	*Documentação Ultramarina Portuguesa*
HPAF	*Historia de la Provincia Agustiniana del Santísimo Nombre de Jesús de Filipinas* (ed. Isacio Rodríguez Rodríguez)
LREIC	*Letters Received by the East India Company* (ed. F. C. Danvers and W. Foster)
PI	*The Philippine Islands* (ed. E. H. Blair and J. A. Robertson)

Journals

JMBRAS	*Journal of the Malayan/ Malaysian Branch of the Royal Asiatic Society*
JSBRAS	*Journal of the Straits Branch of the Royal Asiatic Society*
JSEAH	*Journal of Southeast Asian History*
JSEAS	*Journal of Southeast Asian Studies*
MAS	*Modern Asian Studies*

Introduction

Much work still remains to be done on the history of the Portuguese presence in the Orient. Despite the plethora of several recent studies about Southeast Asia, important lacunae still persist, especially with regard to the period from the end of the 16th century onwards. Portuguese historiography has suffered from two ills—fortunately overcome in recent times—which contributed decisively to this phenomenon.

First, it focused upon Goa, the Malabar coast and the western half of the Indian Ocean or, at the other end of the globe, upon Macao, as areas of a more enduring Portuguese influence. In the midst of this, the Coromandel coast, Bengal, the Malay Peninsula or the Archipelago were frequently overlooked. In Portugal there is no tradition of historiography of Southeast Asia. Yet the discovery of Tomé Pires' *Suma Oriental*, as well as the commendable heuristic and editorial endeavours, in the footsteps of Cunha Rivara, by names such as Silva Rego, Basílio de Sá and Joseph Wicki made a wide array of hitherto unpublished sources available to historiographers. On the other hand, the pioneering work of Luís Filipe Thomaz, endowed with a vast and profound knowledge of the history of Asiatic civilisations, resulted in the creation of a small school of researchers inclined towards studying the Portuguese presence in the Orient, frequently focusing upon areas that were virtually untouched by the national panorama of historiography: Burma, Siam, Sumatra, the Moluccas or the Sea of Sri Lanka, amongst others. Unfortunately, most of this research is available only in Portuguese, which considerably reduces its impact and the circulation that it undoubtedly deserves.

Secondly, the concept of the decadence of the Estado da Índia persisted for a long time, rooted in the idea that the initial rapid advances, especially with the feats of Afonso de Albuquerque, were followed by stagnation and an inevitable decadence, thus reducing a substantial part of the 16th century and subsequent periods to a prolonged and painful decline. According to this traditional idea, the Portuguese retreated on all fronts, steeped in corruption, religious intolerance, administrative in-efficiency and military debacles. It was not unusual to find the utilisation of racial explanations to substantiate this theory, tracing some sort of Portuguese decadence to racial intermixing and the consequent weakening of the stock by the likes of Afonso de Albuquerque, Duarte Pacheco Pereira and so many others. The Habsburg period, long viewed as a dark age in the history of Portugal, further accentuated this idea of decadence. The recent reformulation of this concept and many others, leading to a global reconsideration of the Portuguese expansion at the heart of political, social and economic structures in Asia, tends to open new paths and enables a more profound study of contact between civilisations that began at the end of the 15th century, now that the fog generated by the ideologies of history and the repercussions of the so-called colonial period and its sequels has, to all appearances, been dispelled.

However, the Portuguese panorama of historiography of Southeast Asia still continues to be very meagre. It is even sparser with regard to this particular period. Thus, first and foremost, this work seeks to contribute towards a better understanding of the history of the Portuguese presence in an age and an area which have yet to be studied sufficiently, gathering together in a single work data and approaches which have been dealt with by various authors in a fragmentary manner.

The questions generated around the analysis and study of sources are a fundamental element of any historical study. In the case of this book, many obstacles were encountered along the way. First, despite the work carried out by the aforementioned authors, an important number of the Portuguese sources for this period are still widely scattered and/or unpublished. Many are still waiting to be discovered in Portuguese archives in Simancas or in Seville. What has been published is very often innocuous, repetitive or irrelevant and of limited use, especially with regard to local history.

One of the more serious lacunae of this study is related to my own linguistic limitations: my lack of familiarity with Dutch and an insufficient knowledge of Malay. Owing to the former, Dutch sources, of fundamental importance with regard to the period dating from the early 17th century onwards, were thus out of reach. The same was the case with Malay sources. In both cases I resorted to the available translations in English or French that, despite their undeniable importance, certainly do not fill the breach. In addition, it was possible to access these sources, albeit indirectly, through the works of diverse historians who have cited or utilised them.

Throughout the preparation of this study, another fact gradually became apparent: although Portuguese historiography, in general, is ignorant of Malay and Dutch sources, perhaps on account of linguistic obstacles, it is also obvious that historians working on Southeast Asia are equally ignorant of Portuguese sources, for precisely the same reasons. Names such as Charles Boxer, Denys Lombard, Peter Borschberg and Sanjay Subrahmanyam are distinguished exceptions to this rule, as are those of Alfredo Botelho de Sousa, Luís Filipe Thomaz and Jorge dos Santos Alves on the Portuguese side. Excerpts from the works of Godinho de Erédia and Diogo do Couto are the main sources used by foreign authors as they are available in English translations. Consequently, important document sources for the history of Southeast Asia prior to the arrival of northern Europeans (and even after this) escape great historians who avoid this issue, or gingerly proceed with great care, when they deal with the 16th century. The lacunae about the Portuguese period in general works are themselves highly revealing.[1]

Thus, the second objective of this work can be delineated: to attempt to enrich the Portuguese panorama of studies about Southeast Asia, introducing some of the more important historiography as well as some non-

---

[1]	Some examples are the absence of a chapter dedicated to the Portuguese period in the major work edited by K. Sandhu and P. Wheatley, *Melaka: The Transformation of a Malay Capital c.1400–1980*, the laconic article 'Melaka' in *Encyclopedia of Islam* or the brief chapter about the Portuguese (Khasnor binti Johan's 'The Portuguese in Malaya') in the general work of Malay history *Glimpses of Malay History* edited by Zainal Abidin Wahid.

Portuguese sources, about which there is very little awareness in Portugal. Likewise, it aims to gather, introduce and analyse some Portuguese sources, both published and unpublished, for the period under review so that, in some way, they might comprise a useful contribution to the study of local history, and bring them to the attention of great historians who specialise in the history of these areas. This English edition is definitely a major step in that direction.

A research project in the field of history is not necessarily intended to realise sensational innovations or present revolutionary revelations and proposals. However, one would hope that it contributes in some way to the advancement of the study of the history of human societies, unravelling historical source material in the first instance but also, wherever possible, defining or propounding approaches, issues and problematic questions, putting forth new data or simply reformulating or interpreting in a new light material that is already known but has not yet been analysed in a satisfactory manner. In any case, a careful definition of the starting point, a delineation of the scope of the study and being able to recognise its limitations are of fundamental importance.

In this case, the approach that was chosen defines the very essence of this work itself: the geopolitics of Melaka, at the crossroads of the Estado da Índia and the local structures and environment that surrounded it, within a well-defined span of time of about half a century (between 1575 and 1619). There are two ideas that serve as a unifying element, guideline and the very backbone of this study: placing Portuguese Melaka within the local context that surrounded it and the exhaustion of its role as a great centre of commerce. The concept of decadence is, perhaps, in this particular case not applicable to Melaka and that of exhaustion, which began immediately after the Portuguese conquest and was exacerbated by the transformations of the second half of the 16th century, is perhaps more apt. This rupture was finally and irreversibly hastened from the early years of the following century on account of an easily identifiable factor: the seas of the Archipelago witnessed the arrival of the English and the Dutch. This factor would short-circuit the foundations of Portuguese political stability in the region (in much the same way as it would throughout the Indian Ocean region), deprive the Portuguese strongholds of their economic mainstays, upset the geopolitical balance upon which the city's power depended and act as an effective catalyst for the erosion of the Portuguese structures of the Estado da Índia, which were unable to adjust to this new threat.

What seems equally clear is that, despite all the flaws of the Portuguese administration, all the abuse of power and tyranny of the captains and officials with regard to the merchants and all the decline to which Melaka was subjected throughout the 16th century, the city's position at the heart of the Malay World continued unshaken. One cannot overlook the fact that the last few years of that century witnessed the strengthening of Melaka within the geopolitical balance, the re-establishment of a large part of the mercantile communities who had fled after the sieges of 1568–75, 1582 and 1587 and the overnight fortunes of the officials who held the post of captain of the fortress. It was only with the arrival of a hostile and politically corrosive power that wielded economic strength and military might that the Portuguese edifice caved in, trade shrank and became fragmented, the fleets of the armadas found themselves reduced in terms of power, number and form. Curiously, this gradual contraction that began in the period 1603–06 and accelerated after 1619 emphasised a characteristic that had been obvious throughout the course of the preceding century: the split between the Portuguese presence and the official Estado da Índia. The penetration of the Portuguese had been facilitated by racial intermixing with local societies and the adaptation of Portuguese models to the local environment.

Clearly lacking the qualifications to realise an adequate study of this perspective in global terms, I shall limit myself to endeavouring to trace it from the political point of view, in an attempt to characterise Melaka as a centre of power in its different forms, and trace its evolution throughout the period under study. However, this cannot be done without running some risks. First, the artificiality of examining a single current in a complex whole, in this case focusing upon the political and geopolitical aspect to the detriment of an economic approach, in a historic environment where political life was inextricably associated with commerce and the conditions in which the latter evolved. Secondly, the risk of an excessive reliance on source material, especially Portuguese sources, a potential fount of error and distortion, thus resulting in the risk of overvaluing both the sources themselves as well as the Portuguese structures within the historical context under consideration. Finally, the depth and level of detail that one is sometimes obliged to provide in order to discuss some issues, such as the description of some stages in Melaka's history, could potentially result in a tendency to focus more on description as opposed to an in-depth analysis, thus diverting one's attention from important central issues. The avoidance of these risks or minimising them is a fundamental concern of this study.

It was for precisely this reason that the chapters dedicated to the confusing genealogical history of the sultanates of Johor and Aceh were removed from the main body of the text and converted into annexes.

Why did I delineate the period 1575–1619? The year 1575 was chosen as it represented a fundamental landmark for Melaka: the last siege of the city by Aceh within the context of a vast anti-Portuguese alliance carried out throughout the Indian Ocean region during the 1560s in the aftermath of the Battle of Talikota, and the definitive failure of this movement. An alternative date would undoubtedly have been 1568, as the year of the first of the sieges that took place in this context. Furthermore, 1575 is the year in which the Portuguese lost Ternate, which thus completed the disorganisation of the Portuguese presence in the Eastern Archipelago in a definitive manner and put an end to any pretensions of monopolising the spice trade in this region. This coincided with important changes at the heart of the Portuguese structures in the Indian Ocean that were evident from the middle of the 16th century onwards. As for 1619, it marks the year in which the fate of Melaka was sealed, with the conquest of Jakarta and the foundation of Batavia by Jan Pieterszoon Coen, which would develop into the centre of Dutch power in the East and was situated at the very doorstep of Melaka. The Portuguese lost Melaka in 1641, but it was in 1619 that Melaka 'fell' into the hands of the Dutch, not by conquest but owing to a gradual subordination and suffocation by a hostile rising power.

For a more balanced view of the subject of this study I have proceeded to divide it into segments, defining the internal structure in the following manner. The structure of the scheme has been organised in concentric circles, with a view to approaching questions, tracing the evolution and trajectory of the issues, pointing out contrasts and defining Melaka's positioning. The first two chapters deal with the global context of the Indian Ocean region and the Estado da Índia from an economic, political and military point of view. The next two chapters trace the regional context of the western part of the Archipelago, by means of a chronological approach to the state of affairs followed by a study of the geopolitics of the Straits, dealing separately with each one of the vertices of the region's political triangle. Finally, I shall expand upon the city of Melaka itself, tracing its internal structure and evolution as well as its metamorphosis from a cosmopolitan city to a ghetto-city in the period in question.

Finally, there are the appendices. The tables and maps presented here aim to clarify this study, the former by means of the presentation of supplementary information and the latter by providing a geographical framework for the themes under review. The list of the captains of Melaka was prepared as a result of the errors detected in various works that were consulted. Thus the task of carrying out a suitable correction was realised, in accordance with the available sources. As has already been mentioned, Annexes I and II contain information pertaining to the genealogical history of the sultanates of Johor and Aceh, given that, in reality, they form an autonomous text with regard to the rest of this study.

The important role played by the civilisations of Southeast Asia—and, amongst them, those of the Malay World—in Asian history is something that is already readily acknowledged today. The pioneering studies by J. C. van Leur and B. Schrieke, amongst others, followed by the notable critique and synthesis by M. A. P. Meilink-Roelofsz and a whole new school of historiography would emphasise and highlight the role of this part of the world. Far from being a mere depository for the influence of the great centres of civilisation in India and China, or a simple point of passage for the maritime connections established between them, from very early on Southeast Asia possessed its own distinct identity and played a far greater role in the overall evolution of Asiatic civilisations than the traditional diffusionist visions would have one believe. The development of the maritime factor in the heart of the 'Mediterranean' of the Malay-Indonesian Archipelago with the empire of Sri Vijaya and, later, with the city of Melaka that claimed to be its direct successor played a notable role in the context of the history of Southeast Asia.

Historians lavish a great deal of their attention on Melaka, given that the city played a pivotal role in the great phenomena that took place in the history of Southeast Asia during the Modern Age. Melaka was an important axis that linked the different maritime routes of the Indian Ocean, and it was here that the prized spices of the Eastern Archipelago would mingle together and be redistributed in the light of an ever-increasing demand. Melaka also played a vital role in the diffusion of Islam throughout Southeast Asia, simultaneously acting as a catalyst for the initial process. Finally, it was Melaka that captured the attention of the Portuguese and the conquest of this city heralded the establishment of a permanent European presence in the region. Thus Melaka was the main protagonist in the intensification of economic activities in the Indian Ocean and the development of the maritime factor at the very heart of the Asian scenario that unfolded from the 14th century onwards, which the Portuguese expansion would broaden and intensify.

The spectacular Portuguese exploits in the Indian Ocean region, facilitated by the direct maritime connection with Lisbon, were also felt in Southeast Asia with the conquest of Melaka in 1511, part of Afonso de Albuquerque's game-plan to ensure control over the spice trade of the Malay-Indonesian Archipelago and over navigation in general in the eastern Indian Ocean region. With regard to the specific conditions of the functioning of the emporium, care was taken to try and maintain the structure of the Malay sultanate unaltered: the territorial empire was left in the hands of the sultan, the fiscal policy of attracting mercantile communities was kept intact and the new lords of the city manifested purely commercial intentions. In short, only the political head of the territory was substituted. Even some political and administrative posts of the sultanate were maintained, albeit with different functions. With regard to mercantile traffic, the Portuguese aimed at establishing a monopoly over the most important commodities—spices—and maintain the existing customs policies over other goods. This was the project that the Portuguese tried to implement after the conquest of Melaka.

During the initial decades of the century the Portuguese proceeded to establish, by means of conquests, alliances with local authorities and the transfer of territories, important bases throughout Maritime Asia which would form the structure later known as the Estado da Índia, an empire that was essentially a maritime entity, a multi-polar network linked through an economic, political and military structure aimed at controlling and exploiting trade routes and commerce. With regard to the case of Southeast Asia, one must emphasise that, contrary to the western Indian Ocean where diverse tensions soon necessitated a reinforcement of the military element, here the Portuguese only had Melaka and a few small fortresses in the Moluccas. All of the vast region that extended from the Coromandel coast to Japan lacked the string of fortresses that was so typical of the west coast of India. This is what L. F. Thomaz has termed the 'Guinean model',[2] adopted due to the absence of a climate of endemic war as existed elsewhere.

---

[2]   Thomaz uses it combined with a 'Moroccan model', which defined the other side of the Portuguese Estado da Índia, the result of a process of interaction and learning on African shores; 'Les Portugais dans les Mers de l'Archipel', p. 105; *De Ceuta a Timor*, p. 213.

Once Melaka had been conquered, their presence in the islands that produced spices had been established, and the route to the Far East had been opened up. The Portuguese no doubt hoped for a calm dominion, one that was less turbulent than that which existed in the western Indian Ocean. However, things did not go according to plan. Here, too, an adverse combination of events emerged that would make its presence felt in the second half of the century. The sultanate of Melaka did not disappear; it was transferred to Johor, at the doorstep of Melaka, where it soon began to compete with and directly threaten Portuguese power. The rich and powerful Gujarati community, which had been dominant in the past, withdrew and established itself to the west, in the new Sumatran sultanate of Aceh that gradually emerged as Melaka's main rival.

A substantial part of Melaka's commercial structure as a central hub witnessed considerable fragmentation and dispersion, which then established in new nuclei that competed with Melaka, depriving the city of its primacy in the economic life of the region. Nevertheless, the Portuguese managed to maintain Melaka as a first-rate emporium in the Indian Ocean region, gradually integrating and adapting themselves to prevailing conditions, being prime contenders for control over navigation in the Straits and claiming exclusive access over the spice trade of the Eastern Archipelago. The arrival of the Portuguese in Japan and the foundation of Macao completed the circle, definitively opening up the gates for Portuguese commerce in the region and enabling direct access to the rich wares of the Far East. Portuguese expansion had reached its zenith, and its naval power enabled a substantial capacity for intervention and dissuasion in the region. Here there was no threat that was comparable to the situation that prevailed in, for example, Gujarat or the Malabar area. Any rivalries were, just like the essence of the Portuguese presence in the region, essentially economic, and the attacks to which Melaka was subjected did not constitute a serious cause for alarm.

In the second half of the century, this panorama changed. Anti-Portuguese rivalries appeared throughout Maritime Asia, sometimes organised in a common front united around Islamic solidarity, which competed both economically and militarily with the Estado da Índia. Simultaneously, the Portuguese structures, which had modified and adapted themselves with a greater or lesser degree of success to new times replete with new difficulties, began to evidence signs of wear and tear. The monopolies existed merely on paper, and even control of the routes was increasingly threatened and, on occasion, even lost. The political union of Portugal and Castille would result in new scenarios, eliminate internal attrition and create new economic and political conditions, but would also integrate new elements of tension, attract new dangers and incur new risks. The late 16th century was, thus, a period of economic and military difficulties, a period characterised by growing external tensions and internal changes, and is thus of considerable interest to historians. Finally, the arrival of the English and the Dutch would, unexpectedly, cause an acceleration of the decline in the heart of the Estado da Índia and condemn any attempt to realise processes of reform or recovery to failure. It was only from this point in time onwards that one can discern an accentuated decline and the aggravated contraction, in both economic and political terms, of the Portuguese dominion in the Indian Ocean region, more concretely in Southeast Asia, along with the inefficiency and failure of their attempts to invert an increasingly unfavourable state of affairs.

CHAPTER 1

Melaka and the Estado da Índia: The Economic Backdrop

The union of the crowns of Portugal and Castille under the same king in 1581 had consequences in Asia, namely in the anti-meridian of Tordesillas. As the Spanish already had a presence in the Philippines, midway between Melaka and the Far East, their relations with the Estado da Índia underwent some alterations with this new development. The tension between the two entities was now substantially reduced. Nevertheless, although commercial contacts between the two hemispheres were successively prohibited, Spanish interference in the Archipelago, namely in the Moluccas, as well as an increase of contraband activities, was a constant feature. The blurring of the distinction between the two spheres of influence became evident, as can be seen from the development of the Manila–Macao connection, the support the Portuguese fortress of Tidore received from the Philippines or the penetration of Spanish missionaries into Japan and the resulting dramatic effects upon the local Portuguese presence. However, the most important effect of the political union would take place in Europe, with the hostility of the northern European nations now being extended to the Portuguese, who thus saw themselves dragged into a geopolitical game and a conflict on a worldwide scale that they obviously did not desire. They would also be the first to suffer the devastating effects of this configuration in the short term. When Philip I closed Portuguese ports to English and Dutch vessels, he immediately provoked a race to control the sources of the spice trade, located in the Portuguese hemisphere. In military terms, the seas of the Malay-Indonesian Archipelago were, undoubtedly, the weakest link of the Estado da Índia, and it was here that the European competition struck their deepest blows. The consequences would prove to be disastrous for the Portuguese interests.

Melaka's grandeur had been achieved as a result of the economic traffic that the Straits commanded as a privileged channel for the passage of goods. It was an emporium founded on, and sustained by, trade. Without its usual commercial traffic, without being able to play the role of a junction of different routes for diverse and complementary products, Melaka was worthless. Thus one can understand the interest shown immediately after the Portuguese conquest, which would be incessantly invoked later when their problems multiplied, in maintaining a policy of attracting mercantile communities. In the second half of the century this would become a pressing issue, all the more so because the changes at the heart of the Portuguese structures now considerably aggravated this problem: an increase in the all-pervading power of the captains and the growing pressure exerted upon the city's economic life, the privatisation of commerce and the Crown's withdrawal from the direct exploitation of the routes, the loss of control over the traffic in spices (now dominated by the Javanese)—these were all factors that would increasingly lead to a dissipation of Melaka's former ability to attract traders and deprive it of its long-standing role as a first-rate emporium. The establishment of Dutch and English presence in the region, which was to unleash an intense and inexorable process of competition, resulted in the veritable asphyxiation of the city, which saw itself increasingly isolated and unable to claim its time-honoured role in the face of an emerging hostile power that would surpass it, supplant it and reduce it to a subaltern position.

Melaka and Its Trade

The evolution of Melaka's commerce in the second half of the 16th century evidences some rather disconcerting characteristics. The economic structure ran the risk of collapsing, given that the Portuguese had lost direct control over the most profitable dealings in the spice trade—those of the Moluccas and Banda—which was now almost entirely dominated by the Javanese, and even the Sunda pepper trade was now in the hands of the Chinese, who channelled the commodity towards the Middle Kingdom. Johor directly competed with the city for the commerce of the Eastern Archipelago, while Aceh diverted the pepper production of Sumatra to a rival network that spanned the Indian Ocean region, was sheltered in the Red Sea and competed directly with the Cape route. Both sultanates were serious threats to the city, especially Aceh, which emerged as the great bulwark of Islam in the region. Corruption and inefficiency prevailed within the Portuguese administration and the captains of the fortresses increasingly behaved like despots. Nevertheless, simultaneously we can also observe how the city continued to prosper and how the port still witnessed intense traffic. Never before had the captains and their related agents and interests made such large profits. The captaincy of Melaka, along with those of Hormuz and Mozambique, became the most profitable office in the entire Estado da Índia. The Portuguese residents of the city (the so-called *casados*) were under heavy pressure from the captains but managed to find alternative business and commercial dealings. This can only be wholly understood if we pay close attention to the changes that were made both within the official Portuguese structures as well as in the heart of Luso–Asiatic commerce.

In the case of the former, one must point out that there was a gradual emergence of the Atlantic system, based upon the colonisation of Brazil that took shape from the 1570s onwards. In contrast to the clear Asiatic options of King John III, in successive scenarios epicentres were no longer situated in Goa but rather on the Brazilian and African coasts. Under King Sebastian, the Maghrebian vector emerged as a suitable alternative. In the East, the Portuguese Crown gradually withdrew from direct exploitation of trade, preferring instead to entrust it to private hands, both as a reward for services rendered and also via simple leases, in order to obtain fixed profits paid in advance to the constantly impoverished Royal Treasury. Even the Cape route itself was leased and, as for the monopoly of the spice trade, several solutions were tested that tended to hand over effective exploitation to private individuals.[1] This is what, throughout this study, is

---

[1] Thomaz, 'Les Portugais dans les Mers de l'Archipel', pp. 107–109.

called 'privatisation' of commerce, although, as shall be seen, it did not in any way mean freedom of trade, and was cloaked in peculiar forms fuelled by the flaws of the system itself.

Economic life in Melaka was carried out in two main ways: the exploitation of the numerous lines of traffic that in one way or another terminated in Melaka—the so-called 'voyages' (*viagens*)—which were given out on lease or concession by the Crown to a beneficiary and, secondly, a customs policy that covered the traffic of diverse goods that passed through the port. This included the shorter routes that proliferated throughout the region, as well as the flow of spices from the Moluccas or Banda that was predominantly controlled by the Javanese (although the 'voyage' of the Moluccas continued to exist). We shall shortly see how both facets were affected by the growing influence of the captain's power which, at the end of the 16th century, almost totally dominated Melaka's commercial life, becoming a truly parasitical team or enterprise.

The Estado da Índia suffered from several limitations in terms of its scope, population and the military and financial structures that sustained it, as well as the limits of the age itself. A heavy structure, founded upon a military base to which the economic aspect was coupled, was dispersed across a vast stretch and equipped with technology that, albeit the most advanced of its time, was incapable of responding in a satisfactory manner to all the challenges it faced. So it inevitably suffered from the defects and flaws that time only further worsened and aggravated. Situated at almost the opposite end of the globe from Lisbon, far removed—in terms of both space and time—from Goa (the Estado's headquarters), Melaka was inevitably more sensitive to local economic and political conditions than to the orders, irrespective of how severe and incisive these might have been, that emanated from these decision-making centres. This was what happened in the case of the excessive growth in the captain's power. It was he who wielded the authority inherent in being the king's representative in the city and who controlled the military structure. Therefore, the captain of Melaka seldom encountered obstacles in the course of his tyranny and his abuse of office. When the Estado withdrew from directly intervening in trade affairs, retaining only a position of sovereignty, it was the individual who wielded power locally who took its place and appropriated the main sources of revenue.

In the first place, something may be said about the voyages. It appears to be an established fact that the initial instances of conceding them to private individuals date back to the 1550s, although by the 1560s and

1570s[2] the system would become widespread. In any case, around 1568–70 it was probably still an open question. At this time, freedom of trade and the leasing of a series of routes to private individuals, residents of Melaka or to the captain himself[3] were still advocated. However, this would result in a gradual appropriation, and not mere leasing, of the voyages. As a reliable source amply documents,[4] the captains began to benefit from a substantial number of voyages, exploiting them directly or profiting from their sale,[5] and this constituted a significant source of income. The captain of Melaka wielded ruthless control over these trade routes, establishing exclusivity with regard to the frequenting of ports or trade in their products. However, this source is no more than a global overview of the voyages that the captains were generally granted by the viceroys, or whose control they usurped. One can find specific information pertaining to each concrete case and each captain who, on account of a greater or lesser degree of connections with the viceroy's office, and a greater or lesser degree of scruples, would vary this equilibrium.

One may point to a specific case, that of Captain João da Silva,[6] who arrived in Melaka in 1585 and was one of the main protagonists of the crisis with Johor. This character, a relative of the newly appointed viceroy, Dom Duarte de Meneses, received specific concessions that were different and more extensive than those indicated in the *Livro das Cidades*

---

2   Ibid., pp. 108–109. Thomaz points to the 1570s as the period when the system was implemented. Manuel Lobato in *Política e Comércio* ..., p. 245, corrects this date, bringing it backward by about a decade.

3   'Enformação das fortalezas e lugares da India' [1568]; 'Apontamentos do Arcebispo de Goa' [1569 or 1570] in Wicki (ed.), 'Duas relações sobre a situação da Índia portuguesa ...', pp. 140–146 and 197–199.

4   Luz (ed.), *Livro das Cidades e Fortalezas ... c.1582*, a full report about the Estado da Índia and its revenues written to inform Philip I, who had recently been elected King of Portugal. The data therein have been analysed and studied by Thomaz in 'Les Portugais dans les Mers de l'Archipel', pp. 121–125. In a later period, Justus Schouten sketched the whole frame of Melaka's trade under Portuguese rule; Leupe, 'The Siege and Capture of Malacca', pp. 102–107.

5   The source mentions the voyages from Melaka to Macao, Bengal, Martaban, Tenasserim, Ujang-Selang (Phuket), Kedah, Perak, Bruas, Pahang, Patani, Cambodia, Sunda, Blambangan, Borneo, Makassar, Solor and Timor.

6   'Titulo da prouizões que leuão os capitães das fortalezas de Malaca, para bem da Capitania'. BM, *Add.* 28433, fls. 66–74v.

e Fortalezas. He was granted the voyages from Melaka to Pegu, Bengal and Macao; those from Macao to Tonkin and Java. If it had not already been granted in continental Portugal or in India, or after the grantees had concluded their voyages in 1585, he was further granted, for the duration of his captaincy, the voyages from Melaka to Banda, the Moluccas and Ambon, as well as those from Macao to Japan and Siam. In addition, he was authorised to despatch, through his factors, ships to Japan and Hormuz, and from Macao to Patani. However, the most interesting provision is the declaration allowing him to send his ships annually, 'to whichever lands he so desired'[7]—with the exception of Banda, the Moluccas and from China to Japan—on an exclusive basis. This literally enabled him to reserve for himself all the Melaka voyages and was in addition to a series of complementary powers and privileges,[8] duly justified, as well as all his other privileges, based on the argument that previous captains had received the same concessions. Undoubtedly this is an exceptional case, probably one of those that resulted in complaints from the residents of Melaka and other entities, which led to attempts to curtail these excessive privileges.

Nevertheless, the most contested aspect of the behaviour of the captains of Melaka concerned their constant and oppressive interference in private trade, both trade carried out by the residents of Melaka as well as by Asian traders, especially the Javanese, who frequented the city. These pressures took diverse forms, all aimed at plundering goods that belonged to others. In the first place, there was pure and simple intimidation, with diverse forms of exclusivity imposed both over trade in specified goods (the so-called *estanco*) as well as over journeys to stipulated ports. Secondly, there was real economic coercion with the seizure of property, the reservation of commodities (which they would buy cheaply and sell at inflated prices, frequently without investing a penny), the collection of portage on various goods and cheating on weights—buying with one and selling with another. The majority of these abuses concerned the spices

---

[7] Ibid., fl. 67v.

[8] Amongst other things, he could choose the captain of Solor and the captain-major at the ports of Patani, Siam and Solor and was authorised to purchase about 9.5 tonnes of cloves from the Moluccas, about 26.4 tonnes of nutmeg from the Banda Islands (both exempted from the payment of freights and taxes) as well as 2.5 tonnes of copper from China. About this issue, *see* Pinto, 'Captains, Sultans and *liaisons dangereuses*'.

of the Eastern Archipelago, so much so that they managed to 'obstruct' (*atravessar*) most of the volume of trade carried out in Melaka.[9]

This trend intensified during the 1590s. As far back as the time of Aires de Saldanha (1576–79), this captain had been satisfied with acquiring control over half the volume of spices that poured into the city. At the end of 1588 Bishop Dom João Ribeiro Gaio stated that the majority of duties payable at the customs house were at the rate of 7 per cent. In practice, this did not please anyone nor did it succeed in avoiding abuse by the captains.[10] Pero Lopes de Sousa (1590–93) signed an agreement with the residents in order to put an end to existing abuses of power: the captain reserved one-third for himself, the rest being freely available to residents and merchants, who would pay duties of 12 per cent at the customs house with a further 2 per cent for the weight, thus making a total of 14 per cent.[11] This appears to have been a satisfactory solution for all concerned: the Royal Treasury collected its duties, the captain reserved an important share for himself, and the merchants and the *casados*, despite bearing the brunt of the financial burden, were guaranteed access to the spices. However, in 1599 the city complained that the agreement was not being honoured, as Pero Lopes de Sousa's successors, in this case, Martim Afonso de Melo, who held the post at the time, had once again taken over control of the entire flow of spices, immediately reselling them to India.[12]

---

9   Meilink-Roelofsz, *Asian Trade and European Influence* ..., pp. 167–168. Francesco Carletti estimated the net profit earned by the captain to be about 70–80 per cent, thanks to the way he influenced the market and controlled prices. His abuses are largely corroborated in coeval documentation, after the 1570s. *See* Meilink-Roelofsz, op. cit., and Lobato, *Política e Comércio*, pp. 180–197.

10 Letter from D. João Ribeiro Gaio to the king, Melaka, 31-12-1588, fl. 404v. (*see* Document Appendix, No. 6).

11 Treatise about the trade of Melaka, *c.*1600, AN/TT, *MssLiv.* 805, fl. 158v., included by Lobato in *Política e Comércio dos Portugueses na Mundo Malaio-Indonésio* (thesis), Ap. VI, p. 446. This agreement is implicit in the *regimento* granted by Viceroy Matias de Albuquerque to the city of Melaka ('Alvará em forma de Regimento', 1595, in Pissurlencar (ed.), *Regimentos das Fortalezas da Índia*, pp. 256–257). *See* the document mentioned in note 12.

12 'Notes' from the city of Melaka to the king, 1599, BN, *Res.*, cod. 1573, fl. 57 (*see* Document Appendix, No. 10).

One of the most interesting complaints presented by those who were most affected by these actions concerns the captain's factors, in truth the most important element in this vast and sprawling enterprise that was the captaincy of Melaka. They were the real agents responsible for coercion and commercial control.[13] Their actions were especially effective and predatory in cases allegedly concerning New Christian factors, and especially so in Melaka, owing to which successive orders were issued prohibiting such incidents; these were further extended to include other non-Christians.[14] We can find part of the explanation for the aforementioned complaints made in Melaka in 1599: Captain Martim Afonso de Melo, in collusion with Viceroy Matias de Albuquerque, had employed a particularly voracious Jew as factor.[15]

The captains' power was not limited to these aspects. The control they exercised over the local administration, namely over the officials of the customs house,[16] allowed them a fair degree of peaceful existence. The official inquiries carried out at the end of their mandates were invariably inconclusive.[17] In truth, all efforts to curtail their abuses and illegal acts were in vain. Only a downturn in the city's commerce coupled with a

---

[13]   At the end of the 16th century it was estimated that these factors earned profits in the region of about 50,000–60,000 *cruzados* from 'the spices and products evaluated in customs' over the course of three years; letter from Philip I to Viceroy D. Francisco da Gama, 10-2-1598, *APO*, III, part 2, p. 828.

[14]   Letter from the city of Goa to the king, 1596, *APO*, I, part 2, p. 36; royal *alvará*, 16-1-1598, BN, *Res.*, cod. 2298, fls. 39–39v.; letter from Philip I to Viceroy D. Francisco da Gama, 18-1-1598, AN/TT, *MiscMssCGL*, box 3, vol. VIL, p. 208; letter from Philip I to the city of Goa, 1598, *APO*, I, part 1, p. 120.

[15]   Letter from Viceroy D. Francisco da Gama to the king, date unknown [1600], BN, *Res.*, cod. 1976, fl. 131; *see* 'Notes' quoted in note 12, above.

[16]   By the orders issued in 1585 (cited in note 6, above), fl. 67v., the captain of Melaka was authorised to choose all the officials of the fortress, local affairs, justice and finance. In 1612 the king gave direct orders to stop this practice, which contradicted former royal rights granted to the city; royal letter to Viceroy D. Jerónimo de Azevedo, 27-2-1612, *DRI*, II, p. 182, and royal *alvará*, 27-3-1613, *APO*, VI (ii), pp. 934–935.

[17]   About the evolution of the power of the captains of Melaka, *see* chapter 5, 'The Centres of Power'.

worsening of the political and military conditions prompted by the arrival of the Dutch would lead to a fall in their incomes. Consequently, this would cause a decrease in interest in the post, which waned in equal measure along with the very brilliance of the city itself. Up to that point the captains of Melaka accumulated sizeable revenues during the course of three years of service, which varied substantially in accordance with the scruples of each individual and the opportunities that presented themselves. The estimates for the final decades of the century, prior to the arrival of the Dutch, clearly reveal the profits obtained: Diogo do Couto estimated that Dom João da Gama (1579–82) left Melaka at the end of his tenure with a fortune of 43,200$000.[18] For the subsequent period he declared an average income of 36,000$000.[19] Francisco Rodrigues Silveira, in his pessimistic appraisal of the situation of the Estado da Índia, estimated the same profits to range between 72,000$000 and 108,000$000,[20] sums that are clearly exaggerated. Finally, we have the data contained in the report written by António Barreto da Silva, António Simões and Francisco de Sousa Falcão, who reasonably estimated that the captains' incomes were

---

[18] Couto, *Da Ásia*, X, part 1, III, xiii, p. 355. The coeval *Livro das Cidades e Fortalezas* (ed. Luz, fl. 60v.) presents the figure of 16,000$000 at the very least, as long as he didn't interfere in the spice trade and not including the voyage of Japan. The source mentions 40,000 *cruzados*, a *cruzado* most probably being taken at the standard equivalent of 400 *reis*. The exact value of the *cruzado* is still not completely clear: in Melaka it was equivalent to 360 *reis* (*see* chapter 5, note 27), but some documents and reports (mostly written and issued in Lisbon or Goa, like the *Livro* of Luís de Figueiredo Falcão and the *Lista* of Silva) prefer to use the general equivalent of 400 *reis*. Couto mentions the sum of 120,000 *pardaus*, undoubtedly using the value of 360 *reis* each, this being 'the most used in Goa' (as stated in Nunes' 'Livro dos Pesos da Índia', p. 31), and not the copper one worth 300 *reis*. This general equivalency still posed some doubts at the end of the 16th century: for instance, Viceroy D. Francisco da Gama stated that 4 *pardaus* and 3 *cruzados* had the same value, which is to say that the former was worth 300 *reis* and the latter, 400 (Letter to D. Cristóvão de Moura, unknown date [1597 or 1598], AN/TT, *MiscMssCGL*, box 6, vol. IIE, pp. 11–19).

[19] Or 100,000 *pardaus*; *O Soldado Prático*, p. 212.

[20] Or 200,000–300,000 *pardaus*; *Reformação da Milícia e Governo do Estado da Índia Oriental*, p. 190.

in the range of 48,000$000, although some did not amass more than 12,000$000.[21]

However, the activities of the captain, his abuses and the evolution of his power did not limit Melaka's economic life. In fact, the city maintained a remarkable level of activity and volume of trade. The second half of the century witnessed an increasing tendency to integrate private Portuguese trade into the heart of Asiatic structures, with a distinction between bulk volume traders, who had a firm hold on the markets and had their own capital, and small merchants who were forced to subject themselves to the conditions imposed by the former. These were the individuals who risked their lives on voyages on other people's account, or who simultaneously carried out small volumes of commerce, thus corresponding to the traditional image of *pedlar trade*. In any case, and in contrast to the initial years, the penetration of Portuguese merchants in the trading world of the Indian Ocean region, very often in partnership with Asians, was an established fact.[22]

The Crown's fiscal policy underwent several alterations during this period, with a view to enabling an increase in the volume of trade that passed through the city and the resultant taxation of this commerce. A series of fiscal reform measures was implemented, frequently in a contradictory manner. As for the trade routes, the Crown vacillated between a policy of maintaining privileges and exclusivity or opting for freedom of commerce, counting on the efficiency of a suitable customs policy. This last posture was adopted as early as the *regimento* of 1570, in which one can discern an essential preoccupation with channelling pepper and other spices via Portuguese channels.[23] However, the voyage of the Moluccas continued

---

[21] 30,000–120,000 *cruzados*; 'Lista de todas as Capitanias e Cargos que ha na India', *Revista Portugueza Colonial e Maritima*, 1900–1901 (1st sem.), p. 349. As mentioned above, this particular source says one *cruzado* was equivalent to 400 *reis* ('30,000 *cruzados* … being 40,000 *xerafins*', p. 176).

[22] Lobato, *Política e Comércio dos Portugueses no Mundo Malaio-Indonésio* (thesis), pp. 151–162; *see* Das Gupta, 'The Maritime Trade of Indonesia', p. 253.

[23] 'Regimento sobre a liberdade do trato da pimenta, drogas, e especiarias da India', 1-3-1570, *APO*, V, part 2, pp. 715–726. The debate about liberalising this commerce completely was initiated and was discussed for a few decades. Among those who defended this option was Viceroy D. Duarte de Meneses (*see* his letter to the king, 23-11-1587, AGS, *Secr. Prov.*, book 1551, fls. 72–72v.).

to be an exclusive one in which the Crown eventually accepted the participation of private capital. The galleon of this route departing from Goa or, exceptionally, from Melaka held a formal monopoly[24] of the trade line which was, however, permanently disregarded. Finally, freedom of trade with regard to the spices of the Moluccas and Banda was conceded in 1610 on condition that the customs duties were paid at the customs house in Melaka.[25] As for the rest, the voyage to the Moluccas, despite being very profitable, was long, risky and slow. The Crown sought to give it out on contract, occasionally to the captain of Melaka, but after a certain point nobody was prepared to risk such an enterprise any more.[26] This was not an isolated case: the merchants preferred to pay duties rather than contracting the traffic.[27]

Returning to the spices from the Moluccas, the methods of levying taxes on this commerce were still archaic: the old model of *terços* and *choquéis*, that is, a reservation of one-third of all merchandise to be sold at a lower price to the Royal Treasury and a percentage on account of freight,[28] respectively, still prevailed. Its application also extended to private commerce, but this was difficult to implement: they were either usurped

---

[24] *See*, for instance, the 'Alvará em forma de Regimento' from Viceroy Matias de Albuquerque, 1595 in Pissurlencar, *Regimentos das Fortalezas da Índia*, p. 264; letter from Philip I to this viceroy, 15-4-1597, *APO*, III, part 2, p. 758.

[25] In 1610, the king said that experience had shown that 'the costs to send a single carrack there [to the Moluccas and Banda] exceeded the profits because the Javanese went to the aforementioned islands to purchase these goods and took them and sold them in Melaka the same way they do today'; royal letter to Viceroy Rui Lourenço de Távora, 19-2-1610, *DRI*, I, p. 339.

[26] Letters from Philip I to Viceroy D. Francisco da Gama, 5-2-1597, *APO*, III, part 2, p. 684; 8-1-1598, ibid., p. 807.

[27] The same thing happened with regard to Chinese copper. Nobody wanted to contract this merchandise, so the viceroy decided to free its trade, as long as it was channelled through Melaka and Goa and adequate taxes were paid; letters from Philip I to Viceroy D. Francisco da Gama, 2-1-1596, *APO*, III, part 2, p. 576; 8-1-1598, ibid., p. 807; Couto, *Da Ásia*, XII, I, iii, pp. 20–21.

[28] About these taxes, as well as about the traffic from the Moluccas in general and changes therein, *see* cf. Thomaz, 'Maluco e Malaca' (in *De Ceuta a Timor*) and Manuel Lobato, *Política e Comércio*, pp. 303–322, and the sources mentioned there.

by the captains[29] or were simply not implemented for fear of the possible negative effects on the supply of provisions to the city.[30] Finally, the Crown frequently resorted to despatching ships straight from Lisbon to Melaka to load pepper, thus avoiding the habitual embezzlement. These initiatives were subject to frequent variations; for instance, orders were given to buy spices in Indragiri, Sunda or Jambi, but the Crown would recognise that it was impossible to despatch ships to transport them in the same year, thus running the risk of the Portuguese themselves selling the goods on rival circuits.[31] Opinions were divided about the utility of such initiatives, and the king himself hesitated in the face of opinions that were often contradictory. The Town Hall of Melaka frequently requested that these ships be sent because the *casados* certainly derived great profits as the ships came provided with due payment, thus freeing them from the oppression of the captain. However, the City Hall of Goa, and frequently the viceroys themselves, opposed such moves.[32]

The second half of the century witnessed a flourishing trade with China and Japan, which became—and continued to be, even well into the 17th century—the mainstay of both the city and the Royal Treasury.[33]

---

[29] For instance, *see* the royal letter to Viceroy D. Duarte de Meneses, 11-2-1585, *APO*, III, part 1, p. 39 (also published in *DHMPPO/Insulíndia*, V, p. 36); letter of the *vedor da fazenda* (treasury inspector) to the king, 8-11-1589, BN, *Res.*, cod. 9861, fl. 27v.

[30] Letter from Philip I to Viceroy D. Duarte de Meneses, 28-1-1588, *APO*, III, part 1, pp. 125–126 (also published in *DHMPPO/Insulíndia*, V, p. 82).

[31] As an example, in 1589 there were 800 *bares* (more than 168 tonnes) of pepper in Melaka bought by Portuguese merchants ready to be sent to Lisbon, but there was no way of sending it because the Crown failed to send a carrack directly to the city. The governor recognised that this pepper could be lost or sent to Mecca 'through the Moors of Aceh' (letter from Governor Manuel de Sousa Coutinho to the king, AGS, *Secr. Prov.*, book 1551, fl. 775).

[32] The city suffered, and even the king himself recognised the loss of tax revenues (Letter of Philip I to the city of Goa, 28-1-1588, *APO*, I, part 1, pp. 99–100, and to Viceroy D. Francisco da Gama, *APO*, III, part 2, p. 828; *see* another letter to Viceroy Aires de Saldanha, 25-1-1601, HAG, *MonçReino*, 7, fl. 34v.; other copies of the same letter, fls. 10–24, 53–64 v., 67–77 and 112–122 v., published in *BOGEI*, No. 46 (1880), p. 314).

[33] Luz (ed.), *Livro das Cidades e Fortalezas ...*, fls. 58–59 v.; 'Alvará em forma de Regimento', cited above, p. 260.

The diverse voyages related to this trade, be they from Melaka to Macao, from Macao to Japan or to Tonkin, Siam or Cambodia, were linked with Melaka and therefore were equally liable to pressure on the part of the captains.[34] The Crown's fiscal policy was designed in such a way so as to allow no means of escaping the duties payable on such an important trade, which accounted for the bulk of customs revenues. However, it was unable to prevent abuses and fiscal evasion in much the same way as happened with the spice trade.[35]

In order to complete the scenario, one must also highlight the important westerly trade route in Indian textiles, which complemented the spice trade. This was an important, rich and extremely profitable trade[36] which played a vital role in Melaka's position as a commercial centre. It was with regard to precisely this trade that the Crown would develop, directly and indirectly, considerable fiscal measures: in 1594 it applied a 6 per cent exit tax on all goods bound for the Coromandel coast, as well as for Pegu and Java, as there were no customs houses there. These were goods that were formerly routed to Goa, where they would pay duties, which the astute merchants had thus managed to avoid.[37] However, this measure represented a substantial fiscal surcharge, given that it resulted in a double taxation of Melaka's commerce. Irrespective of whether it was Coromandel textiles that were exchanged for spices, or the reverse, they paid entrance duties in advance. This led to a considerable loss in

[34] *See* the privileges granted to João da Silva in 1585 above, notes 6 and 7. The captain of Melaka took 2 per cent of all the goods on their way to China and controlled the flow of pepper destined for the Middle Kingdom. Pepper was, however, replaced by other goods because Chinese merchants successfully controlled pepper exports from Banten and Sunda; letter from Viceroy D. Jerónimo de Azevedo to the captain-major of the China fleet, 2-5-1613, *APO*, VI (ii), p. 958; royal letter to the same viceroy, 9-3-1614, *DRI*, III, pp. 125–126.

[35] Letter from Philip I to Viceroy D. Francisco da Gama, 9-3-1596, *APO*, III, part A, p. 614; copies of letters from the viceroy to the king, unknown date, [1597?], BN, *Res.*, cod. 1976, fl. 62.

[36] *See* Coutre, 'Vida de Jacques de Coutre', p. 372.

[37] Royal order of 24-1-1594, *APO*, V, part 3, pp. 1364–1365 (also in AHU, *Cons. Ultr.*, cod. 281, fls. 254 v.–255, and in HAG, *Provisões e Regimentos*, 1, fl. 103).

competitiveness as well as jeopardising the city's supply of provisions.[38] Insistent orders were issued to implement this measure, but they were either not carried out or implemented only with great difficulty,[39] which meant the viceroy had to repeat the order several times, without visible success.[40] It was only later, in 1601, that they managed to implement the order, 'to the great reluctance of the people'.[41]

These oscillations in the Crown's fiscal policy, as well as the repetition of orders concerning the collection of duties and the functioning of the customs house, reveal the difficulties in collecting money and, especially, of channelling it into the state's coffers. The entire debate that developed around the issues of fiscal reform, the perpetuation of privileges and exclusivity as opposed to free trade, the direct exploitation of trade as opposed to it being given out on contract, together with the high level of taxation or tax relief also reflects this. With regard to the functioning of

[38] In 1595, the city of Goa showed its solidarity regarding Melaka's complaints about these 'redoubled taxes'. In fact, the revenues did not make up for the loss of traffic; letter from the city of Goa to the king, 1595, *APO*, I, part 2, p. 11; another complaint from Goa in 1599 (ibid., pp. 69–70).

[39] In 1596 the viceroy gave specific orders to the captain of Melaka, Francisco da Silva de Meneses, not to permit any ship to leave the city without paying these taxes (*alvará* of 22-4-1596, HAG, *Regimentos e Instruções*, 2, fls. 130–131); the *ouvidores* (auditors) sent to Melaka were not powerful enough to impose these taxes that everyone in the city refused to pay (*see* 'Resposta [from the king] a algumas cartas [from the viceroy]', s.d. [1597], BN, *Res.*, cod. 1976, fl. 30; copies of letters from the viceroy, ibid., fl. 60).

[40] *Alvará* of 20-4-1598, *APO*, III, part 2, p. 900; letter from the king to Viceroy Aires de Saldanha, 25-1-1601, HAG, *MonçReino*, 7, fl. 43v. (other copies in vol. 8, fls. 10–24, 53–64 v., 67–77 and 112–122 v.; published in *BOGEI*, No. 55 (1880), p. 365; in 1599 D. Francisco da Gama told the king he was still unable to collect the taxes (letter of 23-12-1599, BN, *Res.*, cod. 1976, fl. 174).

[41] Royal letter to Viceroy D. Jerónimo de Azevedo, 27-2-1612, *DRI*, II, p. 178; it was Julião Campos Barreto who achieved this (he went to Melaka to investigate the conduct of Captain Martim Afonso de Melo; letter from Viceroy Aires de Saldanha, to the king, 20-12-1602, AN/TT, *CorCron.*, part 1, bundle 114, doc. 67). However, in this same letter, the king orders that his actions be investigated. The case was still underway in 1615 (AHU, *Índia*, box 3, doc. 140; Bocarro, *Década 13*, I, liii, pp. 224–225).

the customs house, on several occasions decisions were taken to lease it out. The exact terms of any such contracts are not known, nor whether they included all the duties collected at the customs house. The known *alvará* regarding a lease does not clarify anything with regard to this question.[42] However, it was a common practice at least from the 1580s onwards, yielding sums that varied between 18,000$000 and 31,000$000 per year.[43] In the early years of the 17th century, when Melaka already reckoned with Dutch competition, it continued to hover in the range of 26,640$000,[44] only decreasing in a later period. One must take great care with these figures: these are sums calculated according to the lease contract, but it would appear that the Royal Treasury did not always receive the stipulated amount.[45] The lease-holders were subjected to pressure by the captains, and from available documentation one can conclude that, of their own volition or not, they ended up having to submit, either giving in to coercion for fear of the power wielded by the captains, or arriving at agreements to divide the revenues obtained in exchange for their protection. In either

---

[42] *Alvará* from Viceroy Matias de Albuquerque, 25-9-1596, HAG, *Regimentos e Instruções*, 2, fl. 54 (*see* Document Appendix, No. 8).

[43] Or 50,000–86,000 *pardaus* (taking it to be 360 *reis* each); sometimes the calculations were made in *cruzados*, which require a more careful approach because in Melaka it was accepted as 360 *reis* in value but in Portugal and elsewhere the standard equivalent was 400 *reis* (*see* above, note 18); Manuel Lobato presents the general framework of all the revenues of the Melaka customs house (*Política e Comércio* ..., pp. 227–228); Bishop D. João Ribeiro Gaio also provides novel data, stating that before 1587 it was rented for no more than 50,000 *cruzados*, but after the destruction of Johor Lama it rose to 73,000 *cruzados*; letter from the bishop of Melaka to the king, 31-12-1588, AGS, *Secr. Prov.*, book 1551, fl. 409 (*see* Document Appendix, No. 6).

[44] Falcão, *Livro em que se contém toda a Fazenda* ..., p. 78, where he states that this amount corresponds to 66,600 *cruzados* and to 88,800 *xerafins*.

[45] In 1599 the viceroy complained to the king that in the previous year the customs house was leased for 86,000 *pardaus* (almost 31,000$000), but 'to such people and with such sureties and in such conditions that Your Majesty's Treasury will surely lose more than 20,000 *pardaus* [7,200$000]'; letter from Viceroy D. Francisco da Gama to the king, 24-12-1599, BN, *Res.*, cod. 1976, fl. 121 (also in letter issued on 18-12-1599, BM, *Add.* 28432, fl. 16v.).

situation, the interests of the Royal Treasury were harmed.[46] In any case, the effects were minimal: even though the city witnessed a considerable volume of trade and the customs house was leased out with a view to ensuring advance revenues for the Crown, little money reached Goa's coffers, disappearing instead into the administrative mechanisms of the fortress headed by the captain.[47] As early as 1569 the king recognised that never before had there been such large revenues along with such great shortages in the Estado da Índia. In 1587 the viceroy gave vent to his grievances and completed the picture: ever since he had assumed the post of viceroy, not even a *quintal* of cloves nor a *pardao* of customs revenue had arrived from Melaka.[48]

The presence of Asian merchants was a barometer of the city's capacity to capture the trade upon which Melaka's entire existence depended. The truth is that the city was resentful, mainly because of the extortion practised by the captains but also due to oppressive fiscal policies and the dispersion of trade to other centres, especially to Manila, highlighted by Silveira with regard to Javanese and Chinese merchants.[49] This shift was undoubtedly accompanied by an increase in Portuguese contraband, into

---

[46] In the first case, the lease-holder was compelled to exempt the captain and his henchmen from paying taxes; this entailed a loss of his revenues and undoubtedly caused a reduction in the standard bids in the next auction (copies of letters from Viceroy D. Francisco da Gama to the king, unknown date [1597?], BN, *Res.*, cod. 1976, fl. 81). The second situation occurred between 1585 and 1588: a Treasury inspector detected a concealment of profits by the lease-holder, Pero Vieira, in order to cause a reduction in the standard price in the following year which had probably been assured in an agreement with Captain João da Silva. Pero Vieira gave him about one-third of his own profits (about 60,000 *pardaus*) and, in return, João da Silva protected him from being sent to Goa after the investigation; the Treasury inspector's report did not have any effect because the captain was a close relative of the viceroy (letter from the inspector of the Treasury to the king, 8-11-1589, BN, *Res.*, cod. 9861, fl. 28).

[47] Letters from Philip I to former Viceroy D. Francisco da Gama, 2-1-1596, *APO*, III, part 2, p. 576; 8-1-1598, pp. 809–810.

[48] Royal letter to the city of Goa, 16-3-1569, *APO*, I, p. 68; letter from Viceroy D. Duarte de Meneses to the king, 23-11-1587, AGS, *Secr. Prov.*, book 1551, fls. 72–72 v.

[49] *Reformação da Milícia*, p. 183.

which the captain of Melaka sank his talons,[50] mostly of Chinese and Japanese commodities. With regard to spices, trade in this commodity in Manila only made sense when combined with the (obviously illegal) commerce originating in the western Indian Ocean as the Spanish lacked both the markets where they could sell these spices and the main currency for which they were exchanged: textiles from India.[51]

Just as in the geopolitical balance of the Straits, Melaka had to reckon with competition instigated by the rival sultanates of Johor and Aceh, as well as that of Banten. Johor constituted the most classic example. Being the direct heir of the sultanate of Melaka, it continued to be an important centre that diverted commerce at the very doorstep of Melaka, taking advantage of the periodic disturbances that the uncertainties of economic and political life in Melaka caused amongst Asian merchants. In this case, given that both the Portuguese and the rival sultanate of Aceh barred its access to the west, Johor turned towards the commercial traffic of the Eastern Archipelago. It proved to have a remarkable ability to attract Javanese and Chinese merchants, in addition to Malays and even Portuguese, who were thus diverted away from Melaka.[52] The prestige of Johor in the Malay World further enabled it to exercise considerable influence over the sultanates in the Malay Peninsula, in Java or even in

---

[50] About this question *see* Lobato, *Política e Comércio* ..., pp. 212–216; it is rather curious to note how Jacques de Coutre lived and traded in Manila for more than two years as an agent of the captain of Melaka in the city and did not even realise (or, at least, did not mention in his work) that it was illegal (*Vida de Jacques de Coutre* ..., pp. 143–151).

[51] Melaka's close association with the Moluccan trade and the consequences of the Castillian interference in the 1520s and the famous Portuguese–Castillian 'Question' that was resolved in Zaragoza in 1529 are comprehensively analysed by Thomaz in *De Ceuta a Timor* ('Maluco e Malaca'), pp. 564–565.

[52] Coutre, *Vida de Jacques de Coutre*, p. 395; Couto, *Da Ásia*, X, part 1, IV, iv, p. 421; treatise about the commerce of Melaka [*circa* 1600], AN/TT, *MssLiv.*, No. 805, fl. 164v., in Lobato, *Política e Comércio dos Portugueses no Mundo Malaio-Indonésio* (thesis), p. 456; Rodrigues, 'Revista dos casos dos contratos ...' ('do contrato dos bares do calaim'), ibid., fl. 223, in Lobato, *Política e Comércio dos Portugueses no Mundo Malaio-Indonésio*, p. 476. *See* Das Gupta, 'The Maritime Trade of Indonesia', pp. 261–262. The regular presence of Chinese merchants in the sultanate is confirmed by the available Chinese sources (Groeneveldt, 'Notes on the Malay Archipelago...', pp. 254–255).

the Moluccas, namely with the sultanate of Ternate, with whom Johor maintained excellent relations.[53] In this manner, allied with this sultanate (that had expelled the Portuguese in 1575), Johor affirmed itself as a serious rival to Melaka in attracting the spice trade from Banda and the Moluccas. In addition, some time during the 1570s (possibly as early as the captaincy of Dom Leonis Pereira, 1567–70), the sultans arrived at a profitable accord with the captains of Melaka. This agreement was mutually beneficial, and consisted of diverting the movement of Javanese merchants who controlled the supply of spices to Johor, where the sultan collected his duties, and where the captains of Melaka would later acquire their supplies as the sultan exempted them from these duties. In 1585 the new captain, João da Silva Pereira, arrived in Melaka with specific orders to put an end to this situation, which greatly harmed the interests of the Royal Treasury. A crisis broke out and only ended in 1587 with the attack on and destruction of the capital Johor Lama. This state of affairs marked the zenith of Johor's power which had for several years undermined Melaka's fundamental role as a mercantile centre and would only cease in the face of Portuguese military pressure.

If Johor represented competition in the east, Aceh was a significant commercial rival in the west, in addition to being a serious military threat to Melaka's security. This sultanate was the most visible face of an extensive anti-Portuguese structure that emerged, albeit precariously, during the second half of the century. It was based upon the supply of Sumatran pepper, increasingly controlled by Aceh and channelled towards the Levant route via the powerful Gujarati community.[54] With the turn of

---

[53]   In the 1570s, when anti-Portuguese tension was at its peak, the Portuguese noticed how Johor was able to strengthen its prestige and position in Banda and Ternate, having detected the presence of embassies and great ships on these islands; 'A capitania de Amboino', *DHMPPO/Insulíndia*, IV, p. 260; Couto, *Da Ásia*, IX, xxix, p. 262. In 1579 this anti-Christian hostility was compounded by the presence of *ulama* from Mecca and Aceh, as could be expected, but also from the 'Malay land' (*Malaio*), or Johor (letter from Jerónimo Rodrigues to Rui Vicente, Feb. 1579, *DM*, II, p. 38). In the following decade, Johor maintained close relations with Ternate ('Relação' by Paulo de Lima Pereira, 1587, *DUP*, I, p. 15).

[54]   *See*, amongst others, the essential study by Boxer about this theme ('A Note on Portuguese Reactions to the Revival of the Red Sea Spice Trade and the Rise of Atjeh').

the century, the sultanate, under Iskandar Muda, put great emphasis on imperialist inclinations, assuming the role of a hegemonic regional power and establishing a monopoly over the island's pepper, ending up by almost totally dominating trade in this commodity. Likewise, the gold (in the form of dust) found in the interior of Sumatra that had fuelled the avarice of Portuguese ideologues (who advocated that the island be conquered) gradually came under Acehnese control, generally in the form of tributes from satellite sultanates and kingdoms, especially on the west coast. This gold traffic also reached Melaka via the Minangkabau merchants who traded in it more or less freely, but now it began to be carried out under the control of the Acehnese sultans who, as early as the second half of the 16th century,[55] obtained vast profits from it.

The more important political and military aspects, as well as the ideological offensive that transformed Aceh into a champion of Islam in the Far East and an Ottoman supporter, along with the consequent impact on regional geopolitics, will be discussed in more detail in chapter 4. Here, one must stress the connections established by Aceh throughout the Indian Ocean, especially towards the west. It is clear that the most important was the link with the Levant, through which vast quantities of its pepper were channelled,[56] a fact that is clearly corroborated by both the

---

[55] *See* the royal instructions to Viceroy D. Duarte de Meneses, 10-3-1584, AN/ TT, *Fundo Port. da Bibl. Nac. de Paris*, No. 48, fl. 8 (*see* Document Appendix, No. 2); Jorge de Lemos estimates the value of the gold sent annually from Kampar to Melaka before the interference of Aceh to be about 150,000 *cruzados* ('Hystoria dos Cercos ...', fl. 60); this issue was linked to local legends about a 'golden island' that this author located (just like Manuel Godinho de Erédia) on the northern coast of Sumatra; *see* Eredia's 'Lista das Principais Minas ...', saying: 'Diogo Gonçalves and other Portuguese who were kept captive in the kingdom of Aceh spoke of a Golden Island in the sea next to Cape Daia in Sumatra' (pp. 83–84). Bishop D. João Ribeiro Gaio also mentions this island (*O Roteiro*, p. 59).

[56] In 1596 the production was estimated at 15,000 *bares* annually (3.5 *quintais* each or about 3.150 tonnes; letter from Philip I to Viceroy D. Francisco da Gama, 16-3-1596, *APO*, III, part 2, p. 627); in previous decades production seems to have fluctuated between 30,000 and 40,000 *quintais* (1,800–2,400 t.), according to Jorge de Lemos ('Hystoria dos Cercos ...', fl. 60v.) and the bishop of Melaka, D. João Ribeiro Gaio (*O Roteiro*, p. 96). We can compare these figures with those of pepper production in Sunda a few years earlier:

Portuguese[57] and foreign travellers in the Orient.[58] Similarly, in the Persian Gulf, the Portuguese detected the movement of Acehnese ships which, as in other regions, plied these waters without a *cartaz* (a pass issued by the Portuguese authorities), and were thus theoretically liable to be seized.[59]

The rulers of Cochin, long-standing allies of the Portuguese since the times of Duarte Pacheco Pereira, appear to have established permanent contact with the sultanate, although we only find echoes of such suspicions in the sources.[60] A fundamental link was the one connecting Aceh with

Linschoten mentions 4,000–5,000 *quintais* (240–300 t.), but Couto estimates a much higher value:, 8,000 *bares* or more than 1,680 tonnes per year (Linschoten, *The Voyage of* …, II, p. 112; Couto, *Da Ásia*, IV, part 1, III, i, p. 166). These figures and equivalencies have been obtained by reckoning 1 *quintal* = 60 kg (in fact, it had a slightly lesser value), or 1 *bar* = 210 kg, according to the *Livro dos Pesos e Medidas* … by António Nunes. We are referring to the so-called *bar grande dachém* used to weigh pepper (p. 48). However, Couto used different and dubious calculations, for he says that 8,000 *bares* and 30,000 *quintais* were equivalent to each other (1 *quintal* therefore being = 56 kg and 1 *bar* = 225 kg). Lobato, in *Política e Comércio* (p. 210, note 120) also presents different figures.

[57] *See*, for instance, the 'Apontamentos' from Archbishop D. Jorge Temudo to the king (dated 1569 or 1570) in Wicki (ed.), 'Duas Relações …', p. 208, and the letter from Governor Manuel de Sousa Coutinho to the king, 4-12-1589, AGS, *Secr. Prov.*, book 1551, fl. 778v.

[58] Like Ralph Fitch (1583–91), in Foster (ed.), *Early Travels in India*, p. 41, and Filippo Sassetti (letter to Pietro Spina, 20-1-1586, *Lettere da Vari Paesi* …, pp. 480–481).

[59] This was the justification presented by the captain of Melaka in 1585 for sinking a vessel from Johor, saying its captain was Acehnese (Couto, *Da Ásia*, X, part 2, VII, xii, pp. 206–207). By the end of the 1610s, when the Portuguese no longer had pretensions of controlling the sea-routes in their confrontation with both their English and Dutch rivals, Portuguese authorities did not attack Acehnese vessels sailing in the Persian Gulf, thus trying to avoid Acehnese hostility towards Melaka (royal letter to Rui Freire de Andrade, 15-1-1619, *DRI*, V, p. 259; royal letter to Viceroy D. João Coutinho, 15-3-1619, *DRI*, VI, p. 242); however, Governor Fernão de Albuquerque, who had been captain of Melaka from 1600 to 1603, disagreed with such a decision (letter to the king, 7-2-1620, *DRI*, VI, p. 243).

[60] Letter from Philip I to Viceroy D. Duarte de Meneses, 22-2-1589, *APO*, III, part 1, p. 207; royal letter to Viceroy Rui Lourenço de Távora, 21-1-1611, *DRI*, II, p. 4.

the eastern shores of India, namely Masulipatnam, a port situated on the northern Coromandel coast that had been controlled by the Muslim kingdom of Golconda ever since the Battle of Talikota in 1565. Here Aceh found an ideal partner, united by a similar rivalry with the Portuguese, from whom it could acquire armaments and textiles, directly traded for its pepper.[61] Aceh's supply points on the Coromandel coast—sources of rice—likewise seemed to include Nagapattinam, despite Portuguese control over the city.[62] Its influence also extended towards the east, and it was clearly allied with Ternate, the sultanate which headed the opposition to the Portuguese, with whom it signed a treaty in the late 1570s or early 1580s.[63]

Similarly, the sultanates of Java and Sunda were also fierce competitors with Melaka. The most important undoubtedly was Banten, which controlled a substantial part of the pepper production of Sunda and southern Sumatra. In the case of the latter island, it also kept the sultanate of Palembang—an increasingly important port for the traffic in pepper—under control. Banten's main role consisted of its link with China where, from 1567 onwards—when the Ming dynasty authorised a partial opening of Fujian and Guangdong—it became the main supplier of pepper to China and was the great polarising centre of the Chinese mercantile community.[64] As Manuel Lobato has demonstrated, this was the main, although not the sole, reason for the discontinuation of the

---

[61] Luz (ed.), *Livro das Cidades e Fortalezas* ..., fl. 90; Couto, *Da Ásia*, X, part 1, I, iii, pp. 14–16; ibid., part 1, I, x, pp. 75–76; Coutre, 'Vida de Jacques de Coutre ...', p. 373. *See* Subrahmanyam, *A Presença Portuguesa e o Comércio do Coromandel*, pp. 13–17 and Freire (ed.), *Primor e Honra da Vida Soldadesca* ..., fl. 96; the anonymous author of this work claims to have seen a certain number of iron cannon balls being sent to Aceh, estimated to weigh about 3600 *quintais* (about 210 tonnes).

[62] Houtman's first expedition, on his way from Tenasserim to Sri Lanka, took a vessel from Nagapattinam loaded with rice destined for Aceh ('A briefe Relation of Master John Davies ...' in Purchas *His Pilgrimes*, II, p. 323).

[63] Argensola, *Conquista de las Islas Malucas*, p. 142; letter from Jerónimo Rodrigues to Rui Vicente, Feb. 1579, *DM*, II, p. 38.

[64] *See* the Chinese sources in Groeneveldt, 'Notes on the Malay Archipelago...', p. 166.

voyage between Melaka and Sunda.[65] Portuguese attempts to revive
regular trade on this route failed: Banten increasingly became a rival port
connected with mercantile traffic throughout the Indian Ocean region
and was not merely a partner of Melaka dependent on the Indian textiles
that the latter supplied.[66] In the late 1580s, the Portuguese in Melaka
clearly felt the effects of the loss of much of the pepper trade from
Sunda and other ports in the region thanks to the activities of the
Chinese merchants who thus escaped the city's control.[67] For this reason,
the Crown continued to claim, formally and repeatedly, a monopoly that
prohibited the pepper trade from Melaka to China.[68] However, this was
completely disregarded as the Portuguese continued to prefer to carry
pepper to China rather than despatching the commodity to Goa.[69]

Despite the increasing difficulties that Melaka faced during the second
half of the 16th century and the control that the captains exercised over
the city's economic life, it still managed to exhibit a remarkable capacity
to attract commerce. The trade associated with it, including both the
rich spice trade and less important trade in tin or provisions, still ensured
considerable traffic for the port, by both the *casados* and the Javanese or
Keling merchants. The number of Asian traders who engaged in Melaka
was still considerable. At the end of the 1580s, an auditor (*ouvidor*) sent
to Melaka registered the presence of 2,000–3,000 Javanese in the port

---

[65] A later source says the voyage continued to be in the hands of the captain
of Melaka, who used alternative goods such as silver and coral. The voyage
remained profitable even after the arrival of the Dutch; Captain, Martim
Afonso de Melo (1597–1600) allegedly sold it for more than 60,000 *cruzados*,
but Francisco de Miranda Henriques [1609–13?] estimates that its profits
were only about 7,000 *cruzados*, still considered to be 'a lot of money' at the
time (royal letter to Viceroy D. Jerónimo de Azevedo, 9-3-1614, *DRI*, III,
p. 125; letter from the same viceroy to the king, 25-1-1615. AHU, *Índia*,
box 3, doc. 64).

[66] Lobato, *Política e Comércio*, pp. 251–255.

[67] Letter from Philip I to Viceroy Matias de Albuquerque, Jan. 1591, *APO*,
III, part 1, p. 298. Banten seems to have centralised the pepper from other
sultanates like Indragiri and Jambi (Report of Viceroy D. Francisco da Gama,
1603 or 1604, BM, *Add*. 28432, fl. 116v.).

[68] Letter from Philip I to Viceroy Matias de Albuquerque, 16-4-1597, *APO*, III,
part 2, p. 762.

[69] 'Relatório sobre o trato da pimenta', *DUP*, III, pp. 334–335.

and, at the end of the century, the city's Town Hall estimated that more than 20,000 'Moors' frequented the city annually.[70] This was undoubtedly due to the role that Melaka continued to play as a first-rate centre that linked the diverse trade routes of the Indian Ocean which intersected at the Straits. This was a primordial role that had ensured the fortunes of the sultanate in the 15th century and Portuguese Melaka still managed to maintain it albeit at great cost and in the face of serious difficulties.

The fragmentation and destruction that followed the Portuguese conquest and the establishment of new centres of commercial articulation had still not permitted the emergence of a political, economic and military structure sufficiently strong and organised enough to compete in all aspects and supplant Melaka and its supplementary linkages. As long as this was the case, the city would maintain its position, with a greater or lesser degree of difficulty. It was only with the arrival in the region of the English and the Dutch, duly organised into commercial companies and supported by a powerful military structure, that this state of affairs was clearly checkmated, plunging the city into a swift decline.

The 17th Century and the Decline of Melaka

The arrival of the Dutch and the English in the Archipelago's waters served as a powerful catalyst for the seeds of disintegration and erosion that had long undermined the Estado da Índia. Over the course of a few years the Portuguese would find themselves faced with a situation for which they were clearly unprepared. It was no coincidence that the northern Europeans had chosen this region as their prime target as it was the weakest link of the Estado da Índia. The region also produced the most coveted spices and provided quick and easy access to the Far East. In addition, in all of the Indian Ocean, it was the region where Portuguese naval power was the most vulnerable and Portuguese fortresses were few and far between. From an economic point of view, the competition instigated by these new rivals tended to reduce Melaka to a subaltern status: their objective was to acquire spices and channel them directly to Europe,

---

[70] Letter from the *ouvidor*, Duarte Borges Miranda, to the king, 17-12-1588, AGS, *Secr. Prov.*, book 1551, fl. 471; 'Notes' from the city of Melaka, 1599, BN, *Res.*, cod. 1973, fl. 57 (*see* Document Appendix, No. 10). About this issue *see* chapter 5, 'The Structure of the City'.

establishing themselves (by taking over Portuguese positions in the case of Ambon and the Moluccas) in the areas where spices were produced or traded. To this end they naturally sought to establish good relations with local powers. The most important powers in the region had already long been engaged in open or covert conflict with the Portuguese: Ternate had expelled them long ago, Aceh was enjoying a short-lived period of peaceful relations with Melaka, Johor had been forced into an uneasy peace and was waiting for an opportunity to rise against Melaka and, finally, Banten was already completely outside the Portuguese sphere of influence. Thus local conditions were favourable for the newly arrived Europeans who, just like the Portuguese a century earlier, came in search of spices (but not in search of Christians). This movement would be disputed in legal and juridical terms around the issue of freedom of navigation on the high seas and the rights of exclusivity that the Portuguese Crown claimed, a problem that was set in motion with the capture of the *Santa Catarina* in the Johor River in 1603,[71] the incident that initiated the assault on Portuguese navigation and positions.[72]

In 1595 the Dutch made their first incursion into Southeast Asian seas, reaching Banten, where lived a community of Portuguese merchants who, although unable to compete with the Chinese in importance, appeared to be reasonably prosperous.[73] Their influence was still sufficient to spell serious difficulties for the new arrivals who, nevertheless, managed to disentangle themselves without severe damage.[74] Although the conditions

---

[71] About the capture of the ship, *see* Caetano, *Portugal e a Internacionalização dos Problemas Africanos*, pp. 9–48 and Borschberg, 'The seizure of the *Sta Catarina* revisited' and 'The Santa Catarina incident of 1603'.

[72] The most complete Portuguese work that provides a detailed description of the arrival and establishment of the Dutch and the English and their conflicts with the Portuguese is still Sousa, *Subsídios para a História Militar Marítima da Índia*.

[73] Chinese sources confirm the existence of a Portuguese factory in Banten working side-by-side with the Dutch one (Groeneveldt, 'Notes on the Malay Archipelago...', pp. 166 and 182).

[74] The Portuguese seem to have acted in coordination with the deposed sultan of Demak (whom the Dutch called 'Emperor'). According to the Dutch report (*Iovrnal du Voyage de l'Inde Orientale*), the Portuguese in the sultanate acted against the Dutch and not on their behalf as suggested by a Portuguese source

of this voyage hadn't been the best and its results had not been brilliant, a new phase in European expansion had been inaugurated. The Dutch sent new armadas in 1598, on account of several small and newly created commercial companies, an enterprise in which they were closely followed by the English.[75] The political union of Portugal and Castille had thus dragged Portugal into a conflict with unexpected consequences, and Portugal's former friendship with these nations was now sacrificed on the higher altar of global geopolitics.[76] With the foundation of their respective East India companies, the Dutch and the English gradually established themselves throughout the Orient. The Dutch were able to gain ground in the Malay-Indonesian Archipelago, and the English ended up preferring the western Indian Ocean.

In the short span of two decades, from the early voyages to the foundation of Batavia, the Dutch consolidated their position in the main spice-producing centres, obtained important commercial agreements and exercised ever-increasing pressure over Portuguese trade routes. They established a network of factories that stretched from the Moluccas to Aceh, firmly implanting themselves in Jambi, Sukadana (Borneo), Makassar, Java, Solor, Timor, Banda and Ambon, amongst other locations. They likewise interfered in the trade with China and Japan. The circuit was completed with their settlements on the Coromandel coast, in Teganapattam and subsequently in Pulicat. Here they acquired the textiles that were necessary to purchase the spices of the Archipelago, in clear competition with the Portuguese circuits. The effects of this process are plainly evident: Melaka rapidly lost its importance, especially when the last great Portuguese military effort, the enterprise undertaken by Dom Martim Afonso de Castro, failed in its intention of expelling their adversaries and re-establishing the position of Portuguese navigation and trade.

('Roteiro da viagem dos holandeses', *APO*, III, part 2, pp. 885–886); the two sources agree on a single point only: the information given to the newcomers by a Portuguese *casado* from Melaka named Pero de Ataíde.

[75] The English were the first north Europeans to reach Asia by sea, but their initial voyages were merely privateer initiatives such as the ones made by Francis Drake, Thomas Cavendish, Benjamin Wood or even James Lancaster's first voyage.

[76] *See*, amongst others, the evolution of the situation as summarised by Blussé and Winius in 'The Origin and Rhythm of Dutch Aggression against the Estado da India'.

The years 1605–06 marked a fundamental change: it was at this point that it became evident that the Dutch naval power no longer limited itself to attacking ships, but was also a direct threat to Melaka, Tidore, Solor and Ambon. After the initial years of learning about the natural, political and economic conditions of Southeast Asia, during which they avoided direct confrontation, the Dutch took over the Portuguese positions in the Eastern Archipelago[77] and isolated Melaka. This was achieved by following a diplomatic strategy of establishing themselves and exercising pressure upon neighbouring sultanates—Aceh and Johor—and a broader economic enterprise. The strategy aimed at competing directly with the Portuguese in several markets and, above all, at depriving Melaka and its Straits of its age-old role by navigating directly via the Sunda Straits, thus creating an alternative circuit that ensured the confluence of the trade in spices and Coromandel textiles. Sporadically they even managed to blockade the city, against which the debilitated financial and military structures of the Portuguese could do little apart from resisting, often at the cost of enormous risks and losses.

The English, too, tried to obtain an important share in the spice trade and also attacked Portuguese navigation. Initially, the Portuguese confused them with the Dutch, and vice versa. In any case, the subjects of Elizabeth I were following in the footsteps of the Dutch, their erstwhile allies and subsequently fierce rivals. Their corsair attacks on Portuguese ships were equally effective, but they never managed to establish a solid local structure like the Dutch, although they did set up a number of factories. Their lack of strength was a result of their weaker financial and military capabilities and, above all, the lack of a commercial centre on the Coromandel coast, which they never managed to establish. This was a serious impediment to their competitiveness in the markets of Southeast Asia, especially in the great ports that traded in spices: they brought textiles from Gujarat (where they had a factory in Surat), but there was little demand for them here. Therefore, the English were unable to compete with the cheaper and more sought-after Coromandel textiles brought by the Portuguese and the Dutch. This was the case, for example, in Makassar,[78] Jambi[79] and Patani.[80]

---

[77] *See* Lobato, *Política e Comércio* ..., pp. 345–356.

[78] Letter from G. Cokayne to J. Jourdain, 24-4-1614, *LREIC*, II, pp. 31–32.

[79] Letter from J. Tucker to Sir T. Smythe, 11-2-1616, *LREIC*, IV, p. 27.

[80] Letter from B. Farie to the EIC, 24-7-1614, *LREIC*, II, p. 78; letter from A. Denton to the EIC, 5-10-1614, *LREIC*, II, p. 127.

Another equally relevant reason for their weakness was the fierce competition from the Dutch, in addition to the obvious Portuguese hostility.[81] This was especially felt in Java and particularly in Banten, which was the most important centre for the United Dutch East India Company (the Vereenigde Oost-Indische Compagnie, known as VOC) until 1619.[82] Likewise, in Aceh and the areas controlled by this sultanate, the English faced mounting difficulties, just like the Dutch, owing to the fierce control that Iskandar Muda maintained over pepper production and his desire for European ships and artillery. This placed all the European powers in serious difficulties due to the pressure that the sultan exerted upon them to place these means at his disposal for use against Melaka and Johor.[83] In any case, the English were unable to gain the upper hand in their attempt to establish a trading empire in Southeast Asia. In 1612 the Portuguese were still anxious that they would embark upon a policy of conquest,[84] but such fears proved to be unfounded. The famous 'Ambon massacre', carried out by the Dutch in 1623, put a definitive end to English ambitions. They now opted to concentrate on a strategy aimed at the western Indian Ocean—at the Mughal Empire—where they established a solid economic and political base, obviously destined to be detrimental to the interests of the Estado da Índia.

The disintegration of the Portuguese structures in Southeast Asia, in much the same way as had happened throughout the Indian Ocean

---

[81] The Portuguese were obviously aware of this fact and tried to take advantage of it; 'Avisos' from D. Pedro de Castilho to the State Council, 9-11-1611, AN/TT, *MiscMssCGL*, box 6, vol. II E, p. 315; letter [from the viceroy?] to the king, 3-4-1612, AN/TT, *ColVic.*, 26, fl. 128; report of 17-9-[1612?] appended to the royal letter to Viceroy D. Jerónimo de Azevedo, 1-2-1613, *DRI*, II, p. 317.

[82] Letter from J. Jourdain to the EIC, 2-1-1614, *LREIC*, II, pp. 276–277; 'The second Voyage of John Davies' [1605], Purchas, *His Pilgrimes*, II, p. 357; Scot, 'A Discourse of Java and of the first English Factorie there ...' [1604], ibid., II, p. 462; Beaulieu, 'Memoires du Voyage ...' in Thevenot (ed.), *Relations de Divers Voyages Curieux ...*, I, p. 10.

[83] This happened, for instance, in 1613–15, when both their factories were in danger, the Dutch due to the help they provided to Johor and the English because they refused to assist the Acehnese attack on Melaka with their vessels. *See* chapter 4, 'The Sultanate of Aceh'.

[84] Letter [from the viceroy?] to the king, 3-4-1612, AN/TT, *ColVic.*, 26, fl. 128.

region, to the benefit of their European rivals, came about as a result of diverse factors, both internal and external, of a political, administrative and military nature. The economic factor was a consequence of military defeats (especially naval routs), administrative inefficiency and political ineptitude. In truth, it does not seem that the Dutch, despite everything that has been written about the nature of their Company and its functioning, had any substantial advantage over the Portuguese commercial structure, or that they surpassed the competitive potential of the Portuguese (who already had a century of experience with the economic, political and cultural life of Asia and had mingled and merged with Asian populations) in the region.[85]

The Portuguese political and military defeat in the face of Dutch attacks and the decreasing capacity of the Estado da Índia to respond and seize the initiative had an immediate effect: Spanish primacy in combating European enemies. In the Malay Archipelago, the impact was visible, as it was now the Spaniards who frequently came to Melaka's aid because of the distances involved and increasingly risky passage separating the city from Goa. The attempts to re-establish a position in the Moluccas, as well as any initiatives to form a joint Luso–Spanish great armada, were now left to Manila. In practice, it put an end to the division of the two spheres of influence and the prohibition on trade between the two, which had already been disregarded by both the Spaniards and the Portuguese. This became widespread from 1616–17 onwards,[86] coinciding with the enterprise undertaken by Don Juan de Silva, but the Crown continued to maintain its ban and called for transgressors to be severely punished.[87]

Melaka relied upon three main trading links for its survival: Chinese silks and porcelain, Coromandel textiles, and spices from the Malay-Indonesian Archipelago. The Dutch attacked all three commercial connections and obtained results that, despite being uneven, in practice resulted in an increasing reduction in the volume of the city's trade and its decline as a mercantile centre.

Let us begin with the spices. This was a trade in which the Portuguese had encountered very serious problems for quite some time, having lost

---

[85]   Lobato, *Política e Comércio* …, pp. 355–356.
[86]   Bocarro, *Década 13*, I, clxxi, pp. 697–698.
[87]   *Regimento* of Viceroy D. Francisco da Gama, 30-3-1622, AN/TT, *MiscMssCGL*, box 16, vol. 6 F, fl. 128v.

control of the supplies of cloves from the Moluccas and nutmeg from Banda. The Anglo–Dutch competition thus found that the Portuguese commercial structure in the Eastern Archipelago was already disorganised, and that the trade was concentrated in the hands of Asian merchants, especially the Javanese. In spite of these difficulties, Melaka continued to hold its position in the spice trade for two main reasons: merchants were still obliged to go to the city as Southeast Asian markets could not entirely absorb the volumes traded and because Portuguese armadas continuously pressured ships to go to Melaka. All this came under threat when the Dutch arrived and established themselves: they absorbed production profitably and neutralised Portuguese naval power.[88] Furthermore, the merchants, in addition to Dutch pressure not to trade at Melaka, continued to suffer abuse at the hands of the Portuguese captains;[89] consequently they became less inclined to frequent the city.[90] António Bocarro highlights 1615 as the year that witnessed the great rupture in Melaka's commerce, especially evident in the spice trade. This was the last year in which nutmeg and mace were to be found there.[91]

The effects of these changes in the Indonesian spice trade have to be linked with the complementary aspect of this commerce: the trade in textiles of the western Indian Ocean, especially Coromandel textiles.[92] The Portuguese Crown soon realised that the spice trade carried out by the Dutch had another negative fallout for Portuguese commerce: while

---

[88]   Lobato, *Política e Comércio* ..., pp. 204–206.
[89]   Royal letter to Viceroy D. João Coutinho, 7-3-1619, *DRI*, VI, p. 152; reply from Governor Fernão de Albuquerque, 4-2-1620, *DRI*, VI, p. 153.
[90]   Report about the government of Melaka, unknown date [1610s?], AN/TT, *MssLiv.*, No. 1107, p. 289 (copy in BN, *Res.*, Mss. 206, No. 173, pp. 3–4); Coutre, 'Vida de Jacques de Coutre', pp. 172 and 395.
[91]   Bocarro, *Década 13*, I, ciii, p. 461. It seems that this trade, like the trade in cloves, suffered a severe blow but did not disappear; Fr. Belchior dos Santos reports, in 1619, how these spices still managed to circulate from Melaka to the western Indian Ocean in small but swift and well-armed galliots; curiously, he says that Melaka received more nutmeg than cloves ('Discurso sobre as especiarias', 10-10-1619, in Luz (ed.), *O Conselho da Índia*, p. 602).
[92]   This region was an important supplier of textiles but also of provisions to Melaka; about the general evolution of both trades in the late 16th century, *see* Subrahmanyam, *Comércio e Conflito...* ('O Comércio entre Coromandel e Malaca no século XVI'), pp. 45–55.

the Dutch did not have an established emporium on the Coromandel coast, they would buy spices from the Javanese at high prices in exchange for silver *reales de a ocho* and other European commodities, and the Portuguese in Melaka would sell their Coromandel textiles in exchange for these very same *reales*. The Javanese preferred to sell their spices to the Dutch, who paid better rates and absorbed their entire stock, and probably forced the Portuguese to sell their textiles against *reales*. The residents of Melaka accepted the *reales*, probably believing that the silver would be more useful in their private trade than spices, which were subject to abuse by both the captains and customs duties. Thus the spices flowed into the Dutch circuits, not the Portuguese ones. The king forbade this practice as early as 1603,[93] obliging Portuguese sales of cloth to be carried out only in exchange for spices. When this order was not obeyed, he issued a new charter in 1606, which would only be proclaimed in Goa in 1610.[94] However, the inefficiency of this order would result in the provision of pecuniary fines and exile for offenders.[95] However, this issue soon lost importance. The Dutch, after an initial agreement with the Sultan of Golconda and the establishment of a factory in Masulipatnam, established themselves definitively in Pulicat, where they acquired vast supplies of textiles (paying with the same *reales*), which would constitute an excellent base both to compete with Nagapattinam and St. Thomas of Mylapur and also to plunder Portuguese ships arriving from Melaka.[96]

---

[93] Royal letter to Viceroy Aires de Saldanha, 19-2-1603, AHU, *Cons. Ultr.*, cod. 282, fl. 148v., and appended *alvará*, fl. 154 (the latter is published in *APO*, VI (ii), pp. 789–790); *see* royal letter to Viceroy D. Martim Afonso de Castro, 10-3-1605, AN/TT, *ColVic.*, 17, fl. 25. It was made public in Melaka only in 1605 (*alvará* from Viceroy D. Martim Afonso de Castro, 9-11-1605, HAG, *MonçReino*, 6 A, fls. 48–48 v.).

[94] Copy in *DRI*, III, pp. 515–518; *See* royal order to the bishop of Melaka, 5-12-1606, HAG, *MonçReino*, 6 A, fl. 102, and to the viceroy, 16-1-1607, *DRI*, I, p. 72. *See* also royal letters to Viceroy Rui Lourenço de Távora, 23-1-1610, *DRI*, I, pp. 291 and 294.

[95] Four years of exile in Sri Lanka; royal letter to Viceroy D. Jerónimo de Azevedo, 27-2-1612, *DRI*, II, p. 180, and *alvará*, 28-2-1612, ibid., pp. 189–190.

[96] Letter from the city of St Thomas of Mylapur to the king, 19-12-1621, BN, *Res.*, cod., 1975, fl. 375.

This was not achieved without resistance on the part from the Portuguese. The residents of these two cities on the Coromandel coast soon realised that the neighbouring Dutch establishments would be a deadly blow to both their trade and the Estado da Índia itself, given that it completed the rival circuit and reduced the Portuguese structures to a secondary status in addition to posing a military threat. In 1613, shortly after it had been established, the Dutch factory was destroyed by the Portuguese.[97] However, this was quickly rebuilt while the Portuguese could only look on in frustrated impotence, as we can deduce from their account of how the Dutch regained their control over navigation with only two ships.[98] Projects for a new assault on the factory were successively postponed due to a lack of resources, although they recognised that this was the best way of recovering part of the trade they had lost.[99] Thus the Dutch once again took their trade in textiles to Southeast Asia, with visible reinforcements, gradually supplanting the Portuguese circuits.

The Gujaratis also appear to have taken advantage of the debilitation of Portuguese structures to reinforce their trade in the region, overcoming any possible obstacles that the Portuguese armadas could represent: information from 1609 highlights the fact that the merchants of Surat freely sailed to Southeast Asia with large cargoes of textiles, buying off the Portuguese captains of the Northern Armada with bribes (ranging from 10,000 to 12,000 *cruzados*).[100]

The other mainstay of Melaka's economy was the trade with China. This was equally affected, especially due to the lack of security on the Far Eastern routes. The Dutch proceeded to attack the links between Macao and Melaka, the richest traffic that the Portuguese possessed at the time, heralding their presence with the seizure in Johor, in 1603, of the *Santa Catarina* whose sale rendered a veritable fortune in the

---

[97] Royal letter to Viceroy D. Jerónimo de Azevedo, 31-1-1614, *DRI*, III, p. 30; *see* Floris, *His Voyage to the East Indies* ..., p. 67.

[98] Royal letter to Viceroy D. Jerónimo de Azevedo, 6-2-1615, *DRI*, III, pp. 189–190.

[99] Royal letters to Viceroy D. Jerónimo de Azevedo, 21-3-1617, *DRI*, IV, pp. 126–128; 27-2-1619, IV, p. 268.

[100] Letter from the Council of Portugal to the king, 26-11-1609, AGS, *Secr. Prov.*, book 1479, fl. 536; royal letter to Viceroy D. Martim Afonso de Castro, 18-1-1607, *DRI*, I, p. 99.

Netherlands.[101] The preoccupation with ensuring the continuation of the long voyage from Macao to Melaka became a vital problem for the city as this was its main source of revenue. In the light of the Dutch threat, the frequency of this trade became irregular, with years in which the most intense onslaughts of their enemies caused an almost total interruption of their communications with the Far East.[102]

In any case, the voyages ceased to be carried out in large carracks, the merchandise being divided up and transported in speedier galliots that tried to escape Dutch vigilance.[103] The risks involved in this trade intensified substantially, which caused a decline in their auction values and the revenues obtained by the holder of the contract. Even the voyage of Japan declined, due both because the Dutch had a factory there and because the Chinese and Spaniards from Manila inundated Japan with Chinese silk.[104]

In this scenario, Melaka's trade, apart from declining considerably in terms of importance and volume, became fragmented into less profitable trade routes, trafficking in numerous smaller trading circuits that they carried out throughout Southeast Asia as well as to the Coromandel coast and the Far East. From then on these voyages were made in small ships that were quicker and more manoeuvrable so as to be able to slip through Dutch vigilance. The most important was the trade in tin that existed in

---

[101] Caetano, *Portugal e a Internacionalização dos Problemas Africanos*, pp. 26–32 and Borschberg, 'The seizure of the *Sta Catarina* revisited', pp. 54–58; several sources report the capture; beside the ones mentioned in these studies, *see* 'A Description of the East Indies' in Middleton, *The Voyage of … to the Moluccas*, p. 89 and Coutre, 'Vida de Jacques de Coutre', pp. 168–169.

[102] For instance, in 1622, Portuguese communication links with Macao were cut for two years due to the Dutch blockade on the city; letter from Governor Fernão de Albuquerque to the king, 18-2-1622, *DRI*, VII, p. 412; record from the State Council, *ACE*, I, p. 133.

[103] Apparently this change was complete and irreversible in 1618, according to the letter from Governor Fernão de Albuquerque to the king, 8-2-1620, *DRI*, V, p. 276.

[104] In 1616 it was estimated that the profits from the sale of silk in Japan, previously around 100 per cent, had been reduced to 25 per cent; accordingly, the lease-holder of the voyage who formerly obtained some 60,000 *xerafins* (18,000$000) was now unable to get even half of this amount; Silva, 'Lista de todas as Capitanias …', p. 352.

some areas of the Malay Peninsula, especially in Perak. This commodity had already been valuable[105] and, with the rupture in the spice trade and the overall reduction in other profitable goods, it regained prominence, in large measure because it entailed a quick voyage with minimal risks. The Perak tin trade did not receive much attention till the 1610s and appears to have been free for anyone to trade in the commodity, although it is mentioned in the *Livro das Cidades e Fortalezas* as belonging to the captain, who would sell it for 700 *cruzados*.[106]

However, in the 17th century, rights over this trade were fiercely disputed by the residents and captains of the city, both of whom claimed ancient rights over the voyage. The quarrel was caused by Viceroy Rui Lourenço de Távora, who had permitted the residents of the Coromandel coast to buy this tin after their voyage to Melaka with cargoes of textiles, although he immediately revoked this authorisation stating that this was the right of whoever held the contract to the Coromandel voyage.[107] In truth, it seems that the Portuguese of the Coromandel coast indulged in something that was far more profitable: they loaded ships with textiles and sailed directly to Perak, where they bought tin. Therefore they did not go to Melaka and did not pay any duties there. However, this was immediately prohibited.[108] The same viceroy had granted the route to the residents of Melaka, but his successor, Dom Jerónimo de Azevedo, felt that this rightfully belonged to the captains of Melaka and revoked this concession, attributing it instead to Captain João Caiado de Gamboa.

---

[105] For instance, the incident that unleashed the crisis of 1585–87 was the captain of Melaka's greed with regard to the tin carried by a Johor vessel (he actually seized the merchandise and sank the ship), Couto, *Da Ásia*, X, part 2, VII, xii, p. 207. The cargo was around 50–60 *bares*, or more than 10 tonnes (9,180–11, 016 kg, more precisely), if we take it to be the so-called *bar pequeno dachém* used to weigh this metal (Nunes, 'Livro dos Pesos ...', pp. 39 and 48).

[106] Ed. by Luz, fl. 105. *See* Coutre, 'Vida de Jacques de Coutre', p. 376, and Erédia, *Informação da Aurea Chersoneso*, pp. 78–80. About this trade *see* Lobato, *Política e Comércio* ..., pp. 221–223.

[107] *Alvará* of 28-7-1611, correcting the previous one dated 11-5-1611, *APO*, VI (ii), pp. 867–868.

[108] Royal letter to Viceroy D. Jerónimo de Azevedo, 27-2-1612, *DRI*, II, p. 181; *see* the *alvarás* of 28-2-1612, ibid., II, pp. 186–187, and of 28-2-1613, *APO*, VI (ii), pp. 923–924. In his letter of 14-2-1615 to the viceroy, the king extended the interdiction to Java (*DRI*, III, p. 206).

This action evidently displeased the king, who thus saw himself deprived of the respective duties.[109] The trade was again granted to the residents of Melaka, but the governor of Goa disagreed as he felt that this was equivalent to depriving the captains of their main source of income, as they no longer had either the spice trade or the trade with Japan; later, the captains and the *casados* apparently established an agreement to share this trade, according to Dutch sources.[110]

In truth, the captains' fortunes waned in direct proportion to the city's isolation as, apart from losing the main voyages that came along with the post, they were also the main party to suffer losses with the decline of traffic in the port.[111] The Royal Treasury was equally harmed: overburdened by the permanent military efforts, seemingly summoned to assist everywhere at the same time, it saw an accentuated decline in its sources of revenue. The problem was already deeply rooted: whatever customs revenues were obtained, large or small, never reached Goa as they were swallowed up in running expenses, such as the fortification of the city or, more frequently, dissipated thanks to the actions of the captain and officials of the fortress.[112] There was one exceptional year—the only one in which revenues reached Goa—during the viceroyship of Dom Jerónimo

---

[109] Royal letter to Viceroy D. Jerónimo de Azevedo, 4-3-1613, *DRI*, II, p. 362; royal letter to Viceroy D. João Coutinho, 22-3-1617, *DRI*, IV, p. 173, and appended record. About this dispute, *see* Silva, 'Lista de todas as Capitanias …', p. 349.

[110] Royal letter to Viceroy D. João Coutinho, 7-3-1619, *DRI*, VI, pp. 168–169; reply from Governor Fernão de Albuquerque, 5-2-1620, *DRI*, p. 170, and appended *alvará*, pp. 267–269; letter from the same governor to the king, 10-1-1621, *DRI*, VII, pp. 102–103. Schouten's report mentions the agreement between the captains and the *casados* (in Leupe, 'The Siege and Capture of Malacca', p. 95).

[111] The reduction of its revenues was in stark contrast to the vast sums that had proliferated a few years earlier; during the early years of the 17th century it was still the third most profitable captaincy of the Estado da Índia, with sums in the region of 52,000$000 (as compared to 80,000$000 in Sofala and 72,000$000 in Hormuz); Falcão, *Livro em que se contém toda a Fazenda* … [1607], pp. 124–125 (these values were calculated by converting 130,000, 200,000 and 180,000 *cruzados*, respectively, which that author quotes at 400 reis).

[112] Royal letter to Viceroy D. João Coutinho, 18-3-1618, *DRI*, VI, p. 199; Bocarro, *Década 13*, I, xxii, p. 95.

de Azevedo, as the fleets of three voyages from China had joined up and reached Melaka together.[113]

In the light of all these difficulties in acquiring revenues, the Crown resorted to exceptional measures: the most drastic one was the general sale of all the official posts of the Estado da Índia,[114] carried out in April 1615 with a view to resolving all their financial woes, especially the debts left by Rui Lourenço de Távora, and finance a vast joint armada with Manila to expel the Dutch.[115] The captaincy of Melaka was sold to João Caiado de Gamboa for the sum of 32,200 *xerafins* (9,660$000), which was still a substantial amount of money.[116] The funds obtained, which totalled 637,100 *xerafins* (191,130$000), were swallowed up by the administrative apparatus and no armada was ever financed from the proceeds. Viceroy Dom Jerónimo de Azevedo, who was in charge of this action, used the money to other ends, for which reason the king demanded a justification of his acts.[117] The Crown proceeded to send ships directly from Lisbon in an attempt to acquire some pepper from Melaka where, despite everything, it was still possible to buy the commodity. This measure, although nothing new, was aimed at avoiding delays, embezzlement and other sundry difficulties, given that the normal circuits suffered from serious deficiencies.[118] The Crown

---

[113] Letter from Governor Fernão de Albuquerque to the king, 8-2-1620, *DRI*, VI, p. 200.

[114] There is a full description of this general sale, written in 1639 by Gregório de Pina, which is also the theme of a PhD thesis (*Relação de todo o Dinheiro que se fez na Venda dos Cargos e Fortalezas ...*) by Maria Manuela Sobral Blanco.

[115] Bocarro, *Década 13*, I, lxxxviii, pp. 362–366. At this time the governor of Manila, D. Juan de Silva, was preparing a great fleet to join the Portuguese forces in Melaka to expel the Dutch; about this issue *see* chapter 3, 'Disruption'.

[116] Figures from Gregório de Pina's report and from another document dating from 1616 (BN, *Res.*, cod. 1973, fl. 60); other *Relações* mention a slightly inferior value of 30,030 *xerafins* (BN, *Res.*, cod. 206, fl. 90, and cod. 1540, fl. 93v.). The 'Lista de todas as Capitanias ...' by Silva, pp. 348–349, reports the general sale.

[117] At the time, the new viceroy, D. João Coutinho, was already in office, and merely sent the documents pertaining to his predecessor's expenses to Lisbon; royal letter to Viceroy D. João Coutinho (and reply), 21-3-1617, *DRI*, IV, pp. 123–125.

[118] Royal *alvará*, 22-3-1618, *DRI*, V, p. 85, and subsequent *alvará* from the viceroy made public in Melaka, 9-10-1618, *APO*, VI (ii), pp. 1142–1143.

still made some attempts to ensure that the pepper trade continued to flow via Goa by contracting it out, but it would still be necessary to avoid the abuses that the captains continued to exercise over traffic that arrived in Melaka and, likewise, stop it from being diverted to China.[119]

Despite its valiant military and economic efforts, the Estado da Índia never recovered from the shock it had suffered. The military defeats, political ineptitude and failure of its numerous attempts at economic recovery all resulted, slowly but inexorably, in its collapse. On the Dutch side one finds that the initial pretext of defending free trade and freedom of navigation was only defended while they took over privileged centres of Asiatic commerce by force. From the moment they supplanted the Portuguese, the Dutch would themselves make similar attempts to enforce a monopoly, which they later carried out with greater vigour. The project to control all navigation and the main Asiatic trade routes was thanks to the efforts of one man, Jan Pieterszoon Coen, who envisaged the capture of the main Portuguese and Spanish emporia in the eastern Indian Ocean and advocated a hard-line policy of exclusive domination of the seas.[120] It was no coincidence that Bocarro highlighted 1615 as being the year of a definitive rupture in Melaka: it was the year in which the Dutch intensified their activities in the region.

However, 1619 is a far more important year. The Dutch had made Banten their main commercial centre in the Orient. Yet their presence in this sultanate was by no means peaceful as they were subject to the rules of everyday life in the city just like any other foreign mercantile community. The hostility shown to them by the powerful Chinese community, the most important in the city,[121] was particularly visible. The war that Mataram instigated against the sultanate apparently counted upon the support of the Dutch[122] who, in 1619, attacked and destroyed Jakarta, founding their

---

[119] Royal letter to Viceroy D. João Coutinho, 7-3-1619, *DRI*, VI, p. 151, reply from Governor Fernão de Albuquerque, p. 153, and appended document entitled 'Advertencias sobre o trato da pimenta de Malaca', pp. 154–155; *see* the report by Francisco da Costa, *DUP*, III, pp. 333–335.

[120] *See* Vlekke, *Nusantara*, chapter VI, pp. 105–128 and Arasaratnam, 'Monopoly and Free Trade in Dutch-Asian Commercial Policy', pp. 1–5. *See* also the general frameworks presented by Holden Furber, *Rival Empires of Trade in the Orient* and Jonathan Israel, *Dutch Primacy in World Trade*.

[121] Scot, 'A Discourse of Java ...', in Purchas *His Pilgrimes*, II, p. 452.

[122] Letter from N. Ufflet to G. Ball, 13-10-1617, *LREIC*, VI, p. 125.

capital, Batavia, on the site and withdrew from Banten.[123] This action would seal the fate of Melaka, whose enemies, after gaining control of the main trade upon which the city depended, had now settled definitively on its very doorstep. It was from this date onwards that Melaka went into a decline from which it would never recover, thus completing the process of ruin that neither the Dutch take-over in 1641 nor the transfer into English hands would be able to reverse. Melaka shrank, became isolated and fortified itself, exemplified by the image that the chronicler António Bocarro presents us with in the 1630s: a militarised city dominated by its residents, with an indigent and fragmented commercial existence, yielding negligible revenues to the Royal Treasury, apart from some exceptional years in which ships arrived from China or the Coromandel coast. In the global budget, Melaka's deficit was estimated, on average, to be in the range of 6,000$000 per year.[124]

---

[123] Beaulieu, 'Memoires du Voyage ...' in Thevenot (ed.), *Relations de Divers Voyages Curieux*, I, p. 39.

[124] Or 20,000 *xerafins*; Bocarro, 'Livro das Plantas de todas as Fortalezas ...' in *Arquivo Português Oriental*, pp. 14–21 and 24.

CHAPTER 2

Melaka and the Estado da Índia: The Political and Military Framework

The Estado da Índia was the official structure created by the Portuguese in Asia as they established themselves in the East. It underwent a gradual process of decline throughout the 16th century, once the fundamental axes had been established, from Mozambique in East Africa to Macao and Japan in the Far East. The Estado da Índia witnessed an intensification of its current problems, both on account of its dimensions, organisation and maintenance, as well as the external conflicts that the Portuguese experienced in the course of their integration into the heart of the Asiatic world. On the other hand, in the second half of the century, the Portuguese came up against an adverse political scenario which extended throughout the Indian Ocean region. In addition, a new state of affairs emerged from the Habsburg accession to the throne of Portugal. The latter enabled a new geopolitical positioning but also resulted in an intensification of tensions at a global level. Finally, related to this, there was the open challenge from the northern European countries, which directly threatened the foundations of the functioning and maintenance of the Estado da Índia and whose consequences would prove to be harmful to Portuguese interests.

From a political and military point of view, it was an age of stabilisation and decline. However, the accumulated experience of the Portuguese enabled the establishment of a debate about ways of regeneration in administrative, economic and political terms, the containment of problems and deficiencies, and the charting of new courses. Let us take a brief look at two of the most interesting elements in this debate: first, the proposals for creating an autonomous government in Melaka, which came about after the reflexive analysis on a vast structure that extended from the Cape of Good Hope to Japan, and secondly, the projects for territorial conquest, a kind of regenerating project inspired by successful Spanish experiments in America and in the neighbouring Philippine islands. All this happened in a general scenario that differed substantially from that of preceding periods. In fact, the core of the Estado da Índia was inclined towards inertia and, thus, the principal dynamic elements came from initiatives on the peripheries of the system.[1]

Tension, Change and Erosion

The problems that plagued the Estado da Índia did not go unnoticed by the men of the age. The sources that pertain to this period, irrespective of whether they are part of official documentation or a wealth of diverse sources of information ranging from letters to memoirs and reports to chronicles, were all replete with information denouncing the flaws of the system. They are particularly harsh about individual actions, in terms of established practices such as corruption and appropriation of the Crown's goods and wealth by private individuals as well as the defective system that promoted impunity and allowed the perpetuation of errors. Accusations and denouncements are made about the entire edifice of the Estado da Índia. This panorama began with the viceroys themselves: apart from the personal characteristics of each one, their nomination for a short period of three years was complete proof of the system's inefficiency as it allowed them to do little more than correct the errors of their predecessors to guarantee their own revenues and those of their coterie.[2] The scenarios

---

1   Subrahmanyam, 'The Tail Wags the Dog'.
2   'Enformação das fortalezas e lugares da India' [1568], in Wicki (ed.), 'Duas Relações ...', pp. 148–149; 'Apontamentos do Arcebispo de Goa', ibid., p. 188.

painted by some authors, their incisive and caustic tone, particularly Diogo do Couto and Francisco Rodrigues Silveira, has influenced the historiography of our age, shaping the image of an Estado da Índia that was sclerotic, decadent and moribund, dominated by religious fanaticism and widespread corruption.[3] Nevertheless, some authors have demonstrated, often with some amazement, that the Portuguese system, still imbued with a medieval spirit and form of royal service (*serviço del-rei*), continued to function despite all the abuses that took place.[4] However, it is undeniable that many problems remained to be solved in the second half of the 16th century and the situation was considerably aggravated in the 17th century with the arrival of the English and the Dutch.

First, there was the human factor. The problem of effectively managing this eternally scarce resource was a fundamental concern that is evident throughout this period. As is common knowledge, the Portuguese soldiers in India were not subject to a permanent military regime, with the exception of certain specific periods. Occasionally, attempts were made to create orderly and duly organised contingents of troops. Several viceroys proceeded with such initiatives, without any great degree of continuity, although Dutch and English aggression in the 17th century put considerable pressure on the adoption of such measures. Generally, men embarked in Lisbon and, upon arrival in the Orient, habitually placed themselves at the service of a powerful figure, generally a captain or the viceroy, who would manage these forces to serve both the king's and his own ends.[5] From amongst the diverse fates that could befall those who remained in Asia, the most interesting were those of fugitives and renegades. Despite being distinct situations, both derived from the same condition of defection and exclusion from Portuguese structures, very often attracted by the vast world that was Asia and the opportunities offered by a life of adventure, in stark contrast to the misery of those who remained in the fortresses and armadas.[6]

---

3   A recent example is Winius, *The Black Legend of Portuguese India*.
4   For example, Macgregor, 'Notes on the Portuguese in Malaya', pp. 15 and 29.
5   About this issue *see* ibid., pp. 8–11.
6   *See* Cruz, 'Exiles and Renegades in early 16th Century Portuguese India' and 'Degredados e arrenegados portugueses no espaço Índico nos primórdios do século XVI'.

Portuguese soldiers were greatly sought after, especially because of their technical knowledge of the art of war with regard to artillery and light firearms. Between adventurers and mercenaries there were a large number of men who lived on the edge of official structures, especially in the vast geographical area of the Bay of Bengal[7] and the continental kingdoms of Southeast Asia.[8] In the second half of the century, their role in the history of the Portuguese presence in the Orient (increasingly distinct from the history of the official Portuguese empire) became more and more important. It was due to the actions of some of these men that peripheral initiatives were carried out that, by the end of the century, supplanted centralised actions and constituted the most dynamic element *par excellence* of the Portuguese presence in the Orient, as mentioned by Subrahmanyam.[9]

The number of men who deserted from the official circuits of Estado da Índia seems to have increased in direct proportion to the difficulties faced in providing armadas and fortresses with soldiers, to such an extent that, in the light of rising military shortfalls, in 1596 the king granted a general pardon to all those who, having fled for various reasons, flourished in Bengal and Pegu. Official documentation lumped them together under the heading 'fugitives' (*homiziados*). The pardon included all crimes except those of *lèse-majesté*, sodomy, death by treason and counterfeiting of currency.[10] Once the general pardon was circulated in those areas, it soon became obvious that, 'nothing came of it ... because these men live in

---

7   The exact number was uncertain: in the late 16th century, Silveira made an estimate of 2,000 men (*Reformação da Milícia*, p. 151); a document dating from 1608 states that 'the thousand best musketeers of India' were in Bengal (royal letter to Viceroy Martim Afonso de Castro, 4-1-1608, *DRI*, I, p. 174); two reports from the first quarter of the 17th century mention 2,000 and 600, respectively. Espinosa, 'Relação', *DUP*, II, p. 45 and an anonymous report, AN/TT, *MssLiv.*, No. 1116, p. 533.

8   Maria da Conceição Flores presented a paper, 'Mercenaires Portugais au Siam et au Cambodge pendant le XVI Siècle', at the International Seminar on 'A Ásia do Sueste nos Séculos XV a XVIII', Lisbon, Dec. 1989, which was not included in the volume published by Reid (ed.), *Southeast Asia in the Early Modern Era*, which contains the papers presented at the conference.

9   Subrahmanyam, 'The Tail Wags the Dog'.

10 Royal letter of general pardon, 16-3-1596 (copy dated 17-6-1597), made public in Goa on 20-6-1597, HAG, *Livro Morato*, fls. 79–81v.; in August 1597

great freedom and do not want for anything'.[11] In the period under review, on two other occasions (in 1601 and 1615) the king issued a charter granting a general pardon. In the former he reduced sentences by seven years and intended to channel all those who returned to the Portuguese fold into the great armada that was being prepared against the Dutch.[12] In both cases the results were far from encouraging, despite the efforts invested in the enterprise, which included resorting to the services of another adventurer, Filipe de Brito de Nicote, who had built a fortress in Sirian and to whom the king agreed to attribute jurisdiction over the Portuguese who returned to service.[13]

A soldier's life was hard and uncertain and it was not easy to resist the temptation of freedom crowned with wealth, even if it were necessary to serve a Moorish or non-Christian king to obtain it. Tired, famished[14] and badly paid but no less proud on account of this,[15] the Portuguese

---

Viceroy D. Francisco da Gama sent a ship to Bengal with copies of the document to be presented to the Portuguese (copies of letters from the viceroy to the king, 1597, BN, *Res.*, cod. 1976, fl. 69); *see* reply from the king, 21-11-1598, *APO*, III, part 2, p. 925.

[11] Letter from Viceroy D. Francisco da Gama to the king, unknown date [1599], BN, *Res.*, cod. 1976, fl. 146.

[12] Royal letter of pardon, 20-2-1601, HAG, *Livro Morato*, fls. 160–163v.; royal *alvará*, 5-3-1615, *DRI*, III, p. 303.

[13] Letter to the viceroy cited in note 7 above (and *alvará* of 24-3-1608 in *APO*, VI (ii), pp. 811–812). In 1610 the captain of the Coromandel fleet, João Rodrigues Camelo, was authorised to pardon all Portuguese exiles (*alvará* by Viceroy Rui Lourenço de Távora, 18-2-1610, HAG, *Livro Morato*, fls. 241v.–142v.); *see* royal letter to Viceroy D. João Coutinho, 17-1-1618, *DRI*, IV, pp. 262–264, and reply of 14-2-1619, p. 265.

[14] The death rate was quite high among the soldiers who went to the 'South' (Melaka) but there is no systematic data about their alimentary habits. A curious source dating from the late 16th century mentions *arak* (palm-tree wine) and opium, saying it was necessary to send to Melaka 'some casks of *arak* [*urraca*], which is the main sustenance of the seamen in those areas, and also some opium [*anfião*] for those who consume it because they shall not refuse it' (letter from Tomé de Sousa Coutinho to the viceroy, 7-4-1600, AN/TT, *MiscMssCGL*, box 6, vol. II E, p. 349).

[15] The two faces of the Portuguese soldiers in India: 'without pride or self-confidence because they are hungry and abandoned' (letter from the Inquisitor Rui Sodrinho to the General-Inquisitor, Goa, 2-12-1593, in Baião (ed.), *A Inquisição de*

soldiers had to support themselves and buy their arms with their meagre pay, which was very often only paid after long delays. Furthermore, they had to be available to embark on armadas that were frequently poorly conducted and had an uncertain fate. They rarely benefited from the booty or other profits obtained. The temptation to desert was real and widespread, as we can see from Francisco Rodrigues Silveira's accurate portrayal:

> 'Some go to Bengal, others to China, Melaka, Pegu, Diu, Hormuz, Sindh, Cambay; and many serve as soldiers, on board the ships of hucksters (*chatins*) and the carracks of merchants, where although the service is not as honourable as that of the King, it is more profitable for being better paid, leaving aside here those who fight under the standards of non-Christian kings and princes, who are so many in number that one cannot think of them, let alone write about them, without shedding many tears.'[16]

Portuguese soldiers in India were subjected to a series of pressures in order to prevent desertion. From a certain time, their return to Portugal required express authorisation from the viceroy,[17] which shows the permanent shortfall in equipping armadas and fortresses. It appears that the normal period of service in India was fixed at eight years, divided up amongst diverse regions.[18] Indiscipline was a serious problem which

---

Goa, II, p. 157); 'the Portuguese men we receive here [in the Jesuit College of Cochin] are usually former soldiers, therefore imbued with vanity in their bones' (letter from Jerónimo Xavier to C. Acquaviva, 2-1-1587, *DI*, XIV, p. 546).

[16] Silveira, *Reformação da Milícia*, p. 150.

[17] Royal *alvarás* of 17-3-1584 and 12-3-1592, *APO*, III, part 1, doc. 6 and V, part 3, doc. 968, respectively. About the captains, royal consent was requested for their return (royal letter to Viceroy Matias de Albuquerque, 9-3-1594, *APO*, III, part 1, p. 455; also published in *DHMPPO/Insulíndia*, V, pp. 225–226).

[18] By royal *alvará* of 17-12-1611, this period of service was divided into 2 years in Sri Lanka, 2 years in Melaka or in the 'Southern fleets' (east of Cape Comorin, Melaka being the main axis), and 4 in the 'Northern fleets' (north of Goa, including Gujarat, the Persian Gulf and the Red Sea) or the Malabar fleet. There are some clues on how Melaka was effectively a destination that everybody wished to avoid: a soldier could not be forced to stay there for more than the 2 years mentioned above and the noblemen who served there would receive benefits in future official posts (*DRI*, II, p. 123; also published in *APO*, VI (ii), pp. 885–886).

diminished the efficiency of Portuguese military enterprises and the security of fortresses.[19] In the specific case of the 'Southern region' (Melaka and Southeast Asia), the general insecurity of navigation after the arrival of the Dutch made service in this area undesirable; thus soldiers refused to embark for Melaka. There is a very well-documented example of this: the preparation of Dom Martim Afonso de Castro's great armada faced serious difficulties in recruiting men, who would flee after receiving their pay and before embarking.[20] With the permanent shortage of experienced soldiers, a large part of the garrisons of the armadas or fortresses were constituted of men without experience, newly arrived (and often forced into service) from Portugal, who were called 'Reinóis'. They had not yet adjusted to local conditions and were frequently discriminated against by the other soldiers.[21] A lack of qualified personnel was very clearly evident, especially of experienced pilots and bombardiers.[22] The upper ranks were replete with inexperienced officers and the problem was substantially aggravated: the dearth of 'veteran' noblemen and the system of personal favours resulted in the appointment of young, inexperienced noblemen

[19]   The archbishop of Goa refers to the permanent problems of military discipline, saying that the viceroys spent more money on them on land than at sea; 'Apontamentos' from Archbishop D. Jorge Temudo to the king (dated 1569 or 70), in Wicki (ed.), 'Duas relações …', pp. 192–193.

[20]   Royal letter to Viceroy D. Martim Afonso de Castro, 3-1-1608, *DRI*, I, p. 172 (and *alvará* of 14-2-1608, HAG, *Cartas Patentes, Provisões e Alvarás*, 1, fl. 18v.) and to Viceroy Rui Lourenço de Távora, 22-2-1611, *DRI*, II, p. 60. Also *see* the report by Rui Dias de Meneses, AN/TT, *MssLiv.*, No. 1116, p. 731.

[21]   Most soldiers of D. Martim Afonso de Castro's fleet were Reinóis. Luís Coelho de Barbuda describes the general panic caused by the elephants of the Acehnese army when the Portuguese disembarked in the sultanate; one can only imagine the impact of such animals on individuals who had probably never even heard of their existence (*Empresas Militares de Lusitanos*, fl. 322v.); the captains of the Portuguese fleets often refused to admit them in their service; royal letter to Viceroy D. Jerónimo de Azevedo, 14-2-1615, *DRI*, III, p. 242.

[22]   Royal letter to Viceroy D. Francisco da Gama, 12-2-1597, *APO*, III, part 2, pp. 705–706; 'Notes' from the city of Melaka, 1599, BN, *Res.*, cod. 1973, fl. 57v. (*see* Document Appendix, No. 10); royal letter to Viceroy Aires de Saldanha, 31-1-1602. AHU, *Cons. Ultr.*, cod. 282, fls. 72v.–73.

to administrative and military posts and missions with a great degree of responsibility, frequently with serious consequences.[23]

Such problems were not limited to the lower ranks, at the level of ordinary soldiers. Even at the very top, nobles could withdraw from the king's service, likewise preferring a life of trade from which they could obtain profits as not all of them were lucky enough to hold the more profitable posts. An interesting transformation, occasionally mentioned in the sources, reveals a fundamental shift in mentality: the nobles were accused of no longer being as generous with their soldiers as they had been in the past and, instead, economised and saved excessively. This was one of the reasons for the soldiers' poverty.[24] What does seem to have changed was the age-old military function of the nobles as organisers of soldiers in an era when military enterprises and the corresponding booty permitted a generous redistribution of wealth.

In the present scenario, the nobleman who went to India was increasingly either an official who lived off the emoluments of the post he held or a merchant who would invest in profitable trade routes. In both instances he was increasingly far removed from a life of arms.[25] In either case, it does not appear that he squandered any less than his forefathers had

---

[23] Royal letter to Viceroy Matias de Albuquerque, 26-2-1595, *APO*, III, part 2, p. 527; royal letter to Viceroy Aires de Saldanha cited in the previous note, fl. 71.

[24] About this issue, here is an excerpt from a report by Viceroy D. Francisco da Gama to the governor of Portugal, Miguel de Moura: 'This *Estado* has a great dearth of old *fidalgos*, and the few left behave in a very different manner when compared to those of yore because they are only interested in commerce and not in carrying out their duties under the viceroys' command, spending in their service what they had previously extracted in the fortresses and even more, so much so that they all assumed their offices in a state of great debt; today they do exactly the opposite and only think of saving more than they need; this also affects the soldiers because formerly the noblemen used to spend money on them which is a support they lack nowadays, so today they all look out for their own interests and prefer to sail aboard the vessels of merchants and hucksters (*chatins*) instead of serving in our fleets because His Majesty's Treasury cannot pay them more than their wages (...)' (BN, *Res.*, cod. 1975, fls. 252–252v.).

[25] *See* Governor Fernão de Albuquerque's opinion in a letter to the king, 24-1-1621, *DRI*, VII, pp. 150–151.

done.[26] This must be kept in mind when assessing the growing criticism with which the chroniclers (with Diogo do Couto at the forefront) upbraid the arrogance, the laziness or the corruption of the Portuguese noblemen. Similarly, one can better understand some of the astonishment revealed by the chronicles when they relate the personal qualities and military feats of some warriors, such as André Furtado de Mendonça or Nuno Álvares Botelho, considered the last vestiges of the power and heroism of a glorious epoch that had already passed.

These difficulties were obviously linked with material problems. The financial deficit was a permanent headache in a structure that collected vast revenues but proved to be incapable of directing them to the Royal Treasury and, especially, of putting them to use in a productive manner. This was proof of the lack of efficiency of fiscal instruments, of the risk of paralysis that pervaded the entire structure, of the growing divide between the Estado da Índia and the Portuguese presence in Asia. It is the only way to understand the permanent signs of alarm about the fact that revenues were not sufficient to cover ordinary expenses, a situation that the viceroy, although a powerful figure, confessed to being unable to resolve.[27] A second

---

[26] This may be observed in the reserve funds the viceroys had to bestow as benefits to noblemen; until 1587 it was limited to 12,000 *cruzados*, increased by royal command to 20,000 (royal letter to Viceroy D. Duarte de Meneses, 10-1-1587, *APO*, III, part 1, p. 77, also published in *DHMPPO/Insulíndia*, V, p. 59); in 1591 it was considered insufficient; attempting to prevent abuses, the king raised the limit to 30,000 *cruzados*, even mentioning that these benefits put the provisioning of the fleets at risk (royal order of 18-1-1591, *APO*, V, part 3, p. 1282); in 1606 the limit was raised to 40,000 *cruzados* with the curious justification of the war against the Dutch (copy of *alvará* of 11-4-1606, 27-8-1608, *APO*, VI (ii), p. 827); finally, in 1612, the global crisis of the Exchequer forced the king to reduce it to the former level of 30,000 *cruzados* (royal *alvará*, 17-8-1612, *DRI*, II, p. 265).

[27] Royal letter to Viceroy D. Francisco da Gama, 5-2-1597, *APO*, III, part 2, p. 683; letter from the viceroy to the king, 24-12-1599, BN, *Res.*, cod. 1976, fl. 119v.; letter from the viceroy to the governor of Portugal, Miguel de Moura, BN, *Res.*, cod. 1975, fl. 250v.; here he states that 'A viceroy cannot always perform miracles nor strip his men, and without money it is not possible to make war properly or assist anyone in need with due rapidity and quality'; about the 'disorders' caused by this situation, he said, 'They cannot be resolved with such tight limits being imposed on a viceroy by His Majesty'.

problem was the material shortages themselves, the lack of duly equipped ships, munitions and artillery.

The problem of ships was critical for a maritime empire such as the Estado da Índia. The aggravation of political conditions in the second half of the century, particularly in the South, implied a considerable naval effort. Melaka now needed an armada to patrol the Straits and the surrounding region to prevent any possible attack from the rival power, Aceh, as well as to ensure the safety of navigation, especially of the ships from China that passed through the Straits; they were greatly coveted, highly prized and exceedingly vulnerable in these waters. One only needs to look at the urgency involved in sending the armadas of Matias de Albuquerque (in 1576) and Dom Paulo de Lima Pereira (in 1587) to perceive how serious and delicate these issues were considered.

The lack of ships, especially of carracks, became a permanent problem, sometimes even to the point of being ridiculous: there were years in which an abundance of pepper was of no use, as there were no ships available to transport it to Portugal.[28] Considerable efforts were made to improve naval construction, but it was necessary to supply a global empire with increasing demand for ships and military resources but where the weight of Spanish interests seemed to superimpose itself on those of the Portuguese. The arrival of the English and the Dutch considerably worsened the situation, given that the Portuguese Crown found it impossible to match the frequency with which they despatched armadas to the Orient. Nor was it able to contain them due to the debilitated finances of the Estado da Índia. As early as 1598, five armadas, with a total of twenty-two ships, set sail from the United Provinces, while not a single vessel set sail from Lisbon due to the English blockade of the port.[29] The most important fleet in the Orient was that of Jacob van Neck. In 1601, even before the merger of various rival companies which united around the VOC, fourteen

---

[28] This happened, for instance, in 1596; royal letter to Viceroy D. Francisco da Gama, 5-2-1597, *APO*, III, part 2, p. 683.

[29] Portuguese fleets in India rarely exceeded three ships. At the beginning of the 17th century, the king made a contract to build three vessels annually in the shipyards of Lisbon for the fleet of André Furtado de Mendonça; of these three, two ships were supposed to sail directly to Melaka, but in 1604 the entire process was running behind schedule (royal letter to Viceroy Aires de Saldanha, 23-3-1604, AHU, *Cons. Ultr.*, cod. 282, fl. 211).

armadas set sail with a total of sixty-five ships. The Dutch ships would prove to be speedier, more numerous and better equipped, with better and larger quantities of artillery and, similarly, used more efficient naval tactics than those of the Portuguese carracks, as would be plainly evident in the medium term.[30]

In this new scenario, some changes took place in the traditional scheme of the organisation of Portuguese armadas. The Portuguese had arrived in Asia in carracks (*naus*), high-tonnage ships with large capacity for transporting cargoes and equipped with suitable armaments. These ships were specifically designed to sail the high seas, especially on transoceanic routes. However, in the specific case of Melaka and the surrounding territory, the Portuguese realised that smaller vessels, of a lesser gauge, speedier and more manoeuvrable, were far more suited to the treacherous channels and sandbanks of the Straits. They also learned that the use of oars, impossible in the case of high-tonnage vessels, was possible with smaller ships, thus giving them additional speed and the ability to escape the brunt of seasonal winds. Therefore, the armadas that frequented this region generally consisted of a mixed combination of ships, which enabled them to accomplish their mission in different situations.

The arrival of the English and the Dutch would alter this panorama and create additional problems. On one hand, the galliots and other small vessels, although very quick, were not equipped with artillery and had a limited capacity for conflict if they encountered northern European ships, but the large freight-carrying carracks were slow and vulnerable and increased risks by concentrating expensive merchandise in a single ship that could be lost in a single strike. On the other hand, these large ships were generally, for a variety of reasons, badly equipped and badly prepared from a military point of view. Finally, the great armadas of André Furtado de Mendonça and Dom Martim Afonso de Castro failed to drive the European enemies out of Southeast Asian waters, thus considerably weakening the Portuguese naval strength.

Thus a debate arose about the best way to organise the formation of armadas. The result that finally prevailed was not dictated by a strategic choice but, instead, by financial criteria: the high tonnage vessels were dispensed with as they were more expensive than smaller ships. In addition, the Portuguese strategy shifted from an offensive approach, with

---

[30]   *See* Sousa, *Subsídios para a História Militar Marítima da Índia*, I, pp. 429–435.

expeditions aimed at expelling the Dutch, to a defensive one, that is, slipping through chinks in the Dutch web. Oared ships thus started to form the bulk of Portuguese armadas in the region. These vessels became therefore so important that when the sale of ships was banned, a special provision was issued concerning oared craft.[31]

The decline of Melaka was not limited to the city and its trade, but also extended to Portuguese navigation. Rules of navigation were now imposed on ships: the precious and increasingly scarce carracks were prohibited from navigating unless they sailed along with the armada sent by the viceroy.[32] As for navigation in general, ships were now ordered to sail together in a convoy.[33] During the 1610s, the shortage of carracks became critical due to a general worsening of the situation as well as the loss of four galleons near Melaka in Dutch actions immediately after Aceh's siege on the city. The efforts to help the great joint armada the governor of Manila was preparing against the Dutch was an additional factor.[34] The *cartaz*, a means of controlling general navigation that was more political than economic—even though it did not play the same role in Southeast Asia as it did in the western Indian Ocean region—definitively lost its function.[35]

---

[31] Royal *alvará* of 6-3-1613, AN/TT, *MssLiv.*, No. 699, fls. 46v.–47: 'Under no circumstances should any oared ships be sold, no matter how old they may be'.

[32] *Alvará* from Viceroy D. Jerónimo de Azevedo, 1-4-1613, *APO*, VI (ii), p. 925; this provision was extended to the entire South except for Bengal; the captains who did not carry out the order were to lose their office and be exiled to Sri Lanka for four years; *see* Bocarro, *Década 13*, I, lxviii, p. 298.

[33] Royal letter to Viceroy D. João Coutinho, 26-2-1619, *DRI*, V, pp. 275–276.

[34] In 1616 the viceroy considered the possibility of going and assisting Melaka with an oared fleet as there were no carracks available, were he to receive definite information about a new Dutch attack on the city; letter to the king, Jan. 1616, HAG, *MonçReino*, 12, fl. 243v. (published in *BOGEI*, No. 184 (1883), p. 740).

[35] All ships sailing without a *cartaz* were meant to be seized, but at this time the Portuguese hesitated to do so because of the inevitable hostile effects; this happened, for instance, when the Adil Shah of Bijapur asked for more *cartazes* for the 'Southern parts' than those mentioned in the peace treaty (royal letter to Viceroy D. Jerónimo de Azevedo, 21-2-1615, *DRI*, I, p. 267); about navigation from Aceh to Hormuz, *see* chapter 1, note 59.

It has already been mentioned that António Bocarro highlighted 1615 as the year that heralded the irreversible decline of Melaka. The same may be said about this issue: from the time Gaspar Afonso de Melo (captain of Melaka, 1613–15) sent a galleon to China that was captured by the Dutch, the Portuguese ceased to use high-tonnage vessels in the South.[36] Shortly thereafter, the viceroy acknowledged that all Portuguese navigation in the Indian Ocean, including the voyages to Japan, to be carried out in galliots.[37] This vessel soon became the ship of choice. The oared galliot, if properly equipped with artillery, adapted well to these new conditions: it could speedily escape more powerful vessels, but its artillery provided good defences against smaller ships. As a result, all trade, including the spice trade from eastern Indonesia, was soon carried out in these vessels.[38] But the Dutch reply was swift: along with their larger ships, they started using smaller, shallower vessels to such an extent that the Portuguese soon recognised that 'even the galliots can no longer navigate safely'.[39]

From the late 16th century the Estado da Índia stretched from the Cape of Good Hope to Japan and in the 1580s the interaction with Manila and the Spanish sphere of influence became more intense. In an age of structural decline and increasing external pressure, the management

---

[36]   In 1619 Viceroy D. João Coutinho stated that large ocean-going ships only plied the routes to Hormuz, Muscat and Mozambique, all the other vessels being 'small brigantines (*patachos*) and topsail galliots and galliots with round sails … as they were lighter than the carracks'; letter to the king, 8-2-1619, *DRI*, V, p. 13; *see* the Records from the Treasury Council, 22-4-1616, *ACE*, I, part 1, pp. 45–46 and 46–47, with recommendations that the trade with China no longer be carried out in carracks on a definitive basis.

[37]   Letter from Governor Fernão de Albuquerque to the king, 8-2-1620, *DRI*, V, p. 276.

[38]   'Discurso' by F. Belchior dos Anjos, 10-10-1619, in F. Mendes da Luz, *O Conselho da Índia*, p. 602. This information should be compared with the letter from the governor cited in the previous note, referring to the frailty of the galleys that could not support more than two light artillery pieces (*falcões*). He also mentions that this trade carried out in small vessels was not favourable to the interests of the Royal Treasury because it resulted in an evasion of tax payments and customs duties.

[39]   Letter from Governor Fernão de Albuquerque to the king, 18-2-1622, *DRI*, VII, p. 411. He added that the Southern Seas were 'infested' with Dutch ships.

of such a vast expanse faced serious problems, all the more so because it implied an inevitable dispersion of resources and forces.[40] The corrupt practices, the inadequacy of the administrative system, the deeply rooted policy of leasing out trade, the very venality of official posts that had been consecrated by the General Sale, are all aspects to be taken into account. Yet there are also strategic questions to be considered. The most important one concerns the very form of organisation and intervention in this vast area that dated back to the arrival of the Portuguese in the Indian Ocean.

Despite being commonly regarded as ineffective, the Portuguese continued their policy of holding a network of fortresses throughout Maritime Asia. This option was aimed at controlling the most important commercial areas as it was hard, if not impossible, to have effective control over the seas. However, a fortress had considerable human and financial costs, in an undertaking that was frequently ineffective unless accompanied by an armada that complemented its functions. Diogo do Couto even called them 'corrals', badly equipped with men and munitions, which only generated expenses and did not yield any revenue.[41] In the case of Southeast Asia, it has been already emphasised that the Portuguese, due to a lesser degree of military tension than that which prevailed in the western Indian Ocean, had never proceeded with this kind of policy. However, in the late 16th century there was no dearth of suggestions and plans, given that Melaka was now also under increasing pressure. Yet the lack of resources forced the Portuguese authorities to postpone these initiatives. Nevertheless, the intention of carrying them out was plainly evident; they were to be combined with the strategy of large armadas, which was, in fact, executed.

At different points in time the Portuguese intended to build fortresses in diverse locations, first due to Acehnese power and, later, against the Dutch. From the beginning of the 17th century, these plans received a fresh

---

[40] *See*, for instance, the retrospective diagnosis made by João Ribeiro at the end of the 17th century: the dispersal of human and material resources being one of the major causes of the weakness of the Estado da Índia (Ribeiro, *Fatalidade Histórica da Ilha de Ceilão*, III, v, p. 176); Francisco Rodrigues Silveira also argued that the Portuguese should keep only some of the existing fortresses (*Reformação da Milícia*, p. 220).

[41] Couto, *O Soldado Prático*, p. 196.

impetus as the Portuguese sought to resolve two fundamental problems with such an initiative: dominating navigation at key points and controlling the supply of spices, pre-empting the Dutch who were thought to have the same designs. It is no coincidence that careful attention was paid to Melaka's main neighbouring sultanates, Aceh and Johor, and also to Sunda/Banten. Aceh's case is the most interesting as it corresponds to an exceptional period of improved and more intense relations between this sultanate and Melaka. It began in 1591 with the shipwreck of the bishop of Macao on the Sumatran coast and definitively came to an end with the attack by the armada of Dom Martim Afonso de Castro in 1606.

During these fifteen years the Portuguese seriously considered the construction of a fortress in the sultanate,[42] attracted by the sultan's promises of supplying them with his pepper.[43] The earliest information about the plans of Sultan Alauddin Riayat Syah to permit the Portuguese to settle in Aceh dates from 1598, but at this time they had not yet accepted the offer, preferring instead to postpone negotiations until it was possible to conquer the sultanate.[44] Shortly thereafter, the Portuguese demanded that the fortress be located in Gomispola, or the offer should not be accepted, although the Dutch presence was already a cause for concern.[45] In the following years the Portuguese hesitated over signing a formal alliance with the sultanate. Their actions were limited to issuing favourable opinions about the advantages of such an enterprise, which would keep the Dutch away from the sultanate, ensure control over the western entrance to the Straits of Melaka and enable access to supplies of pepper. Diplomatic initiatives by diverse entities, including the captains and residents of Melaka, some Augustinian missionaries and the viceroys

---

[42] About this period there are two important issues to consider: the projects regarding the conquest of the sultanate and the diplomatic process that unfolded over these 15 years in order to obtain a peace treaty, in which the Augustinian friar Amaro de Jesus played an important role.

[43] Royal letters to Viceroy D. Francisco da Gama, 16-3-1596, *APO*, III, part 2, p. 627; 5-2-1597, p. 669; and 30-3-1598, AN/TT, BN, *Res.*, cod. 1975, fl. 331v. (*see* Document Appendix, No. 9).

[44] Letter to Viceroy D. Francisco da Gama, 30-3-1598, BN, *Res.*, cod. 1975, fls. 331–331v. (*see* Document Appendix, No. 9).

[45] The islands of Gomispola, near the northern tip of Sumatra; *see* chapter 3, note 99. Letter from Viceroy D. Francisco da Gama, unknown date [1599 or 1600], BN, *Res.*, cod. 1976, fl. 130v.

themselves kept the channels of communication for reaching an agreement open, but no further steps were taken. At this time, the English who, just like the Dutch, assiduously frequented the sultanate became aware of these efforts.[46]

In the meantime, local political conditions became increasingly unfavourable when the old sultan died, especially after Iskandar Muda ascended the throne. The arrival of Martim Afonso de Castro's armada would, in practice, render any agreement unfeasible, thus bringing a brief period of peace with the old enemy to a close and definitively putting an end to any chance of Portuguese settlement in the sultanate. The Portuguese had lost the diplomatic battle, to the benefit of their European rivals. In Madrid, however, the authorities revealed a remarkable lack of awareness about local realities as the possibility of constructing such a fortress was debated for quite some time.[47] It was only in 1613, when the sultan was already preparing an armada against Melaka, that the impossibility of realising this project was recognised.[48]

The project for the construction of a fortress in Sunda had identical objectives. It is uncertain whether this referred directly to the sultanate of Banten or to the region. The idea was not new,[49] but the arrival of the Dutch resulted in a revival of the project. Once again it was an attempt to capture supplies of pepper and control enemy navigation, which had one of their main bases in this sultanate. Unlike the discussion concerning Aceh, the Portuguese did not request permission from the sultan of Banten to build a fortress. They limited themselves to recognising Banten as a powerful economic and maritime power that was totally outside their control. In any case, such projects were only raised during the preparation of the armada of André Furtado de Mendonça and they were immediately

---

[46] Report of the third voyage of James Lancaster, *The Voyages of ...*, p. 101.

[47] Letter from the Council of Portugal to the king, 26-11-1609, AGS, *Secr. Prov.*, book 1479, fls. 535 and 536v. (based on information from André Furtado de Mendonça); royal letter to Viceroy Rui Lourenço de Távora, 24-12-1610, *DRI*, I, p. 416.

[48] Royal letter to Viceroy D. Jerónimo de Azevedo, 16-1-1613, *DRI*, II, p. 293.

[49] In the 1520s the Portuguese tried to execute a similar project that was doomed to failure because of the political conjuncture; Couto echoes these intentions and those of similar projects in Pegu (Burma) and Aceh (*Da Ásia*, IV, part 1, III, i, p. 168); *see* Thomaz, 'O malogrado estabelecimento oficial dos portugueses em Sunda' and Guillot, 'Les Portugais et Banten'.

dismissed owing to the risks, expenses and ineffectiveness of such an enterprise.[50]

Finally, one should mention the case of Johor, where the Portuguese likewise thought of building a fortress, especially after the destruction of the sultanate's capital in 1587. Immediately after this strike by Dom Paulo de Lima Pereira, a question arose: should one construct a fortress there or, on the contrary, should one invest in a permanent armada to keep an eye on the movements of the sultan in hiding?[51] The first option was raised again much later, well after the Dutch had signed a treaty and established themselves in the sultanate. This time, the Portuguese objectives were mostly strategic as the Dutch made the Johor River a permanent base for attacks on Melaka's shipping. To this end, attempts were made to utilise the good relations that were gradually being established with the sultan, taking advantage of the latter's increasing fears with regard to Aceh. However, he did not appear inclined to make such a concession, to either the Portuguese or the Dutch.[52]

More important than the sultanate of Johor itself was the project of building a fortress in the straits controlled by the sultanate—the Straits of Singapore and of Sabang, through which all shipping to and from the Far East passed.[53] The security of Melaka itself was now in question. It

---

[50] Royal letter to Viceroy Aires de Saldanha, 14-3-1601, AHU, *Cons. Ultr.*, cod. 282, fl. 50; in the following year, with regard to this proposed fortress, the king stated that, 'It will not be sustainable and will not prevent this navigation in the manner that the said fleet will be able to do' (ibid., 10-2-1602, fl. 79v.).

[51] In 1589 the king mentioned both options: letters to Viceroy D. Duarte de Meneses, 6-2-1589, *APO*, III, part 1, p. 178 (also published in *DHMPPO/Insulíndia*, V, p. 132), and of 22-2-1589, ibid., p. 214. In 1591 he already seemed convinced that the construction of such a fortress was useless; letter to Viceroy Matias de Albuquerque, 12-1-1591, ibid., p. 276 (also published in *DHMPPO/Insulíndia*, V, p. 194).

[52] Letter from Viceroy D. Jerónimo de Azevedo to the king, unknown date [Jan. 1617?], HAG, *MonçReino*, 12, fl. 260 (published with errors in *BOGEI*, No. 215 (1883), p. 867; letter from Viceroy D. João Coutinho to the king, 7-2-1619, *DRI*, IV, p. 279.

[53] The straits of Singapore and Sabang were the most important; the former was located between that island and the Karimun Islands and the latter between the island of Sabang (probably Kundur) and Sumatra, according to the most accepted version (*see* below, chapter 4, note 81). Viceroy D. Jerónimo de Azevedo

was here that the problem of which strategic option to implement was debated more vigorously: a patrolling armada or a permanent fortress? The problem dated back at least to the 1570s, a period critically unstable and unsafe for Portuguese navigation in the region. They sought to compete with the fortification of Johor but also with the threatening Acehnese, who intended to control both sides of the Straits through the construction of a fortress in Perak. The warm relations between the two sultanates at this time also raised fears that they could join forces to build a fortress in Singapore, a scenario the Portuguese sought to prevent at all cost.[54] As in other cases, financial difficulties compelled the Portuguese to successively postpone the project. Besides, various opinions proffered by the city of Melaka, as well as by the viceroys, strongly advised against the project and it was shelved for some time.[55] They opted for a permanent armada that, at least after the enterprise undertaken by Matias de Albuquerque (1576), patrolled the Straits.

Once again, the arrival of the Dutch led to this and other projects being taken up anew as it was suddenly necessary to invest in many areas at the same time to try and contain Anglo-Dutch infiltration in the region. Given that the balance of power was increasingly in favour of the enemy, the construction of a fortress in the Straits was considered as a last resort in attempting to control shipping, all the more since it was suspected that the Dutch had similar intentions.[56] However, some

---

knew the region well (because of his sojourn there in 1586–87): with regard to Singapore, he claimed to have discovered a 'new strait', but there were so many islands and channels that, 'if one is obstructed, another one will be found'; about the Sabang Straits, he said that it was too wide and not suitable for the construction of a fortress (letter quoted in the previous note and royal reply, 23-1-1618, *DRI*, IV, p. 278). The Spanish and the Dutch had similar projects. *See* Borschberg, 'Portuguese, Spanish and Dutch Plans to Construct a Fort in the Straits of Singapore, ca. 1584-1625'.

[54] Royal Instructions to Viceroy D. Duarte de Meneses, 10-3-1584, AN/TT, *Fundo Port. da Bibl. Nac. de Paris*, No. 48, fl. 9 (*see* Document Appendix, No. 2).

[55] Copies of letters from Viceroy D. Francisco da Gama to the king, unknown date [1597], BN, *Res.*, cod. 1976, fls. 59v.–60; royal letter to the same viceroy, 21-11-1598, AN/TT, *MiscMssCGL*, box 3, vol. VI L, p. 275.

[56] Royal letter to Viceroy D. Martim Afonso de Castro, 27-1-1607, *DRI*, I, p. 131; royal letters to Viceroy D. Jerónimo de Azevedo, 7-1-1614, ibid., II, p. 473; 6-2-1616, ibid., III, pp. 380–381.

individuals[57] continued to point out the ineffectiveness of such a measure, and the project was never implemented.

The policy of fortresses was, thus, a fundamental instrument of intervention for the Estado da Índia in this region although a dearth of resources never really permitted its implementation in practice. A Portuguese source mentions the existence of a Portuguese fort in Muar, near Melaka, but it is doubtful that such a structure was ever built.[58] They were all merely projects. In 1619, the viceroy confessed that he did not have 'a dime' (*um vintém*) to erect new fortresses, no matter how small.[59] The cases mentioned here only refer to the most important points of this region, those which posed the greatest threat to Melaka and its commercial and political structure. One could also cite other examples, such as Bengal and Martaban.[60]

Another problem that needs to be considered concerns the Portuguese diplomatic policy with regard to local powers. The sultanates of Aceh and Johor, which shaped regional geopolitics, will be dealt with in detail in a subsequent chapter. However, there are other cases, albeit of lesser importance, that show how the Portuguese, which had been minimally effective during the 16th century, proved to be a failure during the subsequent century. The decreasing influence of the Portuguese to the Dutch reduced their diplomatic prestige and political weight and had profound effects on foreign relations with various powers. Just like Aceh during a large part of the 16th century, there was now a new power that capitalised on anti-Portuguese animosity. However, these newcomers were far more dangerous to Melaka than the old Acehnese enemy, for two main reasons. First,

---

[57] *See* the letter from Viceroy D. Jerónimo de Azevedo to the king quoted in notes 52 and 53 above; in 1607 the Portuguese acknowledged that even if they were able to build a fortress in Aceh and were able to control the whole region of the Straits of Melaka, their control over the east Indian Ocean would be ineffective unless they were also able to control Sri Lanka (royal letter to Viceroy D. Martim Afonso de Castro, 12-1-1607, *DRI*, I, p. 60).

[58] The only source about this fort is its presumed builder, Manuel Godinho de Erédia; 'Declaraçam de Malaca ...', fl. 10 and 57v.

[59] Letter from Viceroy D. João Coutinho, 8-2-1619, *DRI*, IV, p. 352.

[60] Royal letter to Viceroy Matias de Albuquerque, 12-1-1591, *APO*, III, part 1, p. 257 (also published in *DHMPPO/Insulíndia*, V, p. 189); Royal letter to Viceroy D. Martim Afonso de Castro, 4-1-1608, *DRI*, I, p. 177; Bocarro, *Década 13*, I, cxvi, p. 518.

Aceh was seen with natural distrust by other sultanates, which viewed its anti-Portuguese moves as an attempt to promote its regional hegemony, while the Dutch claimed to have pure commercial intentions and simply intended to introduce alternative channels to transport spices and other commodities. Secondly, the Dutch possessed a formidable naval presence that, apart from the new factor of economic competition, represented a daunting military challenge for the Portuguese.

Thus, new conditions that aggravated Melaka's diplomatic position gradually emerged. Johor established an alliance that resulted in the siege of 1606 and Aceh put an end to any hopes of friendly relations with the Portuguese, which had prevailed since 1592. Once the Dutch had established their bases in Southeast Asia, they exerted anti-Portuguese pressure throughout the region that, combined with old enmities, began to have an effect. Masulipatnam, for example, had been attempting for quite some time to escape the payment of tribute (*páreas*) to the Portuguese. This was generally paid in rice, in exchange for permits enabling them to navigate in southern waters to go to Aceh and Pegu where they would load cargoes of wood.[61] In 1615 relations were totally cut and the Portuguese on the Coromandel coast were prohibited from trading at this port as it was a declared enemy of the Estado da Índia.[62] Kedah and Perak were drawn into the anti-Portuguese front, and only crossed over to the Portuguese side because they were threatened by Aceh.[63] In Java, a favourite point of settlement for both the English and the Dutch, the Portuguese rapidly lost their influence, in decline since the 1570s, especially because their traditional Hindu allies in Blambangan and Panarukan, in eastern Java, were under increasing pressure from the Muslim sultanates.[64] Patani was a

---

[61] *See* royal letter to Viceroy Matias de Albuquerque, 12-1-1591, *APO*, III, part 1, p. 258 (also published in *DHMPPO/Insulíndia*, V, pp. 190–191); Freire (ed.), *Primor e Honra* ..., p. 96.

[62] Bocarro, *Década 13*, I, clii, pp. 618–619.

[63] Some available information suggests that the sultan of Kedah killed the Portuguese in his port and seized their ships, forcing the Portuguese to send a fleet to punish this sultanate, as also to Perak (summary of letters from Viceroy D. Martim Afonso de Castro, 4-5-1607, and from the city and bishop of Melaka, AGS, *Secr. Prov.*, book 1479, fls. 161–162).

[64] Gresik, in 1597 (*see Iovrnal de l'Inde Orientale* and report of the voyage of Oliver Noort in Purchas, *His Pilgrimes*, II, p. 204).

Dutch base from very early on. In 1605 it captured a Portuguese carrack in collusion with the Dutch,[65] and from that time this sultanate showed a permanent hostility towards the Portuguese that only abated with the peace treaty signed in 1619.[66]

In continental Southeast Asia kingdoms, too, the panorama was not very encouraging, although the principal factor was the Portuguese incapacity to resolve the decline of one of their traditional allies, Pegu, without arousing the animosity of other powers on the rise, such as Siam and Arrakan. As early as the 1580s Aceh offered an armada to assist the kingdom, which the monarch felt inclined to accept if the Portuguese did not assist him, thus placing the latter in a difficult position as they did not have the requisite resources at their disposal.[67] This position was maintained throughout the conflict. The Portuguese revealed a constant preoccupation with keeping Pegu, an excellent source of wood, away from Aceh's clutches. The presence of their old enemy's ships in this region and in Bengal obliged the Portuguese, in the mid-1580s, to send an armada captained by António de Sousa Godinho that was fairly effective in dissuading Aceh's maritime activities in the region.[68] However, the political collapse of Pegu was irreversible and the Portuguese did not have much room to manoeuvre in any possible attempts to alter the process. Viceroy Dom Francisco da Gama tried to coerce the King of Arrakan to alleviate the pressure on Pegu, to no avail as, in the words of this viceroy:

---

[65] J. de Brito Pedroso's 'Relação', 1605, in Luz, *O Conselho da Índia*, p. 430; letter from the city of Melaka to the king, 3-12-1605, *DUP*, II, p. 254; letter from Diogo do Couto to Viceroy D. Francisco da Gama, unknown date, AN/TT, *MiscMssCGL*, box 2, vol. III, p. 372 (copy in BN, *Res.*, box 206, No. 294).

[66] Record from the State Council, 30-4-1619, *ACE*, I, pp. 42–43; *alvará* from the viceroy, 20-4-1619, *APO*, VI (ii), p. 1175. Previous negotiations occurred in 1616, through Siam (Bocarro, *Década 13*, I, cxix, p. 527).

[67] Letter from Governor Manuel de Sousa Coutinho to the king, 4-12-1589, AGS, *Secr. Prov.*, book 1551, fl. 780v.; royal letter to Viceroy Matias de Albuquerque, 12-1-1591, *APO*, III, part 1, pp. 257–258 (also published in *DHMPPO/Insulíndia*, V, pp. 189–190); *see* letter from Philip I to the King of Pegu, 12-1-1591, AHU, *Cons. Ultr.*, cod. 281, fl. 148.

[68] Letter from the king to Viceroy D. Duarte de Meneses, 21-1-1588, *APO*, III, pte. 1ª, p. 116; letter from Governor Manuel de Sousa Coutinho to the king, 10-12-1588, AGS, *Secr. Prov.*, book 1551, fl. 238.

'This State greatly needs him [the king of Arrakan], on account of many provisions that are to be found in his kingdom, where we go when we are unable to obtain them from Pegu. And due to the many Portuguese who are there, he can realise reprisals against any offensive.'[69]

In Siam, too, it was necessary to guarantee a delicate diplomatic position in order to maintain the supply of provisions to Melaka and enable missionary activities in these lands. Despite the good results that the Portuguese embassies managed to obtain, they were unable to prevent the presence of the Dutch[70] (in spite of the projects drawn up to construct a fortress in Martaban), who found Siam to be an excellent trade centre linked with Patani and China. In Tonkin the scenario was more encouraging as the Portuguese were well accepted locally[71] and the Dutch, despite their ambitions of establishing themselves in this region, found it a difficult task to accomplish.[72]

Thus, the diplomatic position of the Estado da Índia weakened considerably from the early 17th century onwards, in large measure due to Portuguese pretensions of imposing exclusive rights and, above all, because the pressure they brought to bear locally to expel the Dutch was not sustainable. However, the Dutch, likewise, aroused similar local animosities, which were partially exploited by the Portuguese. Therefore, the Portuguese defeat was not an economic one, nor was it fundamentally of a political or diplomatic nature but, rather, was a military one, aggravated by the inefficiency of the Portuguese administrative, political and military apparatus. The Portuguese armadas had lost their capacity for dissuasion (already on the wane since the late 16th century) as their new rivals

---

[69] Letters from Viceroy D. Francisco da Gama to the king, 23-12-1599, BN, *Res.*, cod. 1976, fl. 143; unknown date [1599], BN, *Res.*, cod. 1976, fl. 146v.

[70] Royal letter to Viceroy D. Martim Afonso de Castro, 3-1-1608, *DRI*, I, pp. 174–177; Bocarro, *Década 13*, I, pp. 516–526.

[71] *See*, for instance, letter from Viceroy D. Jerónimo de Azevedo to the king, unknown date [Jan. 1617?], HAG, *MonçReino*, 12, fl. 260v. (published with errors in *BOGEI*, No. 216 (1883), p. 872); royal letters to Viceroy D. João Coutinho, 23-1-1618 and 20-2-1618, *DRI*, IV, pp. 280–281 and 351–352; Fr. Félix de Jesus, 'Primeira parte da Chronica e Relação ...', AN/TT, *MssLiv*, No. 731, fls. 29v.–31.

[72] Royal letter to Viceroy D. Jerónimo de Azevedo, 6-2-1616, *DRI*, III, pp. 381–382.

had larger and better managed armadas, with faster ships and better equipment, in both military and general terms. The strategic failure of the great armadas that plied the seas to punish offenders clearly prove this. The lack of a coherent policy for defence and the management of resources, coupled with the inadequacy of tailoring their objectives to available resources aggravated these shortcomings. This does not mean that efforts aimed at recuperation and proposals for reforms were not made. On the contrary, the intensification of difficulties sharpened Portuguese ingenuity and there was no dearth of projects for regeneration during this period, some of which—despite their sheer megalomania—clearly reflect the mentalities of their respective authors in comparison to the reality in which they lived.

Regeneration

The idea that the Estado da Índia faced serious difficulties during the period under review is a constant feature in documents produced in this age. One cannot help but detect the pessimistic tone, the widespread complaints and an awareness of the Estado's shortcomings and difficulties. However, two issues, often omitted or forgotten, must be highlighted when drawing a panorama with sombre overtones about the situation at the time: first, very often the bleak diagnosis, the criticism and denunciation of abuses, errors and shortcomings denote a vision of reality shaped by social, political or ideological factors, or even a calculated act aimed at obtaining personal favours or profits or indirect financing. Secondly, one must duly stress the fact that the period was equally prolific in the lucidity of its diagnosis, ideas for reform and solving problems and projects aimed at making progress in other directions. They prove that debates on ideas and discussions about courses of action were an established feature and a deeply felt necessity during this time. It is clear that this, too, was frequently intentional or linked with personal, social or ideological interests, but a study of this phenomenon enables a better understanding of the spirit of dissatisfaction and disappointment, and also the will and hope, that prevailed amongst the Portuguese during this period.

A few aspects of this question were significantly relevant at the time: the projects for internal reform, namely plans for granting autonomy to a government in Melaka, the proposals for military reform, and projects that envisaged taking the initiative and going on the offensive once again, polarised around plans for territorial conquests and controlling regions instead of the policy of maintaining a maritime network. In this regard one must keep in mind the pretexts already mentioned: personal, social or ideological motivations. The great proposals, or those that contain the most caustic and scathing criticisms, do not derive from a purely individual perception. The most obvious case is that of Diogo do Couto: 'The love of truth, in Couto, is a kind of vice', states the author of the preface to *O Soldado Prático*.[73] Not any truth but, rather, we could say, his own version of the truth. In a system where birth and blood once overrode consider-ations of personal competence and individual qualities in administrative, military and political careers, Couto, from recently ennobled stock, knew perfectly well (and his life was an excellent example of this) that higher offices were beyond his reach due to this insurmountable limitation. His discourse personifies all those elements of Portuguese society in Asia who saw themselves supplanted by blue-blooded nobles, even though they were notoriously associated with incompetence, ignorance or a complete lack of scruples. Thus was born the discourse of an old, courageous and spirited veteran soldier criticising the Portuguese viceroys, captains and assorted noblemen. To a certain extent we can point out similar circumstances in the case of Francisco Rodrigues Silveira.

With regard to projects for conquests we can sketch a similar pano-rama, especially with regard to ideological motivations. Who were the great supporters of plans to conquer Aceh? Dom João Ribeiro Gaio, the bishop of Melaka, Alessandro Valignano, a Jesuit, and Dom Jorge Temudo, the archbishop of Goa, amongst others, viewed these kinds of enterprises as great projects for regenerating and furthering missionary activities. Nevertheless, these proposals were far broader in scope and were defended by diverse sectors: for the captains and great nobles, it would open the door to well-financed great military enterprises and would enable great feats which would be duly rewarded with royal favours; for the less exalted sectors—as can be seen in the case of Couto, who also supported the projects for the conquest of diverse territories—it presented an opportunity for individual initiatives and military glory that occasionally allowed them to penetrate the social system and come to the attention of the king himself, as happened in the cases of Filipe de Brito Nicote and Sebastião Gonçalves Tibau, or even, in the case of Melaka, with some residents who distinguished themselves during the attack on Johor in 1587.

---

[73] M. Rodrigues Lapa, in Couto, *O Soldado Prático*, p. 11.

The viceroys themselves did not scorn these enterprises, which were a potential source of revenues and favour. One can contrast the enthusiasm with which proposals for the conquest of Aceh were received—despite the project being permanently postponed by diverse viceroys—with the hesitation and distinct lack of interest in personally commanding the various armadas that were despatched to repel the Dutch. A good example was Aires de Saldanha, whom the king insistently requested to go personally; he declined and delegated the mission to André Furtado de Mendonça. Or the case of Dom Jerónimo de Azevedo who stated he was willing to go, but cited a lack of means. The only exception was the case of Dom Martim Afonso de Castro, which was certainly due to his inexperience and a lack of awareness of local conditions.

Reform Proposals

Several proposals for the reform of the Estado da Índia emerged throughout the 16th century in a wider context of debate and discussion about the economic and administrative problems. Letters, opinions or reports sent to the viceroy or the king himself were the most common expression of these proposals. They generally identified and focused on an existing problem and presented some measures considered suitable to resolve it, and also adopted a partial approach. The solutions proposed were not always wise or realistic. People who issued such proposals were known as *arbitristas*. The scope covered a wide range of questions and problems concerning several regions of the Habsburg overseas empire.[74]

In Portuguese Asia, two of the most important authors who issued opinions and proposals for reform were Diogo do Couto and Francisco Rodrigues Silveira.[75] Couto was mainly concerned with denouncing injustices and irregularities rather than presenting any coherent proposal. He

---

[74] Curto, *O Discurso Político em Portugal*, pp. 138–142; about Asia, *see* Frutuoso, 'Macau e Manila no Arbitrismo Ibérico'.

[75] Couto's major work in this regard is the 'Diálogo do Soldado Prático'. There are two distinctive versions of this book written in different periods that still await a comparative study by scholars. Silveira's *Reformação da Milícia e Governo do Estado da Índia Oriental* has been recently published, after an old edition of a few excerpts by Costa Lobo, under the title of *Memórias de um Soldado da Índia*.

also had a practical approach, indicating a proposal immediately after the respective denouncement, pointing out the ends but not always justifying the means: as has already been mentioned, he labelled the fortresses as 'corrals', an idea consistent with his opinion of the tribute (*páreas*) paid by vassal Asian kings being 'four bales of rice'. He supported the policy of armadas, but did not indicate how it would be possible to create and sustain it.

Francisco Rodrigues Silveira's life was similar to that of Couto. He was also a 'practical soldier' who experienced the difficulties and harshness of a military life and, in the same way, witnessed the abuse and tyranny of the captains, noblemen and officials. He, too, denounced the system's defects and the ineffectiveness of the policy of fortresses. However, he paid greater attention to problems of a military nature and general disorder and inefficiency. Unlike Couto, his *Reformação*, apart from analysing the problems of the Estado da Índia, presents an overall plan for naval, military and administrative reforms.[76] This was a result of his direct experience with local conditions, especially in military terms, obtained during thirteen years in military service between 1585 and 1598. The military project is the most important element of the work and envisages the implementation of drastic measures to avoid desertion by soldiers as well as a policy of adequate pay and justice, military discipline and reformation of the command structure.[77] The same was applied to the organisation of the fortresses, and a clear distinction was made between mercantile and military functions. To avoid corruption, he suggested a general increase in salaries, with the captains heading the list: 6,000 *cruzados* per year for the captains of Hormuz, Sofala and Melaka, 4,000 for the captain of Gujarat, and lower sums for the others.[78] These represented very large sums,[79] and the effectiveness of this measure in combating corruption

---

[76] *See* the General Introduction by L. F. Barreto and G. Winius in the published version of this work, pp. xxix–lxvii.

[77] Silveira, *Reformação da Milícia*, pp. 96–97, 150–152. *See*, for instance, the 'Parecer sobre o remédio da Índia', unknown date, AN/TT, *MssLiv.*, No. 1116, doc. 45, pp. 528–535, where the author suggests identical measures.

[78] Silveira, *Reformação da Milícia*, p. 185.

[79] His value for the *cruzado* is unknown; he probably followed the general equivalent of 400 *reis*, which would mean 2,400$000 for the captains of Melaka, or four times their regular wages.

was, to say the least, doubtful. However, his diagnosis and observations show a clear thought and his observations about the first incursions of Dutch vessels in the Indian Ocean are of a premonitory nature:

> 'Seeing that, today, these individuals from Zeeland have come in right under the nose of the viceroys, plundering and upsetting the trade and commerce in spices: and tomorrow, due to our own lack of order, they will try and evict us from our own houses. This should certainly be enough to rouse our Portuguese from their slumber.'[80]

Let us now expand upon the question of the creation of an autonomous government in Melaka, which is linked with several issues dealt with in preceding pages. It is clear that a structure as immense as the Estado da Índia would feel the effects of problems derived from its vastness: a dispersal of resources, the difficulties of communications and supplies, administrative and financial centralisation, disarticulation and sometimes friction between the interests of Goa and other centres. The division of the Estado da Índia was a possibility viewed with a certain degree of seriousness during this period and was emphasised by some as being indispensable for its reform. Those who supported this option argued that it would create several decision-making centres with their own spheres of influence, resources and undertakings, thus promoting an improved management and a more effective approach to solving the problems specific to each area.

The proposal was not, however, a novel suggestion. In 1571 King Sebastião had proceeded to divide the Estado da Índia into three parts with their respective headquarters in Mozambique, Goa and Melaka. António Moniz Barreto was entrusted with the autonomous government of the latter, with instructions to proceed with the conquest of Sumatra. The plan was short-lived, given that the three governors immediately clashed over their respective powers and resources; as a result, the king hastened to annul this project shortly thereafter.[81]

However, the project continued to find numerous supporters as a result of an obvious awareness that the problems that had given rise to

---

[80] Silveira, *Reformação da Milícia*, p. 90.
[81] *See* Couto, *Da Ásia*, IX, chapters i and xi, and the report by A. Valignano, 23-12-1586, *DI*, XIV, p. 492. About this question *see* Thomaz, *Os Portugueses em Malaca*, I, pp. 146–147, and the sources mentioned therein.

King Sebastião's initiative were becoming worse; also, the validity of the plan itself had not been questioned. At the beginning of the 1580s, the author of the *Livro das Cidades e Fortalezas ...* declared himself to be in favour of this initiative.[82] However, at the same time the Jesuit Alessandro Valignano voiced serious reservations about any such measure, namely: the 'Southern parts' depended on India, the recruitment of personnel to man the defences and ensure the maintenance of an autonomous government in Melaka would be difficult (as it was impossible to get east of the Ganges River), political power in this region was uncertain and unsafe and, finally, Melaka was impoverished and would not be able to sustain a separate government.[83] Diogo do Couto was also against the proposal that, in his opinion, was doomed to failure.[84]

The debate was revived after the arrival of the Dutch and a worsening of the situation in the Melaka Straits and in the Moluccas. Once it had been recognised that the Portuguese presence in this region was weak and vulnerable to enemy attacks, despite being vital for the Estado da Índia, the separation of Melaka was viewed by some as the only way to face the adversities. An autonomous government in Melaka could solve several problems: it would strengthen the city's defences and fight the Dutch without hindrance on the part of both the captains and the viceroys; the latter were accused of forgetting Melaka and the former of being interested only in trying to enrich themselves at any cost during the three years of their term.[85] On the other hand, a governor in Melaka would respond

---

[82] Luz, fl. 59.

[83] 'Sumario de las cosas que pertencen a la Provincia de la India Oriental ...' (1579 or 1580), BM, *Add.* 9852, chapter xx, fl. 18 (published in *DHMPPO/Índia*, XII, p. 550); however, this author had accepted the separation a few years earlier, as long as the Portuguese were able to successfully conquer Aceh first ('Sumario', 1577, *DI*, XIII, p. 57).

[84] Couto, *Da Ásia*, IX, xvi, p. 116.

[85] *See* the report (date unknown) in AN/TT, *MssLiv*, No. 1107, pp. 277–285; it says that a viceroy, as soon as he sends a captain with a fleet, 'promptly forgets about him, and thus because of the lack of support and provisions the galleons and carracks end up in trouble and run ashore one after another' (p. 283); another report by Rui Dias de Meneses expressed a similar opinion and added that the captain of Melaka 'does no more than look out for the profits he can obtain during his office and in defending his fortress at best' (AN/TT, *MssLiv*, No. 1116, p. 730).

directly to the king. This would put an end to the abuses of merchants by the captain, which was the main reason they preferred to trade with the Dutch.[86]

The greatest problem lay in the question of how to sustain such a separation: the project's opponents stated that Melaka's revenues were not sufficient to meet the expenses involved in creating and maintaining armadas and that the plan would require revenues to be diverted from other fortresses.[87] On the contrary, those who supported the plan affirmed that the shortfall in revenues was linked to the current bad management and widespread abuse by the captains and that if Melaka were well defended and managed and had a separate governor, revenues would increase and would largely be able to sustain the costs involved.[88] One may look at the problem from the inverse point of view: once it was generally accepted that the Estado da Índia depended on the commerce of the 'Southern parts'

---

[86] Report, date unknown [1609?], AN/TT, *MssLiv.*, No. 1107, p. 189 (copy in BN, *Res.*, Mss. 206, No. 173, pp. 3–4); report, date unknown, AN/TT, ibid., pp. 279–280; report, date unknown, AN/TT, ibid., No. 1116, pp. 535–538.

[87] Letter [from Viceroy Rui Lourenço de Távora to the king], date unknown [1610], BN, *Res.*, cod. 1975, fl. 287; the viceroy also mentioned military motives: the 'Southern parts' did not have enough seamen and soldiers and thus it was necessary to procure them in Goa; however, the region was inhospitable and the soldiers refused to go 'as they think that they will end up by staying in that area for a long time, where they all die of disease'.

[88] There are two important reports which include financial projects: the first in AN/TT, *MssLiv.* No. 1107 (quoted in note 86), suggests a reduction of office posts (as most of the expenses were on account of the agents and servants of the captains) and several ways to increase revenues. One suggestion was to lease the customs house in Melaka and the voyage of China that, according to the author, provided a profit of 375,000 *xerafins* (or 108,000$000 as he estimates 1 *xerafim* = 288 *reis*). The second is the report by Rui Dias de Meneses, AN/TT, *MssLiv.*, No. 1116, p. 733 (quoted in note 85) who estimated that the lease of the customs house of Melaka could render 200,000 *cruzados* (72,000$000 if one takes the rate of 360 *reis* each) as long as the Javanese returned to sell their spices in the city; he also considered the voyage 'of the spices' of China (that is, the pepper from Sunda) to be worth 20,000 *cruzados* and envisaged the lease of all Indonesian voyages, without mentioning specific figures.

(namely the one with China), and that Dutch interference represented a serious threat, it seems clear that some sectors opposed the separation of Melaka not because the city was unable to sustain it but, on the contrary, because such a measure would draw away the revenues from Goa and the heart of the administration of the Estado.

The probability of once again attempting a division of the Estado da Índia was apparently growing and the project was well received even by some viceroys, such as Aires de Saldanha, or even the archbishop of Goa.[89] In Lisbon, Madrid or Valladolid, another risk was debated: that of the internal problems that such a measure would cause. The most serious one was the risk involving the viceroys of Goa, that Portuguese Asia could end up with 'two heads', which would further aggravate the functioning of the whole system.[90]

It is possible that one of the fears related to the separation of Melaka was a loss of Portuguese influence and the growing connection with the Philippines, as the city was far from Goa and nearer Manila and the Spanish, who were always interested in extending their influence in the Far East. Even without the separation, it was to Manila that the city appealed for aid when the situation worsened, especially after the 1610s. Melaka was administratively subordinate to Goa, which had enabled a single chain of command extending up to Japan. Therefore, Goa exercised a kind of tutelage over the remaining Portuguese-controlled cities in Asia, and it seems that the capital of the Estado da Índia would not willingly accept losing its status. In any case, the project, although debated and supported by many people, was never put into practice. An obvious symptom of the inertia of Portuguese structures was the extreme difficulty in proceeding with global reforms. The Estado da Índia lost its capacity to take the initiative and limited itself to managing and occasionally correcting practices and procedures and maintaining the fiscal machinery that ensured the collection of duties and revenues.

---

[89] Royal letters to Viceroy Aires de Saldanha, 31-1-1602 and 20-2-1603, AHU, *Cons. Ultr.*, cod. 282, fls. 63v. and 163, respectively; letter from the archbishop of Goa to the king, 6-4-1603, AN/TT, *ColVic*, 12, p. 117 (*see* Document Appendix, No. 13); royal letter to the same archbishop, 23-3-1605, AN/TT, *ColVic.*, 14, fls. 175–175v.

[90] Report from the Council of Portugal, Nov. 1603, British Museum, *Add.* 28432, fl. 76v.

Proposals for Conquest

The proposals for administrative and military reforms were not the only proposals debated during this period with regard to the changes that needed to be implemented at the heart of the Estado da Índia. A new course, different from the existing Portuguese tradition of intervention in the Indian Ocean, gradually took shape and assumed the form of alternative projects: proposals for territorial conquest that emerged in the last quarter of the 16th century and represented a notable shift in the Portuguese vision of their role in Asia. The Spanish example was a powerful driving force to projects of conquest, not only because Portugal and Castille now shared a common king, but also due to the prestige and wealth obtained by the *conquistadores* of the New World. Settled in Manila since 1571, the Spanish cherished ideas of expanding the American experience into Asia (mainly China) for some time. Southeast Asia, on account of being a grey zone between Portuguese and Castillian areas of influence, became a preferred target for those who advocated a domination of the area based on the force of arms, on both Portuguese and Spanish sides.[91]

The conquest proposals emerged due to the transformations taking place at the heart of Portuguese structures and on account of a renewed strengthening of old, deeply entrenched notions. The Estado da Índia was now a stable structure in a defensive position caused by the increasingly hostile scenario from the late 16th century onwards. It was the ideal moment to witness a resurgence of the old ideals of the Crusade, now stimulated by the heightening of tensions with religious motives. The weakening of the Portuguese structures and the worsening of its economic, political and social conditions, combined with the new geopolitical framework deriving from the Iberian Union, completed the picture. Portuguese and Spaniards were now united under the same flag and the same king, the vanguard of the Catholic faith and the empire in Asia as elsewhere.

In terms of mentality, a curious mix of pessimism and despondency triggered by social, economic and moral crises with the idea of Portuguese

---

[91] *See* Boxer, 'Portuguese and Spanish Projects for the Conquest of Southeast Asia, 1580–1600'; also Ollé, *La Empresa de China*, about Spanish projects for conquering the Middle Kingdom. A comparative approach on Portuguese and Spanish *models* of expansion may be seen in Pinto, *No Extremo da Redonda Esfera*.

military superiority over Asian powers continued to prevail. There was a dominant feeling about the idea that the Portuguese military resources were under-exploited and wasted in commercial activities, taken as the cause of the widespread dissolution of customs. A global shift in the right direction—conquest, not trade—was therefore needed to gather resources, motivate men and direct them to military expeditions, which would assure the consolidation of the Estado da Índia, economic prosperity and the expansion and victory of the Catholic faith in Asia. From this point of view, these projects for territorial conquest were, likewise, projects for the regeneration of the Estado and the redemption of men.

There were also more practical reasons accompanying this evolution. The conviction that the Estado da Índia was built upon fragile foundations and needed to firmly root itself in strategically chosen places in order to survive and prosper was one of them. The idea of territoriality was linked to the global evolution of Portuguese expansion, in which the Crown assumed an increasingly distinct sovereign function as opposed to the direct exploitation of trade. This opened the door to conceptions of territorial domination and control over regions, and was no longer restricted merely to routes, ports or trade in commodities.

Successful experiences of territorial domination held an increasing prestige which, inevitably, enticed the men of India: the growing attention on the colonisation of Brazil, which had already enabled the Portuguese to frustrate French incursions and whose success had transformed it into the Crown's main focus from the mid-16th century. In the 1570s other experiments were implemented, with widely differing results: in Africa, the foundation of Luanda by Paulo Dias de Novais and the project to advance towards the interior, the initiative to conquer the Mutapa kingdom, on the eastern side, as well as plans to conquer the African interior and connect the two coasts. More important for Southeast Asia, as it was nearer home, was the success of the Spanish conquest of the Philippines. When the two crowns were united under the same king, all the necessary conditions were in place to once again go on the offensive in the Indian Ocean region, now from a new point of view. These projects for conquest cannot only be viewed as a megalomaniac military venture by some noblemen or missionary fervour on the part of some churchmen. They represent a second wind for Portuguese expansion in the Orient, a strategic wager and an effort at regeneration that the fortunes of history or, more prosaically, the demographic, political, social and financial conditions of the Estado da Índia would postpone and render unfeasible.

The debate over the conquest of key islands in the Indian Ocean region, in order to enable control over navigation—as Afonso de Albuquerque had achieved with his conquest of Hormuz and Melaka—was something that dated back to the very foundation of the Estado da Índia. However, the scenario during the late 16th century would make this an even more pressing issue, given that the solidity of Portuguese fortresses—as one can see by the successive sieges that Melaka suffered—had begun to be called into question. The option of channelling resources to reinforce Portuguese positions once again came into the limelight, with preference given to Sri Lanka and Sumatra, which offered a combination of a wealth of spices along with a strategic location. Both islands had pros and cons.

Another possibility that gained ground, despite the failure of Francisco Barreto's initiative, was that of Mutapa. Diogo do Couto revealed himself to be an enthusiastic supporter of this project.[92] However, it is curious to note how this author changed his perception of prevailing problems, reflecting the very evolution of the men of his times. The first version of *O Soldado Prático* (that may be dated to 1564)[93] merely limits itself to identifying the major problems of the Estado da Índia (Basra, Sri Lanka and Aceh), demonstrating special concern over the rise of the Sumatran potentate on account of the direct threat that this represented for Melaka. The second version, written in the 17th century, already discusses the choice between three distinct and elaborate projects for territorial conquest: Sri Lanka, Aceh and Mutapa.[94]

At the end of the 16th century Spanish interference in the continental kingdoms of Southeast Asia after the attack on Brunei and, likewise, Portuguese initiatives in the same region had a certain impact and incited optimistic prognoses about a successful campaign for the conquest and imminent submission of Pegu, Cambodia, Cochinchina, Siam and Champa.[95] Those who advocated the support and enlargement of these

---

[92]   Couto, *O Soldado Prático*, pp. 195–197; also *see* the discourse by Silveira, *Reformação da Milícia*, p. 220.

[93]   *See* Annex I, note 7.

[94]   The first version in Couto, *O Primeiro Soldado Prático*, pp. 469 and 493–501; the second version in *O Soldado Prático*, pp. 197–203.

[95]   *See*, amongst others, the opinion of San Antonio, 'Breve y Verdadera Relacion de los Sucessos del Reino de Camboxa', pp. 123–127, and the reports about Cambodia and Pegu in Subrahmanyam, 'The Tail Wags the Dog', pp. 157–160.

actions mentioned the riches of this region along with a long list of strategic and economic advantages that could be obtained if they were successfully conquered. Curiously, the potential spiritual bounty did not always head the list of priorities, even in the works by clerics.[96]

From amongst the various proposals for territorial conquest, the proposal by the bishop of Melaka, Dom João Ribeiro Gaio (a singular and central figure in the history of Portuguese Melaka), stands out. His project was vast and ambitious. It envisaged the conquest of Aceh, the main idea and crux of his plan, along with other regions of the Malay Peninsula (beginning with Johor), which would be followed by the kingdoms of Cambodia, Siam and Cochinchina. He even went so far as to include China and Japan, suggesting the formation of a joint attack by Portuguese and Spanish armadas, based in Melaka and Manila, respectively, requiring 4,000 soldiers on the part of the Portuguese.[97] However, the most important element was the conquest of Aceh, of which the bishop was a fervent advocate.

As far as we know, the idea of conquering the sultanate as an official enterprise only emerged in the aftermath of the great siege of 1568. The first known project appeared in that year, still rather vague and written by an anonymous author, who left us a lengthy report about the situation of the Estado da Índia, mentioning how it was necessary for the viceroy to command such an enterprise in person. Nevertheless, the idea had already been mulled over by some before this time.[98] The first justified opinion appeared in the following year: that of the archbishop of Goa, Dom Jorge

---

[96]   *See* the case of Fernão Guerreiro, who supported the conquest of Pegu and Bengal and the military initiatives of Filipe de Brito de Nicote: he presented ten reasons why the Portuguese should proceed with this project for conquest and the missionary arguments were the last on the list: Guerriro, *Relação Anual das Coisas que fizeram os Padres da Companhia de Jesus ...*, I, pp. 290–295; see also II, pp. 317–320 and III, pp. 77–87.

[97]   Gaio, *Roteiro da Cousas do Achém*, p. 76; letter to the bishop of Manila, 11-4-1595, *AIA*, VI, vol. XII, 1919, pp. 452–454. *See* Pinto, *No Extremo da Redonda Esfera*, pp. 286–288, and Boxer, 'Portuguese and Spanish Projects ...', pp. 122–123.

[98]   He affirmed that, 'It is essential that the viceroy go to Aceh, as everyone in India knows'; 'Informação das fortalezas ...' in Wicki (ed.), 'Duas relações ...', p. 148. António Pinto Pereira says that Viceroy D. Luís de Ataíde intended to lead an expedition against the sultanate in person during his first viceroyalty; Pereira, *História da Índia...*, p. [231].

Temudo, who defended the neutralisation of this enemy by means of an armada of four or five galleons and 1,000 men.[99]

Throughout the 1570s there was growing interest in this initiative, which appeared as a handy solution for the ever-increasing problems of Melaka and the Portuguese in the entire region: destroy Aceh, considered to be the greatest threat to the Portuguese, control the island of Sumatra and its resources (especially its pepper and gold) and dominate navigation in the Straits and its routes towards both the west and east. When the Estado da Índia was divided up in 1571, the government of Melaka was entrusted to António Moniz Barreto, along with the mission to conquer Sumatra, Aceh being the most important target. Then Alessandro Valignano, along with his project for Christianisation, appeared on the scene, parallel to plans for the conquest of the sultanate. Therefore, what had been an essentially military and strategic initiative now took on markedly ideological overtones.[100] Other supporters of this project gave their opinions: amongst them were Jorge de Lemos, who wrote his proposal at the end of a description of the sieges that Melaka had been subjected to by Aceh between 1573 and 1575, and the anonymous author of a report dated 1582.[101] In Manila, the Spanish looked at these initiatives with disdain, considering the Portuguese unable to defeat Aceh (which they considered a small power) without Spanish support.[102]

---

[99] 'Apontamentos …', in Wicki (ed.), 'Duas relações …', pp. 207–208.

[100] *See* letter of 18-11-1577, *DM*, II, p. 4; 'Sumario', 1577, *DI*, XIII, pp. 50, 54 and 57; 'Sumario', 1579 or 1580, fl. 10v. (published in *DHMPPO/Índia*, XII, pp. 515–516); letter to C. Acquaviva, 10-12-1583, *DI*, XIII, p. 373 (also published in *DM*, II, p. 141).

[101] Lemos, 'Hystoria dos Cercos que … os Achens, e Iaos puserão a fortaleza de Malaca', fls. 62v.–63, says such an expedition would require 3,000 soldiers; Teensma (ed.), 'An Unknown Portuguese Text on Sumatra from 1582', pp. 311–314, mentions similar figures (3,000–3,500).

[102] In 1576 the governor of Manila, Francisco de Sande, considered supporting the Portuguese to defeat the 'kinglet of Aceh' (*reyezillo de Achen*) because this would prevent 'Moors and Turks' passing east of the Straits of Melaka; letter to the king, 7-6-1576, *HPAF*, XIV, p. 417. In 1588 the Augustinian friar Francisco Manrique said Tonkin, Champa, Cambodia, Siam, Johor or Aceh were minor kingdoms, 'despite being greatly considered here', and all could be conquered with 4,000 Spanish soldiers; letter to the king, 1-3-1588, *HPAF*, XV, p. 333.

It was in 1584 that the bishop of Melaka prepared his careful project for conquering the sultanate.[103] It was a particularly propitious period for the execution of military conquests as, from 1579 onwards, the sultanate had been plunged into great political turmoil, on account of which both the bishop as well as Jorge de Lemos intensified their warnings. In his plan one can catch a glimpse of the fascination with which the Portuguese viewed the Spanish experience in the Philippines, and the desire to imitate this model, which he confessed in a letter to the king:

> 'Our Lord will be served if Your Majesty is victorious in Aceh, for which reason he will give power and order to he who conquers it, as it has many rivers and large urban centres, that can be distributed just like in the Philippines, which will thus result in a great growth of Christianity, and in your wealth, and will give your vassals a means of livelihood.'[104]

After this description of the projects for the conquest of Aceh, one needs to trace the evolution of the enterprise itself, from the time it was considered by Portuguese authorities in the 1560s until its disappearance in the early years of the 17th century.[105] Throughout this period great expectations were raised about this enterprise, a fact that is mentioned in both official documentation and in accounts by travellers.[106] The conquest of Aceh as Melaka's main enemy and that of Sumatra as a future pillar of the Estado da Índia fused together, both because the former controlled part of the island (though not yet as much as it would in the following

---

[103] *Roteiro pera El-Rei Nosso Senhor que Dom João Ribeiro Gaio Bispo de Malaca fez com Diogo Gil e outras pessoas das cousas do Achem*, published by Jorge dos Santos Alves and Pierre-Yves Manguin (Gaio, *O Roteiro das Cousas do Achem de D. João Ribeiro Gaio: Um Olhar Português sobre o Norte de Sumatra em finais do século XVI*).

[104] Letter to the king, 31-12-1588, AGS, *Secr. Prov.*, book 1551, fl. 413 (*see* Document Appendix, No. 6); his determination is also visible in his other writings, such as his letter to Manuel Rodrigues, 7-1-1582, *DI*, XII, p. 564.

[105] There had been several previous initiatives in Melaka or Goa but on a smaller scale and with lesser involvement on the part of the authorities (*see* Alves, 'Une Ville inquiète ...', p. 94).

[106] For instance, an account by Filippo Sassetti in a letter to the Duke of Tuscany, 11-2-1585, *Lettere da Vari Paesi*, p. 447, or by Linschoten, *The Voyage of ... to the East Indies*, I, p. 109.

century) as well as because this would solve several problems that Melaka faced with a single blow. When the Estado da Índia was divided in 1571, the conquest of this sultanate was one of the main tasks entrusted to the governor of Melaka. However, the failure of this political reform resulted in all these plans being aborted.

The first information available revealing a clear intention to proceed with the conquest of the sultanate refers to the armada of Matias de Albuquerque. His fleet set out from Lisbon in 1576, sailing towards Melaka to defend the city and ensure the safety of Portuguese navigation in the Straits. It is clear that he was given instructions to investigate the prevailing conditions for a future military enterprise, to be carried out under his command.[107] However, after his return—although the state of affairs within the sultanate was favourable for a military strike—the enterprise was postponed because the viceroy had capitalised all his resources for Sri Lanka.[108]

The project to conquer Aceh ended up depending on the agenda of various viceroys. Apparently, at this time, the post of 'Captain of the Conquest of Aceh' (or a similar designation) was created, which enjoyed extraordinary funds for the preparation of this enterprise. The project, likewise, seems to have benefited from a Crusader bull, with a value of at least 2,000 *cruzados*, managed by the bishop of Melaka.[109] Viceroy Dom Duarte de Meneses received specific orders from the king—which probably

---

[107] *Alvará* from Viceroy D. Luís de Ataíde, 28-8-1580, *APO*, V, part 3, p. 972; *see* the order by the same viceroy to the Court of Appeals of Goa, 30-8-1580, ibid., p. 804.

[108] 'Vida e Acções de Mathias de Albuquerque', BN, *Res.*, cod. 482, fls. 27–27v. *See* Document Appendix, No. 1.

[109] Both these pieces of information are scarcely documented and are largely conjectural; about the first, Linschoten, *The Voyage of ...*, I, p. 109, mentions the existence of the office, and Couto says that Rui Gonçalves da Câmara, the uncle of Viceroy D. Duarte de Meneses was 'Captain-Major and *Conquistador* of Aceh and received the respective wages' (*Da Ásia*, X, part 2, VIII, xvii, p. 380). With regard to the second, when the bishop of Melaka intended to return to Portugal, one of the questions raised was his refusal to return the 2,000 *cruzados* received from the Crusade bull (which, allegedly, had been granted for the conquest of the sultanate as a major project of the city of Melaka) (*see* chapter 5, note 114).

had been previously drafted in his initial instructions—to proceed with the conquest. It appears that this royal decision was taken in 1587, as it is in this year that one of his letters mentions the 'enterprise of Aceh upon which I have resolved, as you can see in another of my letters'.[110] This other letter is unknown,[111] unlike the viceroy's reply in that same year which elucidates upon the intentions of the king: the despatch of 4,000 men and 300,000 *cruzados* to finance the conquest.[112]

The enterprise was no longer just a mere ideal or a vague hypothesis, but rather a project to which the monarch himself was committed. The following year, the king mentioned that he was unable to fulfil his pledge because of other urgent situations which required assistance, such as the coast of Malindi, Sri Lanka and the crisis in Johor.[113] However, the project was not abandoned. The Acehnese sultan received information about the Portuguese intentions, and probably took this threat seriously, this being one of the reasons for the fortification work carried out in his capital during this period.[114] The viceroyship of Dom Duarte de Meneses was one of the few in which an attempt was made to organise the soldiers

---

[110] Royal letter to Viceroy D. Duarte de Meneses, 30-3-1587, AN/TT, *CorCron.*, part 1, pack 112, doc. 19; in the previous year the viceroy of Portugal had recommended that a swift decision be made; letter to the king, 6-12-1586, AGS, *Secr. Prov.*, book 1550, fl. 701.

[111] This was probably the letter mentioned by Diogo do Couto together with a 'Report' allegedly written by the same viceroy about the conquest of Aceh (*Da Ásia*, X, part 2, X, xix, p. 684).

[112] Letter from Viceroy D. Duarte de Meneses to the king, 6-12-1587, AGS, *Secr. Prov.*, book 1551, fl. 80 (*see* Document Appendix, No. 3). This letter is especially interesting, amongst other aspects, due to the doubts manifested by the viceroy on some issues, such as his statement that the Portuguese soldiers were skilled in naval combat but were not ready to disembark and attack the city.

[113] Royal letter to Viceroy D. Duarte de Meneses, *APO*, III, part 1, pp. 130–132.

[114] The bishop of Melaka, D. João Ribeiro Gaio, gives an interesting but rather confusing piece of information about this issue. He said the Acehnese had built some defensive structures next to the entrance to the harbour, 'to guard and defend it ... at the time when Francisco Barreto was supposed to go to Aceh'. This is an obvious mistake on the part of the bishop, who was referring to António Moniz Barreto, who had been entrusted with the government of Melaka by King Sebastião; Gaio, *Roteiro*, p. 82.

of the Estado in companies. Given that the viceroy himself complained of the risk resulting from military anarchy upon disembarkation in Aceh, the king's immediate order for the division of soldiers into units under captains and flags was probably related to the project that he intended to carry out immediately.[115]

In 1591 there was a new viceroy in Goa, Matias de Albuquerque, who had spent a few years in Melaka and was thus familiar with the city's problems and the conditions for setting this project in motion. His instructions included express orders to proceed with the initiative, being advised to choose the best occasion and exploit the political instability that continued to prevail in the sultanate to maximum advantage.[116] Unexpectedly, the peace proposal that the new Sultan Alauddin Riayat Syah made in 1592 to the captain of Melaka, Pero Lopes de Sousa, resulted in a détente in relations between Aceh and the Portuguese. At least in the short term, Aceh ceased to constitute an immediate threat, and diplomatic ties and closer political relations were established. Ironically, it was this peace that, by ensuring a definitive postponement of the plans for conquest, made any possibility of controlling northern Sumatra and neutralising the old enemy unfeasible.

A diplomatic campaign to foster closer relations with the sultanate was set in motion, but these initiatives did not mean a definitive step towards an alliance. Peace was postponed until the Portuguese were able to undertake a war, given that the instructions of Viceroy Dom Francisco da Gama, written in 1596, included express orders to proceed with efforts aimed at a following military campaign.[117]

---

[115] About the complaints of the viceroy, *see* letter quoted in note 112; the royal order to form units and flags can be found in the letter dated 16-3-1588, *APO*, III, part 1, p. 154.

[116] Fragment of the *Regimento* given to Viceroy Matias de Albuquerque, unknown date [1591], AN/TT, *Cartas dos Vice-Reis*, No. 181; in a letter to the same viceroy, the king stated that, 'This issue is as important as you understood it to be, and that is why I spoke to you of it in my Council, thus summoning you because of it', 18-1-1592, AHU, *Cons. Ultr.*, cod. 281, fl. 195v.

[117] *Regimento* given to Viceroy D. Francisco da Gama, 5-1-1596, AHU, *Cons. Ultr.*, cod. 281, fls. 366–366v.; about the duplicity of the Portuguese policies, *see* the royal letters to the same viceroy, dated 7-3-1596, *APO*, III, part 2, pp. 597–598; 16-3-1596, p. 627; 5-2-1597, pp. 669–670.

No conquest of Aceh was ever attempted, with the exception of the belated expedition of Dom Martim Afonso de Castro in 1606, which was aimed more at forcing the sultan to accept Portuguese conditions for the construction of a fortress locally rather than realising any project for conquest as had been mooted in preceding decades. In fact, the arrival of the Dutch and the English would render the project unfeasible due to the aggravation of the political and economic situation caused by their presence. On the brink of this new scenario, both the viceroy and the king already recognised that the plans for conquest would be hard, if not impossible, to accomplish.[118] Only after the Dutch and the English had established in Aceh and posed a threat to Melaka's shipping and commerce did the Portuguese attempt to arrive at a hasty understanding with the sultan, at a time when the northern European presence now afforded him a position of considerable strength. On account of successive hesitations, not proceeding with the conquest because of the peace proposal, not signing a peace treaty because of hopes of conquest, in practice, the Portuguese ended up rapidly losing ground and wasting successive possibilities of intervention in the sultanate in one way or another.

The projects for the conquest of Aceh soon ceased to be mentioned in documentation of this era. Their final spark before the last (and, curiously, the only project ever put into practice) attempt in 1606 appears to have taken place in 1603, through the efforts of the Augustinian friar Amaro de Jesus, who had gone as an ambassador to Aceh on several occasions: at this time, taking advantage of a new dynastic conflict, the friar managed to obtain the support of one of the pretenders to the throne, the sultan of Pedir, on the condition that the Portuguese would assist him in his attempt to capture the crown. The captain of Melaka, André Furtado de Mendonça, prepared an expedition which was never realised because the capture of the *Santa Catarina* by the Dutch required

---

[118] Copies of letters from Viceroy D. Francisco da Gama to the king, unknown date [1597], BN, *Res.*, cod. 1976, fl. 69v.; letter to the same viceroy, 30-3-1598, ibid., cod. 1975, fls. 331–331v.; copies of letters from the same viceroy to the king, April 1598, BN, *Res.*, cod. 1976, fl. 91v.; royal letters to the same viceroy, 12-1-1599 and 16-1-1599, AN/TT, *MiscMssCGL*, box 3, vol. VI L, pp. 155 and 458, respectively; in the former, the king recognised that, 'The conquest of Aceh is gradually becoming more difficult'.

all forces to be diverted towards Johor.[119] The last-known opinion on the subject probably dates from the years between 1603 and 1607 (before Iskandar Muda's rise to power). The author emphasises the opportunity available for conquest owing to the sultanate's internal problems and also adds a new reason to the older justifications: that the conquest of the sultanate would check Dutch infiltration in the region.[120]

These projects for conquest which were so patiently and ardently prepared by some and supported by so many others never had lasting consequences. The project aimed at Aceh, undoubtedly the most substantial one in the case of Melaka, suffered on account of diverse hesitations and strategic errors and also, principally, due to the lack of resources of the Estado da Índia and the finances of the Crown in general. As for the megalomaniac projects for the conquest of the inland kingdoms in Southeast Asia and elsewhere, these were plans fuelled by the initiatives of some adventurers, without any results. However, these projects for conquest were not just ways of attaining merit or attracting funding. They also constituted efforts to regenerate a debilitated entity and were individual dynamics that only go to show how this age was rife with initiatives and projects, far removed from the vision of a decadent and stagnant Estado da Índia that has been consecrated by tradition.

---

[119] Fr. Félix de Jesus, 'Primeira Parte da Chronica...', AN/TT, *MssLiv.*, No. 731, fls. 66v.–67 (*see* Document Appendix, No. 22).

[120] Report about the conquest of Aceh, unknown date [c. 1603–1607]. BA, Liv. 51-VI-54 $\frac{18}{}$, fls. 36–37v. (*see* Document Appendix, No. 17).

CHAPTER 3

Melaka and the Geopolitics
of the Straits

The strategic importance of the Straits of Melaka and the surrounding region far surpasses a simple recognition of that geographical area as a crossroads that connects various trade routes and links the Asian continent and the Archipelago and the Indian and Chinese civilisations. This small region, which broadly extends from the extreme northern point of Sumatra, the Sunda Straits and the tip of the Malay Peninsula, was, in the global context of the 16th century, a microcosm of the Indian Ocean, not only as a leading centre of the region's economic life but also as a privileged theatre where, on a local scale, political and economic forces jostled for supremacy, linked in a far vaster context that spanned the entire Indian Ocean or even the planet as a whole. The Straits of Melaka reflected a wider reality and, in the same way, the evolution of the city was echoed in places as diverse as Canton or Nagasaki, Manila, Ternate, Goa, Gujarat, Jeddah-Mecca, Cairo, Constantinople, Venice, Amsterdam or Lisbon. We are not referring to the multiple currents of merchandise with extremely diverse points of origin and destinations or to the interdependence between different global economic centres that utilised the Straits as a privileged channel of communication. Our attention is focused on its practical representation in geopolitical terms, that is, the way each local power was supported by and was integrated into a far vaster structure. Melaka, while a fundamental hub of the Portuguese maritime empire, was tied to the vast network that was the Estado da Índia; Aceh, vanguard of Islam in Southeast Asia, embodied the opposing structures that, via the trade in Sumatran pepper, extended to Gujarat and the Red Sea, and from there on to Cairo, Venice and Constantinople. Johor personified the legacy of the sultanate of Melaka and extended to the Eastern Archipelago, exercising a strong attraction over diverse mercantile communities, namely Chinese and Javanese merchants.

The regional balance derived from internal relations within the triangle that comprised Melaka, Johor and Aceh. This underwent diverse modifications throughout the period under study, and suffered a fundamental alteration with the arrival of the English and the Dutch in Southeast Asia. This fourth power destroyed the bases of the triangular balance; Melaka would be the entity that suffered the most damage as the city now had to deal with economic competitors and political adversaries that Portuguese structures were unable to successfully combat.

The notion that this region lived under the sign of an equilibrium between Melaka and the aforementioned two sultanates during the 16th century is not new.[1] One can already clearly detect a great preoccupation with the movements and power of Melaka's two neighbours in official documentation of the era. However, this balance took on specific forms and underwent several changes. The history of this geopolitical scenario in the period under study, from 1575 to 1619, is particularly rich and interesting. This chapter traces the main outlines and articulations of its evolution. First, however, let us go back to the conquest of the city by the Portuguese.

After the conquest of Melaka by Afonso de Albuquerque in 1511, the Portuguese inherited a network of trade routes that can only be understood keeping in mind the grandeur of the sultanate that, at the time, was a leading emporium on a global scale. When the Portuguese conquered the city, it is clear that they intended to seize the sultanate's commercial empire rather than dominate it territorially.[2] This was a result of the nature of

---

[1]   *See* Meilink-Roelofsz, *Asian Trade and European Influence ...*, pp. 140–143, and Boxer, 'Portuguese and Spanish Projects', p. 119.
[2]   Thomaz, *De Ceuta a Timor* ('Estrutura Política ...'), pp. 214–215.

Portuguese expansion in the Indian Ocean region which was, above all, a structure that controlled a network rather than a geographical area,[3] a thalassocracy.[4] However, inheriting a commercial empire by seizing its headquarters by force was something that did not fit local mental standards or practices.[5]

The founding of the sultanate of Johor by the son of the last sultan of Melaka was the culmination of a process of political reorganisation and the logical outcome of the irreversibility of the Portuguese actions. Thus, from 1511 several different Melakas began to exist. First, the city of Melaka, occupied by a foreign power who tried to substitute its former masters and maintain its role intact, at least in the initial phases; second, the sultanate of Melaka, that kept its territorial domination and its web of prior loyalties unaltered, assuming a genealogical continuation of the former sultanate. A third Melaka soon appeared on the scene: Aceh, where the rich and powerful Gujarati community of Melaka sought refuge after the Portuguese conquest of the city. Aceh, brandishing the standard of *jihâd*, would transform itself into the strongest Islamic bulwark in the region, thus continuing the role of Malay Melaka as a nerve centre for the expansion of Islam, as well as into the greatest threat for the newly arrived 'white Bengalis'.[6]

The history of Portuguese Melaka prior to the arrival of the northern Europeans is a history of tension with these two sultanates. It may be said that the hegemony of Malay Melaka was splintered into three pieces, each one unable to rebuild its former power. Until the mid-16th century the Portuguese especially feared Johor, which had stubbornly resisted their military assaults. Yet the tension that directly resulted from the events of 1511 soon came to an end, thanks to new emerging factors. The scenario that prevailed after the middle of the century, with the revival of the Levant

---

[3]   Ibid., p. 515.
[4]   Thomaz, 'Les Portugais dans les Mers de l'Archipel', p. 106.
[5]   Kathirithamby-Wells, 'Forces of Regional and State Integration ...', p. 27. Andaya, *The Kingdom of Johor*, p. 21.
[6]   According to the *Sejarah Melayu* (ed. C. C. Brown, p. 157), this was the name by which the Malays called the Portuguese when they arrived in Melaka for the first time in 1509. They soon became known as 'Franks', a general designation for western Europeans at the time. *See* Thomaz (ed.), 'Os Frangues na terra de Malaca', p. 216, note 6.

route linked to the Red Sea and, in the long term, to Aceh, coincided with the formation of a vast—albeit fragile and ephemeral—league of Islamic solidarity united against the Portuguese and based on Ottoman military power.[7] The apogee of this league, in the 1560s, was afforded by the victory of Talikota, which immediately enabled several attacks by diverse Muslim potentates on Portuguese positions throughout Maritime Asia. In Southeast Asia this role fell to Aceh, which immediately set an assault in motion in 1568.

Aceh's hostility towards Melaka, in the guise of a holy war against the Portuguese, camouflaged a latent imperialism that soon collided with other regional powers, especially with Johor. The expansion of Aceh had begun in the 1520s with their advance towards the east (Pidir, Pasai) and west (Daya).[8] At first it only disturbed the Portuguese, who were banished from Pasai where they had managed to establish a fortress.[9] Acehnese expansion into the Sumatran interior began in 1539, against the Bataks and the Minangkabau. It was supported by Ottoman assistance, but encountered stiff resistance on the part of the other sultanates—Johor, Jambi and Indragiri.[10] The capture of Aru, until then within Johor's orbit, confirmed the worst fears of this sultanate about Aceh's policies. It was at this moment that the bases of the regional balance that would last till the end of the century were drawn up: a tense game of postures, threats and offensive moves between Melaka, Aceh and Johor. The arrival of the English and the Dutch would destroy this equilibrium and form another equation, one that was far more unfavourable to Portuguese interests.

The mutual tension that existed between these three powers, combined with an awareness that each one was incapable of establishing a regional hegemony by itself, meant that any attempts at establishing closer ties, generally sealed with a marriage (in the case of the two sultanates), or with

---

[7]   Couto, *Da Ásia*, VIII, xxxiii, p. 283; Pereira, p. [233]. *See* Boxer, 'A Note on Portuguese Reactions ...', pp. 419–420, and Reid, 'Sixteenth Century Turkish Influence ...', pp. 403–404.

[8]   Mentioned in the Portuguese sources as Pedir, Pacém and Daia.

[9]   About the sultanates of northern Sumatra in the early 16th century, *see* Alves, *O Domínio do Norte de Sumatra*; about the Portuguese fortress in Pasai, *see* pp. 97–111.

[10]   Kathirithamby-Wells, 'Achehnese Control over West Sumatra ...', pp. 455–456.

embassies (in the case of Melaka), had fleeting results. Thus, after a period of latent war in the aftermath of 1511, Johor gradually established contacts with the Portuguese. Two factors contributed decisively to this détente: in the first place, Johor's concerns about Acehnese expansion, confirmed when Aceh attacked Johor in 1564 and took the sultan prisoner. Secondly, the successor of the captive king, Sultan Muzaffar Syah, felt a lesser degree of animosity towards the Portuguese than his forefathers, who had been banished from Melaka.

If we believe Couto, in 1568 Muzaffar Syah would have been around forty years of age and had thus not experienced the defeat of 1511 and the difficult early years before the foundation of Johor.[11] Thus, when Aceh attacked Melaka in that year, Captain Dom Leonis Pereira hastened to warn the sultan about the power of Aceh and the risk it represented for Johor. This had a great impact as the memory of the 1564 attack was still fresh in the sultan's mind.[12] As a result, Muzaffar Syah prepared an armada to assist the Portuguese. Thus the first alliance between Melaka and Johor was eminently political in nature, but with an important economic facet that would be sealed with the sultan being received in the fortress of Melaka after Aceh withdrew its forces.[13]

The sieges of 1573–75 were serious blows for Melaka due to the damage they caused in the city. Three consecutive sieges, carried out by Aceh, by its Javanese allies of Japara, and again by Aceh, took the city to the brink of exhaustion. In this scenario, Johor declared its support for the anti-Portuguese league but, as on other occasions, its support was merely nominal. In truth, its fear of the Sumatran power was greater than ever, and the help it offered was only aimed at keeping an eye on the movements of its rival. Aceh, in its turn, hoped to launch an attack on Johor after the conquest of Melaka. Couto sagely makes the following comment about this apparent understanding:

> 'Some people who wrote about this siege made the mistake of assuming that these things were carried out without any duplicity, it was clear to those who understood the situation well that everything was a stratagem and a ruse, because each one of them wished to consume

---

[11]   Couto, *Da Ásia*, VIII, xxiv, p. 170.
[12]   Ibid., xxii, p. 144.
[13]   Ibid., xxiv, pp. 168–170; Pereira, p. [236].

the other, and that of Viantaná[14] even more so, on account of which fear abounded.'[15]

This lack of confidence was not limited to Johor, but also extended to Aceh's supposed Javanese allies. Only Demak had clearly refused to participate in the Islamic league against Melaka and had even ordered that the ambassadors from Aceh who had transmitted the proposal be killed so that no doubts remained about their decision.[16] When the sultan of Aceh appeared off the coast of Melaka, one of the reasons given to the Portuguese captain to justify his presence was precisely to punish this Javanese sultanate for the grave affront.[17] There are signs which would indicate that Demak's sympathy for the Portuguese did not cease later.[18]

However, the most interesting case was that of Japara. This sultanate already had a long history of hostility towards Melaka (even during the time of the Malay sultanate) and had even attacked the city on previous occasions. Japara was the only power that actively participated in the league. However, the tension with Aceh was clearly evident: it refused to make a joint attack on Melaka. On the contrary, Japara tried its luck after the Acehnese failure in 1573 and cautiously withdrew in the face

---

[14] A corrupted form of spelling, probably due to a misprint in the *Décadas*, of the more common words 'Ujantana' or 'Ujontana', from the Malay *ujung tanah*, 'cape', literally 'headland', that is, the tip of the Malay Peninsula (Johor).

[15] Couto, *Da Ásia*, IX, xxvii, p. 236. It is interesting to note that Couto, despite following the work by Lemos, 'Hystoria dos Cercos ...' (sometimes too closely), still had, unlike this author, a clear perception of the deep tension between these two sultanates. Marsden, *The History of Sumatra*, pp. 430–432, does not mention it while reporting these events, and Macgregor, 'Johor Lama in the Sixteenth Century', p. 86, does not pay any attention to it.

[16] Couto, *Da Ásia*, VIII, xxi, p. 132.

[17] Ibid., xxii, p. 137.

[18] When the Dutch first arrived in Banten in 1596, they noticed the presence of an individual they called the former 'Emperor of Java'. He was, in fact, the sultan of Demak who had briefly ruled over the entire island. The Dutch stated that he spoke Portuguese, had a Portuguese wife from Melaka and that he acted against them in collaboration with the Portuguese settled in the sultanate (*Iovrnal du Voyage de l'Inde Orientale* ...); this character, despite his almost symbolic power, would eventually be murdered in 1604 upon the orders of one of his sons (reports by Edmund Scott in Henry Middleton, *The Voyage of* ..., p. 145, and in Purchas, *His Pilgrimes*, II, p. 440).

of the impasse that resulted from its own attack, alarmed by the news of the impending arrival of a new armada of its supposed allies.[19] Thus the end of the anti-Portuguese league in 1575 brought a cycle to a close: it marked the definitive failure of an attempt to use Islamic solidarity as a unifying factor between different local powers, who never managed to eliminate their mutual mistrust.[20]

Three Decades of Equilibrium

The post-1575 period witnessed an extension of the bases of geopolitical balance in the Straits: the same delicate positioning between the three powers, the same instability and unpredictability in the diplomatic sphere, the same factor—though perhaps now even more pronounced—of the survival of Melaka at the cost of rivalries between the sultanates. The survival, or the occasionally advantageous position that Melaka occupied in the geostrategic equilibrium, was directly proportional to the tension between the two sultanates. When there were signs of closer ties between Johor and Aceh, alarm bells immediately went off in Melaka. And these fears were justified during the period from the late 1570s to 1589, when the two sultanates showed distinct signs of closer ties and it was only Aceh's dynastic problems that prevented an active alliance. Until the end of the century there are two other important factors are worthy of note: the rapid strengthening of Johor under the reign of Ali Jalla Abdul Jalil Syah II and the unexpected détente between Aceh and Melaka. This event brought mutual advantages to both Portuguese and Acehnese but, obviously, had as a consequence the isolation of Johor. At the end of the century the arrival of the northern Europeans would interrupt this period when Melaka had the advantage over her adversaries and would definitively shatter the old model of geopolitical balance in the region.

The end of the period of sieges and attacks on Melaka in 1573–75 marked the definitive failure of the Malay sultanates' joint attempts to conquer Melaka and the end of the Islamic league. However, on the ground, the withdrawal of Aceh's armada did not significantly alter the political instability and insecurity for navigation in the Straits, as is shown

---

[19]   Couto, *Da Ásia*, IX, xxvii, pp. 235 and 239.
[20]   Kathirithamby-Wells, 'Forces of Regional and State Integration ...', pp. 29–32.

by the hasty despatch of Matias de Albuquerque's armada directly from Lisbon. Melaka's position continued to be precarious, even in terms of the city's foreign policy. The sultan of Aceh, Ali Riayat Syah, continued to pressure the city; on account of this, in March 1576 the armada captained by Matias de Albuquerque set sail from Lisbon. After acquiring reinforcements in Melaka, it defeated Aceh's fleet near Johor on 1 January 1577,[21] and continued to patrol the Straits in subsequent years. If Matias de Albuquerque's armada managed to re-establish some degree of security for Portuguese ships, the stability that Melaka managed to achieve, at great cost, during the following years was greatly due to the instability in relations between Aceh and Johor and, above all, to the internal upheavals in Aceh from 1579 onwards.

This period is confusing: in 1579–80, Johor supported Aceh's armadas in their attacks against the Portuguese and one can assume that an understanding existed between the two sultanates. One can find supplementary information that would confirm this support during the captaincy of Dom João da Gama (1579–82).[22] In 1582, Aceh attacked Melaka once again, and later continued on to Johor. The motives for this attitude are unknown, given the recent détente between the two sultanates. In Aceh, a new sultan, Mansur Syah of Perak, now reigned but, contrary to the theory given by Diogo do Couto, this unexpected attack on Johor was probably not caused by dynastic questions.[23] We can accept the second reason pointed out by this chronicler, who gives an account of the flight of a captain from Aceh to Johor in a ship loaded with gold and other merchandise. In any case, the sultan of Johor seems to have requested and obtained the support of the Portuguese captain, Roque de Melo, in yet another episode in this volatile relationship. At this point there was a clear strengthening of Johor's position under the reign of Sultan Ali Jalla, who managed a

---

[21] The main sources about these events are 'Vida e Acções de Mathias de Albuquerque', BN, *Res*, cod. 482, fls. 14v.–17 (*see* Document Appendix, No. 1); Erédia, 'Historia de Serviços com Martirio …', BN, *Res*, cod. 414, fls. 8–8v., and Sousa, *Oriente Conquistado a Jesus Cristo*, pp. 1098–1100.

[22] *See* royal Instructions to Viceroy D. Duarte de Meneses, 10-3-1584, AN/TT, *Fundo Port. da Bibl. Nac. de Paris*, No. 48 (*see* Document Appendix, No. 2).

[23] Couto, *Da Ásia*, X, part 1, III, ii. *See* Annex I. With regard to the strike against Melaka, Bishop D. João Ribeiro Gaio mentioned 120 vessels and 15,000 soldiers, the siege having lasted over a month (Gaio, *O Roteiro*, p. 98).

regional hegemony in the light of Portuguese inefficacy and Aceh's fragile state, obtaining from both parties a peace that was wholly favourable to Johor's interests.

Ali Jalla managed to establish an agreement and a dynastic union with the new Acehnese sultan, Mansur Syah, which enabled him to substantially strengthen his power as the latter sought, at any cost, an external alliance that could, in some way, compensate for his internal fragility. With Melaka, Ali Jalla reinforced the commercial agreement that allowed him to divert Melaka's Javanese trade to his own port by means of an agreement with the captains. Both parties extracted mutual benefits that were as favourable for them as prejudicial to the Melaka customs house and, therefore, to the interests of the Royal Treasury. Having thus neutralised—one can even say having almost bought—the captains of Melaka who were, at the time, the individuals who wielded true power in the city, and having dragged Aceh into its orbit, Johor enjoyed an unprecedented level of power and influence in the region.

In 1585 a crisis suddenly erupted.[24] The new and inexperienced captain, João da Silva, clumsily enforced orders to put an end to the agreement in an attempt to bring back trade to Melaka. The conflict was sparked off by the capture and sinking of a ship from Johor loaded with tin, on the pretext that the captain of the ship was Acehnese. At this time the sultan of Johor felt strong enough to reply accordingly. He prepared a fleet and proceeded to blockade Melaka, both to the east (there is evidence to indicate that Johor even managed to construct a fort on the Straits) and, by means of an alliance with Aceh, closed the blockade to the west

---

[24] The main sources with regard to this crisis are Couto, *Da Ásia*, Década X, part 2, and *Vida de D. Paulo de Lima Pereira*; Gaio, who wrote his *O Roteiro* in 1584, mentions the existence of a fortress and a customs house in Johor, both causing great harm to Melaka's interests (*O Roteiro*, p. 99). A Spaniard called Álvaro de Bolaños Monsalve wrote a curious report in 1586, mentioning the state of affairs in Melaka at that time and the peculiar relationship between the Portuguese captain and the sultan of Johor; he says the sultan was not afraid of the Portuguese because they were 'too greedy, and when they fight him, he would put pepper and cloves in front of them so they would sate'; Report about the Philippines and Portuguese India, 24-3-1586, AGI, *Patronato*, 53, R.1, fl. 38v. *See* Pinto, *No Extremo da Redonda Esfera*, pp. 285–286. Macgregor describes the whole framework in detail in 'Johor Lama in the Sixteenth Century'.

with a fortress that the latter built in Perak. This double strategy enabled an iron control over the Straits and managed him 'to put a noose around Melaka's neck', in the words of Viceroy Dom Duarte de Meneses.[25]

Sultan Ali Jalla proved to have remarkable diplomatic and political skills. His offensive was carefully planned: he waited till Melaka's armada had left for Goa and only then proceeded to enforce a meticulous blockade of the Straits to completely control the city's routes towards the Orient. Two main channels were blocked. The first was the difficult and treacherous Singapore Straits,[26] through which the richly laden Portuguese ships passed on their way back from China. Ali Jalla ordered it to be blockaded by sinking old ships, thus making it impractical for large vessels to sail through. The second was the broader Sabang Straits, through which Javanese trade was channelled. Here, Ali Jalla prepared a roving armada, with orders to divert traffic to Johor.[27] In this manner, Johor not only

---

[25]   Letter from Viceroy D. Duarte de Meneses to the king, 23-11-1587, AGS, *Secr. Prov.*, book 1551, fl. 71v. About Johor's fortress in the Straits, *see* the letter from Luís de Góis de Lacerda to the king, 10-1-1588, AGS, *Secr. Prov.*, book 1551, fl. 314 (*see* Document Appendix, No. 4) and the royal instructions to Viceroy D. Duarte de Meneses, quoted in note 22, fl. 9 (*see* Document Appendix, No. 2). This document specifically refers to the Singapore Straits, while the former only mentions the 'opening of the Strait' in a vague way. About the Acehnese fortress in Perak, *see* chapter 4, 'The Sultanate of Aceh'.

[26]   The *Relação das Plantas & Dezcripções de todas as Fortalezas ...*, p. 45, states: 'The Strait of Singapore has many passages, and some are so narrow that sometimes the yards touch the trees'; Francesco Carletti provides similar information, *Voyage Autour du Monde*, p. 230. The Portuguese avoided going into this maze of narrow and dangerous channels controlled by the Orang Laut loyal to Johor. In 1585, D. Manuel de Almada seems to have found a new passage he called the 'Santa Bárbara channel' (Couto, *Da Ásia*, X, part 2, VII, xii, p. 211); D. Jerónimo de Azevedo would later claim to have also found a new passage (*see* chapter 2, note 53). *See* Peter Borschberg, 'Remapping the Straits of Singapore? New Insights from Old Sources'.

[27]   Royal letter to Viceroy D. Duarte de Meneses, 21-1-1588, *APO*, III, part 1, p. 115; Diogo do Couto, *Da Ásia*, X, part 2, VII, xii. This author says the sultan prepared a fleet and 'sent it to the Straits in order to force the Javanese junks to go to Johor; and with regard to the Straits of Singapore, ... he ordered it to be obstructed with some old junks ...'. About the most probable localisation of both these Straits, *see* chapter 4, note 81.

deprived Melaka of the city's most important trade connections but also threatened to use them for the sultanate's own benefit, thus claiming a commercial hegemony of the region.

The subsequent period was one of permanent alarm for Melaka: Johor did not have sufficient naval power to directly confront the city and thus enforced a policy of attrition, carrying out frequent attacks on Portuguese vessels, depriving the city of supplies and promoting a diplomatic campaign with other regional powers to isolate Melaka. These diplomatic moves were aimed primarily at Aceh and the Malay sultanates, thus forming a true league that was liable to isolate and suffocate Melaka, blockading the city from both the east and west. In the case of Aceh, Johor managed a notable military collaboration, which only failed at the eleventh hour due to a sudden crisis in this sultanate. Johor also exercised its influence over the Minangkabau established in the interior of Melaka, unleashing a revolt in 1586 that caused serious problems to the Portuguese.[28] Johor likewise interceded with the Javanese sultanates and continental kingdoms. Yet, we only have documented information in the case of Cambodia, where the sultan sent an embassy.[29]

Despite these serious difficulties, Melaka managed to extricate itself from this pressure, in large measure due to the prompt assistance—both supplies and military support—sent from Goa. This was the famous armada captained by Dom Paulo de Lima Pereira that managed, with the decisive help of the *casados* of Melaka, to defeat the enemy forces and attack and destroy Johor Lama, the capital of the sultanate, forcing the sultan to flee upriver to new headquarters. In this way, Melaka experienced a decline in the danger from this rival, at least momentarily. The Portuguese military enterprise thus re-established Melaka's links with the Orient and minimal conditions that enabled navigation in the Straits. However, it did not achieve the expected result, which was a complete annihilation of the sultanate's power. The sultan of Johor, in much the same way as his predecessor a few decades earlier, fled and founded a new capital on a site upriver that was more protected and sheltered, where Portuguese ships would find it difficult to penetrate.

---

[28] Couto, *Da Ásia*, X, part 2, VIII, xiv, pp. 357–360; letter from the bishop of Melaka to the king, 15-12-1588, AGS, *Secr. Prov.*, book 1551, fl. 397v.

[29] Cácegas and Sousa, *História de S. Domingos*, II, pp. 343–344.

The sultan requested a peace with the new captain of Melaka, Dom Diogo Lobo, and rebuilt his fortress, which the city's residents managed to destroy, well after the supporting armada returned to Goa.[30] The number of vessels that they found in the port of the new capital goes to prove Johor's power of attraction and the sultanate's rapid regeneration.[31] Johor continued to be a worrisome neighbour for Melaka, although the sultanate would attempt a new assault only in the next century, this time with Dutch support.

However, in the period that extended up to the early years of the following century, the city of Melaka was able to reinforce its security and unhesitatingly affirm its position of strength to its rivals. This was made possible in large measure due to the hostility, which would prove to be a long-lasting phenomenon, that prevailed between Johor and Aceh after Sultan Alauddin Riayat Syah al-Mukammil came to power in Aceh in 1589. The roots of this renewed hostility can be traced to dynastic problems that will be discussed later in this book. This period of Melaka's political advantage thus derived from the enmity between the two sultanates. Each one sought Portuguese support, especially military support, against its rival, giving Melaka a unique and comfortable position in the balance.[32]

Although Johor's defeat of 1587 represented a notable setback for Ali Jalla's hegemonic aspirations, the power of the sultanate continued to be largely intact, albeit reduced. In this scenario it was the new sultan of Aceh who took the daring initiative of openly proposing a peace with the Portuguese, thus putting an end to a latent conflict that had spanned several decades. Although his decision was undoubtedly influenced by

---

[30]   *See* the letter from D. Henrique Bendara to the king, 16-12-1588, AGS, *Secr. Prov.*, book 1551, fls. 524–524v. (*see* Document Appendix, No. 5).

[31]   200 vessels and 5 or 6 'very large trading junks loaded with supplies and spices'; letter from Governor Manuel de Sousa Coutinho to the king, 12-12-1589, AGS, *Secr. Prov.*, book 1551, fl. 746v. D. Henrique Bendara claimed to have sunk more than 100 large vessels loaded with goods (*see* his letter quoted in the previous note).

[32]   This is confirmed by several sources, the most important one being Jacques de Coutre, 'Vida de ...', pp. 104–105 and 166, who describes the despatch of an ambassador from Melaka to Johor with a view to establishing an alliance against Aceh. Also *see* San Antonio, 'Breve y Verdadera Relacion ...', p. 65 and Aduarte, *Historia de la Provincial del Santo Rosario ...*, I, p. 343 and II, p. 527.

internal factors as he had begun a process of political centralisation in his kingdom, it nonetheless appears that external factors played a decisive role. As his conflict with Johor seemed inevitable, the sultan was not in a position to simultaneously sustain his long-standing rivalry with Melaka (now undoubtedly aggravated, according to information available to him, by the projects for conquest taking root in the minds of the Portuguese) along with the internal revolution that he was carrying out. Thus it was necessary to have a détente on one of these fronts, and he opted for better relations with Melaka.

The mutual hostility between the Portuguese and Aceh was a constant, albeit intermittent, feature throughout the history of Portuguese domination in Melaka. The origins of this rivalry dated back to the very conquest of the city by Afonso de Albuquerque, which was followed by the flight of the powerful Gujarati community, which later sought refuge in Aceh and fuelled the commercial network that rivalled the Portuguese one, thus leaving an indelible mark on an apparently irreconcilable antagonism. However, the identical enmity between Melaka and Johor had given way to a readjustment of relations, and even active collaboration, in the light of the threat from Aceh during a good part of the 16th century. In much the same way, the seemingly irreconcilable rivalry between the Portuguese and the Sumatran power only required a suitable opportunity, thanks to geopolitical requirements and the pressures of local *realpolitik*, to transform itself into détente. This opportunity appeared in 1592.

It is now time to pay some attention to this period, with unprecedented characteristics, in which Melaka lived in expectation of a commercial agreement and a political alliance with its traditional and most feared enemy. In practice, it was a true period of *pax portucalensis*.

From 1587 to the period 1603–06, Melaka experienced a period of exceptional strengthening in the regional balance, taking advantage of the state of declared hostility between Johor and Aceh. This was not a new conflict but at this time it was considerably aggravated by a serious dynastic question. Johor, recuperating from the effects of the destruction of its capital and increasingly harassed by its enemy, went through a period of relative decline. Sultan Ali Jalla died in 1597, leaving the throne to his son Alauddin, who had to face the rivalry of his brother Raja Bongsu. Several years would pass before the sultanate returned to playing an important role in the region's geopolitics. Aceh was the focus of everyone's attention during this period. Not because the sultanate was preparing to attack Melaka, as it had already done several times, but for precisely the opposite reason. Unexpectedly, Sultan Alauddin Riayat Syah initiated a thaw in the sultanate's relations with the Portuguese, attempting to attract their attention in order to distance them from his enemy. Thus Melaka witnessed an unprecedented position of simultaneous peace with both its old rivals, each of whom sought to win the sympathies of the city and to attract Portuguese naval power to its realms, conferring upon Melaka the role of pointer on the scale of the regional political balance.

Aceh's overtures to Melaka constituted an exceptional phase in the relationship between the two powers, although it was neither the first nor the last time that peace had reigned between the sultanate and the Portuguese. On the contrary, periods of tension and war alternated with spells of peace and commercial contacts. There was a Portuguese mercantile community in the sultanate, whose presence varied in accordance with the political climate and the sultan's moods, and the Acehnese were also occasionally accepted in Melaka. However, this period was characterised by the fact that this détente did not come about naturally, in the aftermath of a recent conflict. Rather, it resulted from a direct initiative on the part of the sultan, who suddenly became receptive to the idea of an alliance with the Portuguese. We already know what he intended to achieve and likewise what the Portuguese—sometimes in a confused manner—hoped to obtain. Similarly, the gradual evolution of the situation to Melaka's detriment after the arrival of the Dutch, which was aggravated by the sultan's death in 1604, is also nothing new. What is not so well known is the diplomatic process, the steps taken by both parties and, above all, the embassies sent by both sides to sign an agreement that was never actually realised. Historians have not really focused on this issue,[33] in large measure due to the scarcity of information. A history of the Augustinians' missionary activities in the Orient[34] pays some attention to the role that some missionaries of this Order, particularly a friar named

---

[33] The most important works in this regard are Lombard, *Le Sultanat d'Atjéh au Temps d'Iskandar Muda* (the appendix includes an excerpt of the *Hikayat Aceh* that mentions a Portuguese embassy) and Alves' paper about the martyrs in Aceh, 'Os Mártires do Achém nos séculos XVI e XVII: Islão versus Cristianismo?' pp. 399–401.

[34] Fr. Félix de Jesus, 'Crónica e Relação do princípio que teve a congregação da Ordem de Sto. Augto. nas Índias Orientais' (first part), some excerpts in Document Appendix, No. 22.

Amaro de Jesus, played in this process, which shall now be analysed in some detail.

The hazards of history, much like the misfortunes of men, sometimes take unexpected forms. In the present case, Aceh's overtures to the Portuguese had an unusual opportunity with a shipwreck on the shores of Sumatra of a vessel that carried on board the bishop of Macao, Dom Leonardo de Sá. The prelate had participated in the IV Provincial Council in Goa, and set sail for Macao on board the ship of the captain of the Japan voyage, Francisco de Sá. Due to sailing problems, the vessel was shipwrecked on the shores of Aceh in 1592.[35] Friar Félix de Jesus wrote an emotional account of the accident, the shipwreck and contact with Aceh, as well as of the astonishment the survivors felt when they listened to the sultan's words about his intentions to set them free and to make a peace deal with the captain of Melaka. He chose an Augustinian friar, Amaro de Jesus, who, due to his ability to speak Malay, was sent as an ambassador to Melaka to communicate his message to the captain, Pero Lopes de Sousa: the promise to free the survivors of the shipwreck, 'if the Portuguese of Melaka would grant him free access to the seas from there till the kingdom of Johor, where he wished to pass with four hundred ships.'[36]

The die was cast for a period of peace with the sultanate, which would continue for some years and in which the Portuguese hesitated between accepting the sultan's conditions and constructing a fortress in the harbour of the sultanate or taking advantage of the truce to proceed to conquer the city. In any case, the captain gave a favourable response, and Aceh was thus able to carry out its punitive expedition against Johor, which was also described by the same missionary. Given that there is reliable information about the captain having sent a request to Goa for an

---

[35] F. Félix de Jesus does not mention the exact date of this event, but it probably took place in 1592. The first information about this issue was provided by a Jesuit in a letter dated 5-3-1593 (*DI*, XVI, p. 149), and it was mentioned in several Jesuit letters over the following months (letters of 17-12-1593, 8-11-1594 and 20-11-1594, *DI*, XVI, pp. 571, 772 and 846). On the other hand, the bishop was freed in 1595, and stated that he had been kept prisoner in Aceh for three years; copy of certificate in Erédia, 'Historia de Serviços com Martirio ...', BN, *Res.*, cod. 414, fl. 28.

[36] Fr. Félix de Jesus, op. cit., fl. 24v.

armada, and that it arrived in Melaka in June 1592 after having fought an Acehnese fleet in Aru (that had returned to Johor's orbit),[37] one may add yet another motive for the sultan's hasty peace proposal: which is that, having been defeated by Dom Bernardo Coutinho, he did not have sufficient resources to confront the Portuguese armada yet again.

The despatch of Friar Amaro de Jesus was, thus, a skilful manoeuvre to enable him to proceed with his reprisals against Johor without fear of Portuguese strikes, offering a promise of peace in exchange. The Portuguese, who on various occasions had supported one sultanate or the other, gave in willingly, as this war was favourable to Melaka's interests. Aceh's expedition against Johor thus seems to have taken place as early as 1593, their armada of 400 vessels sailing past Melaka. This information caused much confusion in Goa, where it was known that the armada was destined for Johor but concerns about an eventual danger to Melaka continued to prevail.[38]

In subsequent years the two parties exchanged a series of embassies, with a view to reaching an agreement. In 1593 itself, the captain of Melaka and the bishop of Melaka sent the first delegation—an embassy consisting of the Augustinian friar Jerónimo da Madre de Deus, prior of the college in Melaka,[39] and Tomás Pinto—which dealt with the conditions for releasing the bishop of Macao along with the other captives, and a possible future agreement that contemplated the supply of pepper to Melaka.[40] This was possibly the embassy mentioned in the *Hikayat Aceh*,

---

[37] This was the fleet commanded by Bernardo Coutinho; *see* royal letter to Viceroy Matias de Albuquerque, 1-3-1594, *APO*, III, part 1, p. 424, a reminder ('Lembrança') written by Matias de Albuquerque about all the supplies he had sent to the fortresses while viceroy, unknown date [late 16th century], BM, *Add*. 28432, fl. 125 and 'Vida e Acções de Mathias de Albuquerque', fl. 55v. (*see* Document Appendix. No. 1).

[38] Letter from the inquisitor, Rui Sodrinho, to the inquisitor-general, Goa, 2-12-1593, in Baião (ed.), *A Inquisição de Goa*, II, p. 156; anonymous letter against Viceroy Matias de Albuquerque, ('miserable India'), unknown date [1593 or 1594], AN/TT, *MssLiv.*, No. 1112, fl. 88v.

[39] According to a document penned by this friar, the delegation was sent by the bishop, while other sources affirm that it was the captain; certificate dated 6-12-1597 in Erédia, 'Historia de Serviços ...', BN, *Res.*, cod. 414, fls. 28–28v.

[40] Fr. Félix de Jesus, op. cit., fls. 27–27v.; royal letter to Viceroy D. Francisco da Gama, *APO*, III, part 2, p. 627. In January 1594, Tomás Pinto wrote the

naming the Portuguese as 'Don Dawis' and 'Don Tumis'.[41] In any case, the prisoners were released either in the following year or, more probably, in the early months of 1595.[42]

In the wake of this initial contact, the sultan, in his turn, sent an embassy to Goa. This was not a great success as the viceroy did not receive it in a suitable manner and even absented himself while the embassy was in the city before proceeding with negotiations about the agreement. The ambassadors left Goa discontented with the treatment they received and departed without even taking their leave of the archbishop, who governed the city in the viceroy's absence. This failure raised immediate concerns about the consequences of such an act for Melaka.[43] The Goa City Council was aware of the danger and attempted to remedy the situation: during the ambassadors' stay in the city it handed them the goods of an Acehnese ship that had been lost in Surat, whose captain had approached them. After the departure of the ambassadors, the Council also tried to send an embassy with presents to the sultan, but this action did not receive the approval of the very same viceroy, Matias de Albuquerque.[44] This viceroy's hostility, by all appearances, seemed to stem from the project to conquer the sultanate towards which he was greatly inclined, but was unable to implement because he lacked the necessary means to do so. This was aggravated by the fact that the king did not clearly define the

---

king a letter describing his journey to Aceh, but its whereabouts are unknown; one only has news of the king's reply; royal letter to Tomás Pinto, 16-3-1596, AHU, *Cons. Ultr.*, cod. 281, fls. 413v.–414.

[41] Excerpt published in Lombard, *Le Sultanat d'Atjéh au Temps d'Iskandar Muda*, pp. 227–233.

[42] *See* the certificate issued by the bishop and copied in Erédia, 'Historia de Serviços ...', BN, *Res.*, cod. 414, fls. 28–28v. It was written in Melaka on 3 May 1595, soon after his arrival.

[43] Copy of letters from Viceroy D. Francisco da Gama to the king, 1597, BN, *Res.*, cod. 1976, fl. 69; letter from the same viceroy to the king, unknown date [1599 or 1600], ibid., fl. 130v.; royal letters to the same viceroy, 18-1-1598, AN/TT, *MiscMssCGL*, box 3, vol. VI L, pp. 206–207; 26-1-1598, *APO*, III, part 2, p. 824; 5-3-1598, p. 848.

[44] Letter from the city of Goa to the king, 1596, *APO*, I, part 2, p. 35; royal letter to Viceroy D. Francisco da Gama, 5-2-1597, ibid., III, p. 670; royal letter to the city of Goa, 25-1-1598, ibid., I, part 2, p. 120.

strategy to be followed, vacillating between his pretensions of conquest and establishing an agreement.[45]

The new viceroy, Dom Francisco da Gama, Count of Vidigueira, proceeded in a more cautious manner, aware of the delicate nature of the situation because of the arrival of the first Dutch ships in the region. Lourenço de Brito, who was sent to Sunda with the aim of expelling the Dutch and chastising the sultan of Banten, also received orders to contact Aceh and transmit a conciliatory message to the sultanate, in order to prepare a future alliance. However, it seems he did not carry out these orders.[46] In 1599 a new embassy from Aceh arrived at Goa and another embassy was sent to Melaka. The viceroy received the sultan's representatives, who stayed in the city for a short while and left satisfied with the welcome they had received but without any practical results, as the Portuguese now demanded that the future Portuguese fortress in the sultanate be located on the island of Gomispola.[47]

In the meantime, the Dutch and the English penetrated the region. The Dutch reached Aceh on their second voyage to the Orient in 1599, when the armada of Cornelius de Houtman established the initial contact. Luck was not on their side. The Dutch captain's lack of diplomatic skills hindered relations, but Portuguese pressure also seems to have played an important role. The embassy from Aceh that was on its way back from Goa first made a stopover in Melaka before returning to the sultanate, and brought back with them Afonso Vicente, a resident of the city who had been appointed ambassador by the captain of Melaka, Fernão de

---

[45] Royal letter to Viceroy D. Francisco da Gama, 5-2-1597, *APO*, III, part 2, p. 669; royal letter to the same viceroy, 30-3-1598, BN, *Res.*, cod. 1975, fls. 331–331v. (*see* Document Appendix. No. 9).

[46] Royal letter to Viceroy D. Francisco da Gama, 21-11-1598, *APO*, III, part 2, p. 926; letters from the same viceroy to Miguel de Moura, BN, *Res.*, cod. 1975, fl. 245; 23-12-1599, ibid., fl. 285v.

[47] Letters from the viceroy to the king, unknown date [1599 or 1600], BN, *Res.*, cod. 1976, fl. 130v.; 23-12-1599 and April 1600, ibid., fls. 143 and 102, respectively; in his letter to Miguel de Moura (*see* previous note), the viceroy stated: 'The king of Aceh has sent me two ambassadors last April with a long letter and rich presents; I received them very well and sent them home in the same monsoon, they were very satisfied and received many honours and benefits.'

Albuquerque.[48] The Portuguese obviously managed to incite the sultan's hostility against the Dutch as he captured the Dutch vessels by force, killing the captain, Cornelius de Houtman, and imprisoning his brother Frederick.[49]

The Dutch presence in Southeast Asia was now the Portuguese authorities' main cause for concern. Their prime objective was promoting, at any cost, good relations with Aceh in order to prevent the Dutch from gaining a foothold in the sultanate. In 1600 the new viceroy, Aires de Saldanha, arrived in Goa. Owing to the prevailing impasse, he decided to send a new embassy to Aceh, this time headed by Friar Amaro de Jesus, who delivered a letter from the king to the sultan.[50] The Augustinian managed to establish excellent relations with his host, who conferred on him the title of Bintara Orang Kaya Maharaja Lela Putih.[51] Thus he seems to have had some influence with the sultan, safeguarding the continuation of a policy that was still pro-Portuguese, which was evident when a new Dutch armada appeared in Aceh. In addition, the aggressive Dutch attitude resulted in an outbreak of hostilities, an incident that was promptly used by the Augustinian to further Portuguese interests.[52]

---

[48] Letter from Viceroy D. Francisco da Gama to the king, April 1600, BN, *Res.*, cod. 1976, fl. 102; Couto, *Da Ásia*, XII, II, x, p. 242 and V, ix, pp. 512–516. This author states that Fr. Amaro de Jesus went with Afonso Vicente, which is probably incorrect.

[49] *See* the description of these events in 'A Briefe Relation of Master John Davies, chiefe Pilot to the Zelanders in their East-India Voyage ...', in Purchas, *His Pilgrimes*, II, pp. 306–326. *See* the letter from the viceroy quoted in the previous note and the royal letter to Viceroy Aires de Saldanha, 31-1-1602, AHU, *Cons. Ultr.*, cod. 282, fl. 68v.

[50] Royal letter to the sultan of Aceh, 4-3-1600, AHU, *Cons. Ultr.*, cod. 282, fls. 8–8v. (*see* Document Appendix. No. 11). Several sources refer to this embassy, but Fr. Félix de Jesus is the only one who provides a detailed description; *see* royal letter to Viceroy Aires de Saldanha, 20-2-1603, AHU, *Cons. Ultr.*, cod. 282, fl. 163, and the 'Memorial das Missões dos Religiosos que mandou a nossa provincia de Nosso Pe. Santo Augustinho ...', *DHMPPO/Índia*, XII, p. 189.

[51] F. Félix de Jesus, op. cit., fl. 48. This indicates a herald (*bintara*), a title of the royal court (*orang kaya*), a position close to the sultan (*maharaja lela*), and the colour white (*putih*).

[52] F. Félix de Jesus, op. cit., fls. 47v.–48v. A. Botelho de Sousa, *Subsídios para a História Militar Marítima da Índia*, I, pp. 461–464, describes the events according to the Dutch sources.

In 1602 it was the turn of an English armada, captained by James Lancaster, to arrive in the sultanate. Here the accounts differ considerably. The English records emphasise the cordial reception extended to the armada, which signed a commercial agreement with the sultan, and the failure of the Portuguese ambassador's intrigues. The work by Friar Félix de Jesus, on the contrary, states that Friar Amaro de Jesus convinced the sultan to likewise expel these foreigners, who withdrew without obtaining any advantages.[53] This information is incorrect as the sultan signed an agreement with the English captain, issuing a 'charter' allowing the subjects of the queen of England to have access to his ports.[54]

The Portuguese vacillations, the conditional demands made before signing an agreement and, especially, the irritation caused by certain abuses by the residents of Melaka,[55] began to have an effect. However, the most important fact was that the arrival of the English and the Dutch meant that friendship with the Portuguese was no longer indispensable as the sultan now had new forces who were anxious to sign commercial agreements and to whom he could resort in his campaigns against Johor. The sultan welcomed and reciprocated the Portuguese embassies, but simultaneously sent ambassadors to the Netherlands and established contact with the queen of England.[56] Nevertheless, Portuguese diplomatic initiatives had not yet come to an end. Friar Amaro de Jesus—according to the same missionary source—left Aceh accompanying the embassy that the sultan sent for the last time to Goa, where he was received by the viceroy. Finally, in 1603 Aires de Saldanha once again sent him back to Aceh with the same embassy, with orders to make one last effort to arrive at an agreement with the sultan, or else to jointly organise with the captain of Melaka, André Furtado de Mendonça, an armada that would force the construction of a fortress, taking advantage of the internal unrest that plagued the sultanate

---

[53]   Report of the 3rd voyage by Sir James Lancaster, *The Voyages of* ..., pp. 90–101. Fr. Félix de Jesus, op. cit., fls. 48v–49.

[54]   *See* note 105, below.

[55]   For instance, the seizure of an Acehnese vessel sent to Melaka to get supplies mentioned in a royal letter to Viceroy Aires de Saldanha, 31-1-1602, AHU, *Cons. Ultr.*, cod. 282, fl. 68v.

[56]   *See* the letter from the archbishop of Goa to the king, 6-4-1603, AN/TT, *ColVic.*, 12, p. 117 (*see* Document Appendix, No. 13); Argensola, *Conquista de las Islas Malucas*, pp. 343–344.

at that time. Once he returned to Melaka he went to Pedir, where he found the local sultan, the son of the sultan of Aceh, in open rebellion against his father and who promised him permission to build a fortress if the Portuguese would help him to seize power in Aceh. The political scenario was thus already radically different, and the old sultan, who had shown himself to be susceptible to Portuguese influence, was at the end of his rule.

The ascension of Iskandar Muda to the throne brought an end to the period of closer ties with Melaka. Aceh, just like Johor, distanced itself from the Portuguese. It is not known for sure how the diplomatic activities of Friar Amaro de Jesus came to an end. Apparently he was sent to Aceh once again by the captain of Melaka during the siege to which the Dutch and Johor subjected Melaka in 1606; there he was imprisoned by the sultan for some years. However, in 1609 he was already back in Melaka where he was elected prior of the convent.[57]

Thus the period of regional hegemony that the city had managed to exercise for a few years, thanks to the enmity between the two sultanates and the need that they both felt to promote good relations with the Portuguese, came to an end. The turn of the century witnessed the creation of a new conjuncture that the Portuguese, despite the advantage that they held on the ground and the noteworthy diplomatic efforts by some individuals, were unable to overcome.

Meanwhile, the 'enemies from Europe' settled in the region, and the Portuguese did not manage to define a coherent and concerted policy that was capable of successfully opposing them. The Anglo-Dutch strategy was clear: to find the source of the Asian spices that they were now prohibited from buying in Lisbon. They chose the Archipelago as a prime target because this region produced a substantial quantity of these commodities,

---

[57] Fr. Félix de Jesus does not provide any information in this regard; another source refers to his last visit to Aceh, but does not mention his imprisonment (Fr. Simão da Graça, 'Livro Segundo da Origem, extenção e propagação da Religião dos Eremitas ...', AN/TT, *MssLiv*, No. 1699, fl. 140v.); however, another source mentions his captivity, confirmed by Manuel Teixeira ('Memórias da Congregação Agostiniana na Índia Oriental', *DHMPPO/Índia*, XII, pp. 69–70; Teixeira, *The Portuguese Missions in Melaka and Singapore*, II, p. 187).

the Portuguese military might was weaker both in terms of armadas and the number of fortresses and because the area also afforded access to China and Japan. To this goal, they gradually preferred sailing directly through the Sunda Straits, both as a means of avoiding Melaka and the Portuguese forces in the initial stages and, subsequently, a strategy to deprive the city of its political and economic importance.

Melaka by itself was worthless. The city's power derived essentially from the maximisation and profitability, duly sustained by geopolitical and military conditions, of its exceptional geographical location. In other words, Melaka was an important and valuable position as long as it was able to sustain its function as the hub of a multitude of different trade routes associated with the city that were channelled via the Straits. Mainly from the 1570s onwards, the Portuguese gradually lost control over the routes and mercantile traffic of the Eastern Archipelago, Banda, the Moluccas and even of Sunda. With the opening up of other routes that provided an alternative to Melaka, such as the one directly to the Sunda Straits used by the Dutch, further supported by a naval power in its prime, the city saw the very foundations of its survival under threat.

This scenario had a political aspect: the English and the Dutch implemented a policy of contacting the rivals of the Portuguese, especially Aceh, but also Johor and Banten. The Dutch enforced an aggressive naval policy as one of their main instruments for penetrating the East Indies which the Portuguese were unable to emulate. In fact, the cognition that naval supremacy was the key to dominating the trade routes and mercantile traffic, a problem that was as old as the Portuguese presence in Asia, is something that the Dutch seemed to have been quite aware of.

The Portuguese, on the contrary, for a long time still deliberated over a policy of constructing fortresses which, apart from being ineffective, was never really implemented on account of the high costs involved. Nevertheless, despite the various weaknesses of the Estado da Índia, the Portuguese responded to this new and growing challenge with punitive expeditions which, apart from expelling the intruders, were aimed at punishing and dissuading the local powers who harboured their rivals. This formula was not new: they had already resorted to this kind of method, with a fair degree of success, in order to relieve the pressure on Melaka, such as Matias de Albuquerque's armada in 1576 or that of Dom Paulo de Lima Pereira in 1587. However, this policy now failed, for a variety of reasons.

We have already mentioned that duly armed large ships were the only effective means of containing the numerous, swift and well-equipped northern European armadas. However, the financial debility of the Estado da Índia was unable to support the costs of despatching armadas of this kind over a long period of time and increasingly resorted to using oared vessels. Thus these punitive armadas were strategic gambles that involved a pooling of resources, where each failure considerably aggravated naval shortages, until the end of the 1610s.

At this time the viceroys finally confessed the financial exhaustion of the Estado to undertake new ventures. This failure was linked to a shortage of human, material and organisational resources, as well as to the adoption of ineffective strategies. As was witnessed in the case of André Furtado de Mendonça's armada, the preparation and despatch of a great fleet demanded an extraordinary effort to ensure supplies and permanent reinforcements, without which the huge number of ships and men involved simply became an ineffective millstone. Supply lines were a vital factor for the southward-bound armadas. Despite the city's best efforts, Melaka did not have the capacity to provide complete supplies to large armadas, even more so because these fleets were not always duly funded by Goa or Lisbon.[58] This problem was felt by many people, especially those who supported the creation of a separate government in Melaka; they pointed out how the captains of Melaka and the viceroys of Goa had voted to abandon the captain of an armada:

> 'because the moment in which they send him on his mission is when they forget about him, and as there is a dearth of supplies, the galleons and ships are impossible to maintain, and today they beach one, tomorrow another, and very often it is because the captains grow tired of sailing these seas, which do not have as many benefits as in India, and they themselves let the galleons grow weaker and weaker until they soon flounder. And we have seen examples of this such as André

---

[58] The provisions and help provided by the city of Melaka to the armada of André Furtado de Mendonça were recognised by the king, who expressed his gratitude in a letter to the city, 23-3-1604, AHU, *Cons. Ultr.*, cod. 282, fl. 221v.–222. Martim Afonso de Castro's fleet necessitated that a special finance inspector be appointed and sent to Melaka by the king on account of its dimensions and requirements (royal letter to Pedro Mexia, 16-2-1605, HAG, *MonçReino*, 6 B, fls. 112–115).

Furtado de Mendonça, who after they sent him to the South, they did not assist him in any substantial way, and despite suffering every kind of shortage, he sustained the armada for a long time. And the same was seen with the viceroy Dom Martim Afonso de Castro, being senior admiral and viceroy of India, the governor that he left in Goa subordinate to him let him perish on account of a shortage of supplies, with which all the great might he carried with him, which cost more than a million, came to an end, and it will always be like this, on every occasion, as long as there is no governor in Melaka....'[59]

Apart from some partial studies, we only know of one general work where this issue is examined in depth.[60] It would thus not be inappropriate to dedicate some attention to this question. The appearance of the Dutch in Asian waters at the end of the 16th century was not entirely a novelty. On the one hand, the piracy, especially English privateering, that abounded in the Atlantic and had plagued the *Carreira da Índia* meant that the Portuguese were already used to tension with other European powers who, from the 1580s, indiscriminately attacked Portuguese and Spanish interests. Secondly, they had already detected the movements of the pioneering expeditions of Drake and Cavendish, well before the great avalanche of voyages that would be witnessed at the turn of the century. When the Portuguese noted the presence of ships, which they mistook to be English vessels, this time via the Cape route, the information was sent to Goa and was a permanent cause for concern, even more so because the authorities also received information from Flanders about the preparation of armadas bound for the Orient. However, these movements, which threatened the Portuguese monopoly of Indian Ocean waters, were taken seriously only when the new viceroy, Dom Francisco da Gama, took up office.

The first Portuguese armada, under the command of Lourenço de Brito, was prepared during 1597, supposedly to combat the Dutch armada that had been detected in Sunda but which, in fact, had already returned to Europe. The problems that the armada encountered, as well as its failure, could have been avoided if the choice of captain had been pondered upon

---

[59]   Report on a separate government in Melaka, unknown date, AN/TT, *MssLiv.*, No. 1107, pp. 283–284.

[60]   Cf. Boxer and Vasconcelos, *André Furtado de Mendonça*, where these events are analysed in detail; the general work in question is Sousa, *Subsídios para a História Militar Marítima da Índia*.

more carefully. The archbishop, Friar Dom Aleixo de Meneses, in a letter to the king, mentioned his fears about the choice, fears that did come to pass: André Furtado de Mendonça, then occupied in Sri Lanka, had been the first choice, after whom the archbishop was inclined to choose Álvaro de Abranches, but the viceroy favoured Lourenço de Brito.[61] The armada consisted of two galleons, two galleys and nine pinnaces, which would be joined by other vessels in Melaka.[62] It left Goa on 24 September 1597, arriving in Melaka on 28 October.[63]

After discussing the problem with the city's authorities, it was decided that the armada would leave for Sunda (Banten) in December, with a view to lying in wait for Dutch or English ships and dissuade the sultan from accepting these newcomers once again. Lourenço de Brito disregarded his orders as he allowed his captains to seize rice from the local inhabitants, as well as a vessel loaded with pepper, which gave rise to reprisals and resulted in the loss of three galleys. He did not retaliate nor did he attempt to recover the vessels; he neither remained in the region nor patrolled the Javanese coast as he was obliged to do. Instead, he returned to Melaka in July 1598.[64] Thus he did not carry out any of the orders he was given and his actions only served to aggravate Banten's animosity towards the Portuguese.

As will be seen in another chapter, the only positive effect was that it provoked the immediate despatch of various embassies to the kingdoms that neighboured Melaka, bringing about important but short-lived diplomatic

---

[61] Most probably the archbishop agreed to this name in order to prevent the choice of an inexperienced captain who would surely have encountered problems of discipline. Lourenço de Brito was a veteran but, despite this, he faced similar problems; letter from the archbishop to the king, unknown date, AHU, *Índia*, box 1, doc. 20, fls. 9–11v.

[62] Data provided by Diogo do Couto (*see* the following note); in 1598 the viceroy refers to the following information: 2 galleons, 3 galleys, 2 galleons expected from the Moluccas, 8 galliots and 4 *bantins* (letter to the king, Dec. 1598, BN, *Res.*, cod. 1976, fl. 93v.).

[63] Couto, *Da Ásia*, XII, I, vii, pp. 52–54; letter from Viceroy D. Francisco da Gama to the king, April 1598, BN, *Res.*, cod. 1976, fl. 91.

[64] Couto, *Da Ásia*, XII, I, xii, pp. 90–92; letters from Viceroy D. Francisco da Gama to the king, April 1599, BN, *Res.*, cod. 1976, fl. 97v.; 20-12-1599, BN, *Res.*, cod. 1975, fls. 300–300v.; letter from the same viceroy to Pero Guedes, finance inspector and a counsellor to the king, 20-12-1599, ibid., fl. 229v.

benefits. Lourenço de Brito returned to Goa the following April, with the monsoon, without having carried out his orders. When questioned about the course of events, he justified his actions by saying he had returned prematurely to take up his new appointment as captain of Mozambique. The viceroy prosecuted him and the case was discussed by the governing council, but he did not receive any punishment.[65] Thus the chapter of the first Portuguese armada sent to the South to expel the Dutch came to an inglorious end.

The second attempt did not come to pass: Cosme de Lafetá was appointed as Captain of the Sea in Melaka and an armada that would sail directly from Lisbon was prepared. The armada's orders were even issued; these specified that it was to proceed directly to Melaka, where all the ships—vessels that sailed the high seas and oared boats alike—would come together in order to persecute the Dutch and impede the local kings from receiving them. Their powers were not yet as sweeping as the mandate that the 'Generals of the South' would receive in the future, which bestowed them with powers on par with the viceroy's authority. In this case, the king limited himself to ordering the viceroy and the captain of Melaka to provide them with all necessary assistance.[66] The king communicated the despatch of this armada in that same year,[67] but it apparently never left Portugal, probably due to the English blockade of Lisbon which prevented the annual armada from setting sail for India.

Finally, this was followed by the expedition captained by the famous André Furtado de Mendonça.[68] The Crown entrusted Viceroy Aires de Saldanha with the preparation of a powerful armada that could successfully achieve what Lourenço de Brito had failed to do and, likewise, contain

[65] Letters from Viceroy D. Francisco da Gama to the king, 20-12-1599, BN, *Res.*, cod. 1975, fl. 300v.; 23-12-1599, BN, *Res.*, cod. 1976, fls. 156–157v.

[66] Royal orders to Cosme de Lafetá, 17-3-1598, AN/TT, *CorCron*, part 1, pack 114, doc. 19.

[67] Royal letters to Viceroy D. Francisco da Gama, 30-3-1598 and 5-4-1598, *APO*, III, part 2, pp. 877, 883 and 884, respectively. In December 1598 the king stated that he agreed with the choice, but there is no information about the arrival of this armada in India (BN, *Res.*, cod. 1976, fl. 93).

[68] The highlights of this captain's biographical details and career have been presented in Boxer and Vasconcelos, *André Furtado de Mendonça.*

the Dutch penetration of the region, which had grown considerably in the meantime. In 1601 the king ordered the viceroy to go to Melaka and Sunda in person, without delegating the task to anyone else. However, he later accepted the nomination of André Furtado de Mendonça, who had earlier rendered outstanding service in Sri Lanka and the Malabar coast.[69] He set sail from Goa in May 1601, taking a strong armada of six galleons and fourteen light vessels.[70] A storm off the coast of Sri Lanka caused substantial losses for the fleet, considerably reducing its might. It seems that he intended to head for Aceh, where he planned to attempt building the fortress that had been in the process of negotiation between the sultan and the Portuguese for several years.

The unexpected problem mentioned above forced him to postpone this enterprise and sail directly to Melaka.[71] Here he repaired as much of the damage to the armada as was possible and later headed for Sunda, stopping over in Palembang on the way. This sultanate was included in Banten's sphere of influence, but its breakaway tendencies meant that the Portuguese were occasionally able to count upon its support. The documentation of this period mentions the goodwill of this sultan towards the Portuguese captain, providing him with supplies and promising him assistance in his mission. The Portuguese king even wrote him a letter thanking him for this support.[72] In truth, however, this sultan did not fulfil many of the promises he made to André Furtado de Mendonça and, by all appearances, seems even to have gone to Banten's aid.[73]

---

[69] Royal letters to Viceroy Aires de Saldanha, 14-3-1601, 10-2-1602 and 12-2-1602, AHU, *Cons. Ultr.*, cod. 282, fls. 49–50v., 79v.–80, 66 (*see* Document Appendix, No. 12), respectively. *See* Boxer and Vasconcelos, op. cit., Ap. xv.

[70] According to Boxer and Vasconcelos, op. cit., p. 38.

[71] Letter from Nicolau Pimenta to C. Acquaviva, 1-12-1601, *DM*, II, p. 530; letter from Cosme de Lafetá to the king, 15-1-1602, AN/TT, *CorCron.*, part 1, pack 114, doc. 53, fl. 3; letter from the City of Melaka to the king, 3-12-1605, *DUP*, II, p. 257; letter from the archbishop of Goa to the king, 6-4-1603, AN/TT, *ColVic.*, 12, p. 117 (*see* Document Appendix, No. 13).

[72] Royal letters to the viceroy and to the sultan of Palembang, 1604, in AHU, *Cons. Ultr.*, cod. 282, published by Boxer and Vasconcelos, *André Furtado de Mendonça*, pp. 171 and 173.

[73] Letter from Brício Fernandes to Viceroy Aires de Saldanha, 1-5-1602, *DM*, II, p. 554; Argensola, *Conquista de las Islas Malucas*, p. 278.

The armada then proceeded to Banten with a view to punish the sultan for having received the Dutch and to expel any enemy ship found there. It entered into combat with an enemy armada anchored in the port, without any practical results.[74] As they were unable to continue in the region any longer, a decision was made to head for Ambon, where the Portuguese faced a far more serious situation which was of even greater concern. Once again the Portuguese failed in their attempts to intervene decisively in the Melaka region and the consequences would prove to be negative in the short term. The armada's failure in Sunda is not clearly expressed anywhere in Portuguese documentation. On the contrary, the great expectations created around the size of the fleet and the prestige of its captain caused the circulation of news about the armada's supposed victory.[75] André Furtado de Mendonça would only return to the region at the end of his mission in the Eastern Archipelago, which was marked by the failure of the actions that he proposed to carry out. In 1603 he was captain of Melaka in an age that was characterised by the decline of Melaka's regional hegemony which the city had managed to achieve in the 1590s.

Disruption

The years between 1603 and 1606 marked the sudden end of the 'state of grace' in which Melaka had lived for some years. The city's relations with Aceh and Johor deteriorated due to a combination of diverse factors, and the Dutch rapidly established themselves, from this period onwards, as a regional power. The case of Johor is the most glaring example. The first contacts between this sultanate and the Dutch appear to have been established sometime towards the end of 1602 by Jacob van Heemskerk, with whom the sultan's brother, Raja Bongsu, signed an agreement that

---

[74] There is a small report on this battle, usually ignored in books on the subject, in Mills, 'Two Dutch-Portuguese Sea-Fights'.

[75] The Principal of the Jesuits in Melaka said in 1602 that André Furtado de Mendonça 'is lord of Sunda', and that the Dutch 'are moving hither and thither like desperate men' (letter to the Jesuits in Goa, 22-2-1602, *DM*, II, p. 541); a complete description of the battles with the Dutch fleet and the impasse was provided by the chaplain of the Portuguese armada, Brício Fernandes, in his letter to the viceroy quoted in note 73, pp. 554–560.

envisaged Dutch assistance against Patani and the despatch of ambassadors to the United Provinces.[76] The event that caused Johor's rupture with Melaka was, however, the famous capture of the *Santa Catarina*, a Portuguese carrack loaded with a valuable cargo from China, in the Johor River in February 1603, with the connivance of the Malays.[77] Johor's ruler, Sultan Alauddin, seems to have been sympathetic towards the Portuguese and never had a change of heart, unlike his brother, Raja Bongsu, who always preferred the Dutch. Johor's shift towards the Dutch camp thus came about more as a result of the actions of Raja Bongsu than a decision by the sultan himself.[78] Information contained in a contemporaneous source helps one to understand the sultan's sudden animosity towards the Portuguese: the capture of various Johor vessels by the captain of a Portuguese armada, Francisco da Silva de Meneses, and the death of their passengers, among them an ambassador who had been sent to Perak. He was the sultan's brother-in-law and this incident immediately provoked the imprisonment of all the Portuguese in the sultanate[79] and pushed the sultan towards an agreement with the Dutch, thus abetting them in the capture of the *Santa Catarina* as a means of reprisal.

In 1603 André Furtado de Mendonça, the captain of Melaka, was caught off guard by this news as he was busy preparing an armada against Aceh. After demanding that the Dutch be handed over,[80] he channelled these resources against Johor. The attack on Batu Sawar, the sultanate's capital, proved to be a failure because the Malays had access to Dutch military resources and also the Portuguese troops' lack of discipline, which made it impossible to carry out an effective offensive and, curiously,

---

[76] Winstedt, *A History of Johore*, p. 30.

[77] An issue that has been debated in various works at the time and is still debated, especially with regard to the famous theoretical discussion about the freedom of the seas started by Hugo Grotius. Several sources refer to the capture, for example, Valentijn, 'Description of Melaka', Pt 2, p. 128 and Coutre, 'Vida de ...', pp. 168–169. *See* Vink, '*Mare Liberum* and *Dominium Maris*' and Ittersum, *Profit and Principle*.

[78] Erédia explicitly affirms this, 'Declaraçam de Malaca ...', fl. 44v.

[79] Coutre, 'Vida de ...', pp. 165–166.

[80] Raja Bongsu's reply became famous: he said he would rather lose his kingdom than deliver his allies to the Portuguese; Scott, 'A Discourse of Java' (1602–1605), in Purchas, *His Pilgrimes*, II, p. 460.

because the ladders that the Portuguese took to scale the fortress walls were too short.[81] This information indicates a decline in the Portuguese capacity to carry out offensive actions compared with the situation at the time of the attack on Johor Lama in 1587, but it also reveals that a greater effort had been made to fortify the sultanate's capital. In any case, this defeat firmly sealed the alliance between Johor and the Dutch in a common endeavour to try to conquer Melaka. The agreement foresaw a division of the spoils of war and the jurisdictions of each party once Melaka was taken.[82] Thus the Dutch interest in Johor was, above all, political. The English never managed to gain an important position in the sultanate, partly because they did not aspire to conquer Melaka (which they considered to be invincible for a long time)[83] and partly because, until a much later stage, they had an insufficient knowledge of the terrain.[84]

In 1605–06, chance or the caprices of history deemed that two distinct initiatives would take place in the same space, enterprises that would suddenly characterise and reveal, in one fell swoop, diverse factors: the Dutch aggressiveness, after years of exploratory voyages; the failure of the Portuguese naval and military machine, on the brink of rupture; the rapid degeneration of Melaka's geopolitical situation in the light of the arrival of this 'fourth power'. These initiatives consisted of the greatest armada sent

---

[81] Letter from the city of Melaka to the king cited in note 71, p. 255; Valentijn, 'Description of Melaka', Pt 2, p. 128; Fr. Félix de Jesus, op. cit., fl. 67; information by Rafael Carneiro Alcáçova, unknown date [early 17th century], AN/TT, *MiscMssCGL*, box 16, vol. 6 F, fl. 71v.; letter from Diogo do Couto to D. Francisco da Gama, unknown date [1606?], AN/TT, *MiscMssCGL*, box 2, vol. III, p. 372 (published in the compilation of the 'Décadas' by António Baião, Lisbon, Sá da Costa, col. 'Clássicos', 1947, I, p. lviii; 4 pages are missing in the original letter).

[82] Valentijn, 'Description of Melaka', Pt 2, pp. 135–136, transcribed by Winstedt, *A History of Johore*, pp. 31–33.

[83] For instance, in 1615 the English expressed their doubts that the fleet that Iskandar Muda of Aceh was preparing had Melaka as a target because they considered the city to be 'too strong for him to deal with' (letter from Richard Rowe to the EIC, 6-11-1615, *LREIC*, III, p. 210).

[84] In 1615 they confessed that they had insufficient information about the sultanate, as may be seen in the letter from J. Sandcroft and E. Aspinall to the EIC, 12-10-1615, *LREIC*, III, p. 190.

to the South to definitively expel the Dutch, and the simultaneous siege to which the latter subjected Melaka, with the support of Johor.

This was the greatest armada ever prepared by the Portuguese in Asia and the greatest military failure of the age: the armada of Viceroy Dom Martim Afonso de Castro, who would unexpectedly play an important role in the struggle against the Dutch in the Orient. He had never been in India and his inexperience and unfamiliarity with local conditions would prove to be disastrous. Let us deal briefly here with the choice of the individual who succeeded Aires de Saldanha as viceroy.

When Aires de Saldanha was about to conclude his term, the problem of his successor was debated in Lisbon, Madrid and Valladolid. As the results of André Furtado de Mendonça's expedition were not yet known, common sense implied that the next viceroy should be someone with military experience in India, given that the hypothesis of the viceroy going personally to Melaka had already been raised, as would, in fact, happen. The members of the Council of Portugal, summoned in Valladolid, gave their opinions and proceeded to vote. The individual who obtained the most support was Matias de Albuquerque, owing to his military experience and knowledge of the region's problems.[85] Prior to this, when Albuquerque's term as viceroy had come to an end and the question of his successor was being discussed, many had been inclined to let him continue governing India.[86] Dom Martim Afonso de Castro, who was forty-two years of age at the time, was only nominated by Dom Jorge (bishop of Viseu and royal chaplain), who refuted the other choices and passionately advised against the choice of Matias de Albuquerque on account of the enmity he had left behind in India.[87] Thus the king, overruling the majority of the Council,

[85] His name was recommended by the Count of Vila Nova (Statement of 1603, BM, *Add.* 28432, fls. 73–74) and D. Pedro de Castilho, viceroy of Portugal; after the voting, Matias de Albuquerque got five votes, the same as D. Jerónimo Coutinho and D. João Coutinho; Fernão Teles got four and other individuals, including the archbishop of Goa, got fewer votes (Statement of the Council of Portugal and the viceroy of Portugal, ibid., fls. 76–77).

[86] Letter from the governors of Portugal to the king, 8-8-1595, AN/TT, *ColVic.*, 12, pp. 119–120.

[87] Statement of D. Jorge, bishop of Viseu, 24-11-1603, BM, *Add.* 28432, fls. 79–81. The real motives and causes of such choices and votes are unfortunately obscure due to a dearth of appropriate biographical studies and research.

unexpectedly chose Dom Martim Afonso de Castro to proceed to Goa and succeed Aires de Saldanha, captaining the greatest armada ever created in Portuguese Asia.

In 1604 the king drew up a judicious plan to expel the Dutch, which envisaged the viceroy going personally to the South and the maintenance of strict vigilance over the Melaka region after the success of this mission, based on a careful analysis of the steps to be taken, a process in which the advice of Dom Francisco da Gama, Count of Vidigueira, would undoubtedly have played an important role.[88] The viceroy, after some vicissitudes during his voyage, finally arrived in Goa on 20 May 1605.[89] The stage was set for the raising of a powerful armada that, at the very latest, would proceed to Melaka with the monsoon of April 1606. The enterprise entailed a considerable financial effort that diverted resources from other parts of the Estado da Índia and left its coffers empty.[90] The authorities in Goa were forced to make loans that, as on other occasions, took a long time to be repaid.[91] The armada finally left Goa on 13 May 1606 but, before arriving in Melaka, made a stopover in Aceh where, after the failure of talks with the sultan, troops disembarked to try and force the sultanate to cede a fortress to the Portuguese. It was a disaster; men and materials were lost without any benefits as, in the meantime, the Portuguese were forced to re-embark after receiving news of the Dutch attack on Melaka.[92]

---

[88] *See* letter to the viceroy of Portugal, 27-12-1604, AN/TT, *NuclAnt.*, No. 870, fls. 1–4v. (*see* Document Appendix, No. 14). Report by Francisco da Gama, unknown date [1603 or 1604], BM, *Add.* 28432, fls. 116–117.

[89] 'Relação do estado em que estavam as coisas da India no anos de 1605', in Luz, *O Conselho da Índia*, p. 442.

[90] Letter from the archbishop to D. Jerónimo (?), 21-10-1605, AHU, *Índia*, box 1, doc. 20, fls. 20v.–21; Couto stated that, 'The viceroy has gone to Melaka with everything that India had' (letter to D. Francisco da Gama, 20-12-1606, AN/TT, *MiscMssCGL*, box 2, vol. III, p. 367).

[91] In 1613 the loans made by the archbishop of Goa and two Goan Hindus had not yet been repaid (royal letter to Viceroy D. Jerónimo de Azevedo, 14-2-1613 and 22-3-1613, *DRI*, II, pp. 321 and 416, respectively).

[92] This disembarkation in Aceh is described by Queirós, *História da Vida do Venerável Irmão Pedro de Basto*, pp. 334–337 and in the 'Relação do sucesso que teve a armada do viso-rei Dom Martim Afonso', unknown date, AN/TT, *MssLiv.*, No. 1113, fls. 192–192v. (*see* Document Appendix, No. 16). Rafael

In Melaka, they engaged in combat with the Dutch armada—in circumstances that are already well known—which probably saved the city. However, the enormous losses suffered put a definitive end to the grand Portuguese project of defeating and expelling the Dutch from Southern waters.[93] In this clash, it is particularly interesting to note how Portuguese superiority rapidly disappeared in the light of military disorganisation, the viceroy's lack of experience at the helm, rivalry between the viceroy and the captain of Melaka and a series of elementary errors that transformed what could have been a comfortable victory into an impressive disaster.[94] Once the city had been saved, the Portuguese proceeded to evaluate the damages and losses, supervised by Dom Martim Afonso de Castro. However, the support necessary for its personnel and the assistance rendered to the city entailed vast expense, which would only be reimbursed much later.[95] The viceroy, devastated by the defeat and ill, died in the city the following year. The news took some time to reach Goa. The archbishop, who had been entrusted with the governance of the Estado in the interim, revealed his hopes about the results obtained by the expedition, but even before hearing of its fate, he could not avoid a pessimistic tone while referring to the number of Dutch ships that had arrived in the Orient in recent years.[96]

Thus the last great Portuguese attempt to contain Dutch penetration in the region came to nought. The next viceroy, Dom João Pereira Forjaz, the Count of Feira, was lost at sea on his voyage to India, and almost his entire armada—which consisted of more than ten ships—suffered the same fate. Even though André Furtado de Mendonça was appointed to

---

Carneiro Alcáçova estimated that the Portuguese lost about 280 men on the Acehnese enterprise ('Proposta de ...', AN/TT, *MiscMssCGL*, box 16, vol. 6 F, fl. 71v.).

[93] One can find a detailed description of these battles in A. Botelho de Sousa, *Subsídios para a História Militar Marítima da Índia*, II, cap. 1, and in Boxer and Vasconcelos, *André Furtado de Mendonça*, pp. 67–72.

[94] Boxer and Vasconcelos, op. cit., pp. 135–136, mentions 18 Portuguese carracks and 11 Dutch ships, but some sources present different figures: Queiros (*História da Vida* ..., pp. 334–335) refers to 14 Portuguese carracks and Trindade (*Conquista Espiritual do Oriente*, III, p. 406) mentions 12. *See* also *PI*, XV, pp. 312–314.

[95] In 1615, these expenses (about 9,000 *cruzados*) had not yet been paid (royal letter to Viceroy D. Jerónimo de Azevedo, 14-2-1615, *DRI*, III, p. 219).

[96] Letter to D. Jerónimo (?), 29-4-1607, AHU, *Índia*, box 1, doc. 20, fls. 27–30.

lead a new expedition with the title of 'General of the Southern regions', he never returned to Melaka.[97] He would be interim governor in 1609, when the official documents for the succession of the unfortunate Dom Martim Afonso de Castro were opened.[98]

The decline in Melaka's role in local geopolitics soon faced the same situation with regard to the other element in the triangle, the sultanate of Aceh. Here, the main factor in the cooling of relations with Melaka was the ascension to the throne of the new sultan, Iskandar Muda, in 1607, aggravated by the ineptitude of the Portuguese mission to the sultanate in 1606, as we have already seen. Diplomatic relations between Aceh and the Portuguese had been at an impasse for several years, with a series of embassies from both sides, but little progress. The Portuguese intended to build a fortress in the sultanate to prevent the Dutch gaining a foothold. However, their insistence that it be built on the island of Gomispola[99] was stiffly resisted by the sultan, and both Goa and Lisbon hesitated over what should be done next.[100] Both sides avoided making any commitments in

---

[97]   *See* the *Regimento* of the Count of Feira, 4-3-1608, *DRI*, I, pp. 210–213, the royal letter to this viceroy stipulating that André Furtado de Mendonça was to receive 6,000 *cruzados* per year, and the respective *alvará* (*DRI*, I, pp. 215 and 216); *see* the letter from the Council of Portugal to the king, 22-2-1608, AGS, *Secr. Prov.*, book 1479, fls. 52–53v.

[98]   He was also nominated to succeed the Count of Feira, according to the ballot realised by the Council of Portugal, where 5 of the 6 members present voted in his favour (letter to the king, 3-3-1608, AGS, *Secr. Prov.*, book 1479, fls. 92–93). The Council expressed its fears that the transmission of power from the archbishop to Furtado de Mendonça would cause tension in Goa, but there is no evidence to this effect in the documentation (letter to the king, 23-9-1608, ibid., fls. 278–278v.).

[99]   A group of small islands near the tip of Aceh that the Portuguese called the 'islands of Gomispola', mentioned as far back as Tomé Pires' *Suma Oriental*, pp. 255–256, note 230 (fl. 140). The bishop of Melaka, D. João Ribeiro Gaio, stated that they were situated about 5–7 leagues away from the entrance of the port of Aceh (*O Roteiro*, p. 63).

[100]   *See* royal letters to Viceroy Aires de Saldanha, 15-1-1601, AHU, *Cons. Ultr.*, cod. 282, fl. 16v; 25-1-1601, HAG, *MonçReino*, 7, fl. 36 (copies of the same letter in *MonçReino* 8, fls. 10–24, 53–64v., 67–77 and 112–122v.). This letter has been published with errors in *BOGEI*, Nos. 45–55 (1880), pp. 309–364; the excerpt is in No. 49, p. 335.

order to gain time, although the Portuguese did try to hasten negotiations after the Dutch and the English arrived in the region.

André Furtado de Mendonça's armada had received instructions to construct a fortress in the sultanate, but the inopportuneness of the act and the gravity of the situation in other areas prevented any attempt to do so. Aceh had been grappling with internal conflicts from around 1603, and the Portuguese had hoped to use this to their advantage in order to reach their objectives.[101] Dom Martim Afonso de Castro had probably been induced to disembark and attack the sultanate, to no avail, based on the supposition that it would be easy to impose advantageous conditions in the light of the prevailing state of affairs. The new sultan was able to affirm his own power domestically, precisely for having led the defence against the Portuguese, and the latter could therefore not expect any great sympathy from him when he assumed power.

Both the Dutch and the English, and even the French, had already contacted Aceh and, with a greater or lesser degree of ease, had established commercial or even diplomatic relations with the sultanate. All three sultans who ruled in this period were favourably inclined towards the arrival of these new partners, which gradually enabled the sultanate to distance itself from and reduce its dependence on its old enemies in Melaka. In the case of the Dutch, after the disastrous voyage of 1598–99 they reached an agreement with the sultan. The Portuguese received contradictory information: while the events of 1599, in which Alauddin Riayat Syah attacked and expelled the Dutch,[102] were still fresh in their minds, at the same time they received information confirming that the Dutch had established themselves in the sultanate and had eventually opened a factory there.[103]

---

[101] *See* the report about the conquest of the sultanate in BA, Liv. 51-VI-54 $\frac{18}{}$, fls. 36–37v. (*see* Document Appendix, No. 17).

[102] Royal letter to Viceroy Aires de Saldanha, 31-1-1602, AHU, *Cons. Ultr.*, cod. 282, fl. 68v. The data in this letter seem to refer to the events of 1599 and not to those of 1601 (as stated by Alves in 'Os Mártires do Achém ...', p. 400). *See* Sousa, *Subsídios para a História Militar Marítima da Índia*, I, pp. 463–464.

[103] The Dutch 'have a factory built of stone and lime, almost like a fort, and are established there'; letter from the archbishop of Goa to the king, 6-4-1603, AN/TT, *ColVic.*, 12, p. 116 (*see* Document Appendix, No. 13).

After the hostility of the initial contacts and the tension of subsequent attempts, the Dutch did manage to reach an agreement with the sultan. The greatest fear of the Portuguese was that the Dutch would manage to establish a fortification in the sultanate, which would close access to the Straits of Melaka and, combined with the Dutch alliance with Johor, would directly threaten the city. The sultan skilfully played them off against each other, even affirming that he would cede the necessary space for a fortress 'to whosoever arrived first', a fact that hastened the Portuguese diplomatic offensive[104] and precipitated the 1606 strike. In the meantime, the English, and even the French, had followed in the footsteps of the Dutch. The former played an important role during the early years, but later lost ground in the region to the Dutch and focused upon the western Indian Ocean instead. As early as 1602, James Lancaster's armada was well received in the sultanate, and a commercial agreement was signed between the sultan and Elizabeth I of England.[105]

The year 1606 definitively marked the new geopolitical order in the region. Henceforth, the situation would witness the growing precariousness of conditions in Melaka, because the new state of affairs was unfavourable for the city. Simultaneously, both Johor and Aceh definitively broke loose from the Portuguese sphere of influence: Johor established an alliance with the Dutch, and the Portuguese attack on Aceh—rather ironically—hastened the ascension to the throne of Iskandar Muda, who re-established the sultanate's old hostility towards Melaka.

The siege of 1606 revealed, in one fell swoop, the naval and military might of the Dutch and their diplomatic and political strength, not only with Johor but also in their relations with other Malay sultanates. The Dutch strike on Melaka was substantially different from previous assaults on the city by Aceh, both on account of its force as well as, above all, the impact it had locally. The Portuguese were now up against a war in the European fashion, of which they had been the harbingers in the Indian Ocean. The most important aspect, compared with the local way

---

[104] Royal letters to Viceroy D. Martim Afonso de Castro, 5-3-1605, HAG, *MonçReino*, 6B, fl. 13 (another copy on fls. 1–8) (*see* Document Appendix, No. 15); 18-1-1607, *DRI*, I, p. 98.

[105] *Alvará* from the sultan to James Lancaster, 1603, *LREIC*, I, pp. 1–4. Foster (ed.), *The Voyages of Sir James Lancaster* …, pp. 98–100.

of carrying out a war, concerned the destructive effects, in terms of men and materials as well as the city's structures. The Portuguese had never witnessed such destruction. Apart from the inevitable increase in the price of provisions, as usually happens during periods of crisis, the city suffered considerably under the Dutch onslaught. The number of dead reached the thousands, a figure that rose considerably after the siege had ended, with the inevitable appearance of epidemics.[106] The city's defensive structure suffered considerable damage. All the churches within the city walls were affected and the cathedral itself was 'collapsing and ended up buried under a hill'.[107] The city's residents were reduced to penury owing to the systematic destruction of the *duções* (vegetable plots) by the Dutch, who even destroyed the palm trees, something that was inconceivable to the Malay mentality and had therefore never been done in preceding sieges.[108] Melaka abruptly realised that the Dutch were a serious threat if the necessary defensive measures were not taken. Although the Dutch would only launch an attack on the city again in 1640, this time emerging victorious, it was from this moment onwards that the Portuguese began to fortify the city as a whole, maintaining a constant vigilance over the state of the walls and supplies of men, munitions and provisions. Gradually, the city transformed itself into an invincible stronghold, growing stronger and tightening its defences while losing its external connections and became increasingly isolated in a hostile environment.

---

[106] In 1607 the casualties were estimated to be 4,000 but they rose to more than 10,000 (of which 1,000 were Portuguese) due to the 'plague'; 'Relacion de lo que en sustancia contiene una carta del ViRey Don Martin Alfonso de Castro …', AGS, *Secr. Prov.*, book 1479, fl. 162; an anonymous report mentions 5,000 casualties (*MssLiv.*, No. 1113, fl. 193v.). The same figure is given in a report about the armada of D. Martim Afonso de Castro ('Relação do sucesso que teve a armada de…', unknown date, fl. 193v. (*see* Document Appendix, No. 16). Boxer estimates the casualties to have been about 6,000 (Boxer and Vasconcelos, *André Furtado de Mendonça*, p. 68).

[107] Information provided by the bishop of Melaka, mentioned in a royal letter to Viceroy Martim Afonso de Castro, 11-12-1607, *DRI*, I, p. 158.

[108] Royal letter to Viceroy D. Jerónimo de Azevedo, 26-2-1614, *DRI*, III, p. 94; letter from this viceroy to the king, 23-1-1615. AHU, *Índia*, box 3, doc. 21, fl. 1.

Relations with Aceh were not broken off completely, and diplomatic contacts were taken up once again shortly thereafter, albeit without the earlier vigour.[109] Available information enables one to infer that a Portuguese factory existed in the sultanate during this period,[110] although one knows of the presence of Portuguese merchants both before and after this date. As for Johor, the sultan hastened to send embassies to Melaka, as did other powers—Perak, Jambi, Rokan, Siak, Banten and Palembang—with a view to making peace.[111] The survival of the city marked the end of the anti-Portuguese scenario that had preceded the siege, in which various sultanates had attempted an alliance with the Dutch through promises to realise a joint attack on Melaka.[112] The city recovered some of its former prestige but, henceforth, would always live in constant fear of a new Dutch attack. Relations with the neighbouring kingdoms improved, but any measures to punish those who had harboured and helped the Dutch would be constantly postponed. Peace was essential for the replenishment of supplies and the fortification of Melaka, and the king of Portugal ordered that peace treaties should be signed even under unfavourable conditions.[113]

---

[109] *See* Alves, 'Os Mártires do Achém …', pp. 401–402, and the sources quoted therein.

[110] Ibid., p. 401, notes 33 and 35.

[111] Royal letter to Viceroy Rui Lourenço de Távora, 24-12-1610, *DRI*, I, pp. 414–415, quoting a letter from the bishop of Melaka, 3-11-1607. The letter mentions 'Arracam', surely Rokan, next to Siak in Sumatra, and not Arrakan in Burma. *See* chapter 4, note 85.

[112] Valentijn highlights the case of Kedah, while the siege was taking place; Matelieff, disappointed by the unfulfilled promises made by the sultan of Johor, was suspicious and did not accept ('Description of Melaka', Pt 3, p. 299). Barbuda says the Dutch made an alliance with seven neighbouring kings, including those of Johor, Pahang, Patani and Rokan (*Empresas Militares de Lusitanos*, fl. 320v.).

[113] About the peace with Johor, Perak and Kedah, the king says, quoting a letter dated 4-5-1607 from Viceroy D. Martim Afonso de Castro: 'Because the conjuncture does not permit us to punish these kings the way they deserve, and because of the great importance of this peace for the fortress [of Melaka], you shall seek a peace in the most favourable conditions keeping in mind the advantages and the reputation of the *Estado*, in order that they be more secure and firm; this is your first priority; if this is not possible, it should be made in conditions that are the least harmful to us as possible'; royal letter to Viceroy

The Dutch and English continued with their efforts to penetrate the Archipelago, supplanting the Portuguese who had already lost their position in the Moluccas and Ambon. The initiatives to recover these fortresses was entrusted to the Spanish in Manila, who were better placed and prepared for such enterprises. In Melaka, the Portuguese continued in their efforts to contain the Dutch presence, but had scarce means at their disposal after the destruction of a good part of the armada of 1606. Navigation, especially that of the ships that made the voyage of China, now required a permanent patrolling of surrounding waters. The Dutch and the English definitively established their presence in diverse sultanates, directly competing with the Portuguese in each market and port.

One sultanate which saw an increase in its importance with the entrenchment of the northern Europeans was Jambi, due to its wealth of pepper, the warm welcome it extended to foreign merchants, accepting English, Dutch and Portuguese alike, and the sultan's policy of free trade. Although the sultanate was situated next to Indragiri and Lingga, Jambi always maintained a relative autonomy with regard to both Johor and Aceh. As early as the 1610s it became the most profitable factory[114] of the Dutch who, taking advantage of local commercial conditions, preferred it to Aceh and Johor. In the case of Aceh, this was because Iskandar Muda exercised strict control over the pepper trade, which was unfavourable to the Dutch, and also because they were anxious to escape the pressure from the sultan to employ Dutch naval power to his benefit. In the case of Johor, the weakness of the sultanate at that point in time had reduced its former importance, and Dutch interest in the sultanate was, above all, political rather than economic.

Until the end of the period under study, the geopolitical scenario remained stable: a gradual loss of Melaka's influence in the face of the strengthening of Dutch power. The city fortified itself and shrank as its decline became more accentuated. As for the regional balance, these were difficult years for Johor. The kingdom was divided between two sultans, suffered direct strikes from the Acehnese in 1613 and 1615 and managed

---

Rui Lourenço de Távora, 14-2-1609, HAG, *MonçReino*, 11, fl. 200 (published with errors in *BOGEI*, No. 160 (1882), p. 795).

[114] 'A Short Description ... of the Forts ...' (1616) in *The East and West Indian Mirror* ..., p. 157; Jacques de Coutre, p. 400.

to stay intact only at great cost. The constant threat posed by Aceh and the neutral Dutch status in the power play of regional politics resulted in Johor seeking an improvement in ties with Melaka once more. In 1612 the peace agreement had still not been confirmed by Goa.[115] However, after perceiving the consequences of Acehnese victory and control over Johor, the viceroy issued express orders to render assistance to the sultanate,[116] although this collaboration with Melaka was already a reality. However, caution continued to prevail: Governor Fernão de Albuquerque, who had been captain of Melaka, knew the diplomatic entanglements of the region and understood that the sultan's desire for good relations was only because he desperately sought Portuguese support.[117]

Aceh, on the contrary, established itself during this period as a regional hegemonic power, under the iron rule of Sultan Iskandar Muda. He extended the sultanate's power over a large part of Sumatra, control-ling the island's pepper production, as well as over Johor, Pahang, Kedah and Perak. Aceh attacked Melaka in 1615, but immediately signed a truce that, despite all the mutual distrust, lasted for several years. The Portuguese extended the peace and their relations with the sultan in order to counterbalance the Dutch presence and influence and keep an eye on both enemy movements and those of the sultan himself. The tension and mutual distrust that prevailed were clearly evident and Melaka dedicated its energies to trying to prevent Aceh's expansion into other Malay sultanates without breaking the peace that had been established.[118] At this point, the Portuguese hesitated about the measures to be taken, in a context in which the events escaped their control. Thus they encouraged trade with Aceh as a means of distancing the sultanate from the Dutch, even going

---

[115] Royal letter to Viceroy D. Jerónimo de Azevedo, 20-3-1613, *DRI*, II, p. 407.

[116] Letter from Viceroy D. João Coutinho to the king, 9-2-1619, *DRI*, IV, p. 315.

[117] 'He will never be a friend except when he is obliged to be one'; letter to the king, 20-2-1621, *DRI*, VII, p. 146. In the same letter, the governor stated that he did not send the sultan a letter from the king of Portugal in which the latter 'considers him [the sultan] to be a brother-in-arms'.

[118] Royal letter to Viceroy D. João Coutinho, 5-3-1620, *DRI*, VI, p. 300. References to the deceitful nature of the sultan and his hidden hostility towards Melaka are a constant feature in documents of this period.

so far as to open Melaka's doors to Acehnese merchants;[119] but, at the same time, the viceroy issued orders in the opposite direction.[120]

However, relations between Iskandar Muda and the Dutch were already fairly tense. The first sign of instability appeared suddenly at the time of the Acehnese attack on Johor in 1613. A Dutch ship present at the scene took the side of the Malays and Aceh took several prisoners, including an ambassador.[121] Relations deteriorated in 1615 when the Dutch refused to assist in the war that Iskandar Muda was planning against Melaka.[122] The English also encountered difficulties in the sultanate, identical in every respect to those faced by the Dutch. Iskandar Muda proceeded to curtail the privileges of foreign merchants by establishing a pepper monopoly and constant pressure to place European naval power at his service. The difficulties of which English merchants complained during their sojourn in this sultanate were also rooted in these factors: they tried to purchase spices without the sultan's consent and they refused to provide him with military assistance against Melaka.[123] One of the causes of the failure of Iskandar Muda's expedition was, thus, a lack of support by European ships, which he had undoubtedly counted upon.

---

[119] Royal letter to Viceroy D. João Coutinho, 5-2-1618, *DRI*, IV, p. 312 (and reply from the latter, 8-2-1619, ibid., p. 313). Royal letter to the same viceroy, 26-2-1619, *DRI*, V, p. 274. This command was executed in an *alvará* issued by the viceroy on 8-10-1618, *APO*, VI (ii), pp. 1139–1140.

[120] Letter from Viceroy D. João Coutinho to the captain of Melaka, 1-4-1620, HAG, *Reis Vizinhos*, 1, fl. 102 (*see* Document Appendix, No. 20).

[121] *See*, amongst others, Floris, *Peter Floris: His Voyage to the East Indies ...*, p. 97, and 'The Journal of Thomas Best' in Best, *The Voyage of ... to the East Indies*, p. 59.

[122] Letter from J. Millward to the EIC, 13-11-1615, *LREIC*, IV, p. 227; letter from Viceroy D. Jerónimo de Azevedo to the king, 29-12-1616, HAG, *MonçReino*, 12, fl. 297v. (published with errors in *BOGEI*, No. 285 (1883), p. 1149). It is curious to notice a coeval Portuguese letter which stated that it was the Dutch who urged the sultan to attack Melaka and that he refused on account of being afraid of Portuguese naval power; copy of this letter, 26-3-1616, AN/TT, *ColVic.*, 18, fl. 122.

[123] With regard to the former, *see* the letter from P. Floris and G. Chauncey to T. Aldworth, 16-11-1614, *LREIC*, II, p. 165; with regard to the latter, *see* the statement of the factors of the *Solomon*, 9-11-1615, ibid., III, p. 213 and letter from L. Antheunis to T. Roe, 15-2-1616, ibid., IV, p. 30.

1615 was also the year in which the Portuguese made their last great attempt to expel the Dutch by the preparation of a great armada. This was the armada organised by the governor of the Philippines, Don Juan de Silva, who was entrusted with the planning of the enterprise and the preparation of the ships. The Portuguese were merely entrusted with a collaboration that was never accomplished. The idea that the only effective way of combating the Dutch was to unite Portuguese and Spanish resources in a single armada which—from either Manila or Melaka— could reverse the process of debility that had been witnessed since the beginning of the century, was a recurrent feature.[124] The governor of Manila immediately set to work preparing this armada, of which he was a great mentor, and on several occasions requested the Portuguese to send him carracks and other large vessels which would be paid for by cloves from the Moluccas.[125]

Finally, in 1615 the king gave the viceroy express orders to go to Melaka with the armada that he had been able to put together (thanks to the funds obtained from the general sale of the administrative posts and official positions of the Estado da Índia) and join forces with the Spanish, granting him authority above the governor of Manila. The viceroy, clearly reluctant to incur any risks to his person, sent Francisco de Miranda in his stead.[126] This armada, after arriving in Melaka and while preparing to set sail for Manila, met and defeated the Acehnese armada that attacked the city in September that year. Their next skirmish, immediately afterwards, with a Dutch fleet had precisely the opposite result,[127] thus depriving Don Juan de Silva's armada of Portuguese reinforcements. Francisco de Miranda was even accused of disobedience for not having followed his

---

[124] *See* royal letters to the governor of Portugal, 10-1-1617 and 7-2-1617, AN/TT, *ColVic.*, 18, fls. 17–18v. and 133–134, respectively.

[125] Bocarro, *Década 13*, I, p. 105 and 295. *See* the comprehensive and detailed study on the subject by Borschberg, 'Security, VOC Penetration and Luso-Spanish Co-operation'.

[126] Royal letter to Viceroy D. Jerónimo de Azevedo, 5-3-1615, *DRI*, III, p. 291; *alvará* issued on the same date, ibid., pp. 294–295; Bocarro, *Década 13*, I, p. 358.

[127] About both battles, see the description by a cleric present in Melaka [1615], BN, *Res.*, cod. 1975, fls. 193–194v. (*see* Document Appendix, No. 19).

orders to proceed directly to Manila and was only saved by the viceroy's support.[128]

Thus the Manila armada was not able to count on Portuguese reinforcements. There had already been prior instances of captains who had disobeyed orders when requested urgently to go to the Philippines and join forces with the Spaniards. Two cases, at least, are well known: that of João Caiado de Gamboa, before he took up the post of captain of Melaka, and that of Diogo de Vasconcelos in 1612.[129] The governor's preparations could not help but reach the ears of the Dutch and the English. The former simultaneously doubted and expressed fears about the existence of such an armada,[130] and the latter revealed themselves to be well prepared for any such occurrence, maintaining an alert fleet to contain any Spanish assaults.[131] However, this enterprise was condemned to fail in a manner that clearly proved the lack of articulation between the Portuguese and Spanish structures: once the armada finally set sail for Melaka in March 1615, it arrived in the city after patrolling the Singapore Straits. However, the unexpected death of the governor, who had been the driving force behind the undertaking, resulted in the immediate dissolution of the armada whose elements returned to Manila.[132]

The new geopolitical equilibrium of the region enabled Melaka to survive, although the city experienced a progressive decline. In 1620 there were rumours of a new attack against the city by Aceh, which proved to be unfounded. In fact, all that remained for Melaka was the prestige of a great commercial metropolis, the seat of a great mercantile centre from

---

[128] Letter from Viceroy D. Jerónimo de Azevedo to the king, Jan. 1616, HAG, *MonçReino*, 12, fl. 243 (published in *BOGEI*, No. 183 (1883), p. 736); royal letters to the same viceroy, 10-3-1617 and 15-3-1617 (and the respective replies), *DRI*, IV, pp. 52, 63 and 64, respectively.

[129] About the former, *see* Bocarro, *Década 13*, I, pp. 105–106; about the latter, see the order of inquiry in a royal letter to Viceroy D. Jerónimo de Azevedo, 8-3-1613, *DRI*, II, pp. 373–375, and another to the governor of Portugal, 7-2-1617, AN/TT, *ColVic.*, 18, fls. 166–167.

[130] Letter from R. Wickham to Sir T. Smythe, 23-10-1615, *LREIC*, III, p. 291; letter from J. Brown to B. Farie, 30-5-1616, ibid., IV, p. 108.

[131] Letter from W. Eaton to R. Wickham, 22-6-1616, *LREIC*, IV, p. 121; letter from J. Gourney to W. Nicholls, 23-7-1616, ibid., IV, p. 146.

[132] Bocarro, *Década 13*, I, pp. 427–429.

the 15th century onwards. This was the reason why, until 1641, only Aceh attempted to conquer the city. Iskandar Muda's old dream of a great empire with Melaka as its capital, crowning his prestige in the Malay World and permanently supplanting his old rival of Johor, definitively crumbled with the defeat of 1629. The English did not risk a direct attack on the Portuguese stronghold and the Dutch consolidated their supremacy in the eastern Indian Ocean and preferred to deprive Melaka of its role as a commercial emporium rather than risk a new direct confrontation. The Dutch dominated the seas, the Portuguese sought refuge in their fortress. It was in this context that 1619 was a landmark year in the history of Melaka and of the Straits: it was the year that witnessed the foundation of Batavia as the capital of the VOC, which sealed the fate of Melaka, definitively relegating the city to a secondary role.

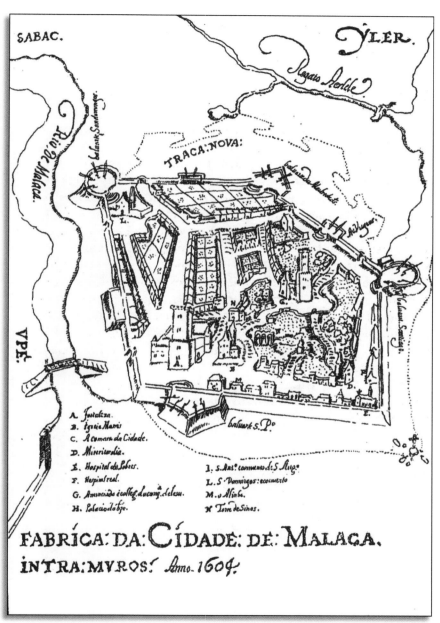

1. The Fortress of Melaka, 1604

Manuel Godinho de Erédia, "Declaraçam de Malaca e India Meridional com o Cathay", published as *Malaca, l'Inde Orientale et le Cathay* by L. Janssen, Brussels, 1881.

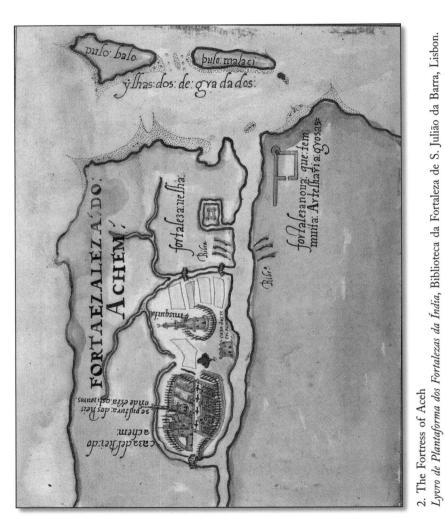

2. The Fortress of Aceh

Lyvro de Plantaforma dos Fortalezas da Índia, Biblioteca da Fortaleza de S. Julião da Barra, Lisbon.

3. Javanese Vessels
Johann Theodore de Bry and Johann Israel de Bry in Jan Huygen van Linschoten's
Itinerario, Oppenheim, 1616.

4. Malays
Johann Theodore de Bry and Johann
Israel de Bry in Jan Huygen van
Linschoten's *Itinerario*, Oppenheim, 1616.

5. The Sultan of Aceh Alauddin of Perak (Mansur Syah)
Manuel Godinho de Erédia, *História de Serviços com Martírio de Luís Monteiro Coutinho*, Biblioteca Nacional, Lisbon, Cod. 414.

6. The Acehnese Sultan Alauddin Riayat Syah and the Dutch, 1599
Isaac Commelin, *Begin ende Voortgangh van de Vereenighde Nederlandtsche Geoctroyeerde Oost–Indische Compagnie...* Amsterdam, Jan Janz., 1646.

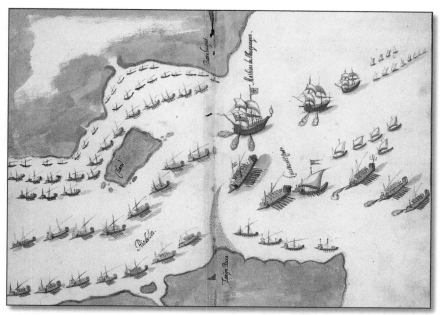

7. Portuguese and Acehnese Fleets Engaged in Battle, Johor River, 1577
Manuel Godinho de Erédia, *História de Serviços com Martírio de Luís Monteiro Coutinho*,
Biblioteca Nacional, Lisbon, Cod. 414.

8. Dutch Strike on Portuguese Ships in Banten, 1601
Cornelis Claesz, Amsterdam, 1608.

9. Luso-Dutch Naval Battle, 1606
Isaac Commelin, *Begin ende Voortgangh van de Vereenighde Nederlandtsche Geoctroyeerde Oost-Indische Compagnie...* Amsterdam, Jan Janz., 1646.

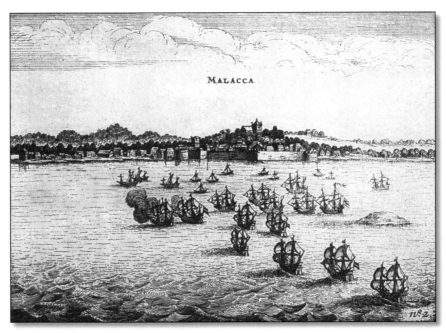

10. Dutch Siege of Melaka, 1606
Isaac Commelin, *Begin ende Voortgangh van de Vereenighde Nederlandtsche Geoctroyeerde Oost-Indische Compagnie...* Amsterdam, Jan Janz., 1646.

11. Aires de Saldanha, Captain of Melaka 1576–79, Viceroy of *Estado da Índia* 1600–05
Museu do Traje, Lisbon.

12. Fernão de Albuquerque, Captain of Melaka 1600–03, Governor of *Estado da Índia* 1619–22
Galeria dos Vice-Reis, Old Goa, Goa, India.

13. André Furtado de Mendonça, Captain of Melaka 1603–06, Governor of *Estado da Índia* 1609
Galeria dos Vice-Reis, Old Goa, Goa, India.

14. D. Martim Afonso de Castro, Viceroy of *Estado da Índia* 1605–07 *Lyvro de Plantaforma dos Fortalezas da Índia*, Biblioteca da Fortaleza de S. Julião da Barra, Lisbon.

CHAPTER 4

Portuguese and Malays

Melaka in the Malay World: Politics, War and Diplomacy

For a better understanding of the integration of Portuguese Melaka in its surrounding environment, one must understand the way in which the city adapted itself to local ways of politics and war. The politico-military balance of the Malay World did not consist of a mere inventory of guns, cannons or soldiers, and the victories that the Portuguese stubbornly achieved when Melaka was under siege acquire a meaningful dimension if we pay some attention to the local mentality, culture and socio-political structure. One fact is universally accepted: the brilliant initial success of the Portuguese was due both to their military superiority as well as the element of surprise in their sudden arrival in the Indian Ocean region. It is also well known that both these factors gradually decreased throughout the early 16th century, in parallel with the process of stabilisation and erosion of Portuguese structures in Asia. A renewed offensive on the part of Asian powers may be added to these factors, both in an economic form (revival of the Levant route, reorganisation of the global commerce of the

Indian Ocean via structures that opposed or were not connected with the Portuguese) as well as in military terms (increased pressure on Portuguese positions, sieges and various offensives, the growing insecurity of routes). Therefore, one may conclude that, in the period under study, Melaka was only one amongst several powers and had to be constantly alert in order to maintain its position at the heart of the regional balance.

The powers of Southeast Asia began to acquire military materials on par with those of the Europeans.[1] The case of Aceh is of special interest, as it began to rely during the 16th and 17th centuries on armaments, training and the adoption of Ottoman military tactics. However, traditional arms, especially the irreplaceable *kris*, continued to play an important role. Another factor also goes well beyond a mere reckoning of military forces in terms of human or military resources when one analyses a conflict or battle.

In the Malay sultanates, the sultan's power was closely linked to one fundamental notion, that of sovereignty of a divine origin (*daulat*), which constituted the essence of political power. Although the term itself was Arabic, this notion of the divine character of royalty predated the arrival of Islam.[2] *Daulat* was a fundamental concept for the Malay sultanates in two ways. First, it marked continuity of power in the long term as sovereignty was legitimated as a legacy of an ancient dynastic connection, a link in a political chain whose origins were as remote as possible, and were often even mythical in origin. The most obvious case was that of the sultanate of Melaka-Johor, which claimed to be a direct heir to the Sri Vijaya empire, thus forming an uninterrupted chain that transmitted royal power.[3] In this case, Prince Parameswara of Palembang had ensured the continuity of *daulat* while founding Melaka. In Aceh,

---

[1] A comprehensive work on warfare and military power in Southeast Asia is yet to be written. *See* Reid, *Southeast Asia in the Age of Commerce*, Vol. 1, pp. 127–129, and Boxer, 'Asian Potentates and European Artillery ...'. With regard to Aceh, *see* Reid, 'Sixteenth Century Turkish Influence in Western Indonesia'.

[2] Andaya, *The Kingdom of Johor 1641–1728*, p. 49.

[3] This can also be witnessed in several other civilisations with different degrees of similarity, and would include the alleged Trojan origin of the foundation of Rome, the successive claims to the authority and heritage of Rome by several European powers and the transfer of the Kinguri title in the Lunda Empire, in Central Africa.

the scenario was different, but attempts to claim a remote legacy were evident, for example, in the ancestry that genealogists attributed to Sultan Iskandar Muda.

Secondly, *daulat* was an important factor for social cohesion around the figure of the sultan. In the case of Melaka-Johor, this was the element that, in spite of all the varied vicissitudes, ensured the continuance of the web of loyalties that sustained the kingdom, ranging from the *orang laut*[4] to the sultanates that were part of its sphere of influence. How deeply Islamic law had penetrated into Malay sultanates is not a question for discussion here.[5] However, generally speaking, the sultan was considered to be above his subjects, a kind of link connecting God and the people, whose power emanated from spiritual sources and was, in principle, indisputable if exercised within the precepts of justice and good government. We may get a clearer image of this concern to keep the ruler above common mortals if we pay closer attention to the efforts at ostentation and visual spectacles realised during festivals and official ceremonies that, more than simply being lavish extravagances, were ways to publicly demonstrate and affirm royal power and status.[6] In Malay literature, and we can once again use the Melaka-Johor model as an example, the king was even viewed as a representative of God:

'a just prince is joined with the Prophet of God like two jewels in one ring. Moreover, the Raja is, as it were, the deputy of God. When you do your duty to the Prophet of God it is as though you were doing it to God Himself, as says the Word of God in the Koran.'[7]

However, the sultan's connection with his dependants was not a mere relationship of authority–submission. This relationship was, at least theo-

---

[4] Literally 'sea people', from the Riau-Lingga archipelago, who were one of the mainstays of the sultanate of Melaka (and later Johor) from its very foundation. *See* 'The Sultanate of Johor', below.

[5] Reid has provided a good, albeit concise, panorama of this question at the heart of Southeast Asia in the chapter dedicated to law and justice in *Southeast Asia in the Age of Commerce*, Vol. 1, pp. 137–146.

[6] In this regard, *see* Reid, 'Elephants and Water in the Feasting of Seventeenth Century Aceh'.

[7] Speech of the *bendahara* of Melaka to his children at his deathbed, in *Sejarah Melayu*, ed. C. C. Brown, p. 118.

retically, a mutual agreement in which the ruler guaranteed his people's security and well-being, which was reciprocated by loyalty and fidelity,[8] a mutual agreement that was a solemn oath according to the history of Sang Seperba (the monarchy) and Demang Lebar Daun (the masses).[9] Nevertheless, the idea of *daulat*—that obviously allowed a far greater freedom of action for royal power—appears to have prevailed over this notion.

However, it is clear that a sultan's authority could be a despotic power only in exceptional cases. The case of Iskandar Muda and his policy of almost absolute power was more an exception than a rule and was the result of peculiar and well-defined political conditions. The mutual dependence between the ruler and his subjects, even though the situation varied from case to case, was a visible reality in the Malay sultanates. In the classic case of Melaka-Johor, power traditionally lay in the reciprocal relationship between royal power and its dependants, the political elite—such as the local chiefs—who ensured its human resources according to a series of conventions established by *adat* (tradition).[10] Fidelity to the sovereign, inherent to *daulat*, was something deeply rooted in the local mentality. *Derhaka*,[11] which constituted a break in fidelity, was something abominable, subject to particularly severe punishments.[12]

An important issue to be kept in mind when dealing with the questions concerning royal power in Southeast Asia is that the true source of power was authority over men and not over the land.[13] The latter was

---

[8]   Cf. Muhammad Haji Salleh, 'Didactism and Conflict Resolution in the *Sejarah Melayu*', p. 9.

[9]   Zainal Abidin Wahid, 'Power and Authority in the Melaka Sultanate', p. 103. One can compare these notions with the *pactum subjectionis* of Medieval European political thought.

[10] Kathirithamby-Wells, 'Royal Authority and the *Orang Kaya* in the Western Archipelago', p. 261.

[11] 'Disobedience' or, more properly, 'treason' or 'rebellion'. *See* Zainal Abidin Wahid, 'Power and Authority…', p. 102.

[12] Andaya, *The Kingdom of Johor 1641–1728*, p. 49.

[13] Valentijn, when describing Johor Lama, the capital of Johor in the post-1587 scenario, says that all the land belonged to the sultan, but that this did not matter because 'If people apply for it, they can get as much as they like' (Valentijn, 'Description of Melaka' , Pt 3, p. 293); Mandelsloe refers to this

vast and covered by dense forests, while the population, on the contrary, was comparatively scarce.[14] Thus, one can better understand the different ties that united men, namely the sultans and their subordinates, with diverse relations and levels of dependence between them. In Aceh, for example, this relationship commonly induced the Europeans to affirm that all the inhabitants were slaves of the sultan.[15] This is a complex question, one of the favourite themes of research of current historiography.[16] In this case, one presently needs only to highlight two main ideas: to understand the figure of the sultan as the centre of political life and consider the relationship between the sultan and his subjects, which was far more complex than a simple relationship between master and slave.

The European mentality, namely that of the Portuguese in Melaka was, in large measure, not familiar with these concepts of power and society. This unfamiliarity began precisely with Afonso de Albuquerque's unexpected act of conquering the city, a notion that was inconceivable by the standards of the local mentality. Contrary to the European tradition, the cities of the Malay-Indonesian world were built, preferentially, along rivers or streams. They were not fortified, and would only be protected

---

issue in similar terms: the king gave land to anyone who would work on it but the Malays were not interested due to their laziness ('The Remaining Voyages of John Albert de Mandelsloe through the Indies' in Harris (ed.), *Navigatium atque Itinerarium Bibliotheca*, I, p. 783). Both reports were certainly based on previous information by Cornelius Matelieff; Borschberg (ed.), 'Description of Batu Sawar'.

[14] Reid, 'The Structure of Cities in Southeast Asia', p. 243. Also *see* Reid, *Southeast Asia in the Age of Commerce*, Vol. 1, pp. 122 and 129. With regard to the demographic questions in Southeast Asia, *see* Reid, 'Low Population Growth and Its Causes in Pre-Colonial Southeast Asia'.

[15] The anonymous author of the project for the conquest of Aceh written in 1582 says the Acehnese did not work in the fields because the king took all their wealth when they died, 'Due to the fact that, by the law of the kingdom all the king's vassals are his slaves.' Therefore, wealthy individuals buried their wealth (Teensma (ed.), 'An Unknown Portuguese Text ...', p. 314).

[16] With regard to slavery and dependence in Southeast Asia *see* Reid, *Southeast Asia in the Age of Commerce*, Vol. 1, pp. 129–136; Reid, '"Closed" and "Open" Slave Systems ...'; Matheson and Hooker, 'Slavery in the Malay Texts'. About the situation in Melaka during the Malay period, *see* Thomaz, 'A Escravatura em Malaca no Século XVI'.

later, owing to European influence. Only the *dalam* (royal palace) was provided with a surrounding wall, and there was no clear frontier between the city and its surrounding environment. It gave it a visibly rural aspect, where one can highlight the enormous importance of fruit trees for the local economy.[17] According to local standards it made no sense to fortify something that could fall into enemy hands. Thus the cities were open spaces, adapted to and fused with their surrounding environment. In the case of an enemy attack which could not be sustained for very long, the sultan would retreat, along with the population that followed him, to the interior, to a site where they could obtain refuge, wait for the enemy to pillage the city, and then return after the enemy had left and rapidly rebuild the structures that had been destroyed.[18] The wooden houses and the fortifications consisting of palisades or partitions could easily be rebuilt. Their wealth, in most cases easily transportable, could be taken with them during their flight and their return. Their fruit trees, which remained intact during the conflict, were their most important element of immovable wealth.

War was not aimed at taking enemy positions, causing them heavy losses or destroying them completely. On the contrary, it was primarily aimed at increasing the number of dependants through the capture of prisoners of war. Similarly, there was a need to conserve an army's forces, avoiding human losses to the maximum extent possible. Wars without quarter or those that caused heavy losses to the enemy were useless. One can imagine the effect that Aceh's successive defeats while attacking Melaka, often with great losses, would have caused. Thus one may understand the reluctance of local kingdoms to supply men of arms to third powers, a fact that the Europeans viewed as yet more evidence of the treacherous nature of the Malay sultans. This happened, for instance, in 1601, with the armada of André Furtado de Mendonça: the king of Palembang, while declaring to be ready to support the Portuguese enterprise, said he could supply 2,000

---

[17] Reid, 'The Structure of Cities …', pp. 241–242.

[18] It happened, for instance, in 1568: when news about the imminent Acehnese raid on Melaka spread, several sultans hid in the hinterland because such a fleet was a threat to them as well; Couto, *Da Ásia*, VIII, xxiv, p. 166. The failure of the Spanish strike on Brunei in 1578 was partially caused by their inability to respond to similar local dynamics. *See* Pinto, *No Extremo da Redonda Esfera*, pp. 236–238.

men (having previously promised 10,000), but later reduced this figure to 700 and ended up by not supplying any.[19] Johor behaved in much the same way during the siege of Melaka in 1606: the sultanate's promises of support to the Dutch in terms of both men and munitions, ended up by never materialising, to the great disappointment of Matelieff.[20]

Thus an attack on a city did not imply capturing it definitively. When the Portuguese conquered Melaka in 1511, the sultan fled, as was to be expected, and was astonished by the continued presence of the intruders in the city and became alarmed when he heard that Afonso de Albuquerque had constructed a fortress as he had believed that they would withdraw after plundering the city.[21] Later, after several years with a roving court, his son founded the sultanate of Johor, thus transferring the political centre to a new capital. As the *daulat* was maintained without perturbations, the sultanate of Melaka survived this audacious strike by the Portuguese intact (in terms of its political structure). The sultanate, along with its consequent economic prosperity, was to be found wherever the sultan was. As the *Sejarah Melayu* states, 'Where there is sovereignty, there is gold.'[22]

This episode would be repeated on other occasions over the course of the 16th century: in 1536 the Portuguese attacked and destroyed the capital of Johor, which was situated in Sayong Pinang, and the sultan established a new capital shortly thereafter, at Johor Lama. In 1564 an attack by Aceh and the capture of the sultan resulted in the court being

---

[19] Letter from Brício Fernandes, chaplain of the fleet, to Viceroy Aires de Saldanha, 1-5-1602, *DM*, II, p. 554.

[20] Valentijn, 'Description of Melaka', Pt 2, pp. 135–138, Pt 3, pp. 290–292.

[21] After escaping to Lingga, the sultan of Melaka 'assuming that Afonso de Albuquerque's intentions were to plunder the city and then leave it and depart with the loot obtained from the sack, waited for about ten days ...'; Brás de Albuquerque, *Comentários do Grande Afonso de Albuquerque*, II, part 3, chapter xxix, pp. 146–147. Barros has a similar version of the events (*Da Ásia*, II, part 2, VI, vi, p. 86).

[22] Ed. C. C. Brown, p. 187; this sentence was said as a conclusion after the *bendahara* had described his doubts to the expelled sultan because the latter had given all his wealth to a daughter in dowry, leaving the heir of the throne, Muda, without any property. The sultan replied thus: 'If Sultan Muda has but the sword of kingship, he will have gold as well.'

temporarily installed at Bukit Seluyut. Finally, in 1587 the Portuguese destroyed Johor Lama and the sultan founded a new capital upriver, at a site called Batu Sawar.[23] The Portuguese-Malay Manuel Godinho de Erédia pointed out that when some misfortune befell a city, it was abandoned and another city was founded. After the destruction wrought by Dom Paulo de Lima,

> 'never again did the said King [Ali Jalla] wish to return to his court at Johor, and he even abandoned his prized fort at Kotabatu, which was the refuge of his empire, and established a new court and city on the Ujontana River, on a high, steep hill called Batusavar....'[24]

The sultans would again rebuild a capital, rapidly reorganising their power. Their approach to war thus differed substantially from the Europeans' concepts in this regard. The power of the latter centred on their armadas and naval might, a rather limiting factor in an environment in which the interior, the hinterland or the mountains were a traditionally safe refuge. The Sundanese of Banten, for example, feared the king of Mataram but not the Europeans, irrespective of whether they were Portuguese or Dutch, as European ships could not follow them into the mountains.[25]

War was associated with a considerable magic component, linked to the individual bravery of the warrior, his invulnerability (*kebal*) or to the *daulat* of the sovereign. However, the most important element was the *amok*, which the Portuguese called '*amouco*', which designated the resolute determination of the warrior to kill the greatest number of his enemies, even if he lost his own life in the process.[26] If a well-aimed assault by an *amouco* managed to strike the enemy leadership, it could prove decisive in a battle.[27]

However, it does not seem that such a statute was only used to designate a special spiritual preparation aimed at assuming magical powers

---

[23] *See* the general framework (for 1530–1720) provided in Gibson-Hill, 'Johor Lama and other ancient sites ...', p. 165.

[24] Erédia, *Informação da Aurea Chersoneso*, p. 71.

[25] Letter from Jan Pieterszoon Coen, 1615, quoted in Reid, *Southeast Asia in the Age of Commerce*, Vol. 1, p. 122.

[26] Couto stated that they were 'men who were determined to die while killing as people many as they could' (*O Primeiro Soldado Prático*, p. 372).

[27] Reid, *Southeast Asia in the Age of Commerce*, Vol. 1, p. 125.

of invulnerability to enemy arms. A common man could become an *amouco* as a desperate response to a dangerous situation or a strong sentiment, such as revenge. At least, one can interpret Diogo do Couto's account of such an episode, which took place in Melaka in 1588 in this way.[28]

The adaptation of the Portuguese to local conditions was not limited to economic or mercantile aspects. On the contrary, they acquired a gradual understanding of local politics, society, mentality and the art of war. This is something that one can perceive while reading Portuguese sources, often when reading between the lines. In the case of warfare, which was something far beyond mere military aspects, the Portuguese seemed to have understood how the outcome of a battle sometimes depended on non-military factors. They observed how a conflict was not bereft of a spiritual component, how a bad omen or a sign that indicated defeat could inflict an important psychological blow and decide the course of a battle.

On the other hand, just as an *amouco* could decide a battle through a well-aimed strike against the enemy leadership, the Portuguese also learnt how to follow the same tactics. When the armada of Tristão Vaz da Viega confronted the Acehnese fleet during the siege of 1573 the Portuguese forces fought from a clearly disadvantageous position, but managed to emerge victorious by destroying the ship that was leading the enemy attack, and the rest of the fleet consequently fled.[29] Likewise, during the attack by Iskandar Muda in 1615, implemented after several years of preparation, the Acehnese forces lost heart after their first skirmish with the Portuguese armada, where they were defeated. The psychological effect of this incident was undoubtedly one of the factors that induced the sultan to immediately send ambassadors to Melaka offering conditions for freeing Portuguese prisoners, including the son-in-law of the captain

---

[28] During a dispute between a Javanese merchant and a Portuguese, Couto stated that, in Melaka 'a rumour of *amoucos* spread throughout the city ... because there were many Javanese junks in the port and many men in the city, and when they run *amok* they are insane and furious ...' (*Da Ásia*, X, part 2, X, xii, p. 625). These were Javanese merchants, not trained warriors spiritually prepared to die in combat.

[29] Joge de Lemos stated that the enemy galleys 'fled when they saw their flagship vessel lose its pennant and be destroyed ...' ('Hystoria dos Cercos ...', fl. 15). *See* Couto, *Da Ásia*, IX, xvii, p. 129.

of Melaka, who had been captured in combat. Iskandar Muda's naval power remained intact, but he would attempt a new offensive only in 1629.

Tenacious resistance was also liable to have an effect on the enemy. During the great siege of 1568, the sultan of Aceh retreated after he had completely surrounded the city with a great army and powerful artillery, discouraged by the tenacity of the city's defenders and fearing that an enemy sally could deprive him of the cannons he was using in the assault.[30] In 1575, after three successive sieges, Melaka was exhausted, without an armada, deprived of the greater number of its soldiers and surrounded by sea and on land by an Acehnese army. Unexpectedly, the sultan retreated, suspecting that the silence of the Portuguese cannons, which in reality was because they had almost run out of resources, camouflaged a crafty stratagem, and withdrew, contenting himself with the naval victory that he managed to achieve.[31] These episodes demonstrate how war was carried out with great care in order to limit losses and damage as far as possible, and was practised in a controlled and prudent manner. Aceh's intention to conquer Melaka was undeniable, especially under Iskandar Muda; however, the quest for prestige and an image of power was something equally important for the sultans when they decided on an attack.

An exhibition of military might was a traditional means of pressure, like many others, to impress and discourage the enemy. There was a kind of diplomacy during war according to which, before hostilities were unleashed, forces were measured, courage and power were put on display and, sometimes, contacts were established and embassies exchanged, as happened during the siege of 1568: the sultan and the captain traded messages whose courtesy sought, on both sides, to measure their enemy's intentions. The Portuguese captain, having been surprised during festivities celebrating the birthday of King Sebastian, ostentatiously went to play in full view of the enemy armada, so as to plainly display his courage and disdain for danger.[32]

---

[30]   Couto, *Da Ásia*, VIII, xxii, p. 160.
[31]   Lemos, 'Hystoria dos Cercos ...', fl. 53; Couto, *Da Ásia*, IX, xxvii, p. 245; Sousa, *Oriente Conquistado ...*, p. 1097.
[32]   Couto, *Da Ásia*, VIII, xxii, pp. 133–134.

In 1586 the sultan of Johor appeared within plain view of Melaka without any intention of attacking the city, intending only to vaunt his armada, as Couto states, 'in a supercilious manner, to show that he was the lord of the sea'. Even when he disembarked and attacked the city in January of the following year, he did not do so without first establishing contact with the bishop, in order to create divisions in the enemy field as well as to use force only as a last resort.[33]

The Portuguese also made use of these tactics of ostentation of power, especially when, paradoxically, they had large armadas. The most notorious case was that of Lourenço de Brito's fleet that, when sent to Sunda in 1597 to expel the Dutch, merely put on a show of strength. The military effects upon the Dutch were nil (the Dutch armada had already returned to Europe), and were negative in Banten (the fleet lost three galleys and their actions resulted in increased animosity against the Portuguese), but it managed an important, although short-lived, political objective: the neighbouring rulers sent embassies to Melaka, and Aceh showed its willingness to allow the Portuguese to construct a fortress in the sultanate.[34]

Embassies played an important role in the panorama of relations between these states, an instrument used to maintain the equilibrium or to exert pressure, a means of espionage or simply to gain economic advantages. The embassies sent to Melaka served as a kind of barometer of the power and prestige of the city in its relations with neighbouring kingdoms. An absence of embassies foretold difficulties and a precarious position in the geopolitical context. Embassies, on the contrary, generally indicated a re-establishment of the regional *status quo*.

In 1568, as soon as it was known that Aceh had been defeated in its attempt to conquer Melaka, the neighbouring rulers who had fled as Aceh's armada approached heaved a sigh of relief and sent embassies to Melaka[35] in a gesture that acknowledged the Portuguese victory. This also happened in 1598, as has been previously noted. In the same way, in the early years of the 17th century, when the Dutch established their presence in the waters of the Archipelago and consolidated their position by contacts

---

[33] Ibid., X, part 2, VIII, ii, p. 272 and xv, p. 365.
[34] Copies of letters from Viceroy D. Francisco da Gama to the king, April 1599, BN, *Res.*, cod. 1976, fl. 97v.
[35] Couto, op. cit., VIII, xxiv, p. 172.

and treaties with various kingdoms, which coincided with the failure of André Furtado de Mendonça's armada, and the possibilities of an attack on Melaka intensified, the embassies that were routine in previous years promptly ceased.[36] In the same way, after the failure of the siege of 1606, various rulers immediately proceeded to send embassies to Melaka; these included the sultan of Johor, who hastened to seek peace after the Dutch retreat (although he did not fulfil its obligations afterwards).[37] Even in other contexts, one can observe the same attitude: the arrival of a strong armada in Melaka immediately reduced tensions and prompted friendly contacts, as happened in 1610 when the armada of Miguel de Sousa Pimentel, which was on its way to China, had an unexpected delay in Melaka due to the monsoon.[38]

These embassies also fulfilled an economic objective: they were a way of skirting fiscal obligations and, in this way, the ambassadors managed to realise commercial transactions without paying duties on them. The captains of Melaka were the main beneficiaries of these initiatives: they worked in collusion with ambassadors from sultanates that traded in spices from the Moluccas, and managed to get these vessels to stop at Melaka, obviously obtaining economic benefits from this stratagem.[39] Another

---

[36] 'The customs house of Melaka has no profits and embassies did not come to the city as they used to; on the contrary, it seems that the neighbouring kings have hostile intentions towards us, judging by the delegations they have been exchanging amongst themselves'; letter from the archbishop of Goa to the king, 6-4-1603. AN/TT, *ColVic.*, vol. 12, p. 117 (*see* Document Appendix, No. 13).

[37] Royal letter to Viceroy Rui Lourenço de Távora, 24-12-1610, *DRI*, I, pp. 414–415.

[38] In his letter to the king, dated 3-4-1612, the viceroy(?) mentioned how the presence of this fleet in Melaka made their neighbours 'calm down, and Johor signed the peace treaty in conditions that were more favourable for us; one still needs to supply these straits with a strong oared fleet, which are the most suitable vessels for the straits and the most feared by the neighbouring kingdoms' (AN/TT, *ColVic.*, vol. 26, fl. 129). *See* Bocarro, *Década 13*, I, xxii, pp. 94–96.

[39] 'Due to our sins, the captains favour the ambassadors who send their vessels to Your Majesty's mines in the Moluccas to procure spices and bring them to Melaka …, but the ambassadors of those kings who welcome Christians into their realms do not receive any favour'; letter from the bishop of Melaka to the king, 31-12-1588. AGS, *Secr. Prov.*, book 1551, fl. 409v. (*see* Document Appendix, No. 6).

practice consisted of keeping the gifts they received from these embassies while reciprocating with presents paid for by the Royal Treasury. This was a common practice that soon became a right inherent to the post. In 1585 the captain of Melaka, João da Silva, arrived in the city with instructions that granted his office precisely this privilege:

> 'he may send whenever he thinks it necessary and of service to His Majesty, presents and *adiás* to the neighbouring kings and lords, as is the customary practice. And if any ambassador comes to the said fortress, he may send him, at the cost of the Treasury of the aforementioned Lord, whatever is in order, this having, likewise, been granted to past captains who served at the said fortress, by the viceroys and governors, and is a customary practice'.[40]

However, attempts were soon made to rectify this situation: in 1595 Matias de Albuquerque's instructions already specified that abuses be contained and stipulated that ambassadors who came only to trade were to pay the necessary duties on their goods.[41] A few years later, as the situation still persisted, the king issued express orders to put an end to this state of affairs.[42]

We have already analysed the triangular balance that prevailed in the Straits region as well as its effects and external links. It is now necessary to reinforce the idea of permanent instability in relations between the sultanates, including Melaka, in which diplomacy—just like war—was an instrument used to maintain and reinforce power. This can be verified by the impressions that the Portuguese sources record, in general terms, with regard to this question: peace treaties were always temporary, alliances precarious and declarations of 'friendship' short-lived. One only needs to

---

[40] 'Titulo da prouizões que leuão os capitães das fortalezas de Malaca', 1585, BM, *Add.* 28433, fl. 66.

[41] The *Regimento* of the fortress of Melaka (1595) in Pissurlencar (ed.), *Regimentos das Fortalezas da Índia*, p. 258, still refers to the alleged need to concede some favours to the ambassadors. The bishop of Melaka (*see* note 39) suggested establishing a limit on exempted trade.

[42] Royal letter to Viceroy D. Jerónimo de Azevedo, 27-2-1612, *DRI*, II, p. 181. The royal order was implemented by an *alvará* dated 26-3-1613, *APO*, VI (ii), pp. 932–933. Another order can be found in a royal letter to the same viceroy, 14-2-1615, *DRI*, III, p. 207.

observe the shifting alliances during the period under study to have a clearer idea about the subject.

Portuguese sources refer constantly to the bad faith of the sultans of Johor and Aceh in peace proposals. In the case of the former, even before the crisis of 1585–87, when a peace treaty was prepared around 1583 with the ambassadors who were sent to Goa, the Portuguese distrusted the real intentions of Sultan Ali Jalla.[43] Likewise, his son Raja Bongsu/ Abdullah Maayat Syah, the main architect of the alliance between Johor and the Dutch which resulted in the joint attack of 1606, would later change his stance due to circumstances: the threat posed by Aceh forced him to go to Melaka in person in 1619 to request help against the common enemy.[44] As for Aceh, although the peace of the final years of the 16th century was viewed with distrust but with some credit, it was, above all, the peace that Iskandar Muda established after the siege of 1615 that prompted the greatest doubts and suspicions.[45] Thus war was a political instrument used according to established rules, in a limited, prudent and cautious manner. Likewise, peace was transient and unstable, subject to stratagems, often employing very subtle tactics (one only needs to observe the dialogue between Aceh and Dom Leonis Pereira in 1568)[46] of diplomacy and the ruses of political intrigues.

---

[43] The *casados* of Melaka informed Philip I that, 'This King signed the peace with different intentions, and he intends to become powerful, so that when he gets the chance he can act according to his own designs'; royal letter to Viceroy D. Duarte de Meneses, 11-2-1585, *APO*, III, p. 33 (also published in *DHMPPO/Insulíndia*, V, p. 27). Years later, they said that 'This King was never our true friend despite having pretended to be so many times'; letter from the city of Melaka to the king, 3-12-1605, *DUP*, II, p. 254.

[44] Letter from Governor Fernão de Albuquerque to the king, 7-2-1620, *DRI*, VI, p. 69.

[45] A constant refrain in coeval Portuguese documents, such as the letters from the viceroy to the king, 8-2-1619, *DRI*, IV, p. 313, from Governor Fernão de Albuquerque to the king, 8-2-1620, *DRI*, V, p. 275; 7-2-1620, VI, p. 243; 10-2-1621, VII, p. 106; letter from the same governor to the captain of Melaka, 1-4-1620, HAG, *Reis Vizinhos*, 1, fl. 102 (*see* Document Appendix, No. 20).

[46] Pereira refers to the 'artful messages from the king', to which 'the captain replied in a shrewd manner, too'; *História da Índia...*, p. [234]. *See* note 32 above.

The Religious Factor

The last issue with regard to this theme concerns the role of the religious factor in relations between these states and the way in which this shaped the integration of Portuguese Melaka into the surrounding environment. The anti-Muslim stance that the Portuguese brought with them to the Indian Ocean region, which dated back to the very origins of the Portuguese expansion, is well known. Likewise, in the case of Melaka, the preference given to non-Muslim neighbouring powers—the Buddhist kingdoms of continental Southeast Asia or the Hindu kingdoms of Java—as natural allies of the Portuguese is also well known. However, it is important to once again emphasise the fact that Southeast Asia was not the Middle East or the west coast of India, where acute religious tension prevailed, where the Portuguese presence was maintained at the cost of a network of fortresses and where the Portuguese concentrated their naval power.

One must keep in mind that, after the conquest of Melaka, Afonso de Albuquerque intended to keep the city open to all merchants, and even reformulated the administrative structure to this effect: the *bendahara* was now the leader and representative of the Keling community, and the *tumenggung*, that of the Muslims. The flight of the Gujaratis from Melaka was linked more to strategic and political issues (they had been the main instigators of the sultan's animosity towards the Portuguese) rather than to the fact that the new masters of the city were Christians.

It is true that from the Catholic Reformation onwards and the renewed vigour of the missionary spirit, combined with other conditions of a political nature, Melaka became an increasingly Portuguese city and the religious factor played a growing important role in the city's life as well as in its functioning, in trade and in politics, as happened through-out the Estado da Índia. However, it is equally undeniable that, in this region, religious tensions often hid conflicts whose origins were purely of a political or economic nature, and constituted yet another means, a pretext or a reinforcing element rather than an end in itself. In the case of Melaka, if the spirit of the Catholic Reformation, intolerance and social discrimination based on religion made their presence felt internally, from an external point of view, and in the light of the unstoppable progress of Islam and ever increasing difficulties, the Portuguese accepted alliances with Muslim powers without reservations. The friendly relationship with neighbouring sultanates, the tacit alliance with Johor during a large part of the second half of the 16th century, or even closer ties with Aceh at the end of the century demonstrate how the realities of geopolitical conditions obliged them to banish any hesitation on account of religious factors.

One of the reasons why there was far less religious tension here than in other regions derived from the fact that Melaka was surrounded by Muslim sultanates where penetration by missionaries appeared to be difficult and it thus seemed preferable to concentrate their efforts elsewhere. The Malays would not convert and in Melaka missionary activities especially focused upon the slave population, as was to be expected.[47] In other regions of the Archipelago, the scenario was quite different, but as Islam was expanding by leaps and bounds, it was in precisely those areas where Catholic and Muslim proselytism clashed— such as in the Moluccas[48]—that the greatest friction arose. In Java, Muslim animosity towards the Portuguese was a result of the disarticulation of Portuguese control over the spice trade of the Eastern Archipelago, but was also due to the expansion of Islam over the island, which clashed with the missionary presence in some areas, such as Panarukan and Blambangan.

Traditionally, the scenario of tension between Christians and Muslims in Southeast Asia has been viewed as antagonism between two distinct camps. Recently, however, new approaches to this issue have emerged.[49] Contesting the idea of an ironclad opposition between these two blocks and refuting the notion of the 'mentality of a holy war',[50] one may conclude that Muslim animosity against the Christians in Aceh that personified the vanguard of Islam in the region was lower than could be expected. Its hostility, far from being permanent and continuous, was actually limited to periods of greater tension and subject to specific political conditions of

---

[47] In 1590 a Jesuit stated that the Malays were 'fierce Moors in the sect of Muhammad', it therefore being easier to convert or, at least baptise, slaves (letter from Pedro Martins, 1590, *DI*, XV, p. 573). Other coeval sources confirm this information: Fr. Félix de Jesus, 'Primeira Parte da Chronica e Relação do principio que teue a congregação da ordem de S. Augto. nas Indias Orientais …', AN/TT, *MssLiv.*, No. 731, chapter 8, and Sousa, *Oriente Conquistado a Jesus Cristo*, p. 1085.

[48] With regard to the struggle between Catholic missionary efforts and Islamic advances in Southeast Asia, *see* Reid, 'Islamization and Christianization in Southeast Asia'.

[49] Alves, 'Os Mártires do Achém nos séculos XVI e XVII'.

[50] Expressed by Reid, quoted by Alves, p. 393, note 9.

the sultanate, both internal and external, rather than to the precepts of *jihâd*. In contrast to some moments of friction and tension, there were also periods of acceptance and tolerance, when there was a regular presence of Portuguese merchants in Aceh, albeit limited in number. As mentioned above, there were even times of declared peace with Melaka and proposals for a political alliance. Malay texts such as the *Hikayat Aceh*, written at a time that was presumably the peak of anti-Christian and anti-Portuguese animosity, do not reveal any trace of this tension.

Aceh's aggressive attitude towards the Portuguese was an exception rather than a rule, which can be verified by the list of individuals who were martyred in the sultanate. Possible pressure by Ottoman ambassadors, the need to affirm Aceh as a champion of Islam in the eyes of the Ottoman rulers, specific internal conditions such as situations of civil war, disastrous breaches of etiquette by the Portuguese or even their uncompromising refusal to convert to Islam, in well-defined political contexts, were the most common reasons that resulted in martyrdom. The case of the unexpected Javanese ferocity towards the passengers of a Portuguese ship during the late 1570s,[51] apart from being an exceptional event, resulted more from the prevailing conditions—be it the growing tension between Melaka and the city's neighbours and the instability of shipping through the Straits, or revenge for damage inflicted by the Portuguese—rather than reasons of an ideological nature.

Returning to the case of the martyrs, and given that the scenario in Aceh is well known, we may add here a case that took place in Johor, another name on the list of Portuguese martyrs: that of Friar Rafael da Madre de Deus, an Augustinian who, while proceeding from Tonkin to Melaka in 1604, was captured in Singapore by the Dutch who left him in Johor as a prisoner, in the hope that he could later be exchanged for Malays imprisoned in Melaka. The missionary was mistreated during his captivity, especially for preaching so strongly against the Muslim religion that the *ulama* managed to have him condemned to death. The sultan attempted to avoid this outcome, granting him a pardon on the condition that he converted to Islam, an offer that the missionary refused. When he was about to be beheaded, the Dutch—fearing Portuguese retaliation against their compatriots held prisoner in Melaka—managed to obtain the

---

[51] This episode has been analysed by Jacobs in 'Un Règlement de comptes entre Portugais et Javanais …'.

release of the missionary, who was handed over to them. However, the Augustinian friar equally irked his new captors by rebelling against the Calvinist heresy. After a brief period of hesitation, they allowed him to leave on a Japanese junk, but on the following day he was found dead on the beach, having probably been killed at the hands of Malays who had information about his fate. The probable date of his death was 2 October 1606. However, the story is only supported by missionary sources, which raises some doubts about its reliability.[52]

This was a situation similar in every respect to the martyrdoms in Aceh: an exacerbated anti-Christian sentiment caused by political conditions and the behaviour of the Augustinian missionary, coupled with the sultan's hesitation to apply capital punishment and his final offer to save his life. This is the only known case of martyrdom in Johor, in an exceptional scenario; in fact, relations between Melaka and Johor had reached a breaking point after the *Santa Catarina* was captured by the Dutch, which resulted in the attack under the command of André Furtado de Mendonça. At the time when the missionary was held prisoner, the alliance between Johor and the Dutch was already taking shape and they carried out a joint attack on Melaka. This martyrdom can be understood better in the light of this state of affairs, highlighting the sultan's avoidance of applying a death sentence, which would be detrimental in future contacts with the Portuguese.

The dichotomy between Islam and Christianity thus has certain specific elements in the regional context under study. One must once again reiterate the idea that Southeast Asia was not the Middle East, and that the Muslim religion had penetrated the Malay mentality in a different manner.[53] At the time, the Malays left much to be desired as

---

[52] These events were reported by Fr. Manuel da Purificação, 'Memórias da Congregação Agostiniana na Índia Oriental', *DHMPPO/Índia*, XII, pp. 38–39; Fr. Félix de Jesus, 'Primeira Parte da Chronica e Relação …', AN/TT, *MssLiv.*, No. 731, fls. 86–87; and Fr. Simão da Graça, 'História dos Agostinhos no Oriente', AN/TT, *MssLiv.*, No. 731, fls. 132–134v. *See* Teófilo Aparicio-López, 'La Orden de San Agustín…', *Stvdia*, No. 40, pp. 88–93.

[53] With regard to the questions concerning the spread of Islam in Southeast Asia, *see* Reid, 'The Islamization of Southeast Asia' and Johns, 'Islam in Southeast Asia: Problems of Perspective', in addition to the classic works by Hall, Schriecke, van Leur and Lombard.

good Muslims according to the Portuguese-Malay Manuel Godinho de Erédia: they did not follow the Koran, they drank wine, ate pork and did not know Arabic.[54] The question of consuming liquor is an important one and is a reflection of this often contradictory penetration of the Islamic faith in the Malay sultanates: Iskandar Muda who, like many other rulers, often applied severe Islamic prohibitions with regard to the distillation and consumption of alcohol,[55] did not himself refrain from drinking copious quantities of liquor, just like his grandfather.[56]

In political terms, Islam was a unifying element between sultanates only fleetingly and in a very limited way. Although religious solidarity was distinctly a common factor with regard to the Portuguese, it was used more as a propaganda weapon by Aceh, as well as an instrument of expansion, with regard to other sultanates than as any real ideological cement between these powers.

Friar Félix de Jesus, once again, provides some information to support the idea that the religious factor was subordinated to political and economic questions in his description of an improvement in relations between the sultan of Aceh, Alauddin Riayat Syah al-Mukammil, and the Portuguese in Melaka. The city sent an embassy to the sultan in 1593 as he had recently shown signs of an intention to pursue amicable relations as a result of the diplomatic actions of Friar Amaro de Jesus. This embassy (which is discussed in another chapter), headed by Tomás Pinto and Friar Jerónimo de Jesus, was aimed at sealing peaceful relations. Encouraged by the sultan's reception, the Augustinian missionary apparently managed to obtain authorisation to publicly hold a solemn Mass in the sultanate. In addition to granting this permission, the sultan and his sons attended the Mass.[57] This indicates that political interests prevailed over any antagonism of a religious nature, which were clearly put aside when important affairs of state were at stake, such as the alliance with Melaka against Johor.

---

[54] Erédia, 'Declaraçam de Malaca ...', fls. 38v.–39.
[55] Reid, *Southeast Asia in the Age of Commerce*, Vol. 1, p. 143.
[56] Letter from J. Sandcroft and E. Aspinall to the EIC, 12-10-1615, *LREIC*, III, p. 190; 'A briefe Relation of Master John Davies ...' in Purchas, *His Pilgrimes*, II, p. 314.
[57] Fr. Félix de Jesus, 'Primeira Parte da Chronica e Relação do principio que teue a congregação da ordem de S. Augto. nas Indias Orientais ...', AN/TT, *MssLiv.*, No. 731, fls. 25 and 27–27v. (*see* Document Appendix, No. 22).

The Sultanate of Johor

The history of Johor during the 'Portuguese period' of Melaka has not yet been studied comprehensively. The authors who have worked on this sultanate have experienced some difficulty in dealing with this period as northern European sources are of little use to them.[58] There is an important lacuna: the studies for the sultanate of Melaka are based upon Malay sources (especially the *Sejarah Melayu*) and the work of Tomé Pires; for the 'Dutch period' there is a vast *corpus* of Dutch sources, as well as some Malay sources. However, for the period from the foundation of the Johor sultanate to the early decades of the 17th century there is a vacuum as local sources are notoriously lacking in information.[59] Most Portuguese sources provide meagre data and, in addition, are disregarded or remain unknown to the majority of historians. At times this has resulted in methodological flaws: that of treating this period as a marginal one, a shadow between the two 'Golden Ages' of the sultanate's history, which have received far more attention. Thus one runs the risk of treating this period as a mere extension of the sultanate of Melaka or, on the contrary, a prologue to the new age of prosperity that was experienced after 1641. The 16th century almost always appears, in diverse studies, as an extrapolation of the 15th or 17th centuries. Thus it is time to restore its particular characteristics.

Unlike Aceh which, except for the unfortunate Portuguese landing in 1606, did not witness direct attacks on its capital, Johor, born out of a military initiative, suffered a succession of pressures and destructive actions during the 16th and 17th centuries by both the Portuguese and the Acehnese. Johor played the role of the weakest link in the balance of the Straits, at least in military terms. Yet, from other points of view, especially

---

[58] The most important works on this subject include Winstedt, *A History of Johore*, a useful but occasionally confusing and outdated work; Macgregor, 'Johor Lama in the Sixteenth Century', and especially the studies by Andaya, *The Kingdom of Johor 1641–1728* and 'The Structure of Power in 17th Century Johor'. Kathirithamby-Wells quotes a forthcoming study entitled *The Johor-Malay World, 1511–1785* in her 'Royal Authority and the *Orang Kaya* ...', p. 261, note 27, but I am not aware of any further information.

[59] The version of the *Sejarah Melayu* that refers to this period and the so-called *Siak Chronicles* are not reliable, according to Andaya, 'The Structure of Power in 17th Century Johor', p. 1.

with regard to its solid position at the heart of the Malay World, where it enjoyed an enviable level of prestige as heir to the sultanate of Melaka, Johor revealed itself to be a powerful entity,[60] having more to fear from Aceh, which attempted to undermine the bases of its power, than from the Portuguese, whose military assaults always proved to be short-lived. Expelled from its natural headquarters, the descendants of the sultans of Melaka tried to recapture the city for a while, but ended up adapting to the undesired Portuguese presence and, especially, became accustomed to the tension resulting from this competition. This relationship was cyclical, oscillating between periods of good relations, or even of alliance, and years of declared hostility. Johor's power, in terms of regional hegemony, varied considerably and was far more vulnerable to the vagaries of the political scenario of the region than that of Melaka or Aceh. Johor witnessed increasing tensions with Aceh that culminated, to Johor's disfavour, in the 1620s and 1630s, at the peak of Iskandar Muda's expansionism.

Johor's relations with Portuguese Melaka reached a turning point in the 1560s with the détente established between Sultan Muzaffar Syah and the captain of Melaka, Dom Leonis Pereira. Until then, these neighbouring powers had been declared enemies. Now, in the face of the common threat posed by the Acehnese expansion, they arrived at a platform of understanding. However, the internal evolution of Portuguese structures also contributed decisively towards this change. While Portuguese naval power was still incisive and had an iron grip over the Straits, while the monopolistic pretensions of this new Melaka still had some effect, while the Portuguese domination of the trade in spices from the Eastern Archipelago flourished, friction with Johor was inevitable. From the moment in which the internal transformations of the Estado da Índia resulted in a lesser degree of intervention by the Crown in trade, as Portugal discarded her

---

[60] It is interesting to note how two European travellers who both visited Johor in the early 17th century have diametrically opposite views about the power of the sultanate: Jacques de Coutre stated that the sultan was the weakest ruler of all the 'Southern parts' ('Vida de ...', p. 170); Pyrard de Laval, on the other hand, affirmed that he was a powerful king and that he controlled the entire hinterland and the regions around Melaka (*Voyage de ...*, II, p. 665). In 1633 the Augustinian friar Andrés de Salazar classified Johor and Pahang as 'very great' (*grandissimi*); 'Relatione del stato della Cristianità nelle Filippine', 16-10-1633, *HPAF*, XIX, p. 385.

monopolistic pretensions and Portuguese control on the flow of spices from Banda and the Moluccas declined (which took place in the late 16th century), in the eyes of Johor, Melaka began to function as any other sultanate of the region, apart from its specific characteristics. The broad mesh of the Portuguese network thus allowed Johor to survive and flourish in Melaka's backyard, in the position, obviously, of a competitor.

As the captains of the fortress increasingly assumed control over the commerce associated with Melaka, acting in the name of the king but comporting themselves like any local despot, nothing was more convenient for Johor than to arrive at an understanding with each one, so as to establish a mutually beneficial *modus vivendi*. This occurred from 1568 to 1585, when a strict order by Philip I, executed at all costs by a particularly clumsy new captain, led to an inevitable conflict, a long period of crisis and the destruction of Johor Lama. The short-lived deal with the captains of Melaka was undoubtedly connected with the power and prosperity of Johor at this time, about which the Portuguese were well aware. The weakness of Aceh, in turmoil at the time due to serious internal instability, completed the favourable scenario for Johor.

From the destruction of Johor Lama until the arrival of the Dutch, Johor—after once again making peace with the Portuguese—remained on the sidelines while seeking support against Aceh, whose rivalry was now aggravated because of dynastic disputes. If the arrival of the Dutch briefly afforded a reinforcement of the sultanate's regional role, it soon proved to be a disappointment for those who placed their hopes on these new foreigners, with the failure of the alliance that sought to conquer Melaka in 1606. The Dutch sought an alliance with Johor for reasons that were essentially political, but this design proved to be unfruitful until 1641, and they favoured other trade centres such as Jambi, Banten, Banda, Ambon or, from 1619 onwards, Batavia. The English, who were soon outmatched in their competition with the Dutch in the region and did not have pretensions of conquering Melaka, never established anything more than tenuous links with Johor, a sultanate that they confessed to not knowing very well.[61]

The unstoppable rise of Aceh relegated Johor to a secondary role within the regional panorama, especially after the crisis of 1613–15 that

---

[61]   Letter from J. Sandcroft and E. Aspinall to the EIC, 12-10-1615, *LREIC*, III, p. 190.

dragged the sultanate into the orbit of its old enemy. It was only later, after the end of the expansionist rule of Iskandar Muda and the destruction of Portuguese power that Johor would be reborn in syntony with the new European lords of the Straits. The basis of its power, however, remained intact, having survived the years of greatest difficulty, and this is a prime explanation for the sultanate's tenacious capacity to resist successive adversities.

The power of Johor—in truth the sultanate of Melaka with a new capital—was based on two essential pillars: the web of loyal vassals that the sultanate's heirs controlled in a series of bordering territories which formed the territorial empire of Melaka that Afonso de Albuquerque had left intact, and its direct domination over the riverside inhabitants of the Riau-Lingga archipelago, whom the Portuguese called '*seletes*' or '*celates*'[62] and were known locally as the *orang laut*,[63] who constituted the heart of Johor's maritime power.

Let us begin here. The origins of the *orang laut*'s links with Johor date back to the times of the Empire of Palembang-Sri Vijaya (7th–10th centuries) when they appear to have played an important role. The flight of Prince Parameswara at the end of the 14th century to the Straits of Melaka, where he founded a new dynasty and a new city, resulted in the transferral of these ties from the moribund maritime empire to this new centre.[64] This fact is mentioned by Tomé Pires, who emphasises the loyalty of these men to the founder of the sultanate and his successors:

> 'Made by the hand of the said Paramiçura, the said Mandarin fishermen always accompanied the said King, and as the said King elevated their ranks to that of nobility, they also recognised the favour that had been done unto them; they accompanied the King to a great extent and served him with great faith and loyalty, giving of their friendship with a good heart, and in this way, they always had love from the King, like the true service and zeal that the said new Mandarins had and sought to please him, and their honour always remained until the arrival of Diogo Lopes de Sequeira....'[65]

---

[62] From the Malay word *selat*, 'strait'; it is possible that these people were called at the time *orang selat*, or 'people of the straits'. With regard to this issue, *see* Lombard, *Le Sultanat d'Atjéh*, p. 92, note 4.

[63] Or 'sea people'.

[64] Andaya, *The Kingdom of Johor 1641–1728*, pp. 45–47.

[65] *Suma Oriental*, VI, pp. 387–388 (fl. 165v.).

In the same way, the fall of Melaka and the foundation of Johor did not cause a break in this chain of fidelity. The *orang laut* remained loyal to the lineage and continued to be one of the mainstays of the sultanate.

The term '*orang laut*' is susceptible to some imprecision. Generally designating 'people of the sea' as opposed to 'people of the land', or 'from the interior', in the western area of the Archipelago it specifies a set of peoples who live on, for and off the sea, generally residing in boats and living an itinerant existence, and one can find diverse parallels in various regions of Southeast Asia.[66] Their homogeneity, even in the Straits region, was not absolute, and it is possible to distinguish different groups according to their origin.[67] Similarly, their adherence to the sultanate also took place at different times. During the 16th century and part of the 17th century, the capital of Johor stood in the river with the same name and the region controlled by the *orang laut* was a secure refuge during periods of crisis.

Dominating the Straits of Melaka and Singapore and their labyrinth of canals, controlling and watching over the maritime traffic of the region, the *orang laut* represented an important power, both in political and military terms, as they supplied men and vessels, as well as in economic terms, as they protected commerce, at the service of the sultans of Johor.[68] There is not very much information about these people in the

---

[66] Lapian, 'Le Rôle des Orang Laut dans l'Histoire de Riau', pp. 216–217; Lombard, *Le Carrefour Javanais*, II, pp. 80–81.

[67] Andaya, *The Kingdom of Johor 1641–1728*, p. 44, identifies several different groups: Orang Suku Bentan (in the Riau Archipelago), Orang Suku Mepar (Lingga), Orang Suku Bulang (Riau), Orang Suku Galang (Riau), and other groups of Singapore.

[68] Ibid., p. 50; Andaya, 'The Structure of Power in 17th Century Johor', p. 7. Some European sources clearly indicate that they were subjects of the sultan of Johor. Gabriel de San Antonio says they were 'vassals of the King of Johor' ('Breve y Verdadera Relacion ...', p. 89); Erédia refers to Sultan Ali Jalla as 'King of Johor and Viontana and ruler of the *selat* people' ('Historia de Serviços ...', BN, *Res*, cod. 414, fl. 8); the Augustinian Andrés de Salazar wrote, in 1633: 'in this realm of Johor there is a certain kind of people who lives in the sea in boats, always residing in them in diverse places, in groups of a thousand. These people are gentile and are called *saletes*'. 'Relatione del stato della Cristianità nelle Filippine', 16-10-1633, *HPAF*, XIX, p. 385.

Portuguese sources during the period under study. It appears that the Portuguese and these lords of the Straits had a mutual respect for each other and the former always avoided taking risks in this region. The *orang laut* were always described as excellent fishermen, always ready to trade in goods.[69] It was only in the 17th century, as the naval power of the city declined, that they began to be viewed as a potential danger for Melaka.[70] When the Dutch suffocated Melaka in an irreversible manner, the chronicler António Bocarro pointed out their hostility towards the Portuguese.[71]

Another pillar of Johor's power was the prestige that the sultanate enjoyed throughout the Malay World as the successor to Sri Vijaya and Melaka. The Portuguese recognised this, attributing to this sultanate a supremacy over other Muslim powers.[72] It is curious to observe how the king of Portugal himself distinguished this sultanate from the others.[73]

---

[69]　Coutre, 'Vida de ...', p. 94; San Antonio, 'Breve y Verdadera Relacion ...; the *Relação das Plantas & Dezcripções* ..., describing the Strait of Singapore, states: 'The water is so transparent that one can see the fish in the depths; the seamen purchase them from the local people whom they call *saletes* ... they go with their women and children in their *balões* and catch them in exchange for the agreed price' (pp. 45–46).

[70]　Royal letter to Viceroy Rui Lourenço de Távora, 24-12-1610, *DRI*, I, p. 415.

[71]　'Very bad people and especially against the Portuguese, knavish and treacherous, the best spies that the Dutch have', this was due to the Dutch-Johor alliance against Melaka; Bocarro, 'Livro das Plantas ...', p. 28.

[72]　Amongst others, one can quote Bocarro, 'Livro das Plantas ...' ('He has always been the Emperor of the Southern parts'); Pereira, 'Relação da Cousas que sucederão a ...' in *DUP*, I, p. 14 ('Rayalle ... having the title of Emperor of the Malay kings among the rulers of the Southern parts'); Couto, *Da Ásia*, VIII, xxiv, p. 166 ('True Emperor of all Malays, legitimate king by the dynastic line of the ancient rulers of Melaka'); and Pereira, *História da Índia* ..., p. [235] ('Long recognised as the greatest and the most honourable, that he seems to have ruled them all as Emperor').

[73]　The Portuguese monarch addressed the sultan as the 'high noble King of Johor'; other sultans only merited a mere 'noble and honourable'; the ruler of Aceh, like that of Pegu, was addressed as 'powerful king'; royal letter to the sultan of Aceh, 4-3-1600, AHU, *Cons. Ultr.*, cod. 282, fls. 8–8v. (*see* Document Appendix, No. 11); also *see* royal letter to the King of Pegu, 12-1-1591, AHU, *Cons. Ultr.*, cod. 281, fl. 148.

The chronicles of Aceh call the sultan of Johor 'Raja Besar'.[74] In addition to a vague and theoretical regional authority, Johor had inherited control over various regions of the Malay Peninsula (Pahang, Muar) and Sumatra (Siak, Kampar, Indragiri, Aru), apart from the Riau-Lingga archipelagos and diverse islands in the Straits. During the 16th century and the early decades of the 17th century, Johor lost a substantial part of these regions to Aceh, whose expansion represented a serious threat to the sultanate's interests.

The first focal point of friction between these two sultanates was Aru, a territory that had traditionally belonged to Johor's orbit and, after various disputes, was captured by Aceh in the 1560s during the period that witnessed the attack on Johor Lama and the imprisonment of the sultan. Johor later managed to reacquire control over this region; in 1613, in the course of his advance over the eastern coast of Sumatra, Iskandar Muda successfully re-conquered Aru,[75] once again during a period when Johor's capital came under attack. However, the date on which Aru had returned to form part of Johor's dominions continues to be uncertain. John Davis, who was in Aceh at the end of the 16th century, indicates that Aru, unlike other kingdoms in Sumatra, refused to submit to Aceh.[76] A small note written by Viceroy Matias de Albuquerque sheds light upon this issue. While giving an account of the despatch of a small armada to Melaka, at the request of the captain of the fortress, he observed:

> 'It arrived in Melaka at the beginning of June [1592] and left from there on the 27th on the orders of the captain, Pero Lopes de Sousa, with 2 galleons, 5 galliots and 4 *bantins* to assist the king of Johor, and the king, with his light armada along the coast, on 18 July, arrived at the kingdom and port of Aru, which is called Gori, as that kingdom was in the possession of Aceh, he set fire to a galley and 30 vessels, and installed the *Rajale* [Ali Jalla] in power; he took 11 more launches and a galley and Sirima Ragilela,[77] nephew of [the sultan of] Aceh,

---

[74] 'Great King'; excerpt from the *Hikayat Aceh* in Alves, *O Domínio do Norte de Sumatra*, pp. 208–212.

[75] Best, *The Voyage ...*, p. 468; *see* Lombard, *Le Sultanat d'Atjéh*, p. 92.

[76] John Davis, 'A briefe Relation of Master ...', chiefe Pilot to the Zelanders in their East-India Voyage' in Purchas, *His Pilgrimes*, II, p. 323.

[77] Probably Sri Nara Rajalela.

governor of the kingdom of Daya,[78] who had come to be captain of Gori, was killed along with some 300 Acehnese in the galley, and he withdrew to Melaka.'[79]

Thus the region of Aru remained under Johor's control for just over 20 years[80] and only succumbed with Iskandar Muda's direct offensive. The evolution of the situation with regard to the other sultanates further to the east such as Siak, Kampar and Indragiri is far less clear. These small states were very important on account of being channels that routed the products from the interior (Minangkabau)—the gold that the Portuguese attempted in vain to access directly and, above all, pepper. Apart from the obvious economic benefits, these sultanates also enabled Johor to control both sides of the Straits of Melaka. During the 1560s, Aceh, in addition to attacking Johor, also managed—according to Couto—to establish its primacy over these neighbouring sultanates and dominate the island of Karimun, which was essential for navigation through the Sabang Straits.[81] There is information which indicates that, at the end of the following decade, Aceh absorbed the supplies of gold from the interior via the Kampar River, but did not succeed in effectively dominating

---

[78] Daya, on the western coast of Sumatra, under Acehnese rule.

[79] Matias de Albuquerque's 'Remark' of all supplies sent to the fortresses when he was viceroy, unknown date [late 16th century], BM, *Add.* 28432, fl. 125. The 'Vida e Acções de Mathias de Albuquerque' (fl. 55v.) confirms this information, albeit with slight differences (*see* Document Appendix, No. 1).

[80] Winstedt states that Johor only ruled Aru from 1599 to 1603 (*A History of Johore*, p. 29).

[81] The Great or the Small Karimun, off the coast of Kampar, dubbed 'carimom' by Tomé Pires (*Suma Oriental*, p. 270 (fl. 143v.)); the passage via the tip of Johor was done via two straits (according to Erédia, *see* Map 3): either via the Straits of Singapore that lay between this island, Bentan, Batam and the Karimun Islands; and secondly, via the straits that the Portuguese called 'Sabam', close to the island of the same name. This reference is not completely clear but probably indicated the channel between the island of Kundur ('Sabam') and Sumatra, according to Erédia and Armando Cortesão (Tomé Pires' *Suma Oriental*, p. 270, note 126). A letter issued by the city of Melaka to the King says that 'Beside the channel we have said is called the Straits of Singapore, the same island of Sumatra forms another called Sabam, next to this one, which has many islands, through which all the vessels come' (3-12-1605, *DUP*, II, p. 255); *see* above, chapter 2, note 53.

the respective sultanates.[82] In the 1580s, these regions, perhaps due to Aceh's fragility at the time, clearly remained in Johor's orbit: Ali Jalla was actively supported by the sultans of Indragiri, Kampar and Tungkal[83] (apart from Bentan and Lingga) in the war he waged against Melaka and these sultanates participated directly in combat against the Portuguese.[84] Information from the end of the 16th century indicates that the panorama had not changed.[85]

However, Aceh's expansion would alter this state of affairs. Although it had managed to advance more rapidly on the western coast of Sumatra, the eastern coast was not immune to the actions of the sultanate, as was soon seen in the case of Aru. The attack of 1613 against Aru and Johor probably resulted in Iskandar Muda appropriating control of this region. When he took Johor in an assault and imprisoned Raja Bongsu, the sultan's brother, he also captured another brother, the sultan of Siak, and thus began to exercise direct control over this kingdom. Shortly thereafter, the region of Siak-Kampar was apparently already under Acehnese control.[86]

Although the kingdom of Jambi was situated alongside Indragiri and opposite Lingga, it seems to have always managed to maintain a degree of autonomy with regard to both Johor and Aceh. The arrival of the English and the Dutch, especially after the establishment of factories by both these powers in 1615, enabled this sultanate to increase its margin

---

[82] Lemos, 'Hystoria dos Cercos ...', fl. 60.

[83] A small sultanate next to the river of the same name, located between Indragiri and Jambi and facing the island of Singkep (Lingga). It was mentioned by Pires: 'Tungkal is beyond Indragiri on the coast' (*Suma Oriental*, p. 417, fl. 172v.).

[84] 'Relação' (*see* note 72 above), p. 14; Couto, *Vida de D. Paulo ...*, p. 110; letter from the bishop of Melaka to the king, 15-12-1588, AGS, *Secr. Prov.*, book 1551, fl. 400 (*see* Document Appendix, No. 6).

[85] 'These *menancabos* [from the west coast] are not the same who come to Melaka but other people who live on the rivers of Sumatra and on the other side [of the straits] facing Melaka, vassals of Johor, as also the rivers of 'Bancales', 'Siaca', 'Arracão' and other places where they have their villages ...'; (copies of letters from Viceroy D. Francisco da Gama to the king, 1597[?], BN, *Res.* cod. 1976, fls. 59–59v.). 'Bancales' is Bengkalis, in Siak; while 'Arracão' is Rokan, near Siak, mentioned by Tomé Pires, pp. 415–416, fl. 172.

[86] Coutre, p. 402, refers to Siak, Kampar, Bengkalis and Aru as being under Acehnese rule.

for manoeuvre within the regional context. Jambi's ties with Johor during this period—in contrast with relations during the subsequent period, which was characterised by open hostility (that even resulted in the destruction of Johor's capital in 1673)[87]—were sealed with a dynastic alliance, the marriage of Sultan Abdullah of Johor with the daughter of the sultan of Jambi. The political effects of this union would only be visible later, and were not unconnected with the crisis that would erupt between the two sultanates.

This alliance is mentioned in European sources in the context of the Anglo–Dutch conflict in Jambi. The English, who were in a weaker position than their Dutch rivals in this region, only managed to establish a factory in the sultanate with great difficulty, as Bongsu/Abdullah, under Dutch pressure, had written to his father-in-law strongly advising him not to allow such an event to take place.[88] However, the sultan ended up acquiescing. The Portuguese also attempted to do the same with regard to the Dutch, as they had done earlier in Johor and Aceh, but, likewise, it did not have an effect.[89]

Pahang was the sultanate whose history was most closely linked with Johor. Although since its very foundation the sultanate had been under the direct influence of Melaka/Johor with which it shared a common origin and there were strong family ties between the two ruling dynasties,[90] the sultanate had never been directly absorbed. During the 16th century Pahang lived in a difficult state of balance between its strong ties with Johor and the neighbouring presence of the Portuguese, with whom the sultan preferred to avoid confrontation. As early as 1518 the sultan accepted a contract of vassalage to the king of Portugal, paying tribute in the form of a golden vase.[91] Although this vassalage was short-lived,

---

[87] About the Johor–Jambi conflict, *see* Andaya, *The Kingdom of Johor 1641–1728*, chapter IV.

[88] Jourdain, *The Journal of* …, p. 332; letter from John Tucker to Sir T. Smythe, 11-2-1616, *LREIC*, IV, p. 26.

[89] Letter from Governor Fernão de Albuquerque to the king, 20-2-1622, *DRI*, VII, p. 408.

[90] Linehan, *A History of Pahang*, Appendix I, pp. 169–177.

[91] Barros, *Ásia*, III, II, iv, p. 151; the tribute was to be an annual one and the vase was to weigh 4 *cates*, or about 3.2 kg (taking each *cate* to be 20 *taéis*, the measure used to weigh gold in Melaka, or about 803 g each); Nunes, 'Livro

Pahang avoided antagonising the Portuguese. This position was maintained even in moments of crisis. Despite providing support to Ali Jalla during his conflict with Melaka, the sultan of Pahang nevertheless refused to shelter him after the destruction of Johor Lama, so as not to incur the wrath of the Portuguese against his kingdom.[92] On the contrary, he offered Captain João da Silva a nugget of gold, thus reviving, in a certain way, the tribute of vassalage to the king of Portugal.[93]

At the beginning of the 1610s, Pahang's ties with Johor suffered a rather serious setback, within the context of a far vaster dynastic conflict which included Patani and Brunei. In 1611 the sultan of Johor, Alauddin Riayat Syah, was in Pahang with his entire fleet[94] and in September 1612 attacked and destroyed a significant part of the city.[95] In the following year, the sultanate's situation worsened, with pressure from Patani and threats of another raid by Johor.[96] Aceh's attack on Johor in the same year was thus facilitated by the climate of instability prevailing in the region. Pahang was not immune to this blow,[97] and was also debilitated for some time.

---

dos pesos …', pp. 39 and 48. A previous source mentions an annual tribute of two *cates* of gold destined to seal the vassal status of the sultan, as it was the same value he formerly used to pay to the sultan of Melaka; letter of Rui de Brito Patalim, captain of Melaka, to the governor, 6-1-1514, *CAA*, III, p. 217.

[92] Santos, *Etiópia Oriental*, p. 551. 'De las Victorias que don Paulo de lima Pereyra tuuo en la India en las partes del Sur …', BNM, cód. 1750, fl. 182v.

[93] Erédia, 'Declaraçam …', fl. 40; in his *Informação da Aurea Chersoneso* (p. 78) he refers to the nugget as having 2,5 *côvados* (about 160 cm); he also tells how Captain João da Silva, curious about the unusual piece, ordered it to be broken and found inside a seam of gold 'as thick as a *vara*' (about 110 cm); Erédia also mention the fact on his 'Lista das principais Minas aurífares …', p. 81.

[94] Bocarro, *Década 13*, I, xxii, p. 95.

[95] Floris, *Peter Floris*, p. 41.

[96] Ibid., p. 72.

[97] The available sources do not agree with regard to the impact of the Acehnese strike on Pahang; Floris says the king of Pahang escaped and arrived in Patani on 12 July 1613 with his family (p. 81); The 'Standish-Croft Journal' says the Acehnese captured him along with the sultans of Johor and Siak (Best, *The Voyage of Thomas Best* …, p. 169).

As we shall shortly study in further detail, in 1615 Sultan Alauddin Riayat Syah of Johor took advantage of the dynastic crisis in Pahang to place his son, Raja Bujang, on the throne. In subsequent years it would be his uncle Abdullah (Alauddin's brother) who would manage to form a common front consisting of diverse sultanates against Aceh,[98] thus reconstituting Johor's ancient suzerainty on both sides of the Straits.[99] As had already happened on many occasions, the capital of the sultanate was transferred, this time to Lingga. Iskandar Muda, the sultan of Aceh, in a continuation of his expansionist policy, attacked Pahang in 1618 as he had not managed to neutralise Johor.[100] However, he was unable to prevent Raja Bujang from occupying the thrones of Johor, Pahang and Siak as early as the 1630s, which thus ensured a merging of dynastic bloodlines,[101] at least in the case of the first two sultanates. When Melaka fell into the hands of the Dutch, Johor was once again a leading regional power, having recovered a substantial part of the ancient empire of Melaka, although it would regain control over some sultanates only later.[102] One last observation concerns the case of Makassar, where the sultanate enjoyed a considerable prestige. The English identified Makassar as an excellent site for supplies of rice as well as gold coins minted in Johor.[103] Apart from the economic factor, Johor appears to have exercised an equally strong political influence.[104]

---

[98] According to Andaya, *The Kingdom of Johor 1641–1728*, p. 25, the alliance included Palembang, Jambi, Indragiri, Kampar and Siak.

[99] A Chinese source dating from 1618 states that Johor had recently taken control of Indragiri, thus worsening the situation of the foreign merchants there; another refers to the permanent pressure exerted by Johor upon Indragiri and Pahang (Groeneveldt (ed.), 'Notes on the Malay Archipelago...', pp. 201 and 254).

[100] Letters from Viceroy D. João Coutinho to the king, 8-2-1619 and 9-2-1619, *DRI*, IV, pp. 313 and 314–315, respectively. 'Warning' from Constantino de Sá appended to a letter from the viceroy to the city of Melaka, 21-5-1620, HAG, *Reis Vizinhos*, 1, fl. 114 (*see* Document Appendix, No. 21).

[101] Bocarro, 'Livro das Plantas ...', pp. 21 and 28.

[102] Andaya, *The Kingdom of Johor 1641–1728*, p. 37; Andaya, 'The Structure of Power ...', p. 2.

[103] Jourdain, *The Journal of ...*, p. 294.

[104] In 1618 a Portuguese delegation headed by Agostinho Lobato arrived at Makassar but the local sultan, 'influenced by the Moors, did not receive the ambassador in an appropriate manner, despite having accepted the gifts, nor did he grant

Another problem of the political structure of Johor concerned the *orang kaya*.[105] An ambiguous term, it designated a title in the Malay courts, and could generally be applied to a set of high court officials. It is possible that its exact meaning varied from sultanate to sultanate. Although it can be interpreted in its general sense of a social and political elite, as European travellers tend to describe it, historians are inclined to thinking that the expression distinguishes, especially from the 17th century onwards, a tier of the nobility directly linked to mercantile trade, and can thus be considered in its literal sense.[106] At least this is what social evolution in Johor would suggest, given that in Aceh, for example, this evolution was substantially different. The problem, owing to the scarcity of information with regard to the period under study, is still not easily understood in its entirety, but we can consider some of its elements here.

The model presented by Kathirithamby-Wells[107] is useful with regard to the internal evolution of the sultanate of Johor during this period. According to this author, Johor, during the course of the 16th and 17th centuries, underwent a process of mutation, which began with the sultanate of Melaka and ended with the situation in Johor at the end of the 17th century and during the 18th century. In the initial phase, relations between the sultan and the political elite were stable and based upon *adat*[108] and tradition, which took the form of reciprocity between the king and the kingdom's constituting elements for the mobilisation of resources, where the elite classes did not play an active role in commercial activities. However, Dutch pressure unleashed a process of internal transformation, which resulted in the development of a tier of mercantile noblemen. This reduced the traditional codes and obligations in relations between the monarch and this group to a secondary plane in favour of joint actions to respond to the challenges imposed by the VOC's monopoly, by means of concerted efforts of diplomacy, war and commercial facilities that the

---

the desired factory, convinced by the reasons of state invoked by the Moorish Johors who dominate him, who said it was a ruse by the Portuguese to take his kingdom'; letter from Manuel Barradas, 1619, BM, *Add.* 9853, fl. 549v.

[105] According to Andaya, the *orang kaya* were the third piece of the political structure of the sultanate, beside the sultan, the 'ministers' and the *orang laut*.

[106] *Kaya*, 'wealthy'. *See* Lombard's 'Le sultanat malais comme modèle socio-économique', pp. 118–119.

[107] Kathirithamby-Wells, 'Royal Authority and the Orang Kaya ...', pp. 260–263.

[108] Custom, customary law or behaviour.

sultan placed at the disposition of the great merchants of the sultanate, the *orang kaya*.

In political terms, power was now more fluid and less rigid with regard to the strict rules of tradition than it had been during the time of the sultanate of Melaka. Kathirithamby-Wells describes the evolution of the situation from its initial phase, in which one can detect the prominence of the council of four ministers, during the time of the sultanate of Melaka, to another phase in Johor during the 17th century in which this same council now included a certain number of *orang kaya*.

Although it is a useful analytical tool, one must make some observations. First, the relationship between the sultan and *orang kaya*, like those of other subordinates, continued to be an association of mutual dependence, and it is still not precisely known to what point *adat* and the traditional model were effectively relegated to a secondary role, or if, on the contrary, they simply incorporated new elements. Secondly, it is still uncertain if the distinction between this new class of upwardly mobile nobles and other groups of the court nobles such as the *hulubalang* or *orang besar* was as clear as is presented in the model. Here is an important example: the *bendahara* and the *laksamana*, who were leading figures in the 'archaic' political structure of the 15th century, were also the greatest merchants of the sultanate in its 'modern' form during the 17th century. Thus it would seem that rather than the appearance of a new mercantilist elite, what probably happened was that the traditional elite adapted to new challenges and the sections of society that were traditionally more powerful in political terms maintained their prominence, albeit with other more outstanding components. Finally, one must also point out the fact that the model does not integrate other political functions in this process: the role of the *hulubalang* (military chieftains) and the *ulama* (religious leaders), amongst other groups in the court, continues to remain undefined with regard to the effects on them over this period, as well as the consequences of this mutation in social mobility.

It seems that we are witnessing two distinct processes: the adaptation of sections of the elite in the sultanate to the challenges posed by European (Dutch) competition, transforming former strata with functions that were merely administrative and political into a group of 'merchant-officials',[109]

---

[109] 'Officials-cum-traders', in the expression of J. Kathirithamby-Wells, 'Royal Authority and the Orang Kaya ...', p. 261.

and an increasing flexibility in the political structure of the sultanate, where relations between the sultan and his subordinates ceased to be regulated by the rigid norms of *adat*. Kathirithamby-Wells approaches both as two sides of the same evolution, but it would appear more correct to understand them as two distinct processes in time. Thus, the first derives from external competition, with regard to the monopolistic policies of the VOC. Although this process perhaps witnessed a prologue during the 16th century, it was only unleashed, as both Kathirithamby-Wells and Andaya mention, during the 17th century with the strengthening of the Dutch position in Southeast Asia, especially after 1641. However, with regard to the second process in question—that is, an increased flexibility of the political structure—everything seems to point towards the fact that it had begun far earlier, probably caused by the Portuguese conquest of Melaka and accelerated with the changes of the 17th century.

Nowadays, the idea that the Portuguese implemented few innovations with regard to the structure of Asiatic commerce is widely accepted and, in the case of Melaka, their role was limited to attempting to substitute the former sultanate.[110] The results of their attempts to implement a monopoly fell far short of achieving the success they desired, and they never had any intention of controlling the means of production or changing routes. In the 16th century Melaka functioned just like any other local sultanate. Thus it did not represent a challenge, in economic terms, powerful enough to bring about a social change like that which the Dutch would later cause in the case of Johor as well as in other instances.

However, the changes in the relationship between the sultan and his subordinates seem to have begun immediately after the foundation of Johor. This process, unlike the other one, did not directly result from economic competition but, rather, derived from causes that were essentially political. This was associated with the weakness or, rather, the urgent need that the sultans of Johor felt to maintain the social and political fabric of the sultanate intact during a period in which it faced external threats from Melaka and Aceh after having been expelled from its headquarters. Thus the need to emerge once again as a regional power at the time of the foundation of the sultanate, the attempt to seek refuge in a secure base when its capital was destroyed on successive occasions or to reconstitute the web of 'vassalities' after 1613–15 would certainly have obliged the sultans

---

[110] *See* Thomaz, 'Les Portugais dans les Mers de l'Archipel', p. 117.

to seek all possible support, irrespective of whether this was from the *orang kaya, orang laut* or small satellite sultanates. The price undoubtedly consisted of ceding powers of consultation and decision: this is why the power of the *orang kaya* council grew. Thus we can see how the mutual reinforcement between the sultan and his subordinates led to a softening in the rigidity of the rules of *adat,* but it would have emerged and developed with the evolution of the sultanate of Johor itself over the course of the 16th century, thus dating to the period before the arrival of the northern Europeans in the waters of the Archipelago and the different process that the establishment of the Dutch presence would unleash a little later.

It is still not possible to clearly determine the structure of the elite classes in Johor during the 16th century, in large measure because a concrete understanding of the power and function of each title has not yet been clarified. L. Andaya, based on Dutch sources, presents a record of the most important *orang kaya* of Johor in 1687 and 1710; in the latter instance the names of ten members of the Council.[111] Unfortunately there are no similar data for the 16th century. The closest document, in terms of information, of which we are aware is a list of the most important captains of the fleet that attacked Melaka in 1587 under the command of Sultan Ali Jalla, which reads thus:

Raja Mahkota, 'renegade, General of the land'
Laksamana, 'General of the sea'
Raja Indragiri, 'King of Andriguiri'
Raja Dampol, 'King of Bintão'
Maharaja Lingga, 'King of Linga'
Maharaja dipati Kampar, 'King of Campar'
Crown Prince [Alauddin]
Raja Itam, 'son of the King'
Raja Bongsu, 'son of the King'
Sri Nara ('Sirimara')
Rajalela ('Raia lela')
Sri Indra ('Silindra')
Sri Nara Rajalela ('Cirinara Raia lela')
Sri Setia ('Siri Sattia')
Maharaja Diraja ('Maraia de Raia'),
Kiai Lantik ? ('Quiai lante')

---

[111] Andaya, *The Kingdom of Johor 1641–1728*, p. 43.

Sri Wangsa ('Simiri bansa')
Paduka Maharaja ('Paduc maraia')[112]

Amongst these names one can distinguish elements of the royal family, including the heir to the throne, sultans from kingdoms neighbouring Johor and a number of Malay court titles whose meanings are still not clearly defined. A substantial number of these titles are present in the two existing versions of the *Sejarah Melayu*.[113] In any case, one can observe the *laksamana* and, possibly, even the *bendahara*, under the title of *Paduka Maharaja*.[114] Raja Mahkota, 'General of the land', was undoubtedly one of the *hulubalang*. It is his designation as 'renegade' that raises doubts. Could it be someone who was originally from another sultanate who had placed himself at the service of Ali Jalla? An interesting case is the presence of a member of the *ulama* as a participant in the armada (*Kiai Lantik*) which proves that, just as on the Portuguese side (the captain of Melaka at the time was the bishop of the city), social functions were diverse and extensive. Some of the other titles probably referred to members of the *orang kaya*.

The Sultanate of Aceh

The political history of Aceh during the 16th and 17th centuries raises fewer doubts than that of Johor. The role of Aceh as a great Sumatran power and a counterpoint to the Portuguese in Melaka was discovered by historians very early on. From the 1530s onwards Aceh was Melaka's great enemy and personified the antithesis of the Portuguese structures in regional terms. When the northern Europeans reached the waters of the Indian Ocean and looked for allies, quite naturally seeking them amongst the enemies of the Portuguese, they selected Aceh as a privileged

---

[112] Letter quoted in note 84 above, fls. 400–400v. Some of the names, including Sri Nara ('Serinará'), Sri Indra ('Serpidra') or Sri Wangsa ('Simirambanca'), are mentioned in the list of the Malay 'captains' killed or captured by the Portuguese (Couto, *Vida de D. Paulo de Lima Pereira*, p. 134).

[113] Cf. Josselin de Jong, 'Who's Who in the Malay Annals'.

[114] According to Braginsky ('Hikayat Hang Tuah …', p. 402), the title of 'Paduka Raja' was strictly reserved for the *bendahara* until the end of the 18th century according to the rules of *adat*. In the source quoted by Andaya (1687), Dato Bendahara and Paduka Raja are distinct characters.

objective. Aceh's hostility towards the Portuguese was a constant factor throughout its history, except for the period of détente, yet tempered with suspicion from 1592 till the end of the century. The rest of the time, relations swung between tense peace and periods of sudden and declared hostility. Aceh's relationship with Melaka (and, to a lesser degree, with Johor) was always carried out by means of a game of pressure and diplomatic and aggressive positions. War, just like peace and political alliances, was never a clear, absolute and definitive undertaking. On the contrary, it was always temporary, limited and judiciously applied, in order to achieve the desired effect; the conquest of Melaka was attempted only on exceptional occasions.

Unlike Johor, whose power varied according to the political conditions of the region and was very sensitive to changes in the geopolitical balance, Aceh assumed the role of a regional power in a more continuous way from the very outset—shortly after the Portuguese conquest of Melaka—until it reached its zenith during the reign of Iskandar Muda. This continuity is clearly visible in its progressive control over Sumatra and the Malay Peninsula, begun in the 1520s with the conquest of Pedir, Pasai and Daya. However, it was during the 1530s that Aceh's expansionism expressed itself more vigorously, based on two interconnected pillars: territorial expansion, with a view to an ever-increasing control of Sumatra's pepper production and terminus of a vast trade structure, rival of the Portuguese one and linked with the Red Sea, the Ottoman empire and Venice. The affirmation of Aceh as a regional power was clearly linked with the military support it received from the Ottomans.

Throughout the 16th century Aceh's role as an Ottoman vanguard seems to have achieved two high points: in 1537 and during the 1560s.[115] On both occasions Aceh utilised the military capacity of its allies to further

---

[115] In his *O Primeiro Soldado Prático*, most probably written in 1564, Couto stated that the zenith of Acehnese military power was due to the reinforcement of Ottoman assistance (p. 498). *See* Reid, 'Sixteenth Century Turkish Influence …', Boxer, 'A Note on Portuguese Reactions …' and the more recent works of Giancarlo Casale, namely 'His Majesty's Servant Lufti', with a translation of a report of an Ottoman ambassador in Aceh, and *The Ottoman Age of Exploration*, pp. 123–125. However, Alves has a different opinion, considering the 1560s as a period of 'cooling of political and military relations between the two states' (*O Domínio do Norte de Sumatra*, p. 168).

its territorial expansion, in the first case against Melaka, the Bataks and Aru, and on the second occasion, once again, not just against Melaka and Aru, but also against Tiku, Priaman and Indrapura on the west coast, where Aceh stimulated the production of pepper, now under its control.[116]

At this time, the anti-Portuguese offensive throughout the Indian Ocean region reached its height, enabling a conjunction of the efforts of various Muslim potentates. In Southeast Asia, far removed from the Middle East and areas that witnessed higher tension, such as the Red Sea or the Persian Gulf, obtaining Ottoman support necessitated a strong ideological motivation. It was Aceh's claim to be a champion of Islam, a bulwark against the infidels (be they the Portuguese or non-Muslim peoples from the Sumatran interior) that enabled it to obtain this support, obviously linked with the island's pepper production. Thus it managed to unite some Javanese sultanates and even Johor into a common, albeit short-lived, front, although distrust with regard to the sultanate's hegemonic temptations always prevailed. The much sought after Ottoman fleet, successively postponed for diverse reasons, would never arrive.

The Portuguese felt the effects of this pooling of forces throughout the Indian Ocean. In the case of Melaka, it was at this time that Aceh began to be viewed as a double threat: a dangerous commercial rival and a permanent hazard for Melaka. It was likewise during these years, especially after the great siege of 1568, that the Portuguese considered the need to conquer this sultanate more seriously.[117] However, once this period of closer contacts between Aceh and the Ottomans passed, hopes of massive Turkish support definitely faded away. Nevertheless, something did remain. Contacts were not abandoned and Aceh maintained its position as a privileged commercial partner of the Ottoman empire throughout the 1580s and 1590s.[118]

---

[116] Reid, 'Sixteenth Century Turkish Influence ...', p. 403.

[117] *See* 'Enformação das fortalezas e lugares da Índia' (1568) and 'Apontamentos do Arcebispo de Goa para o Rei' (1569–70) in Wicki (ed.), 'Duas Relações sobre a situação da Índia Portuguesa ...', pp. 148–149 and 207, respectively.

[118] Loyola, c.1585, refers to the Sumatran supplies of gold to the Ottomans (*Viaje alrededor del Mundo*, p. 189); in the late 16th century, the Portuguese noticed and were concerned about timber supplies from Aceh and Pegu to the Ottoman empire because of their obvious use for naval purposes (copies of letters from Viceroy D. Francisco da Gama to the king, 1597(?), BN, *Res*, cód. 1976, fls.

During Iskandar Muda's rule, contacts were once again reinforced, with Ottoman ambassadors being despatched to the sultanate in 1612.[119] This event served the sultan's objectives of enhancing his reputation and strengthening his hegemony at the heart of the Malay World.[120] The presence of this embassy did not go unobserved by the English who were present in Aceh at the time[121] and the Portuguese detected the presence of an Ottoman factor during these years.[122] As for the rest, and although the period of fears with regard to a great Ottoman naval offensive in the Indian Ocean had already passed, Aceh continued to utilise the military tactics bequeathed by its allies and create elite corps inspired by the Ottoman Janissaries.[123] In addition, Aceh's relentless march forward to conquer a substantial part of Sumatra and the Malay Peninsula during the 1610s and 1620s was inextricably linked with the supply of Ottoman arms, munitions and military advisers.[124]

Thus one can see how Aceh's rise as a power with hegemonic pretensions in the regional context was due, in great part, to this external factor. If the driving motto during the 16th century was the *jihâd* against the Portuguese, it would be interesting to know how the sultanate would justify aggression against Muslim sultanates, especially Johor, the heir to Melaka.

69–69v; royal letter to the same viceroy, 21-11-1598, *APO*, III, part 2, p. 926; in the former, the viceroy states: 'However, they currently do not have the same reputation here as before').

[119] *See* the description of this embassy in the *Hikayat Aceh* in Lombard, *Le Sultanat d'Atjéh* ..., pp. 222–227.

[120] The *Hikayat Aceh* attributes a statement about the existence of two great rulers in the world to the Ottoman ruler: himself in the West and Iskandar Muda in the East; *see* Reid, 'Sixteenth Century Turkish Influence ...', p. 399 and Brakel, 'State and Statecraft ...', p. 59.

[121] In 1613 the English became aware of the intentions of the Ottomans in Aceh to contact Captain Thomas Best ('The Standish-Croft Journal' in Best, p. 159).

[122] The *Relação das Plantas & Dezcripções* ... (unknown date, post-1615) states, 'The Turk has a factor there with one *conto* in gold' [i.e., 1,000$000] (p. 46).

[123] According to Reid, 'Sixteenth Century Turkish Influence ...', pp. 410–411, supported by Beaulieu, 'Memoires du Voyage aux Indes Orientales', pp. 100–101.

[124] Governor Fernão de Albuquerque, while referring to Aceh, mentioned that the Ottomans 'come to serve him in his kingdom with fleets of bombardiers and naval experts' (letter to the king, 7-2-1620, *DRI*, VI, p. 243).

Acehnese progress along the western coast of Sumatra took place at a more accelerated pace than in the case of the eastern coast, where it came up against Johor's ties with various sultanates such as Aru, Kampar or Siak. After a period of notorious strength during the reign of Alauddin Riayat Syah al-Kahar, Aceh lost ground, to Johor's advantage, during the 1580s and 1590s. The latter managed to re-establish its control over Aru in 1592 and Aceh contented itself with an increase in pepper production on the western coast, which would prove to be an important attraction for the English and the Dutch. Nevertheless, even its control over this coast was not tight. Political instability within the sultanate during the final decades of the century provided the pretext for various revolts. The most serious one was that of the Minangkabau, around 1588, shortly after a prince of Minang origin seized power. The internal upheavals and the sultanate's weakness enabled a transient period of emancipation in the region. One does not know the exact relationship between the usurpation of the throne in 1586, the revolt and the new palace coup of 1589, although they must certainly be linked. Local sources are silent in this regard and Portuguese sources limit themselves to recording the carnage, epidemics and wars:

> [Aceh] 'has not been coming to these parts with armadas for some time now, because they are occupied in their war against the Monancabos, who disobey them, who inhabit the opposite coast of the island of Sumatra, and because there is much dissension and plague, and many of their people are dying....'[125]

This question is obviously linked with the internal history of the sultanate, which experienced a new phase of centralisation of power with Alauddin Riayat Syah al-Mukammil's rise to power in 1589. Externally, however, Aceh would only manage to consolidate its dependants, its dominion over most of Sumatra and its pepper production and, likewise, control over various sultanates of the Malay Peninsula during the following century, thus dominating both sides of the Straits. However, there was one moment during the 16th century when the sultan of Aceh (Alauddin of

---

[125] Letter from the auditor (*ouvidor*) of Melaka to the king, 17-12-1588, AGS, *Secr. Prov.*, book 1551, fl. 470. The bishop of Melaka describes a similar scenario (letter to the king, 31-12-1588, AGS, *Secr. Prov.*, book 1551, fls. 404 and 407v.; *see* Document Appendix, No. 6).

Perak or Mansur Syah), having wed one of his daughters to Sultan Ali Jalla of Johor, established a short-lived common strategy to dominate the Straits of Melaka when he erected a fortress in Perak, the land of his birth, in 1584.[126] This is the first known evidence of Acehnese control on both sides of the Straits.[127] a fact that rapidly alarmed the Portuguese. This sultan was assassinated in 1586. If this had not happened, Johor's siege of Melaka (which was to have been supported by an armada from Aceh that never set sail), which prevented Portuguese access to the east, would have been completed with this blockade to the west, completely suffocating the city, and the evolution of the crisis of 1585–87 would surely have been different.

Acehnese expansion during the reign of Iskandar Muda is well known. After his ascension to the throne in 1607 he prepared to definitively subdue the Sumatran sultanates after imposing order and royal authority within his kingdom. The first campaign took place against Deli and Aru in 1612, coinciding with the arrival of the Ottoman embassy. In the case of the former, Aceh met with strong resistance headed by the Portuguese,[128] perhaps even by the captain of Melaka himself,[129] while in the latter it regained control over the sultanate after a brief period during which Aru had been subordinated to Johor.

In 1613 Aceh attacked and neutralised its old rival, attempting to control its satellites, namely the region of Siak-Kampar. For the first time, Aceh managed to establish a minimally stable domination over both banks of the Straits. The Acehnese strategy would fail in two essential aspects:

---

[126] Letter from the viceroy of Portugal to the king, 6-12-1586, AGS, *Secr. Prov.*, book 1550, fl. 701; royal letter to Viceroy D. Duarte de Meneses, 22-1-1587, *APO*, III, part 1, p. 80 (also published in *DHMPPO/Insulíndia*, V, p. 63). In his *O Roteiro*, the bishop of Melaka, D. João Ribeiro Gaio, mentions the presence of the sultan in Perak in this year but does not refer to the construction of any kind of fort; on the contrary, he states that the intentions of the sultan were to build a fortress in the Straits of Singapore, which, in fact, was being done by Johor at the time (*O Roteiro*, p. 98).

[127] Previous attempts had failed: in 1548 the fort built in Kedah after the strike on the sultanate did not last more than a few months, and the attack on Johor in 1564, followed by the capture of the sultan, did not have political effects.

[128] Beaulieu, 'Memoires du Voyage aux Indes Orientales', p. 100.

[129] According to Beaulieu, ibid. At the time, the captain was Francisco Miranda Henriques, but no Portuguese sources confirm this hypothesis.

first, the difficulties encountered in controlling Johor. Sultan Alauddin, who fled in 1613, regained power shortly thereafter, forcing Aceh to carry out a raid to dislodge him, and his brother Abdullah, who definitely seized the throne after 1615, revealed a latent streak of insubordination and promoted a common front of diverse sultanates against his powerful Acehnese brother-in-law. Later, Aceh's strike on Melaka in 1615 failed, and a hasty peace was made with the Portuguese in order to try and control Johor. This period of peace with the Portuguese was the immediate step that Aceh took to divide the common front that was developing, where Johor and Pahang came together under Portuguese agreement.

Shortly thereafter, Aceh went on the offensive once again, attacking Pahang. Here, as in Johor, Acehnese intentions were to control the sultanate both economically and politically.[130] This attack took place in 1617 or 1618, and Aceh managed to imprison the sultan and, once again, gained the advantage over Johor. In this regard there is no doubt that Melaka's passivity contributed towards this success, more so Aceh's growing hegemony was a constant cause for alarm. Nevertheless, this strange inactivity is easily explained: during the 1615 attack the Acehnese forces had captured the son-in-law of the captain of Melaka, João Caiado de Gamboa,[131] handing him over after the peace negotiations. Thus this captain proceeded to favour Aceh as long as he remained in Melaka, and he was succeeded in his post by his son-in-law, João da Silveira.[132] Various sources testify the preferential treatment they both gave to Aceh despite being Melaka's prime enemy, to the detriment of Johor.[133]

In 1619 Iskandar Muda attacked Kedah, submitted after a three-month siege in which the queen and some members of the royal family

---

[130] Lombard, *Le Sultanat d'Atjéh* …, p. 93. Iskandar Muda would eventually marry his daughter to a Prince of Pahang, who claimed the Acehnese throne in 1637 as Iskandar Thani.

[131] Among others, in Bocarro, *Década 13*, I, xciii, p. 414. These events are mentioned in the *Bustan-us-Salatin*, which states that the Acehnese fleet 'captured a son-in-law of the [Portuguese] viceroy' after striking Johor and Bentan (translated in Lombard, *Le Sultanat d'Atjéh* …, p. 200).

[132] João Caiado de Gamboa was captain of Melaka from 1615 to 1616; his successor was his son-in-law João da Silveira until 1618.

[133] Letters from Viceroy D. João Coutinho, 8-2-1619 and 9-2-1619, *DRI*, IV, pp. 313 and 315, respectively.

were captured and the sultan was obliged to flee.[134] Here, too, Johor led the resistance against Acehnese expansionism: it was on this occasion that Sultan Abdullah went personally to Melaka to ask for Portuguese help against the enemy armada.[135] In the following year, Aceh attacked Perak, which it managed to conquer despite the Portuguese assistance captained by Fernão da Costa.[136] Thus it managed to reinforce its hegemony over the Malay sultanates. These campaigns continued till the end of his reign, against the island of Nias, Melaka, Pahang and the western coast of Sumatra. In these areas, where Acehnese influence had waned during the final years of the 16th century and early 17th century, Iskandar Muda obtained total control.[137] All these campaigns, except the one against Perak, are described in the *Bustan us-Salatin*.[138] Thus Aceh's territorial expansion reached its greatest heights, from the times it dominated only some regions in Sumatra[139] until it managed to claim sovereignty over vast areas on both sides of the Straits.[140]

---

[134] Lombard, *Le Sultanat d'Atjéh* ..., p. 93; Beaulieu, 'Memoires du Voyage aux Indes Orientales', pp. 77 and 83. On 8 February 1620 Governor Fernão de Albuquerque wrote to the king saying that 'Aceh sent a fleet of 50 galleys against the kingdom of Kedah this year and destroyed it, capturing the Queen and many noblemen of that kingdom, killing many of them and many other people, forcing the king to escape to the woods'. (*DRI*, V, p. 274.)

[135] Letter from Governor Fernão de Albuquerque, 7-2-1620, *DRI*, VI, p. 69.

[136] Letter from Governor Fernão de Albuquerque to the king, 10-2-1621, *DRI*, VII, p. 106; he stated that the Portuguese destroyed several Acehnese ships but refers to a letter from the captain of Melaka, currently unknown. *See* another letter from the same governor, 20-2-1621, ibid., p. 225.

[137] Kathirithamby-Wells does not accept that this control had been accomplished by military force ('Achehnese Control over West Sumatra ...', pp. 458–459).

[138] Translated in Lombard, *Le Sultanat d'Atjéh* ..., p. 200. This author quotes the information from Beaulieu about the arrival of the Acehnese fleet in Perak (p. 93) in 1620, but does not mention it in Map XIV, 1.

[139] In 1539, while addressing the sultan of Johor, Iskandar Muda called himself the king of Aceh, Barus, Pedir, Pasai, Daya, Aru, ruling over the Bataks and the mines of Minangkabau (according to Fernão Mendes Pinto; *see* Alves, *A Hegemonia no Norte de Sumatra* ..., II, doc. 6).

[140] In 1616 he called himself king of Aceh and other parts of Sumatra 'with authority over Johor' (letter from Iskandar Muda to the king of England, *LREIC*, IV, p. 123). Yet, in 1621 he claimed to be king of the kingdom, land and realms of Deli and Johor, and of Pahang, Kedah, Perak, Tiku and Priaman

Let us now take a look at the internal evolution of the sultanate. Once again, this is slightly better known and clearer, and has been studied in greater detail, than that of Johor. In general, we can distinguish two main stages during the period under study: a phase in which power was divided between the figure of the sultan and various sections of the nobility and court and a new phase with a drastic curtailment of the broad powers of the latter, after Alauddin Riayat Syah al-Mukammil's rise to power in 1589. This set in motion a process of centralisation of power that, after a brief interregnum, would be continued and intensified by Iskandar Muda from 1607 onwards. The power that the *orang kaya* wielded during the 16th century is well known, namely, in controlling the sultans' room for manoeuvre. In periods of political crisis, especially when the sultan in power did not exercise his authority in an uncontested manner (which happened throughout Aceh's turbulent political history during the 16th century), the throne was successively disputed and, especially during the period between 1579 and 1589, the sultanate witnessed a succession of sultans, including two foreign monarchs (from Perak and Indrapura), who were invariably assassinated.

The struggle for the throne was merely the most visible face of a wider conflict, where opposing sections of the court as well as external forces from neighbouring or satellite sultanates battled it out for supremacy. During the crisis of 1579, over the course of a few brief months, the son of the preceding sultan, his uncle[141] from Priaman and a nephew of the latter from Aru succeeded each other on the throne in quick succession. In 1586–89, as has already been mentioned, elements of the royal houses of Perak and Indrapura seized power. This scenario was quite different from the rather simplistic but widespread idea that Aceh witnessed a scenario in which the *orang kaya* placed and deposed a series of weak sultans on the throne, manipulating them at will.[142] This idea perhaps denotes an overly

---

(letter from Iskandar Muda to the king of France in Beaulieu, 'Memoires du Voyage aux Indes Orientales', p. 73).

[141] About the different versions of Lombard and Alves, *see* Annex II, note 7.

[142] Kathirithamby-Wells, 'Royal Authority and the Orang Kaya ...', p. 263, says: 'Power was manipulated by both the secular and religious chiefs (ulama) in the interest generally of eliminating weak rulers through a succession of assassinations.' Alves, 'Os mártires do Achém ...', p. 398, says: 'The *orang kaya* (in association with foreign merchants) took the Acehnese throne through several puppet sultans, who were easily manipulated.'

literal reading of a Malay source, the *Hikayat Aceh*, which describes the decision of the power brokers of the sultanate to successively overthrow the new sultan and elect another in his place.[143] One must keep in mind that this work was intended to exalt Iskandar Muda and, therefore, by glorifying the justness of the process of centralisation carried out by this sultan, denigrates the image of the aristocracy that allegedly caused the preceding chaos in the sultanate. Thus it was very convenient to attribute a deliberate action of consecutively assassinating various sultans to the powerful figures of the Aceh court.

A more judicious reading of this question points to an alternative scenario. In truth this was a situation of political turbulence where opposing forces strove to gain the upper hand, in which there was no single prominent candidate and where none was able to achieve more than fleeting power, weakly supported by an opportunistic faction. Diverse forces within the sultanate, momentarily acting in harmony, placed a new sultan on the throne (more evident when the sultan in question was a youngster, like Sultan Muda in 1579) who was plainly manipulated and immediately assassinated. Or, as possibly happened in 1586 and 1589, these were adventurers and military chiefs who took the initiative, trying their luck in one fell swoop. In any case, these were factions that tried to obtain control over the sultanate: in 1580 Mansur Syah of Perak's rise to the throne was brought about, in the words of Jorge de Lemos, by '*some* captains', as they had suspicions of 'thoughts of rebellion' of 'figures amongst the most powerful in the land'.[144] The idea of a united, cohesive and all-powerful aristocracy which successively placed and assassinated different sultans does not seem defensible. This idea is transmitted by Augustin de Beaulieu who, just like the *Hikayat Aceh*, transmits the 'official' version that was current in Aceh during the zenith of Iskandar Muda's power.[145]

Historians are not unanimous in their identification of these various sectors of aristocracy in Aceh. The term *orang kaya* is generally utilised to

---

[143] According to Reid, 'Trade and the Problem of Royal Power ...', p. 47.

[144] 'Hystoria dos Cercos ...', fl. 62v. (the italics are mine). Alves uses this excerpt incorrectly, attributing the death of Zainal Abidin to these 'captains' (*O Domínio do Norte de Sumatra*, p. 172).

[145] Beaulieu, 'Memoires du Voyage aux Indes Orientales', pp. 110–111. However, Lombard accepts the idea of solidarity and homogeneity among this group (*Le Sultanat d'Atjéh ...*, p. 57).

designate groups of powerful individuals in the court, usually connected with trade and the commercial and urban life of Aceh, who wielded great political influence in the sultanate until 1589 and after the death of Iskandar Muda in 1636. This is the path followed by Denys Lombard and Anthony Reid.[146] Kathirithamby-Wells makes the distinction between secular chiefs (*orang kaya*) and religious chiefs (*ulama*), but attributes the same political role to them. Jorge dos Santos Alves presents a position that differs substantially from this: based on a presupposed opposition between royalty, supported by officialdom (the 'mandarins') and military chiefs (*hulubalang*), and the *orang kaya*, who dominated political life in the sultanate, he makes a clear distinction between this mercantile aristocracy and the nobility in Aceh. As for the decade of political instability, he characterises it as a period in which this nobility was distanced from power by the *orang kaya*.[147]

We are still nowhere close to having a clear picture of the political balance in Aceh, in much the same way as in the case of the other sultanates, and the evolution of the situation over the course of the 16th and 17th centuries. In the case of Aceh, and once again using the decade of 1579–89 as a privileged moment, it is a legitimate question to ask up to what point is it possible to clearly distinguish the *hulubalang* from the *orang kaya* and place them on a collision course (as Alves does), or these elements from the *ulama* (as Kathirithamby-Wells does). We are referring, in many cases, to people with the title and function of the *orang kaya*, who are distinctive in social terms but are rarely specific. The title essentially designates a social distinction of a generic nature, an association with court life and royal officialdom and which, from the end of the 16th century, also began to be (if it was not already so) an honorific title bestowed by the sultan. Alauddin Riayat Syah al-Mukammil conferred it upon the Portuguese friar Amaro de Jesus, and Iskandar Muda upon the Englishman Thomas Best and the Frenchman Augustin de Beaulieu; at least in the case of the former, this was due to reasons that were solely political and not of an economic nature.[148] Even in European accounts, which always

---

[146] For Brakel, for instance, the term only refers to the four most important officers in the Acehnese court ('State and Statecraft ...', p. 63).

[147] Alves, *O Domínio do Norte de Sumatra*, p. 172.

[148] About the granting of this title to the Portuguese Augustinian friar, *see* chapter 3, note 51.

use the term *orang kaya* to refer to the elite sections of the sultanate, it seems clear that nowadays attempts are made to make distinctions that, at the time, did not fully make sense.

The decapitation of the more powerful groups of the court, carried out by Alauddin Riayat Syah from 1589 onwards, was later continued with undeniable success by his grandson, Iskandar Muda. This sultan instigated a true social revolution by definitively regulating society and the administration. As Beaulieu mentions,[149] Muda almost totally eliminated the old nobility and created a new one. Here one can clearly distinguish strata of prominent aristocracy, inevitably linked to the court and to the sultan, as also to the administrative apparatus that Muda developed, especially for the governance of the sultanate's dependencies namely, the pepper-producing regions. We are no longer dealing with a, more or less archaic, system that handed over dependencies to elements of the royal family, as Alauddin Riayat Syah al-Kahar had done, which posed a potential danger to the throne itself in the long term (as did happen after Alauddin's death). Instead, we have a structure where the sultan had direct control over the provinces, through governors (*panglima*), appointed for three years like the Portuguese viceroys and captains, who were directly responsible for the strict enforcement of the royal monopoly (especially of pepper and gold) and reported to the sultan himself. However, it is true that this was never fully enforced, either on the western or eastern coast of Sumatra,[150] although European sources refer to this, and also mention the fear the inhabitants of Tiku or Priaman felt in selling pepper without the sultan's authorisation.[151]

Alongside this new nobility of officials and the court, it is undeniable that Iskandar Muda was supported, perhaps more than is supposed, by a warrior aristocracy, relying upon their resources to promote the military expeditions that he almost permanently undertook against diverse neighbouring kingdoms. One only needs to establish what kind of relationship prevailed between these *hulubalang* and the old military elite in Aceh. In

---

[149] Beaulieu, 'Memoires du Voyage aux Indes Orientales', p. 63.
[150] Kathirithamby-Wells, 'Royal Authority and the *Orang Kaya* …', p. 263; Kathirithamby-Wells, 'Achehnese Control over West Sumatra …', p. 459.
[151] Beaulieu, 'Memoires du Voyage aux Indes Orientales', p. 56; Jourdain, *The Journal of* …, p. 232; letter from A. Spraight to N. Downton, 18-4-1615, *LREIC*, III, p. 103; letter from A. Spike, 23-6-1615, ibid., p. 122.

any case, the role they played was now an extremely important one: it is enough, as Kathirithamby-Wells observes, to see the prominence that the *Hikayat Aceh* gives to both the *hulubalang* as well as the sultan, while it omits all mention of the *orang kaya* and only occasionally refers to the *orang besar*.[152] Territorial benefits were bestowed upon this military elite who, according to Reid, would later give rise to a land-holding aristocracy, but the tight control exercised over them by Iskandar Muda shows up to what point it constituted a potential threat for the sultan.[153]

Thus, in this way, one can observe how the internal evolution of Aceh was, in a certain way, inverse to that of Johor. Here, first the growing military dependence of the sultan upon his subordinates and, later, the VOC's monopolistic policies resulted in a modification of the strict rules of the traditions of political relations, bringing about a growing division of power on the part of the sultan and the transformation of the old court elite into economically active and competitive strata. In Aceh, on the contrary, the traditional interdependence between the power of the sultan and the aristocracy (it does not seem that the latter felt itself in any way impeded from participating actively in trade, contrary to the aristocracy in Johor) ended up having disastrous political effects that only profound and decisive actions could contain. Thus the process was more radical than in Johor, where everything was characterised by continuity: a new aristocracy was born, both in administrative and military terms, forged by the forced centralisation of power, in which the sultanate's political, economic and social life revolved around the figure of the sultan. The death of Iskandar Muda would, however, result in the reversal of this process to new situations where royal power lost ground to the aristocracy.

---

[152] Kathirithamby-Wells, 'Royal Authority ...', p. 264; this information is more significant if compared with the *Bustan*, which was written in an age of a weak political authority, in which the title of *orang kaya* is frequently used.

[153] Reid, 'Trade and the Problem of Royal Power ...', p. 50.

CHAPTER 5

The City of Melaka

The history of Melaka is not limited to a political or economic approach at the level of regional geopolitics or that of the entire Indian Ocean. One must also consider its local history, the result of power play by the city's authorities in which royal officials (with the captain at the forefront), the bishop, the *casados* as well as the various Asian communities played a central role. One must also bear geographical conditions in mind, a surrounding environment that, in large measure, determined the daily life of the city's inhabitants and a seasonal fluctuation of the population. This was an inherent part of the very condition of being an emporium, conditioned by the monsoons. Apart from being geographically equidistant from both Johor and Aceh, which moulded the region's geopolitics, Melaka also experienced an isolation that resulted from the distance that separated the city from the capital of the Estado da Índia. It was Goa where decisions were taken about this fortress, and the centre that Melaka looked to whenever the city required assistance, very often in vain. One must also reflect upon the problem of the city's defence and security, which became a pressing issue in times of crisis and was a permanent feature from the early years of the 17th century. Finally, it is necessary to consider the city's internal evolution in which Melaka adapted, in various ways, to its surrounding environment and the specific conditions of each period.

The available sources do not allow a sufficiently deep analysis of all these questions. However, given the dearth of a study exclusively dedicated to the internal history of the city during this period,[1] this book would inevitably be truncated if some pages were not dedicated to this issue. The focus will be on two questions, given their connection with the theme of this work: the balance among the various powers in the city and the problems of Melaka's security, namely from 1606 onwards.

The Structure of the City: Population and Society

Just as Egypt is a gift of the Nile, Melaka is likewise a gift of the Straits. The history of the city's grandeur is closely related to the exceptional geographical position that the Straits occupy in the Indian Ocean region. However, this factor, which was responsible for the city's prosperity, was also the cause of its decline. The city suffered from several weaknesses, created or aggravated during the Portuguese period: a precarious military situation, an almost total dependence on the outside world for its food supplies, an unstable position in its external relations and isolation with regard to Portuguese structures. Melaka depended on the sea and its maritime connections; it was disconnected from its surrounding environment and turned its back on the hinterland, following the model of the sultanate.[2]

The city was divided into three main areas: the city itself, delimited by a fortified perimeter, and the districts of Hilir and Upeh on the left and right banks, respectively, of the river. Clusters of palm groves and vegetable plots, along with the *duções*,[3] completed the picture. Proceeding upriver, there were some more vegetable plots which belonged to the city's residents,[4] also a chapel and some villages, the most important of which was Naning, inhabited by people of Minangkabau origin.[5] After

---

[1] Luís Filipe Thomaz's graduation thesis presents the most complete study about this issue so far, but it is limited in terms of the time span covered despite using later sources such as Manuel Godinho de Erédia.

[2] Lombard, 'Le Sultanat Malais comme modèle socio-économique', p. 118.

[3] Used in Portuguese sources to designate a village or a village house (from the Malay *dusun*, 'village').

[4] Bocarro, 'Livro das Plantas de todas as Fortalezas …', p. 22.

[5] Erédia, 'Declaraçam de Malaca …', fls. 11–11v.

the Portuguese conquest, some of these villages came under Melaka's jurisdiction but continued, nevertheless, to be strongly influenced by Johor as the only known revolt coincided with the crisis of 1585–87, probably having been promoted by Sultan Ali Jalla. It was the rebellion of November 1586, promptly subdued by Diogo de Azambuja and Dom Manuel de Almada.[6] In the interior regions were pre-Malay populations, isolated in the hinterland, whom the Portuguese did not know very well.[7] These were the Orang Asli,[8] some groups of whom can still be found today in various regions of Malaysia.[9]

The most important members of Melaka's population were the *casados*, a heterogeneous group of Portuguese or descendants of Portuguese who safeguarded the city's defence and ensured that it remained in the hands of the Portuguese Crown. A large segment of the population, consisting of merchant communities of diverse origins, resided in the city on a seasonal basis.[10] The Kelings (Hindu merchants from the Coromandel coast), the Chinese and the Javanese were the most important communities, and were established in specific quarters in the city (*kampung*[11] *keling, kampung cina*), situated in Upeh, the economic heart of the city, although some of the Javanese resided in Hilir.[12] Some of the *casados* of the city lived outside

---

[6] Couto, *Da Ásia*, X, part 2, VIII, xiv, pp. 357–360; letter from the bishop of Melaka to the king, 15-12-1588, AGS, *Secr. Prov.*, book 1551, fl. 397v. At least some of these local groups were ruled by Pahang as in 1614 the sultan asked Melaka for help to suppress a revolt (Bocarro, *Década 13*, I, lxvii, p. 293).

[7] Erédia says they were 'the *banuas*, wild people ... cannibals, black people with hair like the satyrs' ('Declaraçam ...', fl. 11).

[8] Literally 'primitive people' (from *asli*, 'original, primitive').

[9] *See* Anderson and Vorster, 'Diversity and Interdependence in the Trade Hinterlands of Melaka', pp. 447–449.

[10] Sousa clearly states: 'Melaka's inhabitants were forever changing because it was a common inn for all nations and sects of the Orient' (*Oriente Conquistado a Jesus Cristo*, p. 1082).

[11] Malay, 'village'.

[12] Thomaz, 'Les Portugais dans les Mers de l'Archipel', p. 116; *Os Portugueses em Malaca*, I, p. 181; chapter IV of this work ('The city and its inhabitants') is still the most complete study on the subject. In 1641 Schouten reported: 'here [Hilir] most of the mestics, the blacks and some Portuguese citizens lived happily under the shade of coconut trees and surrounded by beautiful gardens and pleasure grounds' (Leupe, 'The Siege and Capture of Malacca', p. 88).

the perimeter of the fortress, also in Upeh.[13] The interior of the fortified
perimeter, which was a rather small area, was, in large part, occupied
by churches and convents, which left little space for residential houses
or other buildings. The houses, constructed in perishable materials, faced
constant danger from fire, such as the particularly destructive blaze that
broke out in 1597.[14]

Melaka depended greatly on the outside world. The *duções* and
vegetable plots in the areas around the city were clearly not sufficient
to sustain it. Thus Melaka was almost totally dependent upon external
supplies of food, despite the city's propitious agricultural conditions.[15]
The main centres that supplied provisions to Melaka in the period
under study were Java and Pegu. These regions were abundant in rice,
although the political turmoil in both areas resulted in a search for
alternative markets such as Siam, Bengal or even the Coromandel coast.
Any one of these sources was preferable to despatching food supplies
from India, in terms of distance and speed as well as price.[16] The flow
of provisions to Melaka was, however, vaster. A small but permanent
stream of light vessels continuously provided supplies to the city in times
of peace, from several regions.[17] For the period under study, there is
evidence that Melaka received food supplies from Arrakan,[18] Cambodia,[19]

---

[13] Bocarro, 'Livro da Plantas …', p. 14.

[14] Coutre, 'Vida de …', pp. 130 and 143, refers to about 1,000 houses
      destroyed.

[15] Mentioned by Erédia, 'Declaraçam …', fls. 10v.–11 and 19, among other sources.
      About this question, *see* Hill, 'The History of Rice Cultivation in Melaka',
      pp. 540–542.

[16] Royal letter to Viceroy D. Jerónimo de Azevedo, 19-3-1612, *DRI*, II, p. 225.
      It quotes a letter from the bishop of Mylapur who stated that apart from the
      fact that the food supplies were of better quality, provisions could be acquired
      on the Coromandel coast at about two-fifths of the price of those on the west
      coast of India.

[17] *See* Lobato, *Política e Comércio*, pp. 218–221.

[18] Royal letter to Viceroy Aires de Saldanha, 15-1-1601, HAG, *MonçReino*, 8,
      fl. 49.

[19] Letter from the king of Cambodia to the Portuguese viceroy, unknown date
      (late 16th century), AN/TT, *MiscMssCGL*, box 2, vol. III, p. 338; letter from
      Viceroy D. Francisco da Gama to the king, 23-12-1599, BN, *Res.*, cod. 1976,
      fl. 143v.

Kedah,[20] Makassar,[21] Manila,[22] Pahang,[23] Patani,[24] Perak[25] and even Johor.[26]

This dependence on the outside world had two immediate effects: on the one hand, it resulted in the permanent scarcity of which everybody complained; and, on the other hand, it compounded the city's debility in times of crisis, which considerably aggravated the military situation and made help from Goa or a rapid supply of provisions from neighbouring kingdoms that produced these food items an issue of great urgency. The price of rice fluctuated considerably. In periods of siege it quickly became scarce, and prices rose swiftly: taking, as was habitual during this period, the *cruzado*[27] to be a standard norm, during the 1575 siege a *cruzado*

---

[20] 'Relação' by D. Paulo de Lima, 8-11-1587, *DUP*, I, p. 15; royal letter to Viceroy Rui Lourenço de Távora, 14-2-1609, HAG, *MonçReino*, No. 11, fl. 200 (published with errors in *BOGEI*, No. 160 (1882), p. 795.

[21] Fr. Félix de Jesus, 'Primeira Parte da Chronica …', AN/TT, *MssLiv.*, No. 731, fl. 25v.

[22] Bocarro, *Década 13*, I, xciii, p. 415.

[23] Ibid., lxvii, p. 293.

[24] Letter from the city of Melaka to the king, 3-12-1605, *DUP*, II, p. 254; Coutre, 'Vida de…', p. 155; *Relação das Plantas, & dezcripções* …, p. 44; Record from the State Council, 30-4-1619, *ACE*, I, p. 42.

[25] 'Relação' by D. Paulo de Lima quoted in note 20, above.

[26] Record from the State Council, 13-4-1622, *ACE*, I, p. 134.

[27] The exact value of the *cruzado* is not completely clear to this period. I have followed the Melaka standard of 360 *reis* being equivalent to 5 silver *tangas*; these values were correct in 1554 (Nunes, 'Livro dos pesos …', p. 40), and are the figures most commonly accepted by scholars (*see* Godinho, *Os Descobrimentos e a Economia Mundial*, II, pp. 125–126, who takes the *cruzado* and the *pardau de larins* to be equivalent, the former being the standard currency worth 360 *reis*); *see* Godinho, *Les Finances de l'État* …, pp. 115 and 332 and Matos, *O Estado da Índia nos anos de 1581–1588*, table I. However, the 'Lista de Moedas …', p. 142, published by J. Wicki, compiled in 1582, says the golden *pardaus* were also called *cruzados* in Melaka but were not worth more than 300 *reis* there; when transported to India, they were worth 330 *reis*. However, it seems that the *cruzado* would have continued to be the standard currency with a value of 360 *reis*: a report written in 1613 by the Treasury Council refers to the *cruzado* 'of 360 *reis* each which is the common currency in Melaka' (record of 21-11-1613, *ACF*, I, part 1, p. 5). Another report of an unknown vintage, but probably dating from the first quarter of the 17th century, states:

would buy only 2 *gantas*[28] of this cereal, and the price gradually dropped with the retreat of Aceh's forces and the arrival of replenishment supplies until a *cruzado* purchased 70 *gantas* of rice.[29] In 1587 prices rose to such an extent that 1 *cruzado* would only buy 1 *ganta*. After the help rendered by Dom Paulo de Lima, it would buy 40 *gantas*, but it was still expensive.[30] Furthermore, the price of foodstuffs in Melaka was one of the signs, keenly felt in the city's daily life, of the worsening of the situation after the arrival of the northern Europeans, that is, after 1606.

The years of an abundance of provisions became increasingly rarer, and the average price of the cereal clearly reveals this: during the 1570s, the normal price in times of peace was 1/70 or 1/80; in years of plenty, it touched 1/120,[31] a figure that was very much cheaper than the prices found in the first half of the century.[32] During the 17th century this proportion had already worsened substantially. After the siege of 1568 there was such an abundance of rice that the viceroy ordered that 3,000 *candis*[33] of this commodity be bought in Melaka to supply Sri Lanka and Goa.[34] However, in 1610, although the city was at peace, the arrival of the armada of Miguel de Sousa Pimentel and the capture of ships loaded

---

'The customs house of Melaka, in the past, used to register a profit of 80,000 *cruzados* at 18 *vinténs* [20 *reis* each = 360 *reis*] for each *cruzado*, which is the local currency, or 100,000 *xerafins*' (report about an autonomous government in Melaka, unknown date, AN/TT, *MssLiv.*, No. 1107, p. 282). Anyway, in the present case of the price of rice, and in order to prevent confusion, it is best to establish a ratio between one *cruzado* and the equivalent amount of grain irrespective of the intrinsic value of the former.

[28] Measure of capacity, from the Malay *gantang*, equivalent to 1.25 *canadas* or 1.75 litres; Nunes, 'Livro dos Pesos e Medidas', pp. 39 and 58.

[29] Lemos, 'Hystoria dos Cercos ...', fl. 55.

[30] 'Relação' by D. Paulo de Lima in *DUP*, I, p. 15; letter from the bishop of Melaka to the king, 15-12-1588, AGS, *Secr. Prov.*, book 1551, fl. 398.

[31] Lemos, 'Hystoria dos Cercos ...'; Luz, *Livro das Cidades e Fortalezas ...*' (about 1582), fl. 102v., presents similar figures.

[32] *See* Macgregor, 'Notes on the Portuguese in Malaya', pp. 7, note 18. The values are presented in *reis* and not in the equivalent *gantas* per *cruzado*.

[33] Each *candil* was equivalent to 140 *gantas* of Melaka (1.75 l), or 245 l; therefore, 3,000 *candis* were 735,000 l, which corresponded to 721,510.8 kg according to Lima Felner (Nunes, 'Livro dos Pesos e Medidas', pp. 31, 39 and 58, note 6).

[34] Couto, *Da Ásia*, VIII, xxx, p. 255.

with foodstuffs resulted in a lowering of prices from 1/10 to 1/60, which was already considered to be exceptional.[35] Even the bishop complained of these high prices, emphasising the permanent scarcity of food and revealing the prices of meat of an unspecified origin (presumably beef) at the end of 1606 or 1607: one *cruzado* for two *arráteis* (about 900 g).[36]

Various attempts were made to put a stop to this dearth of provisions. As already mentioned, the areas surrounding the city had favourable conditions for agriculture, but the cause of its rudimentary state was not just 'because the locals are negligent and slipshod in this service', as Erédia stated.[37] Various attempts were made to increase agriculture in the surrounding environs, but all proved unsuccessful. During the captaincy of Francisco da Silva Meneses (1594–97) fifteen ships with Chinese aboard[38] arrived in Melaka; they proposed to cultivate the land on the same side of the river as Hilir to regularly provide the city with victuals; the captain and the city council did not allow this.[39] A statement about this question, dating from the end of the 1610s, is very revealing:

> 'The orders particularly emphasised that all care must be taken to continue to sow rice, taking advantage of the ease with which the land gives an abundance and surfeit of this, it seems to me very necessary to bring the *chinchéus*, a very industrious and hardworking people, and when they flock here in overly large numbers, one can impose the charges that Governor Dom João da Silva ordered in Manila—a convenient means of interrupting the tyranny that the *casados* use, there being a continuous scarcity of bread and meat, and the other provisions that the lack of people and the dereliction of lands causes in this state, which is by nature abundant and bountiful'.[40]

---

35   Bocarro, *Década 13*, I, xxii, p. 95.
36   More precisely, 919 g; royal letter to Viceroy D. Martim Afonso de Castro, 3-1-1608, *DRI*, I, p. 172.
37   Erédia, 'Declaraçam ...', fl. 10v.–11.
38   The source refers to *chinchéus*, or people from Fujian.
39   Coutre, 'Vida de ...', p. 423.
40   'Sobre a Fazenda de sua Magestade', unknown date [between 1616 and 1622], AN/TT, *MiscMssCGL*, box 16, vol. 6 F, fl. 103. The word *chinchéus* refers generally to Chinese people from Fujian (the cities of Quanzhou or Zhangzhou); it designates an ethnic, a linguistic or even a religious distinction in relation to the *chins* (people from Guangdong); Thomaz, 'Chinchéu' in *Dicionário de História dos Descobrimentos Portugueses*, I, p. 250.

In the early 16th century the Crown's factor still had the power to acquire rice at the minimum market price in order to provision the armadas.[41] However, in the period under study it was already the *casados* of Melaka who dominated the flow of provisions into the city, earning considerable profits from this trade and, quite naturally, they opposed any attempts to increase local production. This was true, at least from the end of the century onwards.[42] This situation was certainly linked, directly or indirectly, to the growing tyranny of the captain of the fortress over the merchants, appropriating the city's most lucrative commercial traffic for himself. This would have caused the *casados* to explore other, less profitable trading avenues, such as that of provisions.

The society and population in Melaka situation underwent considerable changes from 1511 onwards. Let us go back in time to the date of the Portuguese conquest. In the time of the Malay sultanate, two communities contended for supremacy over the sultanate's trade: the Kelings (Hindus), and the Gujaratis (Muslims), who held the advantage over the former. The Kelings became the natural allies of the recently arrived Portuguese, spotting an opportunity to supplant their rivals. In the same way, just as they had done throughout the Orient, the Portuguese sought support in non-Islamic sectors. The initial policy, aimed at keeping the structure of the Malay sultanate unaltered, ended up promoting the primacy of the Kelings as the Gujaratis abandoned the city and subsequently settled in Aceh. This policy took advantage of the administrative structure of the sultanate to regroup the mercantile communities into Moors and Gentiles, creating separate jurisdictions.

Thus the *tumenggung*[43] (who had earlier been responsible for the security of the city) was transformed into the representative of the Muslims, and the *bendahara*[44] (a post that wielded executive power within

---

[41] Lobato, *Política e Comércio*, pp. 219–220.

[42] Coutre also stated that the *casados* were all bakers and that they purchased one *candil* of wheat for 15 *ducados* [at the time 1 *ducado* being equivalent to 1 *cruzado*] and later sold the bread for 50 *ducados* ('Vida de ...', pp. 423–424). *See* Bocarro, *Década 13*, I, xlvi, p. 195.

[43] Mentioned in the Portuguese sources as 'tumugão' or 'tomungão', adopted hereafter.

[44] The Portuguese sources mention 'bendara', 'bandara', 'bandará' or even 'bandarra'.

the sultanate, immediately below the sultan) was made the representative of the Gentiles. The former post was entrusted to a Muslim from Luzón and the latter to a Keling called Nina Chatu, who played a very important role during the early years of Portuguese rule.[45] During this initial phase, in continuance of the policy of maintaining the structure of the Malay sultanate unaltered, the Crown tended to favour the Keling mercantile community by means of a policy of low customs duties (6 per cent), while the Christians paid 10 per cent. This was possibly aimed at ensuring that Portuguese soldiers did not exchange a career of arms for one of commerce, which would be prejudicial to the interests of the Estado da Índia.[46]

This scenario underwent significant changes during the second half of the century: the stabilisation of Portuguese structures instead of expansion, an increase in the number of Portuguese merchants or mixed race Portuguese, as well as the ideological environment of the Catholic Reformation, caused alterations within the heart of Melakan society.[47] The Christians now paid customs duties of 6 per cent, while 14 per cent was demanded from Gentiles and Muslims.[48] The number of converts increased significantly due to the pressures on the non-Christians, the privileges granted to converts and the missionary activities of various religious orders that established themselves in the city from 1549 onwards. Christianity made inroads, above all, in the lower social classes (namely the slaves),[49] but the Hindu community was also affected.

Melaka society was increasingly dominated by miscegenation, which progressed more by way of concubines than by marriages. There were more concubines than legitimate wives, but neither category frequented

---

[45] About this issue *see* the articles by Thomaz, 'Nina Chatu e o Comércio Português em Malaca' and 'Malaca e suas comunidades mercantis na viragem do século XVI' in *De Ceuta a Timor*, and 'Indian Merchant Communities in Melaka' in Souza (ed.), *Indo-Portuguese History, Old Issues, New Questions*.

[46] Thomaz, 'Les Portugais dans les Mers de l'Archipel', pp. 111 and 113.

[47] Thomaz, 'Indian Merchant Communities ...', p. 63; *see* also Lobato, *Política e Comércio*, pp. 77–83.

[48] These figures are to be found in the 'Alvará em forma de Regimento' granted by Viceroy Matias de Albuquerque to the city of Melaka in 1595 (in Pissurlencar (ed.), *Regimentos das Fortalezas da Índia*, pp. 256–257), referring to the 'Javanese and other foreigners' dealing in Indonesian spices.

[49] *See* chapter 4, note 47.

the churches.[50] However, one element is worthy of note in this regard: Portuguese sources remark that the women of Melaka earned their own livelihood, not being economically dependent upon their husbands,[51] which would indicate that here—in the same manner as throughout all of Southeast Asia—women traditionally enjoyed greater freedom and carried out more visible social functions than in Europe.[52] As the city became increasingly more 'Portuguese', Melaka simultaneously also accentuated certain 'Malay' characteristics.

It is clear that the mercantile communities, irrespective of whether they were Muslim or other non-Christian groups, would witness a decline in their importance over the course of the 16th century to the advantage of the Christians in the city. The roles of the Malay sultanate officials that had been adapted by Afonso de Albuquerque—the *bendara* and the *tomungão*—were altered significantly, as we shall see shortly. The Chinese frequented Melaka in increasingly smaller numbers, especially after the foundation of Macao,[53] but did not abandon the city totally. There are data to confirm their presence in Melaka during the period under study: in 1586 Dom Jerónimo de Azevedo attacked a junk of Fujianese in the Straits and killed almost the entire crew, causing 'tumult' in Melaka;[54] in 1589 the Chinese sold pepper in Melaka, all of which was bought and sent to India;[55] in the official orders given to Viceroy Dom Martim Afonso de

---

[50]   Sousa, *Oriente Conquistado* …, p. 1085; *see* Lobato, *Política e Comércio*, p. 81.

[51]   'The women of this city are not dependent upon their husbands for their domestic expenses, because with their manual labour they assure their own maintenance' (*Relação das Plantas* …, p. 44); Bocarro confirms this information in his 'Livro das Plantas …', p. 25.

[52]   *See* Reid, *Southeast Asia in the Age of Commerce*, I, pp. 162–163.

[53]   Pinto, 'Traços da Presença Chinesa em Malaca', p. 139; Lobato, *Política e Comércio*, p. 81; Meilink-Roelofsz, *Asian Trade and European Influence* …, p. 158. The history of the Ming Dynasty confirms the reduction in the number of Chinese vessels in the city due to the alleged plunder and pressure on them (Groeneveldt, 'Notes on the Malay Archipelago…', p. 253). *See* also Purcell, 'Chinese Settlement in Melaka' despite its minimal data on the Portuguese period.

[54]   Couto, *Da Ásia*, X, part 2, VIII, ii, p. 273.

[55]   Royal letter to António Fernandes de Ilher, *casado* of Malaca, 12-1-1591, AHU, *Cons. Ultr.*, cod. 281, fl. 164v. (*see* Document Appendix, No. 7). The king stated that this was to be attempted again in order to attract the Chinese

Castro in 1605 the king forbade his subjects to bother the ships of the *'chinchéus'*;[56] finally, in Melaka during the 1620s there was an official post of 'interpreter of the *chinchéus*'.[57] The presence of the Muslims in the city is rather more confusing. There was a regular and important presence of Javanese in Melaka. However, for the period under study it is not clear whether they consisted exclusively of Muslims. For Muslims originating from other regions, there is a dearth of records. One can point out the presence of a 'Coja Ibrahim', a rich merchant in Melaka who also served as the city's ambassador to Johor[58] and was executed during the siege of 1606, accused of treason.[59]

The Kelings and the Javanese continued to play an important role in the city. Several documents mention the continuous presence and residence of the Kelings in Melaka.[60] They would probably no longer have been as rich as in earlier periods, in which they had managed to accumulate great

---

to Melaka and also agreed with Fernandes de Ilher that the Portuguese should prevent the Chinese from going to Sunda, Patani and other ports.

[56] 'to the vessels belonging to the *chinchéus*, with whom this Estado is not at war ..., no harm shall be done and, instead, you shall order that they all be treated well, in order to bring them to my service ...'; royal letter, 5-3-1605, HAG, *MonçReino*, No. 6B, fls. 12v.–13 (*see* Document Appendix, No. 15).

[57] On 4 May 1621 the viceroy issued a confirmation of this office to Paulo Fernandes, who was born in Melaka and was the *bendara* at the time; the office already existed: the document states that he would serve three years, 'the same way his predecessors did with the same rights and duties' (HAG, *Mercês Gerais*, vol. 2, fl. 384).

[58] Coutre, 'Vida de ...', p. 166; it is possibly the same embassy mentioned by Valentijn, 'Description of Malacca', Pt 2, p. 129.

[59] Barbuda, *Empresas Militares de Lusitanos*, xviii, fl. 321v. and Queirós, *História da Vida do Venerável Irmão Pedro de Basto*, p. 333. The work by Queirós, written and published later, seems to repeat the information provided by Barbuda, contrary to what has been stated by some authors, such as Boxer and Vasconcelos, *André Furtado de Mendonça*, p. 72.

[60] 'Riquesas que produs o Estado da India', unknown date [probably late 16th century], *DUP*, II, p. 112, refers to an episode that took place in Melaka involving 'a Keling merchant born in Melaka'. In 1603, while in Johor and due to the unexpected events, J. Coutre sought refuge in the house of a Muslim (*see* note 58, above) along with other two Keling merchants of Melaka, 'Nina Gadin' and 'Nina Aure' ('Vida de ...', p. 166).

fortunes.[61] However, the most interesting aspect is to observe that their performance in the defence of the city was undoubtedly trustworthy: in 1568 the captain of Melaka himself defended them when rumours were circulating in the city about a supposed agreement between them and the Acehnese, and in 1575 they proceeded to man the city's bastions, along with the *casados* and the soldiers.[62] Their influence was such that, even in the 1580s, they were able to practice Hindu ceremonies with the connivance of the bishop and the captain[63] although, in the very same decade, they complained to the king about the abuses to which they were subjected.[64] Even at the end of the 1610s, when the city's commerce already showed a notable decline due to the Anglo–Dutch competition, the Kelings' trade in clothes was still so profitable that the authorities in Goa considered applying an extraordinary tax on this activity.[65]

The case of the Javanese was quite different and can be summed up in a few words: despite all the abuses to which they were subjected by the Portuguese captain, and the preference that they would subsequently give to other ports, their activities in Melaka continued to be important as—due to the disorganisation of the Portuguese trade in spices from the Eastern Archipelago—Melaka now depended almost entirely on the Javanese for the supply of spices. They also played an equally important role in the supply of provisions to the city.[66] The movement of Javanese merchants at

---

[61] Couto states that in the early 1560s there were rich Keling merchants in Melaka who, in his opinion, even possessed 12–15 *bares* of gold (*Da Ásia*, VII, part 1, IX, xvi, p. 427), or 2,202.3–2,754 kg, according to the 'Livro dos Pesos …' by António Nunes, pp. 39 and 48 (using the *bar pequeno dachém* (183.6 kg), used to weigh metals, like tin, and not the *bar grande* (about 210 kg).

[62] Ibid., VIII, xxii, p. 150; IX, xxvii, p.243; in the latter, the author refers to the 'Keling born there'.

[63] Letter from the *ouvidor* of Melaka to the king, 17-12-1588, AGS, *Secr. Prov.*, book 1551, fl. 469v.

[64] Royal instructions to Viceroy D. Duarte de Meneses, 10-3-1584, AN/TT, *Fundo Português da Bibl. Nac. de Paris*, No. 48, fls. 11v–12 (*see* Document Appendix, No. 2).

[65] Letter from Governor Fernão de Albuquerque, 8-2-1620, *DRI*, VI, p. 201.

[66] Royal letter to Viceroy Rui Lourenço de Távora, 23-1-1610, *DRI*, I, p. 291; Couto, *Da Ásia*, X, part 2, X, xii, p. 626; Erédia even refers to the place he calls the 'market of the Javanese' (*bazar de jaus*) where the food supplies they brought to the city were sold ('Declaraçam de Malaca …', fls. 6, 10v. and 19).

the port of Melaka continued to be intensive right until the turn of the century and the establishment of the northern Europeans,[67] later declining in an accelerated manner with the worsening of the economic and political conditions mentioned in the course of this study, especially after the great siege of 1606. This shift can be detected even in the concerns about the city's security, mentioned above: documental information about the risks involving the presence of a large number of foreigners in the city and the absence of a suitable military garrison[68] disappear during the 17th century, being replaced by a constant preoccupation with a Dutch offensive.

Tracing the evolution of Melaka's population during the period under study is no easy task. The information contained in the sources is very irregular, as shown in the table on pp. 184–185. Some remarks may be added: first, with regard to the very nature of the sources themselves. There are glaring discrepancies in the figures on the number of inhabitants, which are connected with each author's viewpoint: the Europeans tended to consider only the Portuguese to be 'inhabitants', and only edifices built within city walls and near the nucleus of the city to be 'houses'. One must not forget that part of this data did not result directly from first-hand observation, but was obtained from accounts or information from third parties. Another important variable was the seasonal nature of part of the city's population, regulated by the monsoons which dictated the rhythm of navigation and the trade upon which the city depended: we do not know at what time of the year the data were recorded. It is curious to note how the highest numbers of inhabitants and hearths come from local sources: Manuel Godinho de Erédia, born in Melaka, and the records of the city council.

There is no doubt that the total population declined, if one compares these numbers—even allowing for omissions—with the figures available for the early years of Portuguese rule, which range between 100,000

---

[67] Carletti, *Voyage autour du Monde*, p. 236. *See* the data about the presence of 2,000–3,000 Javanese in the port of Melaka in 1588 and the calculations of the presence of about 20,000 'Moors' in the city each year, chapter 1, note 70.

[68] The *regimento* granted by Viceroy D. Duarte de Meneses to Melaka in 1585 refers to the imminent risk of 'raids from Aceh, who is such a powerful enemy, as everyone knows, and the fears about the Javanese and many other nations who come to Melaka everyday with their fleets' (HAG, *Cartas Patentes e Provisões*, 3, fl. 8).

Population of Melaka, 1577–1630s

	INHABITANTS	HEARTHS	CHRISTIANS	SLAVES	MEN OF ARMS	CASADOS	SOLDIERS
1577[1]	4,000	< 100 (houses of Portuguese)					
1579–80[2]		70–80 (houses of Portuguese)					
1580s[3]						< 100	
End of the 16th century[4]				2,000 ('vassals', incl. suburbs)		600 (including suburbs)	
1600–1610[5]	1,200 (including suburbs)				300	200 (Portuguese)	
1605[6]		10,500 (1,500 in each parish)					
1606[7]					100		
1606[8]					< 180 (*casados* and soldiers)		
Decade of 1610[9]				2,000		200 (including suburbs)	
1613[10]			7,400 (including suburbs)			300 (within the walls)	

Year			
1614[11]			500
1618[12]			150
1620[13]	2,500 (including female slaves)	< 100	
1626[14]		about 120	75
1630s[15]	2,000	250 (including 150 in Upeh)	

The calculation refers to the total between the fortress and suburbs.

Sources:

(1) "Sumário da província dos jesuítas da Índia", by Alessandro Valignano, 1577, *DI*, XIII, p. 49.

(2) "Sumario de las cosas que pertencen a la Província de la India Oriental", by Alessandro Valignano, 1579 or 1580, British Museum, *Add.* 9852, fl. 10 (published in *DHMPPO/India*, vol. 12, p. 514).

(3) J. H. Linschoten, *The Voyage of … to the East Indies*, I, p. 104.

(4) M. Godinho de Erédia, *Informação da Aurea Chersoneso*, p. 72. The calculation refers to the total between the fortress and suburbs.

(5) "The Remaining Voyages of John Albert of Mandelsloe" in Harris (ed.), *Itinerarium*, I, p. 783.

(6) Letter from the City Council of Melaka to the King, 3-12-1605, DUP, II, p. 259.

(7) L. Coelho de Barbuda, *Empresas Militares de Lvsitanos*, xviii, fl. 320v.

(8) P. Fernão Guerreiro, *Relação Anual das Coisas que fizeram os Padres da Cª de Jesus…*, II, p. 313.

(9) *Relação das Plantas, & dezcripções de todas as Fortalezas…*, p. 44; mentions "casais" ("couples").

(10) M. Godinho de Erédia, "Declaraçam de Malaca…", fls. 5-10.

(11) Letter from the Viceroy to the King, 31-12-1614, HAG, *Mon;Reino*, 12, fl. 163 (published in *BOGEI*, No. 92 (1883), p. 368.

(12) Information provided by A. Pinto da Fonseca mentioned in a letter from the Viceroy, Dom João Coutinho, to the King, undated [1618], *DRI*, IV, p. 64.

(13) Letter from the Governor, Fernão de Albuquerque, to the King, 20-2-1621, *DRI*, VII, p. 226.

(14) "Relação" of the Bishop of Melaka, D. Gonçalo da Silva, in Sanjay Subrahmanyam, 'Commerce and Conflict', appendix.

(15) António Bocarro, "Livro das Plantas de todas as Fortalezas…", p. 14.

and 200,000 inhabitants.[69] These numbers reflect the exodus of part of the city's population, which slowly debilitated Melaka over the course of the 16th century (beginning with the Gujarati community just after the Portuguese conquest), a phenomenon undoubtedly aggravated both by the competition from other commercial centres and the worsening in the political conditions of the city. Melaka's role as a centre where mercantile communities established themselves or resided decreased. The city no longer wielded the immense power of commercial attraction that had ensured its grandeur during the 15th century, which the Portuguese tried to maintain over a good part of the following century.

Melaka had become a 'Portuguese' city, where Christians (be they *casados* or their dependants) held centre-stage. The number of *casados* during this period is clearly higher than in the first half of the 16th century, during which it never surpassed a hundred or so individuals.[70] The 17th century and the worsening of the city's political conditions does not, at least during the early decades, appear to have resulted in a decline in the number of *casados* or Christians. On the contrary, they seem to have grown in number, everything pointing towards a greater dispersal in the region, settlements in the city's suburbs or along the river, perhaps because security conditions were better there than within the fortress itself. Probably a large part of this population ceased to seek refuge there during times of crisis, and instead proceeded to follow the Malay tradition of hiding out in the interior until security was restored. Melaka was becoming increasingly more 'Portuguese', but also more 'Malay'.

One can observe disproportionate figures between the number of *casados* and slaves: during the early years of Portuguese dominion, the percentage of slaves ranged from 2.5 to 5.5 per cent of the total population.[71] During the period under study, the number of slaves was far higher. A common factor in these sources confirms the scenario in the city during this period: a few hundred *casados*, who constituted the core of the city, as an axis of Estado da Índia's network, and a large number (quite stable throughout the period in question) of slaves and dependants,

---

[69] Thomaz, 'A Escravatura em Malaca no século XVI', p. 4; Reid, 'The Structure of Cities in Southeast Asia', p. 238.

[70] 38 in 1525, 33 in 1528, 40 in 1532, 60 in 1539 (Macgregor, 'Notes on the Portuguese in Malaya', p. 12, note 37).

[71] Thomaz, 'A Escravatura em Malaca no século XVI', p. 4.

surely converts and mixed race individuals. This imbalance was, at a certain point, so asymmetrical that it became necessary to reduce the number of slaves by deporting them to Manila.[72] The 'foreign' communities, in their turn—although they continued to be vital for the survival of the city—declined in quantitative and qualitative terms and became marginal factors for the centres of political decisions. All this was symptomatic of Melaka's decline, from a city that was a model of cosmopolitanism to the fortified ghetto into which it was transformed.

The Centres of Power: Captain, Bishop and *Casados*

The period 1575–1619 reveals important changes at the heart of Melakan society. Apart from the demographic aspects and the notable qualitative changes in the city's social structure, there is also an important political facet that must not be forgotten. Just like the external balance, one must also analyse the internal political factors in play, which accompanied and compounded the transformations taking place in the city at various levels. First, Melaka's loss of the ability to attract mercantile communities; secondly, the transformation into a 'Portuguese' city, in which the *casados* were the leading figures in society; then, the hypertrophy of the captain's power and its decline; and, finally, the impoverishment and slow suffocation of the city during the 17th century after the failure of Portuguese attempts to expel the northern Europeans from East Asian waters.

The growth in the captains' power, which had started in the middle of the century but was more marked from the 1570s onwards, is closely linked to the 'privatisation' of the trade that took place at the heart of the Estado da Índia, that is, the Crown's tendency to withdraw from direct exploitation of trade and commercial routes. Handing over trade routes as a reward for services rendered, as a way of financing expenses, or simply selling them to help the Crown's debilitated coffers, became a generalised practice. In Melaka, the captain now sought to control the concession of trade voyages emanating from the city.[73] In the same way, the disorganisation of Portuguese structures, the loss of control and even direct access to the spice-producing sources did not, however, imply that these commodities

---

[72] Letter from Governor Fernão de Albuquerque, 18-2-1622, *DRI*, VII, p. 392; ibid., p. 407.
[73] Thomaz, 'Les Portugais dans les Mers de l'Archipel', p. 109.

ceased to flow through Melaka. This trade was now concentrated, above all, in the hands of the Javanese. Here, too, the power of the captains was felt in the form of all kinds of tyranny and extortion.[74]

When one speaks of the captain of Melaka, one is not referring merely to the figure of one individual, but rather to a set of people, sometimes an entire administrative machine. It was centred in the city, but included trading agents established in several ports according to the different trade routes whose profits they ensured and, quite logically, lived off. The merchants were obviously the first to suffer the captain's pressures, irrespective of whether they were *casados* or Asian traders, namely the Javanese who ensured the greater volume of the port's traffic and income of the customs house. The extortion of the captains, as has already been duly analysed, took several forms: buying cheap and selling at inflated prices, very often without any investment or risk; cheating on weights; claiming various exclusive privileges, in terms of both buying and selling; reserving the best merchandise for themselves and paying with others of a lesser quality; making seizures without justification; or charging excessive taxes.[75] During the three years in which they held the post the captains grew rich,[76] generally using all means at their disposal.

The abuse and tyranny was not new. What is of interest for the period in question is that the power of the captains now enabled them to exert increasing pressure on other local powers—the *casados*, who complained regularly to the king. What irritated the *casados* most was the constant interference of the captain or his men in their commercial affairs and

---

[74] Lobato, *Política e Comércio*, p. 191.

[75] The pressure and constraints of the captain of Melaka over trade are a permanent issue in Portuguese documentation. *See* chapter 1, 'Melaka and Its Trade'.

[76] Not all of them became wealthy, even in the most profitable years; for instance, Roque de Melo [1582–85] declared that he had completed his three years having earned 'little wealth'; however, this is clearly an argument used to obtain a grant from the monarch (letter to the king, 8-1-1587, AGS, *Secr. Prov.*, book 1551, fls. 127–127v.). Martim Afonso de Melo [1597–1600] seems to have left Melaka poor and in debt: D. Francisco da Gama says it was due to his lack of 'concern with regard to his duties' (letter to the king, unknown date [1599], BN, *Res.*, cod. 1976, fl. 140). However, Viceroy Aires de Saldanha refers to the lack of spices in Melaka due to the Dutch and also because he fully bore the expenses of a galleon sent to assist Tidore and Ambon (letter to the king, 20-12-1602, AN/TT, *CorCron*, part 1, pack 114, doc. 6, fl. 1).

even in their daily lives, which they considered to be an affront to their status.[77] The event that took place after the crisis with Johor in 1587 is revealing: after having played an important role in the defence of the city, the *casados* wrote to the king not asking for grants or privileges as a reward, but simply relief from the oppression the captains put on all commercial activities.[78] The captains, likewise, exercised their power over the officials of the fortress, especially the customs officials, who generally gave in to this pressure.[79]

The power of the captain was also felt in ecclesiastical affairs. In the late 1570s the captain of Melaka, Dom João da Gama (1579–82), controlled the Jesuit College by means of the appointment of a director, Father Gomes Vaz, who supported him in his extortion. This Jesuit later resigned after falling out with the captain, and his successor faced great difficulties in exercising the post in the light of the constant hostility of the same captain.[80] Curiously, during this period there are no signs of conflict with the bishop. This was undoubtedly due to the extraordinary figure who held the post at the time, Dom João Ribeiro Gaio (1579–1601) who, being one of the most powerful individuals in the city and someone who exercised his power well beyond the three short years for which each captain governed, was a figure who even the captains themselves feared. They thus avoided entering into conflicts with him. One cannot say the

---

[77] For instance, in 1583 or 1584 they complained about the captains who 'do not respect their rights but, instead, for the slightest reason arrest them and insult them, and harass them greatly'; royal letter to Viceroy D. Duarte de Meneses, 11-2-1585, *APO*, III, part 1, p. 34 (also published in *DHMPPO/Insulíndia*, V, p. 27).

[78] Royal letter to Viceroy Matias de Albuquerque, 12-1-1591, *APO*, III, part 1, p. 275 (also published in *DHMPPO/Insulíndia*, V, p. 194). A summary of their claims may be found in the 'notes' they sent to Viceroy D. Francisco da Gama in the final years of the 16th century (BN, *Res.*, cod. 1973, fls. 57–58; *see* Document Appendix, No. 10).

[79] Royal letter to Viceroy D. Francisco da Gama, 10-2-1598, *APO*, III, part 2, p. 828.

[80] This case is described by several Jesuits: letter from Diogo Pinto, 25-11-1580, *DI*, XII, p. 145; letter from Fernando Meneses, 31-12-1580, ibid., pp. 183–184; letter from Duarte Leitão, 4-1-1582, ibid., pp. 546–548. Gomes Vaz had New Christian ancestors and was able to achieve that position thanks to the support he received from the captain.

same about his successor, Dom Gonçalo da Silva (1613–36): the various conflicts with the captains during his tenure include a famous episode when Captain João da Silveira entered the church with his armed Japanese guards in 1616 or 1617.[81]

The captains' abuse of their power was the cause of constant complaints to both the viceroy and the king himself. In all these cases, attempts were made to stop the abuses by successive orders to strictly carry out their instructions and avoid irregularities. This repetition is the best proof of how ineffective these orders were. As Melaka was far removed from Goa and even further away from Lisbon, the authorities were unable to limit the abuses due to the frequent alarms caused by enemy attacks. On the contrary, as the captain was the highest authority in Melaka, his figure was necessary to ensure the city's defences. For this reason many irregularities were permitted, not to speak of slow and ineffective justice. Some of the captains who were notorious for various abuses of power received favourable judgements due to their performance in defending or ensuring provisions for the city.[82]

The officials who were usually sent to the fortresses were the auditors (*ouvidores*) who, generally at the end of each captain's term, proceeded to carry out an inquiry, the so-called 'official inquiry' or 'residence', which investigated possible irregularities that had taken place. These inquiries about the conduct of each captain were a mere formality, with negligible results. There were also inspectors from the Royal Treasury who the viceroy sent to Melaka on exceptional occasions when serious anomalies were revealed in financial affairs. It appears that they were not sent after the final years of the 16th century as in 1599 Viceroy Dom Francisco da

---

[81] Royal letter to Viceroy D. João Coutinho, 1-2-1618, *DRI*, IV, p. 297. Also *see* the orders for the arrests of the captains João Caiado de Gamboa (already deceased at the time) and João da Silveira for offences against the bishop and other irregularities, 1-2-1618, HAG, *Livro Verde*, fl. 32, and royal letter to the same viceroy, 21-3-1619, *DRI*, VI, pp. 253–254.

[82] Some examples were Diogo Lobo (letter from Viceroy D. Francisco da Gama to the king, 1597, BN, *Res.*, cod. 1976, 20), Martim Afonso de Melo (ibid., fl. 19; royal letter to M. Afonso de Melo, 25-1-1601, AHU, *Cons. Ultr.*, cod. 282, fl. 32) and Pero Lopes de Sousa (royal letter to Viceroy Matias de Albuquerque, 26-2-1595, *APO*, III, part 2, p. 504); no complaints against this last captain are known.

Gama complained that he had been deprived of this instrument, which he considered the only effective way of containing the abuses of the captain of Melaka and his agents over the trade and revenues of the city.[83] In any case, the officials sent from Goa, who were strangers to the city and generally unfamiliar with the ways of everyday functioning, frequently came into conflict with the city's most important figures, especially the captains. The most notorious case was, once again, that of Captain Dom João da Gama who, in the light of the activities of the auditor Cosme de Ruão, proceeded in such a manner that orders were given for him to be immediately suspended and sent back to Lisbon; subsequently, explicit orders were issued to imprison him.[84] Likewise, orders were issued to imprison at least three other captains: Francisco da Silva de Meneses (1594–97), João Caiado de Gamboa (1615–16) and João da Silveira (1616–18).[85]

However, at a certain point, the power of the captains of Melaka began to decline. This was not due to measures on the part of the authorities in Goa or Lisbon, but rather to two distinct factors, which appear to be linked in a way. The first factor was an economic one: the post ceased to be one of the most lucrative offices of the Estado da Índia as its profitability gradually declined. With northern European competition in Southeast Asian waters, the process of the city's decline—which had already been

---

[83]   He stated that 'The irregularities committed by the captains and their factors are increasing' because written admonitions were not effective and the inquiries were limited to a mere record of the abuses and were unable to prevent them (letter from Viceroy D. Francisco da Gama to the king, 23-12-1599, BN, *Res.*, cod. 1975, fls. 297–297v.).

[84]   Royal letter to the viceroy, unknown date, AN/TT, *Cartas dos Vice-reis da Índia*, No. 41; Couto, *Da Ásia*, X, part 1, II, ix, pp. 211–212. This case took several years to be resolved because D. João was permitted to go to China in the meantime. The king ordered a new inquiry and his immediate arrest, admonishing the governor of India for his connivance in 'such a horrible, public and prolonged crime committed by the said D. João' (royal letter to Governor Manuel de Sousa Coutinho, 9-2-1589, HAG, *MonçReino*, 2A, fls. 48–48v.). *See* royal letter to the same governor, 6-2-1589, AHU, *Cons. Ultr.*, cod. 281, fls. 27v.–28.

[85]   On Silva de Meneses, *see* the royal letter to Viceroy D. Martim Afonso de Castro, *DRI*, I, pp. 41–42. About the other two figures, the royal letter to Viceroy D. João Coutinho, 1-2-1618, HAG, *Livro Verde*, fl. 32.

underway for some decades and had been aggravated by the tyranny of
the captains—was accelerated. Once its capacity to attract mercantile
communities had diminished, once it had lost control of and access to the
vast trade in spices that the Dutch gradually began to dominate, once some
of its most profitable routes had been lost, Portuguese navigation in the
region had become precarious and the shipping routes were no longer safe,
Melaka slowly collapsed. Melaka's revenues diminished, the city shrank,
the captains got fewer commodities (spices) to tax, confiscate or trade in.
Furthermore, even when attracting foreign merchants to Melaka became
an urgent question upon which the very survival of the city depended,
taking advantage of the enmities that the Dutch created throughout the
region, the abuses do not appear to have ceased. Similarly, it does not
seem that the markets began to function in a really free way.

In the meanwhile, another factor also needs to be analysed here, one
of a predominantly political nature: the 'militarisation' of Melaka, especially
after the arrival of the Dutch and the English, resulted in the creation of
a post that rivalled and eventually superseded the captain of the fortress:
the 'captain of the Sea of Melaka' or the 'general of the South' or other
titles that were used to designate the commander of an armada, with
exceptional powers, whose jurisdiction extended over the naval forces of
the region which were deployed in predefined missions or simply used
to watch over shipping. These figures, who initially appeared in well-
defined time periods, generally during moments of crisis or great military
undertakings, became permanent entities based in Melaka. They were
the ones who controlled the armadas, seized enemy vessels, guaranteed
the security of the city and of navigation, and they wielded a good deal
of power. Therefore the captain of the fortress saw himself relegated to
a secondary role, confined to a city that was undergoing a process of
isolation and decline. The captain had formerly derived his riches by
profiting from the goods that passed through the city or what he was
able to seize by force. Without an armada and without the port's former
traffic, the post was no longer profitable and was therefore no longer
in demand.

The armada of Matias de Albuquerque who, in 1576, set sail for
Melaka directly from Lisbon to re-establish the security of Portuguese
navigation in the Straits and deflect the threat posed by Aceh, was the
first instance of an exceptional power that rivalled the authority of the
captain of Melaka. It is not clear exactly what powers were bestowed
upon Albuquerque, but there is evidence of friction with the captain of

Melaka, Dom João da Gama.[86] This does not seem to have happened with the armada of Dom Paulo de Lima Pereira, undoubtedly for two reasons: the gravity of the situation attenuated any rivalries (even though one can nevertheless note the tension that prevailed between Dom Paulo de Lima Pereira and Dom António de Noronha), and the fact that the booty from the conquest of Johor, as well as the rewards that Philip I distributed, were sufficient to satisfy all concerned. The effectiveness of an armada sent to Melaka could be seriously compromised if there was any incompatibility between the captain of the fortress and the armada's commander and, thus, it was necessary to keep the name of the individual who then occupied the post of captain of Melaka in mind when making an appointment to this post.[87] However, till the turn of the century the post was somewhat of an appendage and was viewed as complementary to the figure of the captain of the fortress, who was the one who exercised power in the city in reality.

From the time of the great armadas of André Furtado de Mendonça (1601–03) and Viceroy Martim Afonso de Castro (1605–06) the picture changed substantially: Melaka and the commerce associated with the city, especially after the great scare of 1606, were in dire need of urgent and permanent vigilance and, thus, a commander of an armada to patrol the Straits and accompany the ships to China was appointed. Sometimes, when more ambitious undertakings were envisaged, these captains were provided with powers on par with those of the viceroy, with jurisdiction over Melaka and the city's officials, as happened in the case of André Furtado de Mendonça, and was once again contemplated in 1608. Although the specific post of 'captain of the Sea of Melaka' began to exist on a permanent basis, it was sometimes endowed with exceptional powers: this was what happened in 1610 with Manuel de Mascarenhas Homem, and the powers

---

[86] 'Vida e Acções de Mathias de Albuquerque ...', BN, *Res.*, cod. 482, fls. 22–23. A fragment of an *alvará* issued by Viceroy D. Luís de Ataíde refers to a dispute between Matias de Albuquerque, who had been sent to Melaka as captain-major of the sea and the captain of the city; *alvará* dated 28-8-1580, *APO*, V, part 3, pp. 970–972.

[87] In a report issued in 1603 or 1604 about the Estado da Índia's priorities, ex-Viceroy D. Francisco da Gama recommended that command of the fleet destined for Melaka be handed over to someone 'eager for honour' and a friend of the captain of the fortress (BM, *Add.* 28432, fl. 117).

given to this individual were considered to be excessive and unnecessary by the monarch himself.[88]

From some point during the 1610s these captains of the Sea of Melaka acquired authority over Melaka's soldiers, which meant that they supplanted the role of the captains of the fortress.[89] This evolution did not, however, take place without some hesitation. The king himself hesitated between subordinating the captain of the armada to the authority of the captain of Melaka or separating the two powers, with the former having complete jurisdiction over the armada and military questions and limiting the latter to matters of the fortress, which was what finally happened.[90] In practice, the captain of the armada put the captain of the fortress in the shade. In 1616 it was already acknowledged that the 'captain-general', as he came to be called, 'diminished the power and authority of the captains'.[91] The 'captain-general' thus became the leading figure of the city.

At this time the office was in the hands of António Pinto da Fonseca, who organised the city's defences, proceeded to arrange provisions and began new repairs on the walls of the fortress, as well as the construction of a fortress in the Ilha das Naus ('Carracks' Island'), facing Melaka. He did not, however, fail to come into conflict with the captain of the fortress, João Caiado de Gamboa.[92] Even control over the soldiers of the fortress now escaped the captain and was gradually absorbed by António Pinto da Fonseca, to whom the viceroy entrusted the entire defence of the city.[93] Melaka's impoverishment is also evident at the level of the more important posts: the office of captain-general remained in the hands of the same António Pinto da Fonseca for several years, a sign that it was not a coveted

---

[88]	Royal letter to Viceroy D. Jerónimo de Azevedo, 20-3-1613, *DRI*, II, p. 407.

[89]	*See*, for instance, the royal letter to Viceroy D. Jerónimo de Azevedo about Diogo de Mendonça Furtado (1613–16), 14-2-1615, *DRI*, III, p. 231, and the information provided by Bocarro about João Pinto de Morais (who was granted the office in 1614 but never occupied the post), *Década 13*, I, lxiv, p. 280.

[90]	Royal letter to Viceroy D. Jerónimo de Azevedo, 14-2-1615, *DRI*, III, p. 232, where these options are discussed by the king.

[91]	Silva and others, 'Lista de todas as Capitanias …', p. 349.

[92]	Letter from Viceroy D. João Coutinho to the king, 9-2-1619, *DRI*, IV, p. 315.

[93]	In 1618 a Spaniard was sent, 'A veteran soldier, to be a sergeant of those people', which clearly indicates that the captain was now a secondary figure; letter from Viceroy D. João Coutinho to the king, 9-2-1619, *DRI*, IV, p. 256.

office, and that of the captain of the fortress became so ineffectual that in 1633 nobody accepted the post, the viceroy being obliged to nominate and send a new captain from Goa.[94]

The city of Melaka also counted upon other political figures who, especially in the previous period, when the omnipresent domination of the captains tended to extend to all sectors, served to moderate or counterbalance their power. The most important of these was the bishop. An important player in the city's political balance, his margin for manoeuvre depended upon the charisma and individual prestige that he was able to establish. The first bishop, Friar Dom Jorge de Santa Luzia (1558–77), appears to have kept a low profile or, at least, acted with a certain degree of discretion. However, his prestige was sufficient to resolve a succession dispute for the captaincy in 1574.[95] In the same way, other bishops left the same image of acting with circumspection with regard to the city's affairs. Dom Gonçalo da Silva (1613–36) achieved some prominence. This can be appreciated as a result of a direct comparison with Dom João Ribeiro Gaio,[96] who was bishop between 1579 and 1601[97] and was, without doubt, the most important prelate in Melaka's history.

Dom João Ribeiro Gaio wielded profound influence over the city and was a leading figure in both political and military terms. It is enough to mention that he assumed the captaincy of Melaka, taking command of this post to defend the city during the siege of 1587, and exercised his office with remarkable courage and efficiency. His attitude and conduct, sometimes excessive, demonstrate his internal power and external prestige, which rivalled those of the captain himself. When the sultan of Johor

---

[94] Bocarro, 'Livro das Plantas ...', p. 31; this author says António Pinto da Fonseca held the post for more than 20 years and that his salary was triple (4,000 *xerafins*) the amount the captain received; ibid., pp. 15–16.

[95] This came about due to the death of Captain Francisco Henriques de Meneses, whose nomination of Tristão Vaz da Veiga as his successor was not accepted by other candidates (Sousa, *Oriente Conquistado* ..., p. 1089).

[96] A complete biography of this figure still does not exist. The latest work by Alves and Manguin (*O Roteiro das Cousas do Achem de D. João Ribeiro Gaio*) does not add significant new information, nor does it present a complete synthesis of known data.

[97] These dates, just like the ones with regard to other bishops, were taken from Teixeira, *The Portuguese Missions in Melaka and Singapore*, I.

appeared in Melaka in January 1587, he went to the bishop with proposals for peace in order to create divisions within the city.[98] When the English arrived in eastern Java in 1558, they wrote letters—undoubtedly on the advice of the Portuguese they contacted—to Captain Dom Diogo Lobo, but also to the bishop, which reflects the political parity that prevailed at this time.[99] His prestige in the sultanates was also clearly evident: at the end of the century, just like the captain, the bishop wrote letters of recommendation to the sultan of Johor.[100] In both political and economic terms, the bishop behaved in an identical manner to the captains.

Just like other members of the administration, he had important interests in the spice trade which were exempt from the payment of duties at the customs house,[101] a fact that leads one to infer that this would have been done in agreement with the captains. The dissolution of morals was a fact that does not seem to have bothered him, in much the same way as his predecessor. The officials of the inquisition in Goa became aware of this and requested that his jurisdiction over the affairs of the inquisition be withdrawn and entrusted to the Visitors of the Holy Office.[102] The way in which he intervened in secular issues earned him great enmity, especially from the auditors who periodically arrived in the city from Goa. In 1587, when he was also at the helm of the captaincy, and even later, Dom João Ribeiro Gaio reached the zenith of his power, being, during this period, the great authority of the city and was 'empowered with all the jurisdiction of His Majesty, and uses it along with his ecclesiastical authority as he wishes'.[103]

---

[98] Couto, *Da Ásia*, X, part 2, VIII, xv, pp. 365–366.

[99] Letter from D. João Ribeiro Gaio to the king, 31-12-1588, AGS, *Secr. Prov.*, book 1551, fl. 406 (*see* Document Appendix, No. 6).

[100] Jacques de Coutre, 'Vida de ...', p. 104.

[101] *Alvará* by Viceroy Matias de Albuquerque, 22-4-1596, HAG, *Regimentos e Instruções*, 2, fl. 135v.

[102] 'There has been no arrest nor even a denunciation sent from China or Melaka to this Court for many years; it is well-known that those parts are on fire'; letter from the inquisitor Rui Sodrinho to the inquisitor-general, Goa, 24-12-1585 in Baião (ed.), *A Inquisição de Goa*, II, p. 102.

[103] Letter from the *ouvidor*, Duarte Borges Miranda, 17-12-1588, AGS, *Secr. Prov.*, book 1551, fls. 469v.-470. He describes the abuses committed by the bishop, namely presiding over summary judgements and not respecting the decisions of the court; imposing heavy pecuniary penalties; and controlling the city with the

Excommunication was one of his chief weapons, which he used with-out reservation or clemency[104] and was especially applied to the auditors. Just the threat of using it was generally enough to keep the captains at a respectful distance and permissiveness.[105] Dom Ribeiro Gaio himself suggests having excommunicated the captain of Tidore on account of an offence that this individual committed against the vicar and visitor of the fortress.[106] The constant conflicts that he provoked earned him ever-increasing hostility from various sectors and ended up permeating the captain himself, who was not immune from excommunication. The bishop did excommunicate Francisco da Silva de Meneses (captain of Melaka, 1594–97) and his successors who perpetrated abuses over merchants and appropriated the spice trade.[107] During his captaincy, the bishop ordered

---

complicity of the captains. This official disturbed this *status quo* and the local residents mutinied against him. The bishop was accused of causing 'disputes and disorders' against even D. Paulo de Lima Pereira (letter from Viceroy D. Duarte de Meneses to the king, AGS, *Secr. Prov.*, book 1551, fl. 558v.; copy of the same letter in fls. 295–302).

[104] In 1588 the same *ouvidor* arrested a nephew of the bishop for having murdered a nobleman; he got timid support from the captain and both were excommunicated by the bishop (letter quoted in previous note, fl. 471). In 1596 Viceroy Matias de Albuquerque sent his officers to put an end to the abuses committed in the customs house of Melaka despite the risk of excommunication by the bishop (*alvará* quoted in note 101, fl. 136); in 1598 the king was informed that the bishop had excommunicated officials and inhabitants of Melaka and asked the viceroy to put an end to the situation (royal letter to Viceroy D. Francisco da Gama, 10-3-1598, *APO*, III, part 2, p. 853).

[105] Letter from the *ouvidor* quoted in previous notes, fls. 469v.-470. One of the most scandalous cases from his point of view was the bishop's tolerance of Hindu rituals, described as follows: 'I was informed that some Kelings of this fortress [of Melaka] performed a certain pagan ceremony, so I registered it in an official record, questioned some witnesses and then ordered their arrest. After they were sent to prison, [the bishop] ordered my excommunication and fines of a thousand *cruzados*, to release them immediately ...; João da Silva, who was the captain at the time, feared the bishop and ordered that the Kelings be released.'

[106] Letter quoted in note 99 above, fl. 412.

[107] Treatise about the trade of Melaka, *circa* 1600, AN/TT, *MssLiv.* 805, fl. 163v., in Lobato, *Política e Comércio dos Portugueses no Mundo Malaio-Indonésio* (thesis), Ap. VI, p. 454.

that a procurator (*procurador do número*) be imprisoned. However, his orders were not obeyed; on the contrary, armed by the captain and other officials (and possibly counting upon the connivance of the *casados*), the latter surrounded the bishop's residence and attempted to imprison and deport him, the excommunication orders uttered against him being of no avail.[108]

In 1596 Dom João Ribeiro Gaio was to be found in Goa, requesting (apparently for the second time) that he be allowed to renounce the post and seeking authorisation to return to Portugal via Manila. The king expressly forbade him the latter request[109] but, at the same time, placed the case before the viceroy and the Archbishop of Goa.[110] From the time of his return to Melaka until his definitive departure, his actions were marked by constant conflicts, especially with the auditors. Shortly thereafter—in 1596 or 1597—supported by the city's clergy, he thwarted an official inquiry about trade with the Philippines.[111] These conflicts were replete with convoluted episodes: in the same year, when an attempt was made to imprison a woman who lived with him, the bishop responded with a mob, trying to free the prisoner at all costs and persecuting the auditor, who was obliged to seek refuge in the captain's fortress.[112]

---

[108] Royal letter to Viceroy D. Francisco da Gama, 11-3-1598, *APO*, III, part 2, p. 867; *see* also AN/TT, *MiscMssCGL*, box 3, vol. VI L, pp. 9–12.

[109] Royal letter to the bishop of Melaka, 12-2-1597, AN/TT, *CorCron*, part 1, pack 114, doc. 2.

[110] Letter from Viceroy D. Francisco da Gama, 1597, BN, *Res.*, cod. 1976, fl. 12; royal letter to the same viceroy, 12-2-1597, AN/TT, *CorCron*, part 1, pack 114, doc. 2.

[111] Royal letter to Viceroy D. Francisco da Gama, 10-3-1598, *APO*, III, part 2, p. 826.

[112] Her name was Isabel Ferreira and the *ouvidor* was ordered by the archbishop to take her in chains to Goa; letter from *ouvidor* Domingos Toscano to the king, 24-2-1597, *APO*, III, part 2, pp. 868–869 (the fragment of the letter referring to this episode is not identified in *APO*, but by comparing it with a copy in BN, *Res.*, cod. 1975, fl. 338 one may conclude that it is actually part of the letter). Also *see* a royal letter to Viceroy D. Francisco da Gama, 21-1-1599, AN/TT, *MiscMssCGL*, box 3, vol. VI L, p. 457, referring to 'some indecencies' of the case. Oddly enough, Teixeira says that this episode took place in Goa (*The Portuguese Missions* ..., I, p. 186).

In 1597 or 1598 Dom João Ribeiro Gaio appears to have left for Goa.[113] The bishop intended to return to Portugal, but demanded diverse emoluments for this, alleging the many expenses that he bore while he discharged his post as well as the expensive living costs in Melaka. Amongst the demands he claimed in order to return to Portugal one can find the payment of debts owed to him by the royal exchequer and the concession of 30 *bares* of cloves from the Moluccas.[114] At this time he was undoubtedly of a fairly advanced age, although his date of birth is not known. His obstinacy ended up causing great irritation in Goa, where the viceroy voiced the following opinion:

> 'The bishop of Melaka, on account of his advanced age, is so decrepit, that while I tried to persuade him to embark for Portugal, in conformance with a letter that I received from Your Majesty and the archbishop also tried to get him to do the same, he resolved not to do so unless he was given eighteen thousand *pardaus* in money and benefits and other things ... the bishop of China died in October 1597, and as for the bishop of Melaka, it would have been better not to have had him due to his many impertinent acts, which are insufferable, apart from having antagonised almost all the residents of that city....'[115]

Dom João Ribeiro Gaio never returned to Portugal. It is possible that he died in Goa in 1601; however, one can find information that would

---

[113] Teixeira (ibid.) refers to the first date, but the second is also plausible. There is not a single document stating clearly that the bishop had left Melaka for Goa. The best clue is provided by Fr. Gabriel de San Antonio, who travelled from Manila to Melaka in February 1598 and did not find the bishop in the city when he arrived there ('Breve y Verdadera Relacion ...', p. 89).

[114] In 1601 the king clearly refused his claims, saying it would be tantamount 'to paying fantastic wages'; royal letter to the bishop of Melaka, 25-1-1601, AHU, *Cons. Ultr.*, cod. 282, fl. 41v. D. João Ribeiro Gaio was also in debt to the Crown, namely to the tune of 2,000 *cruzados* of the Crusade bull that he had kept for himself (*see* the copies of letters from Viceroy D. Francisco da Gama to the king, 1597 [?], BN, *Res.*, cod. 1976, fl. 77v., and royal letter, 12-2-1597, quoted in note 110 above).

[115] Letter from Viceroy D. Francisco da Gama to the governor of Portugal, Miguel de Moura, 28-12-1599. BN, *Res.*, cod. 1975, fls. 239v.–240. *See* royal letter to Viceroy Aires de Saldanha, 15-1-1601, AHU, *Cons. Ultr.*, cod. 282, fl. 22.

indicate that he returned to Melaka during the monsoon of 1600.[116] His obstinacy in returning via Manila would seem to confirm the interests he held there. There is no doubt that he did not comply with the prohibition on commerce with these islands while he was bishop. In any case, with his death the situation of the diocese went into a rapid decline until the arrival of the new bishop in 1605.[117]

The *casados* constituted another political nucleus, another power that one must not overlook or underestimate. The 'Portuguese' of Melaka, who at this time were, above all, *mestiços* of mixed blood, formed the backbone of the city, although in both political and economic terms they were frequently surpassed by the captain. However, the *casados* were the ones who dominated the city with their networks of family members, dependants and slaves. They ensured the city's defence at a time when the soldiers stationed there were few, undisciplined and badly paid. This happened during the siege of 1568, when the slaves played an exceedingly important role.[118] Likewise, during the crisis of 1587, which was particularly difficult for Melaka in many aspects, it was the *casados*, under the bishop's orders,

---

[116] Teixeira refers to 1601 and Goa as the date and place of his death (*The Portuguese Missions ...*, I, p. 188). Teófilo Aparicio-López mentions an interesting piece of information. He says that the bishop was the godfather of a converted Muslim prince whose baptism took place in Goa on 17 April 1601 ('La Orden de San Agustín en la India...', Pt 1, p. 689). There is a version of a letter by D. João Ribeiro Gaio himself which has inherent contradictions: the letter informs the king that he had returned to Melaka but is dated Goa, 30 April 1600. I am grateful to Dr Martine van Ittersum who kindly sent me this letter. The closest coeval information referring to the death of the bishop is a royal letter to Viceroy Aires de Saldanha (15-2-1603, AHU, *Cons. Ultr.*, cod. 282, fl. 109v.).

[117] One finds mention of the fact that the diocese was 'governed by foolish clerics who set a bad example, due to which there are many scandals'; royal letter to Viceroy Aires de Saldanha, 15-2-1603, AHU, *Cons. Ultr.*, cod. 282, fl. 130.

[118] António Pinto Pereira says the Portuguese 'made great use of the slaves, and the presence of the lords gave them more courage than their disposition and nature gave them'; he then acknowledges that despite all the difficulties suffered in the course of the siege, 'With the service and help of the slaves, and continuous and immense efforts on the part of all, they always put up a far stronger resistance than one could expect from a large garrison in such a site, and so weak'; *História da Índia...*, p. [234].

who checked Johor's advance, and financed and played an important role in the city's defences. Dom Paulo de Lima's expedition only struck the final blow. Similarly, during the siege of 1606 and Aceh's attack in 1615, the *casados* played a fundamental role. Their military and defensive functions, which became increasingly well known, shall be discussed below. For now, one only needs to mention that this defensive function was associated with another role, a political and diplomatic one. On account of their knowledge and their contacts in the world in which Melaka was integrated, the *casados* were a privileged channel of communication with neighbouring sultanates. At this time the influence of non-Christian communities had tended to diminish, and even their supposed representatives—the *bendara* and the *tomungão*—were *casados*, converted Hindus in the case of the former and Portuguese or individuals of mixed blood in the case of the latter, as we shall see below.

The *casados* represented local interests, which generally conflicted with those of outside elements who came from Portugal, be they captains, administrative officials or auditors. They faced the same abuses as those suffered by Asians, and for this reason their complaints to the king were sent in the name of Christians and heathens alike.[119] One of the most important requests, which was granted by the king although he queried its real application, was that of electing *casados* to official posts—generally in the hands of the captain's retainers and henchmen—in the administration of the city.[120] Their constant complaints to the king reflect the rapacious actions of the captains, but can also be viewed as the reaction of a group that perceived itself to be under threat and hindered in his privileges, power and freedom of movement.

The control they wielded over the city's supplies has already been mentioned: they exercised this in an effective manner and putting an end

---

[119] Royal instructions to Viceroy D. Duarte de Meneses, 10-3-1584, AN/TT, *Fundo Português da Bibl. Nac. de Paris*, No. 48 (*see* Document Appendix, No. 2); soon after, Bishop D. João Ribeiro Gaio alerted the king to the fact that even the *casados* were gradually moving away from the city because of the extortion they suffered (letter to the king, 31-12-1588, fl. 413 (*see* Document Appendix, No. 6).

[120] Ibid., fls. 10v.–11; royal letter to Viceroy D. Duarte de Meneses, 11-2-1585, *APO*, III, part 1, pp. 39–40 (also published in *DHMPPO/Insulíndia*, V, p. 35).

to their abuses proved to be a difficult task.[121] This sometimes became very useful, especially when the Dutch competition obliged armadas to constantly be sent to the 'Southern Parts', which frequently arrived in Melaka badly equipped and provisioned. In such cases, the *casados*, making obvious profits, proceeded to provide the ships with supplies, as happened with the armada of André Furtado de Mendonça.[122] They did not hesitate to exercise their power against anyone who threatened their privileges: once again, the auditors were prominent opponents. The most serious case was undoubtedly the assassination, under the protection of the captain—which proves how their interests did not always clash—of the auditor (*ouvidor*) António Marques Ribeiro, who was sent to Melaka in 1598 to ascertain the veracity of alleged abuses against the bishop.[123] The case was investigated, but without any conclusive results.[124]

During the 17th century, accompanying the city's evolution, the *casados* of Melaka became impoverished on account of the decline and fragmentation of Portuguese trade. They particularly felt the ruinous effects of the siege of 1606, which devastated their vegetable gardens and palm groves.[125] The minor commerce that supplied the city, very often in collusion with the interests of neighbouring sultanates, remained in their hands, which explains their remarkable resistance in the face of increasing

---

[121] Jacques de Coutre stated, 'There is no justice against them; they are all relatives and mates' ('Vida de …', pp. 423–424). *Ouvidor* António Barreto da Silva was also aware of this situation in 1613 (Bocarro, *Década 13*, I, xlvi, p. 195). *See* document quoted in note 40, above.

[122] The king expressed his gratitude for their 'readiness and efficiency'; royal letter to the city of Melaka, 23-3-1604, AHU, *Cons. Ultr.*, cod. 282, fls. 221v.–222.

[123] This episode is described by Fr. Gabriel de San Antonio, whose own life was endangered by the conspiracies of the *casados* and by the attacks made on the Dominican convent, where the *ouvidor* sought refuge ('Breve y Verdadera Relacion …, pp. 92–98).

[124] *Ouvidor* Julião de Campos Barreto went to Melaka to conduct a judicial inquiry against Captain Martim Afonso de Melo, and to investigate the charges against him. Later, the *ouvidor* himself was the subject of an inquiry about his actions and wages which may suggest that, unlike his predecessor, he eventually got involved with local interests (judicial proceedings against Julião de Campos Barreto, 8-11-1615. AHU, *Índia*, box 3, doc. 140).

[125] *See* the sources mentioned in chapter 3, note 108.

difficulties. Their internal power inevitably grew, due to the isolation for which the city was progressively destined. The decline of the power of the captains seems to have reinforced the strength of the *casados*, who became equally responsible for the depredation wrought upon the merchants, to such an extent that the viceroy even requested that Melaka's city council be abolished due to the abuses that were committed.[126] It appears that this process had already been completed in the 1630s. The post of captain was no longer desirable and had already been totally eclipsed by the 'captain-general' who, however, had lived in Melaka for over twenty years and, thus, could scarcely be differentiated from the *casados*. In fact, as the city was isolated, whoever lived there was in command, and Bocarro highlights this fact: the *casados* dominated the city with their slaves, all of whom were well armed, and their aggressiveness did not fail to arouse his admiration. After falling into Dutch hands, the Commissary Justus Schouten reported an identical conclusion.[127]

The Bendara and the Tomungão

The history of these two offices during the period under study merits special attention and individual treatment. The little information available which pertains especially to the preceding period can be found in diverse articles.[128] As already mentioned, the former office, which designated a kind

---

[126] 'The men suitable for government offices are very few and they are usually the same, and with the power of their offices they greatly vex the people'; he also stated that in Diu, as in Melaka, there were 4,000–5,000 Gentiles, who gradually moved away from both cities because of the abuses they suffered at the hands of the Portuguese; letter from Viceroy D. Jerónimo de Azevedo to the king, 23-12-1613, HAG, *MonçReino*, 12, fl. 66v. (published in *BOGEI*, No. 54 (1883), p. 216).

[127] 'In all occasions of war they are ready and diligent, most of them looking for a way to earn a living and take so many risks that they stick a *kris* into someone's belly at the slightest provocation' (Bocarro, 'Livro das Plantas ...', p. 15). Schouten wrote in his report that the Portuguese garrison consisted of 260 men, 'but the Portuguese mestics and the native inhabitants in all about two to three thousand formed the best fighting men for the defence' (Schouten's report in Leupe, 'The Siege and Capture of Malacca', p. 87).

[128] *See* note 45, above. About the *bendahara*, *see* Pinto, 'Purse and Sword: D. Henrique *Bendahara* and Portuguese Melaka in the late 16th century'.

of Prime Minister of the sultanate of Melaka (as in other sultanates), had been transformed by Afonso de Albuquerque into a representative of the city's gentile elements and handed over to Nina Chatu, a leading merchant of the Keling community and a valuable ally of the Portuguese during the period of the conquest of the city. The latter who, similarly, had been responsible for the city's security prior to 1511, now exercised jurisdiction over the Moors of Melaka, and was handed over to a Muslim from Luzón.[129] An initial analysis of this panorama highlights the predominant role of the Keling community as the *bendara* had more privileges (the hereditary nature of the post) and double the pay of the *tomungão*, that is, 100$000 and 50$000, being the fourth most well-paid functionary in the city, after the bishop, the captain and the factor.[130]

However, over the course of the 16th century, these offices underwent various changes: with the decline in the number of foreign merchants in Melaka and the reversal of the policy that initially favoured them to the detriment of the Portuguese, these posts, especially the *bendara*, lost their former prominent function. The orders of Dom Antão de Noronha, in 1564, stipulated the wages of all the officials of the city, but did not mention either of the two posts in question. Likewise, the 'Tombo do Estado da Índia' by Simão Botelho (1554) does not refer to these offices.[131] They did not disappear, but their jurisdiction became increasingly diluted and sometimes even confused. The budget for 1574 calls the *bendara* the 'administrator of the local people' and the *tomungão* the 'chief-justice of the local people', but does not go into specifics with regard to either of the two posts.[132] However, after a period of a certain lack of definition or

---

[129] According to Thomaz, 'Indian Merchant …', p. 60 and 'Les Portugais dans les Mers de l'Archipel', pp. 115–116. Castanheda refers to an *ulama* ('um caciz') (*História do Descobrimento e Conquista* …, I, p. 682), and Barros mentions a Javanese called 'Utimutiraja' (*Ásia*, II, pte. 2ª, VI, vi, p. 84).

[130] *See*, for instance, Jean Aubin (ed.) 'Le Orçamento do Estado da Índia …', p. 271.

[131] Pissurlencar (ed.), *Regimentos das Fortalezas da Índia*, pp. 245–255; Botelho, 'Tombo do Estado da Índia', pp. 108–111.

[132] Jean Aubin (ed.), 'Le Orçamento do Estado da Índia …' (also in Godinho, *Les Finances de l'État Portugais* …, p. 329). Other sources are vague about the functions of the offices; for instance, the report 'Despezas da fortaleza de Malaca', date unknown, refers to the *bendara* only as the 'captain of local people' (*DHMPPO/Insulíndia*, V, p. 254).

even overlapping of their authority, they ended up having clearly distinct jurisdictions.

Let us begin with the *bendara*. Nina Chatu's tenure came to a tragic end, and he was replaced by the king of Kampar, who suffered a similar fate, partially due to the pressure brought to bear by Nina Chatu's sons. In 1564 the *bendara*, probably a grandson of Nina Chatu, converted to Christianity, entrusting the education of his son to the care of the College of the Jesuits.[133] It was a sign of the times, an indication that pressure of a religious nature was already clearly evident. From this moment onwards, the distinction between the *bendara*, as the representative of the Keling community, and the *casados* of Melaka, as the 'Portuguese' component, which had been very clear prior to this, became increasingly smaller. Most probably it was the *bendara* called Dom João, who died in the siege by Aceh in 1573 while defending Upeh from an enemy disembarkation.[134] The individual who appeared as *bendara* in the siege of the subsequent year, this time by Japara, was already another figure called Dom Henrique.

This one was, without doubt, a notable figure who left his mark on life in the city for more than a decade, during the crisis of 1585–87. He was neither Keling nor Malay, but a member of the royal family of Tidore and also related to the royal house of Ternate. He was a Muslim, whose original name was 'Cachil Labuzaza'.[135] During the 1550s, according to Diogo do Couto, he had been a tenacious enemy of the Portuguese in the Moluccas and had distinguished himself on the battlefield for his skills and courage.[136] The date of his conversion to Christianity is not

---

[133] Thomaz, 'Indian Communities …', p. 64, note 41.

[134] Couto, *Da Ásia*, IX, xvii, p. 123; Lemos, 'Hystoria dos Cercos …', fl. 7. This D. João was not the *bendara* who became a Christian in 1564 but his son. His successor, D. Henrique, was asked to take the office because the son of D. João was still a child at the time.

[135] Portuguese sources are not unanimous with regard to these events. Despite the most common version by Diogo do Couto and others (*see* the next note), one source refers to the existence of this personage, a relative of the ruler of Tidore, saying he was in Melaka when Aires de Saldanha was captain (1576–79), which does not match the common version presented here ('Acção de Gonçalo Pereira Marramaque', *DHMPPO/Insulíndia*, IV, p. 472).

[136] Couto, *Da Ásia*, VII, part 1, IV, vii, pp. 332–333 identifies this character with D. Henrique; this author describes his exploits in VII, part 1, V, iii, pp. 362–366,

known, but can be dated to between 1563 and 1568, during the regency of Cardinal Dom Henrique, and he then received the insignia of the Order of Christ.[137] In any case, in 1574 he was to be found in Melaka, holding the posts of *bendara* and *xabandar*,[138] where he participated in the defence of the city and gave ample proof of his military abilities.[139] The choice of Dom Henrique to exercise this post, towards which he seemed to be little inclined (being a converted Muslim chosen to head a community of Hindus), can be understood in two ways: in the first place, the urgency of the military situation of the city that had suffered successive attacks and needed a captain who had proved himself and would assist in organising the city's defences; and secondly, the opportunity to gratify the sultans of Tidore, whose support the Portuguese were now trying to win after the revolt in Ternate in 1570.[140] Dom Henrique married—on an unknown date, but perhaps in 1579, when he went to Goa—a Christian granddaughter of Ali bin Yusuf Adil Khan, called 'Mealecão' by the Portuguese, an exiled prince of Bijapur, and at the time received a dowry from the Crown.[141]

During the 1580s Dom Henrique became a central figure in Melaka and achieved great fame. As early as 1577, in the celebrated battle that

---

referring to the way he was seriously injured and defeated by the Portuguese. *See* also 'A Capitania de Amboino' (anonymous text presumably written by A. Bocarro) in *DHMPPO/Insulíndia*, IV, p. 272, and letter from A. Monserrate, 26-10-1579, *DM*, II, p. 44.

[137] H. Jacobs refers to 1572–73 (*DM*, ibid., note 11); *see* Couto, *Da Ásia*, VIII, part 1, IV, vii, p. 333.

[138] Port-master.

[139] Lemos, 'Hystoria dos Cercos ...', fl. 44v.

[140] Thomaz, 'Indian Merchant ...', p. 64; *De Ceuta a Timor* ('Nina Chatu e o Comércio Português em Malaca'), p. 507.

[141] 'Dom Henrique Bendara of Melaka is paid an annuity of 20,000 *reis*, granted to him by our lord the king with the habit of [the Order of] Christ; he also receives 60,000 *reis* each year, that 'Mamedequão', son of 'Mealequão', gave to him as a dowry with his daughter.' *Receita e Despesa do Estado da Índia*, unknown date [probably 1580s], AHU, *Cons. Ultr.*, cod. 500, fl. 58v; also *see* the letter from António Monserrate quoted in note 136, above. About Ali bin Yusuf Adil Khan, *see* Subrahmanyam, 'Notas sobre um rei congelado'.

Matias de Albuquerque engaged in with the armada from Aceh, Dom Henrique was present and captured five ships loaded with pepper.[142] In Aceh's raid against Melaka in 1582, he once again played a prominent role.[143] At this point, news of his services had already reached Lisbon. The king began by advising the viceroy to reward his actions in battle in some way,[144] but ended up granting him a series of royal favours a few years later: two voyages of the Moluccas, two voyages of the Coromandel coast for his son João Henriques and the post of captain of the stockade of Melaka (*capitão da tranqueira*), with a salary of 80$000.[145] During the crisis of 1585–87 with Johor, Dom Henrique was once again at the frontline of the city's defences, defending the stockade of Upeh against the attacks of Sultan Ali Jalla.[146] After Dom Paulo de Lima's expedition, he was successful in actions against the sultanate's attempts at renewed fortification, services for which the king thanked him personally.[147]

It seems certain that Dom Henrique did not bequeath the office to one of his descendants. On the contrary, the post returned to the hands of the line of Nina Chatu, which had been interrupted in 1573 with the death of Dom João. Dom Henrique held the post on an exceptional basis, only while Dom João's son attained the necessary age to be able to discharge the office himself. In 1587 King Philip I confirmed him in the post of *bendara*, 'To which he was elected upon the death of Dom João Leal Bendara, and that he serve in it until the son of the said Dom João is of age to serve it, and he will avail of all the advantages and benefits.'[148]

---

[142] 'Vida e Acções de Mathias de Albuquerque', BN, Res., cod. 482, fl. 17v. (*see* Document Appendix, No. 1).

[143] Couto, *Da Ásia*, X, part 1, III, ii, pp. 273–274.

[144] Royal letter to Viceroy D. Duarte de Meneses, 10-1-1587, *APO*, III, part 1, p. 75 (also published in *DHMPPO/Insulíndia*, V, pp. 46–60).

[145] AN/TT, *Chancelaria de Filipe I*, Doações, book 18, fls. 21, 21v. and 22, respectively.

[146] Couto, *Da Ásia*, X, part 2, VIII, xv, pp. 367–369. This chronicler also mentions the exploits of his son, D. Pedro.

[147] Royal letters to D. Henrique Bendara, 7-3-1590 and 20-12-1590, AHU, *Cons. Ultr.*, cod. 281, fls. 87v. and 133v., respectively, and to Diogo Lobo, captain of Melaka, ibid., fl. 132v.

[148] Royal letter to D. Henrique Bendara, 21-11-1587, AN/TT, *Chancelaria de Filipe I*, Doações, book 18, fls. 21v.–22.

In 1588 or 1589 this son had attained the necessary age, and Dom Henrique prepared to leave office, writing to the king complaining of his misery, reminding him of his services and requesting royal favours.[149] The individual who appeared as *bendara* in 1613, when Erédia wrote his 'Declaraçam de Malaca', was a certain Dom Fernando Leal, who this author confirms as being a descendant of the first *bendara*.[150] All things considered, it seems probable that this was the son who had been left an orphan by Dom João's death in 1573. In 1616 this Dom Fernando still held the post,[151] but by 1620 he had already died, and the story was repeated. Paulo Fernandes, born in Melaka, was appointed to hold the office, 'To have it and serve while the orphaned son of Dom Fernando Leal, on account of whose death the said post became vacant, is not of age to serve in person.'[152] In this way the hereditary nature of the office attributed to Nina Chatu was respected, having only been interrupted by exceptional circumstances.

Nothing more is known about the evolution of the *bendara* of Melaka. The office already had functions that were different from those initially attributed to the post. As seen above, the sources sometimes refer to

---

[149] 'Seeing that, this year I will leave the office of *bendara* which I served and from which I met my needs, because it will go to the son of Dom João Leal, whose post it is'; letter from D. Henrique Bendara to the king, 16-12-1588, AGS, *Secr. Prov.*, book 1551, fls. 524–524v. (*see* Document Appendix, No. 5).

[150] Erédia, 'Declaraçam de Malaca …', fl. 42; this author fails in the following two details: he says this D. Fernando ('Leal', like his father) was a grandson of the first *bendara* (he was actually his great-grandson to all appearances), and says this one had converted to Christianity during the time of Afonso de Albuquerque (in fact this happened only in 1564).

[151] Silva *et al.*, 'Lista de todas as Capitanias …', p. 351. In this report he is incorrectly mentioned as 'Dom Fernando Leal, Christian from the Moluccas', which would hint at him being a descendant of D. Henrique. Based on this information, Manuel Lobato suggests that he could have been the son of D. Henrique and a daughter or granddaughter of the *bendara* who had converted to Christianity (*Política e Comércio*, p. 80, note 88).

[152] He was duty bound to provide for the said orphan; HAG, *Mercês Gerais*, 2, fl. 260. This Paulo Fernandes was also the 'interpreter of the *chinchéus*' (*see* note 57, above).

the post in a vague manner, as the 'captain of the local people'[153] or similar terms. The appointment of Dom Henrique clearly questions the representative nature of the *bendara* with regard to the Keling community. At the beginning of the 1580s this divorce appeared to be fairly evident.[154] At this point the function of the post already seems to have been rather vague and diffused, possibly varying with the profile and characteristics of each personage: with Dom Henrique, the military function, with the organisation of the city's defences along with the *casados*, is well known; with Paulo Fernandes, and perhaps already with Dom Fernando Leal, the diplomatic function associated with that of being an interpreter would prevail.[155] The specific jurisdiction as a representative of the Keling community was diminished, and the post now seemed to avail of a vague power over the city's mercantile communities, from whence it reaped its profits, given that the office was generally clubbed together with the function of *xabandar* or port-master.[156] In this manner, in 1616 it was still defined as the 'Judge of the Keling community from the Coromandel coast' and after the Dutch conquest it was described as the governor 'for the foreign Indians who came to Malacca and lived together as a large group'.[157]

In 1622 an attempt was made to abolish the post that, at the time, was considered to be the 'head of the Malays', probably in reference to Paulo Fernandes. At this point the *bendara* (or rather, this *bendara*) was a kind of intermediary between Melaka and Johor, being very well accepted by the sultan; he was also his ambassador in the city and hosted the Malays

---

[153] As mentioned in the budget of 1612, still with a salary of 100$000; BN, *Res.*, cod. 11410, fl. 120.

[154] The Kelings complained directly to the king about the extortion they suffered and made several requests but there is no mention of their alleged representative, the *bendara*; *see* the Royal instructions quoted in note 119, above, fls. 11v.–12v.

[155] Despite the fact that in 1612 the office of *bendara* was quite distinct from the one described as 'interpreter and translator of the letters the kings send to the captain', which had a salary of 15$120 (Budget of 1612, BN, *Res.*, cod. 11410, fl. 120).

[156] Silva *et al.*, 'Lista das Capitanias ...' (1616) says this office had a salary of 800 *xerafins* if exercised along with the one of *xabandar* (p. 351).

[157] Ibid.; Schouten's report in Leupe, 'The Siege and Capture of Malacca', p. 98.

who passed through the city at his residence. This had its advantages and benefits: he was a privileged source of information about Johor and a valuable instrument to exert pressure on other sultanates. However, at the same time there was a risk that this power could result in a double game, and that he could become an agent of Johor in Melaka. Nevertheless, the abolishment was postponed.[158]

Let us now discuss the *tomungão*. The evolution of this office took place parallel to that of the *bendara* although, from the very outset it had been of lesser importance. As mentioned, the post was created by Afonso de Albuquerque, adapted from the Malay *tumenggung*, to head the Muslim community, having been handed over to a Moor from Luzón called 'Aregimute Raja'.[159]

---

[158] This information is mentioned in two letters from Governor Fernão de Albuquerque to the king, dated 18-2-1622 and 20-2-1622, published in *DRI*, VII, pp. 393 and 407, respectively. Both say the office had no jurisdiction at the time and, 'only acts as a mediator of the foreigners in their affairs with the captain of that fortress and the other ministers and officials that Your Majesty has there, in which affairs the said foreigners obtained great profits and no vexation ...; the man who serves in the office was very well received by the king of Johor and by his procurator in that city; so I sent him as an ambassador with a letter from Your Majesty and another written by myself trying to persuade him to reject the intentions of his father-in-law, the king of Jambi, who was trying to promote an agreement between him and the Dutch, and for this purpose and other very important matters this man was very useful there; the bishop also wrote to me with similar information ...'. It is interesting to note that the governor worried about possible implications as the *bendara* 'is a local and it is an ancient and important office of the city'. This distrust was intensified by the news of the treason committed by a *bendara* and 'because justice has already been made there to one of them, for a breach of loyalty'. This is probably an odd and vague reference to Raja Abdullah, king of Kampar, who succeeded Nina Chatu and was *bendara* from 1514 to 1515. *See* Thomaz, *De Ceuta a Timor* ('Nina Chatu e o Comércio Português em Malaca'), p. 505.

[159] *See* note 129, above. João de Barros mentions 'Utimutiraja' as the leader of the Muslims of Melaka but does not refer to the office of *tomungão*. Shortly thereafter he refers to this office ('tamungo'), saying it was 'almost like the port-master', and mentions that the individual who was serving in this office was 'Tuan Mohamed Tamungo of Melaka, a trustworthy man' (*Ásia*, II, part 2, IX, iii, p. 345 and iv, p. 357).

Unlike the case of the *bendara*, we cannot trace the succession of individuals who held the post of *tomungão*; from the very beginning it was a minor office, which evidently was because the Muslim community—unlike the Kelings—had never had a leading role in the internal history of Portuguese Melaka. There was also no 'Dom Henrique *tomungão*' whose feats would be registered in the chronicles. Just as in the case of the *bendara*, the functions of the *tomungão* were now also confused. In 1551 the *bendara* was still the 'governor' of the Keling community, and the *tomungão* that of the 'natives'; both participated in the defence of the city.[160] However, during the siege of 1568 Couto does not mention the *bendara*, and a careful reading of his writings seems to reveal that the *tomungão* would have had authority over the Keling community.[161] It was also at this time that both offices appear to have had jurisdiction over the 'people of the land'.[162] This period of a lack of definition coincides precisely with the transformation of Melaka into a 'Portuguese' city, with a growth in the number of converts and an increase in the power of the *casados* over foreign mercantile communities.

In 1585, at the beginning of the conflict with Johor, a certain 'Dom Sebastião Tamugão', of unknown origin but who probably converted during the reign of King Sebastião, given the name he had adopted, held the post. In that year the captain of Melaka, João da Silva Pereira, sent him to Johor as ambassador.[163] The office undoubtedly declined in importance as a few years later, the bishop would request that it be abolished.[164] Probably whoever held the office at the time did not distinguish himself in military battles like Dom Henrique Bendara. This lack of definition did not last very long: at an unknown date, the *tomungão* began to govern the villages of the *menancabos* of the city's

---

[160] Couto, *Da Ásia*, VI, part 2, IX, vi, pp. 258–259.

[161] Ibid., VIII, xxi, p. 150. This is the episode, which has already been mentioned, of the rumour that the sultan of Aceh was able to spread in Melaka according to which he had established a secret agreement with the Keling community, suggested by the *tomungão* of the city. It is probably an error by this chronicler who possibly wished to refer to the *bendara*.

[162] *See* sources quoted in note 132.

[163] Couto, *Da Ásia*, X, part 2, VII, xii, pp. 207–209.

[164] Letter from the bishop of Melaka to the king, 31-12-1588. AGS, *Secr. Prov.*, book 1551, fl. 405v. (*see* Document Appendix, No. 6).

hinterland.[165] This new function was possibly associated with the rebellion of these villages during the crisis of 1585–87, resulting in the necessity to control them more directly so as to avoid future setbacks. During the 1610s this statute had already been defined:

> 'In the hinterland, the king has many Moorish subjects, governed by one of the governors of Melaka, who is called Tamungão, whose office is appointed by the viceroy of India, and has 10 per cent of the revenues derived from them ....'[166]

The individual who occupied this post, at least from 1610 onwards, was a certain João Lopes de Amoreira, a local *casado*. At this time, a little like the *bendara*, the *tomungão* played an important diplomatic role with regard to Johor, having been appointed as ambassador to conclude the peace negotiations and, eventually, a treaty.[167] A few years later he provided support to the sultan against Aceh, in 1615 or 1616.[168] This João Lopes de Amoreira appears to have been 'a great friend of the father of the King of Jor',[169] that is, of Ali Jalla Abdul Jalil Syah II, who died in 1597. This would possibly indicate that he was already *tomungão* at that time. In any case, the intrigues plotted against him had an effect: the post was abolished sometime around 1621 due to the complaints of the sultan

---

[165] The Portuguese way of designating the people from Minangkabau, in inland Sumatra. The *menancabos* of Melaka were groups who came from this region and established themselves upstream from Melaka and had been partially controlled by the Portuguese since 1511. At this time they were undoubtedly Muslims. *See* note 5, above.

[166] *Relação das Plantas, & dezcripções ...*, p. 44.

[167] Borschberg, 'Portuguese, Spanish and Dutch Plans to Construct a Fort', p. 77, note 106. About this character, *see* also Silva *et al.*, 'Lista de todas as capitanias ...', p. 351.

[168] Letters from Viceroy D. João Coutinho to the king, 8-2-1619 and 9-2-1619, *DRI*, IV, pp. 313–314 and 314–315, respectively. They report that this was the reason why João Lopes de Amoreira incurred the hostility of Captain João Caiado de Gamboa, who had a good relationship with Iskandar Muda after the strike on Melaka in 1615. Lopes de Amoreira was even put in jail and sent to Goa but the viceroy considered the charges to be unfounded and sent him back to Melaka. In these letters he is referred to as the '*tomungão* of the foreign people'.

[169] Letter from the viceroy, 9-2-1619, ibid., p. 315.

of Johor and other neighbouring kings, who accused the said *tomungão* of extorting money from the Malay merchants who went to the city to sell provisions and who were, just like the *menancabos*, under his jurisdiction.

It is known that João Lopes had a large warehouse where he would assemble the Malays and *menancabos*. From this *bangaçal* he would charge important revenues, which raised protests when they became excessive. With the abolishment of the post, it was estimated at the time that the leasing of this warehouse to the *menancabos* would provide sufficient revenue to sustain the constables and bombardiers that were ordered to be permanently stationed in the city.[170] However, the abolishment was not carried out, as during the 1630s the office was again mentioned by António Bocarro, who set out the functions of this post: it governed around five or six thousand *menancabo* Moors, keeping ten per cent 'of everything he sees fit' and confiscating the property of those who died without descendants; at this time the post was held by a *casado*, but Bocarro does not mention his name.[171] Unlike the *bendara*, whose system of nomination respected the initial form (the hereditary nature granted to Nina Chatu), it appears that the *tomungão* ceased to be elected and later confirmed by the authorities; on the contrary, he was appointed by the viceroy or by the king, at least from the time of João Lopes de Amoreira.[172]

Security: Fortifications, Material and Human Resources

The problems related to the security and defence of Melaka date back to the very conquest of the city by Afonso de Albuquerque, since the

---

[170] In letters from Governor Fernão de Albuquerque to the king, 18-2-1622 and 20-2-1622, *DRI*, VII, pp. 393–394 and 407, respectively; Record from the State Council, 13-4-1622, *ACE*, I, pp. 133–134.

[171] 'Livro das Plantas de todas as Fortalezas ...', p. 22. The list of all offices of the Portuguese fortresses in India in BN, *Res.*, cod. 11410, fls. 1–4v., post-1622, also refers to the *tomungão*, 'judge of the *menancabos* of Melaka'. Schouten, in 1641, also mentions the Minangkabau people, about 1,000 in number, who lived in the village of Naning and were 'governed by one or two Orang Kaya, under a Portuguese Tommagon or Chief'; Schouten's report in Leupe, 'The Siege and Capture of Malacca', pp. 88–89 and 98.

[172] *See* sources mentioned in notes 166 and 167, above.

construction of the tower that was the residence of the captain and was, for a long time, the city's sole fortified structure. Melaka lived for decades without sturdy walls, provided only with perishable defences of adobe walls and wooden palisades. This was the scenario in the mid-16th century,[173] a clear sign of how Portuguese naval power was sufficient to ensure the defence of Melaka. External attacks by both Johor and Aceh posed no serious threat. However, as early as 1537 the attack by Aceh had been repelled at some cost and caused obvious concern about the problems of defending the city. Increasing pressure from Melaka's enemies forced the city to be fortified, a process that was begun between 1564 and 1568.[174] The siege of 1568 amply justified these measures, due to the use of heavy artillery by the Acehnese.[175]

The scenario definitively changed. The problem of Melaka's security would never cease to be the prime concern of official correspondence. Henceforth, Melaka was a city at risk: the anti-Portuguese league that had formed throughout the Indian Ocean and whose ramifications reached Melaka through Aceh and, above all, the subsequent arrival of the Dutch and the English in Southeast Asia, meant that the city could never be allowed to let its guard down. The problem became a perennial factor and accompanied the economic, social and political evolution of the city until its fall in 1641. The great siege of 1606, due to its sheer scale and the risks that the city faced, would aggravate the problem, making the adoption of measures to ensure defence an urgent necessity. As we shall see, although persistent attempts were made to reinforce security in three sectors—fortifications, men and materials—it was only in the first sector that these efforts were successful, and even then only at great expense and rather slowly. Melaka fortified itself, but this did not mean the city was stronger. This is the development that will be discussed in the following pages.

The fortified perimeter of the city remained unchanged throughout the entire period under study, and even subsequently. It had a pentagonal

---

[173] As seen in the drawing in *Lendas da Índia*, by Gaspar Correia; reproduced by Macgregor in 'Notes on the Portuguese in Malaya', p. 38.
[174] *See* Manguin, 'Of Fortresses and Galleys', p. 614.
[175] Couto, *Da Ásia*, VIII, xxii, p. 155. Pereira, p. [234].

plan, interrupted by bulwarks and various gates.[176] Outside the city there was a further palisade or stockade in Upeh, where the most important of the merchants and *casados* lived. The pace of fortification was slow: at the beginning of the 1580s only part of the perimeter was fortified, and Captain Dom João da Gama pointed out that the city lacked sufficient funds to proceed with the task in a satisfactory manner.[177] At the time, these funds derived from a 1 per cent tax created by Philip I in order to reinforce fortresses.[178] The captain also refers to a voyage of China, whose revenues were applied for the same purpose, but stated that from these funds not even a penny had remained for the intended objectives. Sometime during this decade the Italian architect Giovanni Batista Cairati, who was inspecting the Portuguese fortresses of the Estado da Índia, arrived in Melaka. In Melaka's case, he drew up a plan for the construction of a series of fortified bulwarks that, however, was never accomplished.[179] The Portuguese limited themselves to constructing a bastion on the Hilir bank, improving the remaining bulwarks and completing, to the extent possible—and as pressure increased—the fortification of the city's perimeter.

When the Dutch and the English arrived in the waters of the Archipelago, this scenario had not changed significantly. Almost no progress had been made on the task of fortifying Melaka. One can find information from the turn of the century indicating that some works had

---

[176] Depicted in several drawings, such as those of Erédia, 'Declaraçam de Malaca' (reproduced by Irwin, 'Melaka Fort', p. 786) or the anonymous image dating from the 1560s, studied by Manguin in 'Of Fortresses and Galleys'.

[177] Royal instructions to the viceroy, 10-3-1584, AN/TT, *Fundo Português da Bibl. Nac. de Paris*, No. 48, fl. 9v. (*see* Document Appendix, No. 2).

[178] Mentioned by the 'Alvará em forma de Regimento' issued by Viceroy Matias de Albuquerque, 1595, in Pissurlencar, *Regimentos das Fortalezas da Índia*, p. 256.

[179] This is what Erédia describes as 'the new scheme' (*traça nova*) in his plan contained in the 'Declaraçam de Malaca'; about this issue, *see* Irwin, 'Melaka Fort', pp. 785–787. Following Erédia, this author states that the architect was in Melaka in 1588. In fact, it was in this year that the king issued the following order to Viceroy D. Duarte de Meneses: 'I entrust you to send engineer João Baptista [to Melaka] to visit and evaluate the fortification works that are underway there' (royal letter, 21-1-1588, *APO*, III, part 1, pp. 115–116).

been completed.[180] Yet, in 1605, on the eve of the great Dutch siege, the city council revealed that there was only a wall of adobe and wood, and that they were proceeding to raise another wooden one.[181] It was only after 1606, partially due to the damage caused by the Dutch attack, that the viceroy ordered the construction of 'a trench from sea to sea' made of stone and lime. However, at the same time, the *casados* complained about the lack of funds and the dearth of revenues from the 1 per cent tax, and of the fact that the withdrawal of noblemen after the siege had forced them to bear this expense 'with their slaves and the local people'.[182] In any case, it was at this time, and on the suggestion of the viceroy, that it was also decided to construct a fortress on the small island called the Ilha das Naus, opposite Melaka, to ensure the defence of the city, the security of shipping and to avoid future incursions by Dutch armadas. As one shall see, it was never built. Another project, which similarly lacked continuity, was the plan to erect a fort on top of the city's main hill beside the Jesuit College.[183]

The 1 per cent tax that was levied to assist fortification was manifestly insufficient, and was eventually raised to 2 per cent, along with

---

[180] Royal letter to Viceroy D. Martim Afonso de Castro based on prior information provided by the former viceroy, Aires de Saldanha, and the archbishop of Goa, 26-2-1605, *DRI*, I, p. 7.

[181] The only source of income was the tax of 1 per cent and a voyage of China, which was considered insufficient, so the city asked for a voyage of Japan; letter from the city of Melaka to the king, 3-12-1605, *DUP*, II, p. 258. The information about the city having just a wall of wood and adobe is not completely correct because a portion of the perimeter already consisted of a stone wall. Viceroy D. Martim Afonso de Castro (*see* the following note) said that the city was vulnerable on one side, with a wall made of wood and brick, referring to 'the land side'; Luís Coelho de Barbuda stated: 'On the side of Hilir, the fortress had no strong wall because the existing one was made of adobe and partially of wood' (*Empresas Militares de Lvsitanos*, fl. 321v.).

[182] Information contained in a summary of a letter from the viceroy (4-5-1607) and others from the city and the Bishop of Melaka, AGS, *Secr. Prov.*, book 1479, fls. 162–162v. and 168v. *See* the information provided by Schouten after the fall of Melaka in 1641 in Leupe, 'The Siege and Capture of Malacca', p. 86.

[183] 'Sobre a fazenda de Sua Magestade', undated report (between 1617 and 1622); AN/TT, *MiscMssCGL*, box 16, vol. 6 F, fl. 103.

other stern fiscal measures aimed at financing these defensive efforts.[184] Melaka, after a series of refusals, accepted payment of only the 2 per cent, and that, too, on the condition that these revenues be destined exclusively for this purpose and not be diverted elsewhere.[185] This was nothing new as the channelling of funds, especially those sent from Lisbon or Goa, for other purposes, or even their appropriation by the administration or the captain, was not uncommon. The money that André Furtado de Mendonça and the archbishop sent to Melaka for the fortification efforts disappeared without any justification whatsoever,[186] as a result of which it was now considered preferable to raise funds from the city's revenues, where the various authorities could control the process better and avoid embezzlements. Other revenues were granted for this purpose, namely a voyage of Japan, in 1607 and 1619.[187]

The situation of the fortress did not progress in a satisfactory manner, even when money for the fortification efforts arrived, which can be attributed to the corruption that prevailed amongst the officials of the fortress from where funds were embezzled. In 1610 Melaka continued to be a city unprotected on its inland side. At the time, Viceroy Rui Lourenço de Távora summed up the situation thus:

'The city, on the side where is surrounded by water (from where it is more defensible), is well surrounded by walls and bulwarks; however, on the inland flank, where the danger is greater, it does not have more than a wall of adobe and wood and, outside this, a layer of sticks and

---

[184] Among others, the taxes on palm-tree wine, betel and the retail sales of cotton clothes from the 'Kelings' bazar'; letter from Governor Fernão de Albuquerque to the king, 8-2-1620, *DRI*, VI, p. 201; *see* letter from the same governor to the king, 7-2-1620, ibid., p. 33.

[185] Record from the State Council, 30-4-1619, *ACE*, I, p. 41; *alvará* by the viceroy, 5-4-1619, *APO*, VI (ii), pp. 1174–1175. *See* letters mentioned in the previous note.

[186] In 1610 Viceroy Lourenço de Távora issued an order to investigate the use of these funds, but the results of this inquiry are unknown (provision by the viceroy, 27-4-1610, HAG, *Provisões dos Vice-Reis*, 2, fl. 118v.).

[187] Royal letter to Viceroy D. Martim Afonso de Castro, 18-1-1607, *DRI*, I, p. 92; royal letter to Viceroy D. João Coutinho, 20-3-1620, *DRI*, VI, p. 375 (*see* replies from the governor, 15-1-1622 and 18-2-1622, *DRI*, VII, pp. 155 and 401–402, respectively).

palm trees, that quickly rot, and if it were not for the necessities of these past years, the damages are not mended, and when the need is urgent, the work is done with great difficulty, and from the said terrestrial side from the bastion of São Domingos, that is alongside the river, to the bulwark of Santiago, that is next to the sea, there is only the bulwark of Madre de Deus, which is of adobe and is small, and another of Onze Mil Virgens, made of stone and lime, small and not very strong, which was made as a remedy and to serve as a wall, when that land flank is enclosed, so as to make a bulwark from there towards the outside, and it is so easy to climb, in the corner where it joins the adobe wall, and there is such little vigilance, that some people use it, when they find the doors of the city closed, and the slaves do so without this being the case.'[188]

The fortification of the city was finally completed despite the delays and funding problems. The arrival of António Pinto da Fonseca, whose main mission was precisely to resolve the problems of the city's defences, was a decisive contribution to this goal.[189] In 1620 the work was about to end[190] and was finally completed in the following decade.[191] As for the fort on the Ilha das Naus, the problem was far more complex, for two main reasons. First, there were substantial costs involved: to construct a fort from scratch, equip it with artillery and keep it operational was an expensive task, the total cost of the project being calculated at 30,000 *cruzados*, for which the king granted a voyage 'of spices'.[192] Secondly, there were risks involved: a fortress on the island could be a serious threat to the city and to Portuguese navigation if it fell into enemy hands. The Portuguese now reasoned in much the same way as throughout Southeast Asia. The Dutch were powerful at sea, but did not have bases of their own on land. In any attack on Melaka, they would be subject to the caprices of their allies in

---

[188] Letter to the king [1610], BN, *Res.*, cod. 1975, fl. 288v.

[189] Royal letter to Viceroy D. João Coutinho, 21-3-1617, *DRI*, IV, xxx, pp. 142–143. For further information about this figure, *see* Macgregor, 'Notes on the Portuguese in Malaya', pp. 33–34.

[190] Letter from Governor Fernão de Albuquerque to the king, 16-12-1620, *DRI*, VII, p. 207.

[191] Bocarro, 'Livro das Plantas ...', p. 15.

[192] Or two voyages from the Coromandel coast to Melaka, if those proved to belong to the captain of the fortress; royal letter to Viceroy D. João Coutinho, 18-3-1619, *DRI*, VI, p. 15.

Johor, as happened in 1606, which was one of the reasons why the siege failed. If they conquered the fort, once entrenched and supplied by their armadas, they would be able to launch a lethal strike on Melaka. Be that as it may, in 1620 construction on the fort had not yet begun, and during the 1630s only work on the foundations was underway.[193]

However, fortification alone was not sufficient to ensure the city's security. It is clear that an indispensable component of Melaka's defences consisted of protection from the sea, by means of an armada for vigilance. However, this problem was closely linked to questions of strategic defence options throughout the Estado da Índia, from the initial years of the 17th century onwards: oared armadas or sea-going fleets, supplies and provisions for them, routes and bases, tactics of naval combat, a policy of armadas or of fortresses, etc. Even concerning specific naval issues, the city had unfavourable characteristics: not possessing a shipbuilding yard, all the vessels sent there could not be repaired, and ended up rotting.[194]

One of the most interesting aspects of the 'militarisation' of Melaka has to do with the very organisation of the city's internal space. As has already been mentioned briefly, available space within the city's fortified perimeter was minimal. At a time when the city's defence became an urgent priority, this problem assumed rather serious proportions. Monasteries and churches occupied most of the space, so few people actually lived within the city.[195] However, the successive sieges that the city suffered caused the population to seek refuge within the city walls. This was particularly accentuated after the siege of 1606, houses being built over the fortress walls. The viceroy ordered the demolition of these houses immediately on account of the danger they constituted for the city's security.[196] There had

---

[193] Information provided by António Pinto da Fonseca mentioned in a royal letter to Viceroy D. João Coutinho, 5-3-1620, *DRI*, VI, p. 300; Bocarro, 'Livro das Plantas ...', p. 23.

[194] Report from Rui Dias de Meneses, unknown date [1623?], AN/TT, *MssLiv.*, No. 1116, p. 731.

[195] Summary of a letter from Viceroy D. Martim Afonso de Castro, 4-5-1607, AGS, *Secr. Prov.*, book 1479, fl. 163.

[196] Royal letter to Viceroy Rui Lourenço de Távora, 14-2-1609, HAG, *MonçReino*, 11, fl. 200 (also published in *BOGEI*, No. 161 (1882), p. 799); the viceroy refers to the orders issued by D. Martim Afonso de Castro to 'knock down the houses that the inhabitants had built on top of the walls because the city was small and there was no space left'.

already been previous reports of terraces and balconies on the wall from where goods were furtively smuggled in, thus avoiding the payment of customs duties.[197]

However, the most important aspect of the houses in Melaka— obviously including those outside the fortress, in Upeh and Hilir—is that they were built of wood and other perishable materials, being thatched with palm leaves, which constituted a permanent fire risk and was a grave danger in case of attack. As early as the assault in 1568 Diogo do Couto highlights this fact,[198] which did not change during subsequent decades. In 1599 the city council requested the viceroy to force the city's residents to substitute the palm leaf thatch with tiles, which were produced in abundance in the city.[199] The order was eventually given later, along with another one: to cut down the palm groves on the outskirts of the city so that Melaka's enemies (that could only have been the Dutch) could not use them against the city.[200] This had been unthinkable a short while previously and had serious repercussions on the everyday life of the local people. In any case, neither order was ever carried out;[201] on account of this, during the 1630s Bocarro continued to chronicle the straw houses in which the Portuguese of Melaka lived.[202]

Equipping the city with armaments, especially artillery, munitions and supplies was vital for Melaka's survival. Yet the picture that emerges from Portuguese documentation is one of laxity and negligence in this regard, due to greed or simply carelessness. There are constant references to a lack of artillery and supplies in the city, as well as orders to urgently remedy the situation. In the first case, the main accusations were directed

---

[197] *Alvará* issued by Viceroy Matias de Albuquerque, 22-4-1596, HAG, *Regimentos e Instruções*, 2, fl. 133.
[198] Couto, *Da Ásia*, VIII, xxii, p. 150.
[199] 'Apontamentos que a Cidade de Malaca ...', [1599], BN, *Res.*, cod. 1973, fl. 57v. (*see* Document Appendix, No. 10).
[200] Letter from Governor Fernão de Albuquerque to the king, 20-2-1621, *DRI*, VII, p. 226; 18-2-1622, ibid., pp. 392–393.
[201] In the former case, because any building works apart from the fortification of the city were forbidden; in the latter, because it was feared that it might create panic among the locals, who might think that a siege was imminent; letter from the governor to the king, 20-2-1622, ibid., p. 407.
[202] Bocarro, 'Livro das Plantas ...', p. 15.

at the Royal officers and the captains of the city, as the former sold artillery and munitions and the latter used them for their own ends, leaving the city without provisions.[203]

An exemplary case took place in 1587 after the attack on Johor Lama: despite the fact that several hundred pieces of brass artillery had been captured in the course of the raid, almost none arrived at the Royal warehouses, having immediately been appropriated by the captains, *casados* and soldiers who participated in the enterprise.[204] Thus the city constantly lacked materials for war. There had once been a foundry and a powder warehouse in Melaka, but in 1613 nothing remained of them and they could not be rebuilt because, owing to the limited confines of the city, the space they occupied had already been taken over by houses.[205]

The same situation prevailed with regard to provisions. The *casados*, who dominated the trade in victuals and profited from shortages in the city, were not interested in promoting local agriculture. The city was thus permanently dependent on imported supplies. When the Dutch gradually began to dominate navigation in the waters of the Archipelago, the situation became more serious, even more so because the Dutch sought to impede the flow of provisions to the city.[206] Aid from Goa or Lisbon, which had already been constantly requested previously, now became an urgent necessity because the break in Melaka's revenues and the endemic corruption ensured that the coffers of the royal exchequer remained empty.

---

[203] *See*, for instance, the royal letters to Viceroy D. Francisco da Gama, 9-3-1596, *APO*, III, part 2, pp. 614–615, and to Viceroy Aires de Saldanha, 31-1-1602, AHU, *Cons. Ultr.*, cod. 282, fl. 73.

[204] Letter from Governor Manuel de Sousa Coutinho to the king, 4-12-1589, AGS, *Secr. Prov.*, book 1551, fl. 778v: 'despite the fact that a large number of pieces of artillery were captured in Johor, as some people have reported to Your Majesty, no more than seven or eight of them have been deposited in your warehouses; this occurred despite the proceedings I have ordered including excommunications, without effect. All the artillery vanished because they were all small cannons, so captains, soldiers and *casados* from Melaka were able to take them aboard their vessels on the sly, in order to use them later or sell them elsewhere, as I have been informed some actually did ...'.

[205] Bocarro, *Década 13*, I, xlvii, pp. 196–197.

[206] They were successful in Java (from where Melaka obtained most of its supplies) in the early 1620s; letter from Governor Fernão de Albuquerque to the king, 18-2-1622, *DRI*, VII, p. 412.

Thus there was a growing need to resort to external funding in order to supply the city with provisions. The supplies that did arrive were naturally consumed and were not replenished. In 1613 the auditor António Barreto da Silva supplied the city with a large quantity of rice, and came equipped with an order from the viceroy to replenish the city's reserves annually. However, after his departure this measure was not continued.[207] In the same way, the instructions given to António Pinto da Fonseca included an express order to construct a rice depot in the city that was apparently never built.[208]

The central factor of Melaka's security was, however, the human element. Theoretically, the soldiers constituted the most important corps for the defence of the fortresses but the military structure of the Estado da Índia suffered from diverse ills and shortages that, from the beginning of the 17th century, were further aggravated by the competition from the northern Europeans. There were also several projects and efforts for military reform that successively took place with some effect, but without managing to achieve the desired objectives. In the concrete case of Melaka, what can be seen throughout the period under study is that the fragility of this military structure resulted in the burden of Melaka's defences being gradually transferred to the city's resources: the *casados*, along with their dependants and slaves, the captain and his men, and even Asian communities, especially the Kelings.

As is known, during most of the 16th century soldiers in India were not organised into companies, and were subject to the protection of a powerful figure, generally the viceroy or captain of the fortress, for their livelihood. They generally lived in difficult conditions and associated war with plunder and, whenever possible, with trade. Many became mercenaries or renegades, placing their services at the service of Asian kings. It was only in exceptional cases that soldiers in India were organised into companies and were duly paid, commanded and disciplined: Afonso de Albuquerque and Dom João de Castro constituted the best-known cases. During the period under study Viceroy Dom Duarte de Meneses also attempted to adopt the same policy, which was abandoned after his death in 1588.

---

[207] Bocarro, *Década 13*, I, xlvi, pp. 195–196.
[208] *See* letter quoted in note 189, above.

Orders to supply the fortress of Melaka with soldiers, generally indicating several hundred in number, were issued on a regular basis. In 1564 the viceroy ordered that there be 300 men stationed at the fortress, including the captain's men and the bombardiers.[209] Subsequent orders of this nature, just like other instructions referring to the supply of provisions, munitions or fortification of the city walls, invariably fell on deaf ears on account of the city's financial incapacity, negligence, or other more obscure motives. In any case, in 1585 Viceroy Dom Duarte de Meneses drew up a general list of orders (a *regimento*) for the city of Melaka, which referred, above all, to the military restructuring that he intended to implement: there should be 250 men to guard the fortress, duly organised into units and paid and controlled in such a way as to avoid desertions and flights.[210] He must not have met with much success as, at the end of his tenure, the king pressed him to put the very same orders into effect.[211] At this time, the bishop of Melaka stated that there were 300 soldiers in the city, but some had already settled and married. He advised that only those who remained on board the ships should be paid, as the soldiers who were at the fortress received payments from the captain's men who, in their turn, charged these funds on the *casados*.[212]

In any case, it was only later, after the arrival of the Dutch and the English, and this time with a far greater urgency, that new attempts were made. The first attempt was implemented by Dom Martim Afonso de Castro as a result of the siege of 1606 and was clearly impractical for a city exhausted of men and resources: he ordered that a permanent garrison of 600 men be raised.[213] However, from this time, this issue became more serious and, from the early 1610s, the fortress had a permanent contingent of soldiers organised into companies. The initiative was taken by Viceroy

---

[209] *Regimento* of Viceroy D. Antão de Noronha, 1564, in Pissurlencar (ed.), *Regimentos das Fortalezas da Índia*, p. 249.

[210] *Regimento* issued by Viceroy D. Duarte de Meneses to the fortress of Melaka, 1585, HAG, *Cartas Patentes e Provisões*, 3, fls. 8–10v.

[211] Royal letter to Viceroy D. Duarte de Meneses, 16-3-1588, *APO*, III, part 1, p. 154.

[212] Letter to the king, 31-12-1588, AGS, *Secr. Prov.*, book 1551, fls. 405v.–406 (*see* Document Appendix, No. 6).

[213] Information provided by Rafael Alcáçova Carneiro, unknown date [early 17th century], AN/TT, *MiscMssCGL*, box 16, vol. 6 F, fl. 73.

Dom Jerónimo de Azevedo in 1613.[214] In 1615 the process was underway, apparently with a fair degree of success.[215] However, the coeval sources, especially the letters of the viceroys, clearly tend to exaggerate: in 1614 Dom Jerónimo de Azevedo stated that there were 500 soldiers in Melaka; the auditor António Barreto da Silva, who was in the city at the time, only found 18 men available.[216] Later, António Pinto da Fonseca arrived at the figure of 150.[217]

The process of creating companies would, however, undergo some modifications, linked with the tendency of the decline of the captains of the fortress: in 1617 the king removed their command and authority over the soldiers.[218] They were placed under the jurisdiction of António Pinto da Fonseca, captain-general of Melaka, thus completing the afore-mentioned decline of the importance and role of the captains of the fortress. Despite all the setbacks and difficulties, the provisioning of soldiers for Melaka's fortresses became—just as in Mozambique and Hormuz—a reality.[219]

The Portuguese authorities, in both Madrid and Lisbon as well as in Goa, were constantly preoccupied with providing Melaka with soldiers. However, the defence of the city was primarily based on the *casados* and the local people. The soldiers arrived in auxiliary armadas, but their permanence in the fortress was problematic as they frequently fled or sailed to other areas. They were undisciplined, badly paid, badly trained, frequently caused all kinds of problems and were generally ignorant

---

[214] In a letter to the king he refers to 240 soldiers divided into 4 squadrons of 60 men each (HAG, *MonçReino*, 12, fl. 12). *See alvará*, 15-8-1613, HAG, *Cartas Patentes e Alvarás*, 3, fls. 109v.–110v. (published in *APO*, VI, (ii), pp. 972–973, albeit with a different date [13-8-1613] and folio [117]), and also the record from the Treasury Council, 21-11-1613, *ACF*, I, part 1, p. 5.

[215] Royal letter to Viceroy D. Jerónimo de Azevedo, 14-2-1615, *DRI*, III, p. 231.

[216] Letter from the viceroy to the king, 31-12-1614, HAG, *MonçReino*, 12, fl. 163 (also published in *BOGEI*, No. 92 (1883), p. 368); Bocarro, *Década 13*, I, xlvii, p. 198.

[217] Letter from Viceroy D. João Coutinho to the king, unknown date [1617 or 1618], *DRI*, IV, p. 64.

[218] Royal letter to Viceroy D. João Coutinho, 27-3-1617, *DRI*, IV, p. 194.

[219] Letter from Governor Fernão de Albuquerque to the king, 8-2-1620, *DRI*, VI, p. 65.

of the environment in which they were operating.[220] Furthermore, the concentration of soldiers in the city, although important for Melaka's security, proved to be a permanent focus of disturbances about which the Jesuits, amongst others, complained.[221] This instability was aggravated by the pressure exerted by Lisbon and Goa to form permanent companies which, along with the delay in payments and the insalubrity of the region, resulted in desertions by both soldiers and the bombardiers.[222]

A brief remark about the presence of mercenaries in Melaka is needed. It is true that some of the inhabitants of Melaka—the slaves and dependants of the *casados*—were of Chinese, Malay or Javanese origin or came from the Eastern Archipelago, and formed an important and active nucleus in the city's defences. There were also Japanese retainers, whose behaviour sometimes proved to be unpredictable.[223] However, during the 1610s there were true mercenaries who generally served as the captains' guards; they were mainly Japanese, but it seems that there were also some Javanese and Malays.[224] Their presence in the city has been attested as

---

[220] The king admitted that the captains were the first to disobey the orders and *regimentos*, which set an example for their subordinates and soldiers; royal letter to Viceroy D. João Coutinho, 10-3-1617, *DRI*, IV, p. 52. In 1611 Pyrard de Laval stated that most of the soldiers were convicts; *Voyage de ...*, II, p. 668.

[221] Letter from Simão de Sá, 1-1-1589, *DI*, XVIII, p. 920.

[222] Information provided by António Pinto da Fonseca mentioned in a royal letter to Viceroy D. João Coutinho, 18-3-1619, *DRI*, VI, p. 199. *See* letter quoted in note 216, above.

[223] The most remarkable incident took place in the case of the Dominican friar Agostinho Lobato, missionary in Solor and Timor. He was murdered by a Japanese servant who had been punished, and then proceeded to commit suicide; letter from Governor Fernão de Albuquerque to the king, 6-2-1620, *DRI*, VI, p. 12.

[224] Royal letter to Viceroy D. João Coutinho, 1-2-1618, *DRI*, IV, pp. 297–298, and reply, 9-2-1619, ibid., pp. 298–299. This was the famous episode when the captain stormed into the church with his men, causing a protest by the bishop. They were not slaves but mercenaries, for the captain sent them away at once and the factor received specific orders to pay them. A specific order was then issued not to allow any Japanese, Malay or Javanese to serve as guards, but only Portuguese or *topazes* (half-bloods).

early as the siege of 1606, and they played an active role in the defence of the city.[225]

Let us now consider a few aspects concerning the *casados*. Their evolution at the heart of local society during the period under study has already been described, highlighting the growing importance of this group in the defence of the city as well as in other functions. Yet let us open a small postscript to describe the role of three cases as examples—three *casados* who played a leading role in the defence of Melaka. They were also the ones who achieved great renown and whose biographical details are better known:[226] António de Andria, António Fernandes de Ilher and Fernão da Costa.

António de Andria is the best-documented one. His name first appears during the crisis of 1585–87, although a certain Mateus de Andria, possibly a relative, had participated (and possibly died) in prior campaigns against Aceh.[227] During the crisis of 1585–87 António de Andria commanded diverse Melakan armadas against the forces of Johor and defended the city before the arrival of the fleet of Paulo de Lima Pereira, which put an end to the conflict.[228] In this final attack, in which two armadas combined, he was the captain-major of the city's ships.[229] After the attack, the habitual scenario that was usually witnessed in the aftermath of situations of crisis was repeated: the armada from Goa withdrew, and the Portuguese soldiers and noblemen returned to the capital satisfied with their booty and intent on presenting the king with requests for rewards for their services. The *casados* remained in Melaka and had to deal with a delicate situation in which the sultan of Johor had been defeated but not destroyed and

---

[225] Barbuda, *Empresas Militares de Lvsitanos*, fl. 321.

[226] D. Henrique Bendara is not mentioned because he was not formally a *casado* and because he has already been analysed in previous pages.

[227] He was still a young man in 1583, when he was kept prisoner with Luís Monteiro Coutinho in Aceh. He managed to escape but was recaptured; whether he suffered the same fate as Coutinho is unknown; *see* Erédia, 'História de serviços com martírio …', and Francisco de Sousa, *Oriente Conquistado …*, pp. 1112–1113.

[228] Couto, *Da Ásia*, X, part 2, VII, xii, p. 209; part 2, VIII, ii, p. 270; part 2, IX, vii, p. 448.

[229] Letter from the bishop of Melaka to the king, 15-12-1588, AGS, *Secr. Prov.*, book 1551, fl. 399v.

continued to be a potential threat for the city. Thus, in 1588 the *casados* of Melaka prepared an armada at their own cost, brushing aside the hesitation of the captain of the fortress, Dom Diogo Lobo. António de Andria, along with Dom Henrique Bendara, who commanded the renewed attack on Johor's new fortifications, destroyed the recently constructed stockade.[230]

News of these services reached the king's ears. In 1593, as a reward for his long services, António de Andria was granted the captaincy of Solor and Timor.[231] He seems to have been the second captain of Solor after the construction of the fortress by the Dominicans and the creation of the captaincy by the Crown.[232] News from him only emerged again in 1604, in charge of an armada of *bantins* from Melaka which intercepted a Dutch armada on the Johor River, an episode related with Friar Rafael da Madre de Deus' odyssey.[233] Finally, during the siege of 1606 he was once again active in the defence of Melaka, commanding the city's forces in sorties against the Dutch.[234]

António Fernandes de Ilher possibly had a similar, albeit less prominent, career. His name indicates his place of birth or residence (the suburb of Hilir). Although the economic heart of Melaka was situated in Upeh, which was richer and more important than Hilir, it is possible that he was a descendant of the most powerful merchant in the city during the 1550s.[235] In any case, only scant biographical information is available. In

---

[230] Letter from Governor Manuel de Sousa Coutinho to the king, 12-12-1589, AGS, *Secr. Prov.*, book 1551, fls. 746–747; he said that António de Andria took the place of D. Paulo de Lima Pereira after he left Melaka; *see* Fr. Paulo da Trindade, *Conquista Espiritual do Oriente*, III, p. 487.

[231] Letter bestowing a royal grant to António de Andria, AN/TT, *Chancelaria de Filipe I*, Doações, book 28, fls. 81–81v. (published in *DHMPPO/Insulíndia*, V, pp. 23–24).

[232] Couto, *Da Ásia*, XI, xxxiv, pp. 181–182.

[233] *See* chapter 4, 'The Religious Factor'.

[234] Barbuda in *Empresas Militares ...*, fl. 321, describes his exploits on the battlefield with only 40 men (information that can also be found in Queirós, *História do Venerável Irmão Pedro de Basto*, p. 332, amongst others).

[235] While describing the siege of Melaka in 1551, Couto refers to a homonym, the 'oldest and wealthiest [*casado*]', who established diplomatic contacts with Johor; it is possible that he was a relative of the António Fernandes mentioned above (*Da Ásia*, VI, part 2, IX, v, p. 255).

1582 he participated in the defence of Melaka during the attack launched against the city by an armada from Aceh.[236] In 1587 he commanded a ship in the armada from Melaka that, along with the armada of Dom Paulo de Lima Pereira, attacked and destroyed Johor.[237] He did not earn favours like António de Andria and certainly was no great warrior. On the contrary, one gets the impression that he was a man of great wealth and that his greatest talents lay in trade and commerce. His importance in this field must have been so prominent that he was the one entrusted with buying pepper (from Sunda or Sumatra) and despatching it to India or directly to Lisbon, which he did on his own account and risk, as the money that should have been sent annually for this purpose suffered successive delays.[238]

Finally, we have Fernão da Costa. This individual was undoubtedly a warrior, but was also a diplomat. During the siege of 1606 he appears at António de Andria's side in the defence of the city.[239] We only find mention of him again some years later, around 1614, when he was sent as an ambassador to Johor, attempting to establish closer ties with the sultan (who, at the time, was Raja Bongsu/Abdullah Maayat Syah) and trying to ensure that he maintained his distance from Aceh, ruled by his brother-in-law who had put him on the throne of Johor.[240] With an attack on Melaka by Aceh seeming an imminent possibility, in February 1615 Fernão da Costa commanded an armada to guard the coast, capturing several ships from Aceh and Kedah loaded with supplies.[241] When Aceh attacked the city in September or October of the same year he distinguished himself

---

[236] Ibid., X, part 1, III, iii, p. 285.

[237] *See* letter quoted in note 230, above.

[238] Royal letter to Viceroy Matias de Albuquerque, Jan. 1591, *APO*, III, part 1, pp. 297–298; royal letter to António Fernandes de Ilher, 12-1-1591, AHU, *Cons. Ultr.*, cod. 281, fl. 164v. (*see* Document Appendix, No. 7).

[239] *See* note 234, above.

[240] Bocarro, *Década 13*, I, xciv, p. 418. He states that Fernão da Costa was a well-known and prestigious figure in the region, therefore being the ideal choice for the position of ambassador.

[241] On 23-5-1615 Fernão da Costa wrote a report and certificate about Luís Pereira who served as a soldier during these events (AHU, *Índia*, box 3, doc. 114, fl. 1).

in naval battles, supporting the armada of Francisco de Miranda, who inflicted a heavy defeat on the enemy forces.[242]

Little else is known about the life of Fernão da Costa. He did not receive favours from the king, as so many others did. However, it is known that in 1618 he was in Goa when Viceroy Dom João Coutinho sent him back to Melaka with 100 men, as the captain of an armada to assist the city.[243] In 1620 he was the one who came to Perak's aid during the attack that Iskandar Muda of Aceh launched against this sultanate during one of his campaigns to conquer Sumatra and the Malay Peninsula.[244] Very probably he had died by 1626 as his name does not appear on the list enumerating the *casados* of the city prepared by the bishop in that year.[245]

---

[242] Anonymous letter [1615], BN, *Res.*, cod. 1975, fls. 193–194v. (*see* Document Appendix, No. 19).

[243] Grant bestowed upon Fernão da Costa, 12-5-1618, HAG, *Mercês Gerais*, 2, fl. 85; letter from Viceroy D. João Coutinho to the king, 1619, *DRI*, V, pp. 239–240.

[244] Letter from Governor Fernão de Albuquerque to the king, 10-2-1621, *DRI*, VII, p. 106.

[245] Published by Subrahmanyam, 'Commerce and Conflict', pp. 76–79.

Conclusion

The work presented in the preceding pages represents an attempt to approach the history of the city of Melaka in concentric circles or successive convergences between two fundamental watersheds: the end of the cycle of the three successive sieges to which the sultanate of Aceh subjected the city between 1573 and 1575 and the foundation of Batavia by the VOC in 1619.

The concentric circles that approach the various parallel and concurrent processes that took place during this period of history, which spanned almost half a century, define the structure of the internal organisation of this work. Thus the initial part provides a general overview that concentrates upon the political conditions pertaining to Melaka within the heart of the Estado da Índia and the evolution of the situation, and then traces the prevailing scenario from an economic point of view. Subsequently, it then proceeds to a more specific approach about the fundamental question that constituted the crux of this study: an analysis of the triangle formed by Portuguese Melaka and the two most important sultanates of the region around the Straits of Melaka, Johor and Aceh, that shared a common geographic space and competed and collaborated with the former in the regional balance.

For a better understanding of the manifold factors in play in this historical process, this work then takes a closer look at some fundamental characteristics of the surrounding environment that enabled the city, far removed from the heart of the Estado da Índia in logistical terms, to survive and integrate itself within local structures. In conclusion, it provides a portrait, albeit a rather general one, of the internal history of Melaka and her neighbours, a kind of close-up that enables the reader to visualise the players, events and tonalities that shaped the city's evolution. On account of their specific nature, the questions concerning the genealogical history of the two sultanates, which includes the information contained in Portuguese sources about the region's history, which shall be expounded upon further over the following pages, have been highlighted and grouped into two separate annexes about the respective sultanates. Finally, a compilation of documents, which are almost entirely unpublished, that were examined in the course of researching this work and are of interest for the topics dealt with in this book is included.

The diverse contents of the various issues studied herein required several different approaches, which, perforce, were quite distinct: 'horizontal' or diachronic cuts whenever it was necessary to understand the evolution of a situation, scenario or trajectory, or define starting and ending points, or enable a more detailed analysis of the aspects that were modified by time and new factors in play and novel conditions. However, one also finds 'vertical' or synchronic approaches whenever it was necessary to characterise or define issues at precise moments in time and to obtain an overview of the space and interaction of the various players or, likewise, whenever it was necessary to expound upon a certain question—often in greater detail—that was intrinsically interesting or was capable of shedding light upon other issues. Thus there is an intersection of views that hopefully will enable a more complete and multifaceted vision of the city that was, for more than a century, a veritable 'jewel of the crown' of the Portuguese empire in Asia.

When the Portuguese Governor Afonso de Albuquerque conquered Melaka in January 1511 he was not only executing a fundamental stage in his blueprint to control the main axes of maritime trade in Asia, which likewise included Goa, Aden and Hormuz. He was also bringing to fruition, although in a rather excessive manner, the pressure brought to bear by King Manuel I to 'discover' the great Malay metropolis, which his predecessor, Viceroy Dom Francisco de Almeida, had neglected to fulfil. For the Portuguese monarch, conquering this city had become an objective of prime importance given the confusing information that had spread throughout Europe about its wealth and location, possibly within the hemisphere of influence that had been attributed to Castille by the premises of the Treaty of Tordesillas.

Vasco da Gama's arrival in India would culminate a long process of disputes with Castille over navigation and control in Atlantic waters and access to the Indian Ocean. However, a few years later, the scenario of Luso-Castillian competition extended to the far side of the earth, at the very limits of the anti-meridian of the line that had divided the world in 1494. This haste to be the first to arrive in Melaka and affirm the Portuguese claim to the city explains the urgency in advancing towards the East before the Spaniards did so via the New World, as Ferdinand Magellan would do a few years later.

Neither the monarch nor his bellicose governor was aware of the far-reaching impact of this conquest, which gave Portugal precocious access to the Far East and the Spice Islands and possession of one of the most important nerve-centres of Maritime Asia for over a century and a quarter. However, the city occupied a remote position in the network of maritime links that would, shortly thereafter, be dubbed the Estado da Índia. Melaka was a singular case amongst all the Portuguese possessions in Asia. Due to its odd location, far removed from the western coast of India and the western Indian Ocean where the Portuguese Crown concentrated its attention and resources, it became a kind of isolated island in the midst of a vast ocean that extended from southern India to Japan, if one excludes the small fortress in Ternate and, later, the one in Tidore, strongholds that existed in permanently precarious conditions and were dependent upon the goodwill of local kingdoms. What dictated the fortunes of Portuguese Melaka was, in large measure, the fact that the waters in the region were not predominantly controlled by Muslims and, at least in an initial phase, even they did not evince any special animosity towards the Portuguese.

The Portuguese rapidly managed to stabilise their position, substituting the existing political power and adapting to local conditions as a way of guaranteeing the survival and, if possible, the prosperity of this trade centre. Prosperity was obtained by exploring three great commercial routes that intersected at the Straits and were responsible for the fortunes of the city: spices from the Indonesian archipelago, Indian textiles and Chinese silks and porcelain. Over the course of the 16th century, in different ways, the Portuguese attempted to profit from each one of these trade routes, and their northern European rivals set upon precisely these commercial links at the beginning of the subsequent century.

Thus, from the very outset, Melaka was rather remote with regard to the political and economic centre of the Estado da Índia and Portuguese power in the Indian Ocean. The city had to learn to guarantee its survival in accordance with local conditions, given that the distance separating Melaka from Goa and the non-existence of neighbouring fortresses meant that external support in times of crisis was rare. The fact that there was no Muslim power in the region immediately surrounding Melaka that could place this Portuguese stronghold at serious risk meant that preoccupations with security were relegated to a secondary plane despite the almost permanent skirmishes with the sultan of Melaka who had been dispossessed in 1511.

It was only when the tide turned and the situation gradually became more hostile in the mid-16th century that Melaka made the city's armadas and defences an urgent priority, so as to guarantee the necessary conditions that would enable the circulation and security of goods and people. It was at this point that the city was fortified and a permanent armada to patrol the Straits was created. In the meantime, the arrival of the Portuguese in Japan and the growth of a small community of merchants on the Chinese coast enabled the city to play a role of renewed importance in links with the Far East at the same time that the definitive implantation of the Spanish presence in the Philippine Islands posed new challenges for the city's role as a first-rate commercial centre.

In 1581 Philip II of Castille and Aragon was elected as Philip I of Portugal, and the Habsburg rule lasted for six decades. The effects of this Iberian Union were inevitably felt on the other side of the planet. The gradual wear and tear on Portuguese structures in the Indian Ocean, based on a maritime network sustained by commercial ports and defended by patrolling armadas, faced a new challenge with the proximity of the Spanish model, based on territorial conquest and executed in the New World and in the Philippines. However, the main effect of the political union was far more dramatic. The end of the 16th century witnessed the arrival of new European powers in the Indian Ocean and, especially, in the waters of the Malay-Indonesian archipelago. The war in Europe that pitted the Catholic Habsburgs against their Protestant enemies—Anglican England and the *rebeldes* from the United Provinces—spread to the Atlantic and, later, to the Indian Ocean, thus becoming the first truly global conflict in history. Melaka, which was the 'weakest link' in the Portuguese maritime network, but which paradoxically held an enviable position with regard to access to Indonesian spices and Chinese silk, was a prime target for the northern Europeans from the very outset, with profound and long-lasting consequences.

Considering the three entities of Melaka, Johor and Aceh as the most important powers in the region of the Straits is nothing new. From the point of view of the Portuguese expansion in Asia, the two sultanates had long been the greatest military threats, the most powerful politico-diplomatic rivals and the greatest economic competitors of Melaka. However, the relationship between these three powers has never merited an autonomous approach and has never been studied with a reasonable level of acuity and depth. In truth, the Melaka-Johor-Aceh triangle goes far beyond a simple division of regional influence or mere economic rivalry. There is a series of important characteristics that makes this relationship a subject of study that is of undeniable interest and that, in addition, gives it a solidity and autonomy as a pertinent object of analysis.

It is a relatively well-known consensus that the 15th century was the 'Golden Age' of Melaka, which emerged and was established as the most important Malay sultanate of the period, a driving force for the diffusion of Islam and the Malay language throughout the Archipelago, a key position in the acceleration of the economic life of Maritime Asia and a veritable mercantile emporium whose fame even reached, in remote echoes, the shores of Europe. Its unexpected capture by the newly arrived Franks was cause for great surprise and rapidly gave way to adjustments in the commercial routines of the Straits region. Despite the Portuguese policy of maintaining pre-existing practices and regulations, so as to ensure the continuity of trade and avoid any reduction in Melaka's capacity to attract mercantile communities, Melaka never again regained its erstwhile prominence. Part of this commerce accompanied the deposed sultan and his court who, after a period of some turbulence, established on the banks of the Johor River a new sultanate which maintained the dynastic line and inherited the prestige it had enjoyed in the past. Part of it disappeared with the withdrawal of the Gujarati mercantile community, bitter rivals of the Portuguese throughout the Indian Ocean, who would later settle in the up-and-coming sultanate of Aceh, located on the northern tip of the island of Sumatra. This is why it is said in the course of this study that Malay Melaka broke into three pieces, each one of which claimed the ancient legacy of the sultanate. Similarly, each one of the three parts was linked with far broader structures that extended throughout the Indian Ocean or, in some cases, as far as the Middle East and Europe. Melaka was part of the Portuguese network of fortresses and maritime links that stretched from Japan to Goa and from there to Lisbon; Aceh, due to the activities of the Gujarati community, extended its interests to Cambay, the east coast of India, the Persian Gulf and the Red Sea, while it reinforced its ties with the Ottoman empire and, locally, expanded its territories in Sumatra and the Malay Peninsula. As for Johor, it retained the prestige that the erstwhile sultanate had enjoyed throughout Southeast Asia, especially in Banda and the Moluccas. This small region around the Straits of Melaka was thus a veritable micro-cosmos of the Indian Ocean.

The relationship amongst the three main players that interacted against the backdrop of the Straits was, at first glance, quite simple: each one attempted to obtain the greatest possible benefits from the others and sought to prevent the other two parties in this triangle from forming an alliance against itself. However, a deeper and more careful analysis of this triangle reveals far more interesting details and allows an understanding of some of the reasons why Melaka, despite its inadequate fortifications, almost non-existent defensive infrastructure and an eternally absent patrolling armada, managed to survive amongst the diplomatic intrigues, political mistrust and mutual fear that vitiated relations between Johor and Aceh. They likewise enable one to obtain a more or less clear picture of the peaks in tension between the three rivals and the turbulent evolution of the alliances that were formed and broken, especially during the period between 1592 and 1606 when, for the first time, the Portuguese managed to establish cordial relations and almost achieved a formal alliance and a commercial treaty with Aceh.

One of the most interesting—and at the same time, most dis-concerting—questions that involve the history of Portuguese Melaka, especially during this period, is the contradictory nature of all aspects of life in the city, from politics to economic contingencies, everyday life to the diplomatic balance, from social status to existing conditions of defence. In every one of these facets one can detect contradictions and, in a few exemplary cases, veritable paradoxes between the apparent and the real, what is stated in coeval documentation and what can be detected by reading between the lines, in plays of light and shadows and reflections, intentions, words and deeds.

In order to achieve greater clarity in the panorama presented herein it was necessary to take local and regional conditions and the city's adapt-ation to the Malay World into consideration. At the turn of the century,

Melaka was apparently a more 'Portuguese' city than in the decades immediately after 1511. The number of *casados* was greater than ever before and this segment of society now constituted the main pillar of the city's defences, on account of which they had progressively obtained many privileges—fiscal benefits—in comparison to the Asian communities. On the other hand, the former policy of religious tolerance, when not an assumed privilege, with regard to the Hindu Kelings and other communities now came to an end and pressure to convert to Christianity, influenced by the winds of the Catholic Reformation, was effective and real. A clear sign of this tendency was the evolution of the nature of the posts of *bendahara* and *tumenggung*, which from being representatives of non-Christian communities now became offices with widely differing responsibilities that were, however, unequivocally linked to the defensive and diplomatic functions of the city as a whole.

However, the way in which the city and its main powers began to act according to local practices, the way they rapidly acquired and internalised this way of behaving, trading and guaranteeing the security that was characteristic of the other sultanates and, especially, the manner in which the social strata that ensured the routine functioning of the city, such as the *casados*, acted with regard to local interests and conditions and not according to the orders and directives that emanated from Goa or Lisbon, provide an element of contradiction in the scenario described above, as can be better ascertained in chapters 4 and 5 of this book.

During the early stages of this work the internal history of the sultanates of Johor and Aceh was merely the subject of curiosity and, at the time, considered to be of lesser interest. The initial concern of this study was to understand the way in which the Portuguese adjusted to local conditions and to study the relationship between Melaka and its two powerful neighbours. However, as this work progressed, a dual necessity became obvious: first, the authors who had produced works about the sultanates in question generally ignored the contribution of the Portuguese sources with regard to local history as the overwhelming majority were not acquainted with the Portuguese language and required English or French translations, thus considerably reducing the amplitude of available information. Ian MacGregor and Charles Boxer are two notable exceptions to this generalisation.

Secondly, works about the Portuguese presence in Southeast Asia have not paid particular attention to the internal history of Melaka's neighbours, focusing instead on the peculiar forms this presence assumed in the Archipelago and on military, political and, especially, economic aspects of Melaka and its links with the Far East and the Moluccas.

Thus, one became progressively interested in attempting, in some way, to remedy this double lacuna that gradually assumed an increasingly important place in the overall research that this work entailed, especially when it became clear that the Portuguese sources could shed some light on diverse obscure questions about the genealogy of the sultans of Johor. This was an unprecedented approach that enabled a better understanding of the history of Johor and Aceh during the period under study, despite the fact that several of the problems that came up in the course of this cross-referencing of sources had to be dealt with in a superficial and unsatisfactory manner.

It would be a useful and highly desirable exercise if some of the information and conclusions that resulted from this process, presented especially in chapter 4 and the annexes, were rigorously reviewed by specialists in the field, since they were produced with a clearly insufficient knowledge of the Malay-Indonesian language and culture and were based, in large measure, on conjecture, theoretical models and a dash of imagination. The dynastic crisis in Aceh in 1579, the chronology of the sultans of Johor between 1570–71 and 1615 and the explicatory model of the socio-political mutations that took place in this sultanate during this period are some examples of questions that were dealt with mainly on the basis of the information contained in Portuguese sources and thus lack, in some cases, a critique that, as is evident, should ideally be extended to the entire work.

ANNEX I

The Sultanate of Johor: Genealogical Questions and Problems

The genealogy of the sultans of Johor during the 16th century is still quite confused and controversial. The available sources manifest a great many lacunae and, above all, contradictory information. Portuguese sources could shed some light on this nebulous period despite their deficiencies. Therefore it would be of interest to compare the information they provide with other sources of a different origin so as to enable them to contribute, in some way, towards the political history of the sultanate.

The difficulties involved in reconciling European sources (Portuguese in the present case) and the information obtained from Malay sources are quite evident from the very first approach. In the specific case of Johor, there are additional difficulties concerning the 'Malay' period of the sultanate's history, that is, since its foundation until the crisis of 1699. This is due to various reasons: the sultanate's political instability from its foundation to 1641, the peculiar characteristics of the Malay sources, both in their essential features as well as in the particular case of the period under study. This political instability needs a supplementary clarification: it does not mean internal instability or dynastic disputes; on the contrary, the sultanate was quite stable from this point of view. It consists of the constant transfers of the capital after the conquest of Melaka by Afonso de Albuquerque, and the fact that the sultanate was under permanent pressure from both the Portuguese and Aceh. The lack of clarity, or even the downright contradiction of the sources, generally produced in a later period, thus has a preliminary explanation. But there are other, more important ones that concern the very characteristics of the Malay sources.

The use of Malay sources regarding this particular period requires special caution. In the specific case of the genealogies, and in political terms, one must keep in mind the fact that they were prepared and later transcribed and modified with political objectives. To begin with, in the case of Johor, one must stress the most important political aspect: to show the continuity of *daulat*, or royal power in the broader sense of sovereignty tinged with sacredness, claiming a continuity of transmission from the first king of Palembang.[1] The legitimacy of the sultan's power depended upon his success in claiming *daulat*, and this resulted in genealogies serving as a political instrument. For the historian, however, one can imagine the problems of interpretation that such a situation causes, and that only a painstaking cross-checking of sources can, to a certain extent, mitigate.

For the period under study there is a further difficulty connected with the specific characteristics of coeval Malay sources. For this period there are two main sources to consider: the second version of the *Sejarah Melayu*,[2] dated to the 18th century,[3] and the *Bustan us-Salatin*, written in the mid-17th century in Aceh on the orders of Sultan Iskandar Thani.[4]

---

[1]   Bowen, 'Cultural Models for Historical Genealogies ...', p. 163.
[2]   Known as the 'Shellabear version' because it was first published by W. G. Shellabear in the late 19th century and was subsequently re-published several times. The first version, translated into English and published by C. C. Brown, was written in the early 17th century but the events described therein do not go beyond the early 16th century.
[3]   According to Bowen, 'Cultural Models for Historical Genealogies', p. 170. The exact date of this version is still not accepted by all scholars; part of the preface was written on the orders of Sultan Abdullah Maayat Syah (who ruled from 1613 to 1623), but the appendix was written after his death (Winstedt, *A History of Johore*, p. 26). As for the central portion of the book, some authors accept 1612 as the most probable date of composition of both versions; in this regard, *see* Wake, 'Melaka in the 15th Century...', pp. 129–131.
[4]   Lombard, *Le Sultanat d'Atjéh...*, pp. 19–20. Bottoms presents a list of partially or fully published Malay sources in 'Malay Historical Works'. Alves describes the main chronicles of Aceh in *O Domínio do Norte de Sumatra*, pp. 28–30.

However, they are not consistent in the data they provide. The *Sejarah Melayu* is, clearly, more complete, on account of not being a foreign chronicle but—just like other identical sources of the same period, such as the *Tuhfat al-Nafis* or the *Silsilah Melayu dan Bugis*—it was written after the 1699 crisis in Johor. And this is a fundamental piece of information with regard to understanding its contents.

The year 1699 witnessed the assassination of the sultan, an event that marked the end of Johor's Malay dynasty and gave rise, after various vicissitudes, to the preponderance of the Bugis (from the Celebes). Johor, which, since the times of the Melaka sultanate, had not suffered dynastic disputes that implied serious ruptures, namely in the *daulat*, witnessed a civil war for possession of the throne at the beginning of the 18th century. The throne was finally taken by the *bendahara* who, with the support of the Bugis, inaugurated a new dynasty. Thus there was a rupture in the political lineage of the sultanate. However, the new Bugis hegemony that transferred the centre of the sultanate to the archipelago of Riau-Lingga assimilated and claimed the sultanate's Malay heritage, and would later transform itself into an ardent champion of Malay culture and traditions.[5]

However, during the 18th century there was a need to legitimate this new power that, in the case that is of interest here, took the form of a vast range of court literature aimed at legitimising the fusion of two ancestries, explaining the new situation. Consequently, this literature tends, on the one hand, to lay claim to the direct transferral of the *daulat* since the times of Sri Vijaya until the sultan who was assassinated in 1699 and, on the other hand, seeks to attribute a royal origin to the lineage of the *bendahara* of Johor, so that the new sultan could, in this manner, claim the *daulat*.[6] Thus one must understand the context and the purposes for which the works were elaborated. In the *Tuhfat al-Nafis* and in the *Silsilah Melayu dan Bugis*, the period prior to 1699 is generally summarised, presented only in order to prepare the link between the Malays and the Bugis. In the *Sejarah Melayu*, as this is probably a later version of an earlier work, one can find an incorporation of information, with the same objectives, but via a different route, as we shall shortly see.

---

5   Matheson, 'Strategies of Survival', p. 6.
6   Andaya, *The Kingdom of Johor*, p. 313. About this model, *see* Bowen, 'Cultural Models for Historical Genealogies', pp. 170–172.

It is now commonly accepted that the sultanate of Johor was founded by the son of the last sultan of Melaka, Mahmud Syah. He was called Alauddin Riayat Syah II and ruled from 1528 to 1564 when, after a long conflict with Aceh, he succumbed to a surprise attack, lost Aru and was taken prisoner by the Acehnese.[7] Here, Malay sources differ substantially: the appendix of the *Sejarah Melayu* does not mention conflicts with Aceh at this time, only pointing out that the sultan died in his capital, Johor Lama, and left a son, Muzaffar Syah, who succeeded him, and a daughter, Raja Fatimah. The *Bustan us-Salatin* states that he was taken to Aceh as a prisoner, along with his family, but that his captor, Sultan Alauddin Riayat Syah al-Kahar, gave his daughter in marriage to a son of the captured sultan, called Radin Bahr, and sent him to Johor to succeed his father.[8] It is obvious that the *Bustan*, written in Aceh, avoids mentioning the assassination of the Malay sultan, preferring instead to show the magnanimity of the sultan of Aceh in offering his daughter as a bride. The *Hikayat Aceh*, a panegyric to Iskandar Muda, sultan of Aceh, only records Alauddin's capture.[9]

According to all the sources except the *Bustan*, Alauddin was suc-ceeded by Muzaffar Syah. Could he be the 'Radin Bahr' who is mentioned

---

[7] Date mentioned by Fernão Mendes Pinto but compatible with data presented by Malay sources. *See* Alves, *O Domínio do Norte de Sumatra*, p. 166, note 82. It is interesting to note how this fact is mentioned by Diogo do Couto in the first version of his *Soldado Prático*, whose precise date of composition is not known. Referring to the hostility of Aceh towards neighbouring Malay sultanates, Couto states that 'He wages war on them with his armadas, as he did a few days ago against Johor, where he took the local King prisoner, along with a large number of souls and a wealthy sack' (*O Primeiro Soldado Prático*, p. 498). *See* Pereira, p. [233]. If one accepts the information provided by Mendes Pinto, then 1564 would therefore be the exact date when Couto's work was written.

[8] Information presented by Winstedt, *A History of Johore*, p. 24. *See* Macgregor, 'Johor Lama in the Sixteenth Century', pp. 85–86.

[9] According to this work, the sultan of Aceh married a daughter of the sultan of Johor, who fled to the hinterland when he heard that his son-in-law was arriving with his fleet. He was captured and taken prisoner to Aceh (excerpt in Alves, *O Primeiro Soldado Prático*, pp. 208–212).

in this work? Some authors acknowledge the possibility.[10] In any case, Muzaffar Syah reigned from 1564 to 1569 or 1570. This period is the most obscure and the most confused period of Johor's genealogical history with regard to his descendants and those of the following sultan, Ali Jalla Abdul Jalil Syah II (the 'Rajale' of the Portuguese sources).

Let us summarise this history in a few lines, to later proceed to analyse the sources and reconstruct the genealogy. According to the Malay genealogies, with the *Sejarah Melayu* at the forefront,[11] Muzaffar was the son of Alauddin,[12] and had a sister, Raja Fatimah, as has already been mentioned. She was married to a certain Raja Omar of Pahang (whose origins are obscure), who had earlier married a daughter of a prominent personage of Pahang, called Sri Nara Diraja Pahang in the sources. It so happened that the throne passed from Muzaffar to the young Abdul Jalil Syah I, the son of Raja Omar and Raja Fatimah, who would have ruled for a brief span of time (*c*.1570), and died at the age of nine. Thus, power passed to his father, Raja Omar, who took the name Ali Jalla Abdul Jalil Syah II, as has already been mentioned.

The confusion is compounded by the uncertainty of a piece of information: the paternity of Abdullah (who would later ascend to the throne with the name Abdullah Maayat Syah and reign from 1613 to 1623), son of the *anak* Sri Nara Diraja. This source casts a doubt over whether he was the son of Raja Omar, or the result of a relationship of Muzaffar. As Winstedt points out, it seems clear that the history included in the appendix of the *Sejarah Melayu* that describes the divorce between Raja Omar and his wife, and the secret wedding of the latter with Muzaffar, only seeks to legitimate Abdullah's lineage, attributing his ancestry to the line of Melaka, personified by Muzaffar.[13] One must, therefore, keep in mind the efforts of the genealogists to minimise the

---

[10] *See*, for instance, Gibson-Hill, 'On the Alleged Death of Sultan Ala'u'd-din II of Johor', p. 135; Andaya, 'The Structure of Power in 17th Century Johor', p. 2. Winstedt raises questions in this regard.

[11] Generally accepted by scholars like Gibson-Hill, 'On the Alleged Death of Sultan Ala'u'd-din II of Johor' and Buyong, *Sejarah Johor*, p. 97.

[12] There are at least two Portuguese sources that state he was a brother and not a son: Pereira, *História da Índia...*, p. [235], and Couto, *Da Ásia*, VIII, xxi, p. 144.

[13] Winstedt, *A History of Johore*, pp. 25–26.

role of Raja Omar and his son Alauddin (his successor), attributing a direct descent from Muzaffar, and thus a continuance of the *daulat*,[14] to Abdullah's lineage, which lasted till 1699. The *Silsilah Melayu dan Bugis* does not hesitate to present this version,[15] while the *Tuhfat al-Nafis* purely and simply omits Raja Omar from the genealogy.[16] In the same way, the young Abdul Jalil I himself is seen as the biological son of Raja Omar, but political 'son' of Muzaffar, by means of a narrative of the *Sejarah* that enables one to establish a (political, not biological) continuity between Muzaffar Syah and his nephew.[17] Raja Omar is, once again, relegated to an inferior plane. The *Bustan* attributes Muzaffar's death to poisoning, thus bringing the lineage of Melaka to an end.[18] Even Diogo do Couto, as we shall see, adds a few words about these issues.

Until now we have limited ourselves to mentioning the information contained in the Malay sources. The Portuguese sources provide data that do not always coincide with their Malay counterparts. However, it seems that from all of the available material that it is possible to present an alternative to the traditional version. There are four important extracts from Portuguese texts to consider: two from Diogo do Couto, one that was probably written by António Bocarro, and an anonymous text. It seems preferable to immediately present the excerpts and analyse them later. Thus, we have:

1. *Da Ásia*, by Diogo do Couto:

'In Decade IX one mentioned how Sultan Malafaxa, King of Viantana, who was married to a daughter of Aceh, died, and not without suspicions

---

[14] Bowen, 'Cultural Models for Historical Genealogies ...', pp. 174–175. It is clear that one is accepting here the hypothesis of the Shellabear version that the *Sejarah Melayu* was composed in the 18th century; if one considers the possibility, as others have done (*see* note 3, above), that it was composed during the reign of Abdullah, it becomes easier to understand the preoccupation with legitimating this sultan to the detriment of his brother, reinforcing his links with Muzaffar.

[15] Ed. by Hans Overbeck, p. 348.

[16] Ed. by Virginia Matheson and B. W. Andaya, p. 18.

[17] *See* Bowen, 'Cultural Models for Historical Genealogies ...', p. 175. The father/son (*bapak/anak*) duality may have a 'generational' sense and not a strictly biological one.

[18] Winstedt, *A History of Johore*, p. 25.

of poisoning, that they say was ordered to be administered to him by Enchisadel, who we commonly call Rasale, who was his mother's brother, to take his kingdom from him, as he subsequently did, because there was no other heir; and as soon as he was obeyed by everyone, he immediately married his nephew's wife, the daughter of Aceh, who was so offended, that he decided to avenge the affront.'[19]

2. *Vida de D. Paulo de Lima Pereira*, by Diogo do Couto:

'The King of Melaka, from whom Afonso de Albuquerque took that city, was called Mamed Xá, who, after losing the city went to Ujantana and founded the city of Jor, where he established his base; and there, being very old, the King of Aceh captured him, and took him to his kingdom, where he died. He was succeeded in his kingdom by Sultan Alaudin, who always engaged in many wars with Melaka. On his death, he was succeeded by his son Mala Faxá, who was a boy held under the power of his uncle, who is this Rajale King of Jor, against whom Dom Paulo Lima fought; who after a while killed his nephew, being this one already married to a daughter of the King of Aceh, whom he subsequently wed himself, and took his kingdom from him, his given name is Sultan Abdal Jalel.'[20]

3. Text attributed to António Bocarro, published as 'A Capitania de Amboino':

'At that time, Jor was at war with Melaka, and united with Aceh, and as the galleon [of Martim Afonso de Melo] made its way to Ambon, already being in the Straits of Sabang, as far along as the Diamões, at daybreak they came across Aceh's armada, which was very large and powerful, because it consisted of two hundred sails, which included forty royal galleys.

The Rayale was aboard this armada and was bringing the daughter of the King of Aceh, married to the little king, who was the Raiale's nephew: because the Raiale was not King; he was merely a governor, as the little king was not yet of age to govern. And this Raiale made peace with Aceh and went to his kingdom, as the King of Aceh had done him harm, because the father of that little king, the Acehnese had captured him and put his eyes out, and after that they killed him.

---

[19]   Década X, part 1, III, ii, p. 272.
[20]   Ch. xxiv, p. 108.

This armada was coming to assist the Raiale against Melaka, and was so large that it amazed the onlooker.'[21]

4. 'Vida e Acções de Mathias de Albuquerque', by an unknown author. About the despatch of Mathias de Albuquerque's armada to Melaka in 1576, it states that he went:

'to protect the seas of Melaka, that the King of Aceh had overrun with a large number of ships and soldiers, as well as due to the old and natural enmity that he always had with us, and his own interests that he hoped to obtain from this, as by having a daughter married to Recalale, nephew and heir of the King of Jor, descended from the ancient line of the Kings of Melaka, who when evicted from the city went to establish their settlements alongside this river of Jor, preserving the title and empire over these few Malays who withdrew with them ..., and with the renewed help of Aceh, they sought to strike us, a rather arduous and difficult business for our men ....'[22]

Later, while describing the expedition by Luís Carvalho to the Johor River, he narrates how he ran into an armada from Aceh:

'Recalale, the nephew and heir of the King of Jor, with whom we say that the King of Aceh had married a daughter and to whom he wished to restore the sceptre of Melaka, which had formerly belonged to his ancestors, was also on board ....'[23]

According to these sources, one can immediately draw one conclusion: Ali Jalla/Raja Omar was the one responsible for the death of his nephew, the sultan or heir to the throne. All of them contain partial and imperfect versions of the same political phenomenon, but it seems reasonable to acknowledge that this nephew could not have been Muzaffar, who was not a youth at the time of his death. As Couto states in another chapter of his 'Décadas' that he was about forty years old in 1568,[24] it is, surely, Abdul Jalil Syah I, as everything points towards him being the son of Muzaffar, and not of Ali Jalla. The information provided by Bocarro is conclusive, where he speaks of the 'little King' who reigned under the protection of his uncle. Likewise, the 'Vida e Acções'

---

[21]   Published in *DHMPPO/Insulíndia*, IV, ch. 53, p. 335.
[22]   Ch. 6, fl. 14v. *See* Document Appendix, No. 1.
[23]   Ibid., fl. 16. *See* Document Appendix, No. 1.
[24]   Couto, Década VIII, xxiv, p. 170.

speaks of the nephew of the sultan 'descendant of the ancient line of the Kings of Melaka'; except it calls him 'Recalale', that is, Ali Jalla who, as Bocarro says, was the one who was to be found on board the armada from Aceh. Couto errs in calling him 'Mala Faxá' (Muzaffar Syah) since, as we have already seen, he was not a 'boy'. Thus he mistakes the father for the son. Couto defines Ali Jalla as his uncle, but makes a mistake while explaining their relationship: he was not his uncle on account of being 'a brother of his mother' but rather, as the husband of his paternal aunt.

It also seems reasonable to accept that Abdul Jalil I, the young son of Muzaffar Syah, would have married a daughter of the sultan of Aceh due to pressure exerted by his uncle Ali Jalla, who governed Johor while he was a minor. This marriage undoubtedly took place in 1576, after Aceh's siege of Melaka in 1575, when, as we have already seen, Johor's distrust of Aceh was evident. The rules of the triangular balance ensured that the weakness of one of the vertices after a confrontation with another almost always resulted in the former seeking the support of the third party. Aceh, defeated in 1573 and 1575 by the Portuguese, would certainly have sought Johor's assistance, sealed by a wedding. As Bocarro mentions, at a certain point Ali Jalla 'made peace' with his rival, thus increasing joint pressure against Melaka and coinciding with the arrival of Matias de Albuquerque's armada.

The death of Abdul Jalil at the hands of his uncle is another aspect in which we are obliged to reject the Malay sources: he could not have died in 1570, as they claim. The most probable date is 1580, that is after the death of his father-in-law in 1579 and before the attack by Aceh against Melaka and Johor in August 1582. However, contrary to what Couto says, this sudden hostility by Aceh should not be taken as the main cause of Ali Jalla's seizure of the daughter of the sultan of Aceh who was married to Abdul Jalil. The reason is simple: from 1579 or 1580 onwards, the Acehnese throne was in the hands of a foreigner from Perak, known as Alauddin or Mansur Syah,[25] and it does not seem that he would have viewed this act by the sultan of Johor to be a great offence. The inverse is more probable: that Ali Jalla killed his nephew and took his wife precisely

---

[25]   The version presented by Erédia (also followed by Winstedt), which states that the new sultan sent a daughter of his to Ali Jalla as a bride is implausible because he says the event took place when Matias de Albuquerque arrived in Melaka (that is, late 1576) ('Vida e Acções...', fl. 8).

by taking advantage of the death of the sultan of Aceh in 1579. As we shall see in the following pages dedicated to Aceh, there are clear indications that point to the marriage of Ali Jalla with a daughter of this new sultan of Aceh sometime during the 1580s.

To bring this period to a close, it only remains to determine the date of Muzaffar Syah's death, and whether it was caused by his brother-in-law, who ascended to power as his nephew's regent. Generally, the date attributed to this change has been held to be 1570–71.[26] However, the information provided by a Portuguese source would suggest that Ali Jalla held the reins of power as early as 1569. The work in question is a transcription of two letters from 'Resatalle, King and Regent of the Malay', dated August and 6 September 1569, hailing Mem Lopes for his victory in the battle he engaged in with an armada from Aceh that was bound for Johor.[27]

Ali Jalla died in 1597[28] in Batu Sawar, the capital of his sultanate. The Malay sources do not say anything about the cause of his death, but it is possible that it was induced by the attack that Aceh probably unleashed at that time.[29]

The following genealogical question concerns the dynastic problem created between his two sons, Alauddin Riayat Syah III (the successor to the throne) and the future Abdullah Maayat Syah. It is necessary to refute the version provided by the Malay sources that make the latter out to be the son of Muzaffar, as has already been mentioned. Two additional reasons: one cannot understand how Ali Jalla could have proceeded to

---

[26] *See* the works quoted in notes 10 and 11, above.

[27] 'Relação da victoria milagrosa que Nosso Senhor deu a huma nao dos christãos contra os Dachens', 16-1-1570, *DHMPPO/Insulíndia*, VI, 326.

[28] Date mentioned by Erédia, *Informação da Aurea Chersoneso*, p. 71.

[29] The 'Shellabear version' only states that he 'died in Batu Sawar' (Gibson-Hill, 'On the alleged death...', pp. 125 and 135); however, information provided by a Portuguese source points to a probable strike by Aceh against Johor at this time. In a letter to the king dated April 1598, Viceroy D. Francisco da Gama wrote: 'I received reliable information from Melaka stating that Aceh, with all his might, was on his way to Johor, who is expecting him with considerable preparations for war and has already sunk a large number of his vessels; with Our Lord's help, they will destroy each other' (BN, *Res.*, cod. 1976, fl. 91v.).

eliminate his nephew Abdul Jalil, a condition *sine qua non* to obtain power, and not do the same with Abdullah, if the latter was also his nephew; secondly, because European sources in general, and Portuguese sources in particular, say that the two were brothers; one particular source, that deserves some credibility, clearly states that Abdullah was the 'son of the King'.[30]

Abdullah appears in the sources under two names, the first being 'Raja Bongsu', and the second 'Raja Seberang'.[31] Alauddin is only 'the sultan'. The most interesting aspect of this question is the division of power between them, from the time of the death of Ali Jalla in 1597 until the attack on and destruction of the capital of Johor by the sultan of Aceh, Iskandar Muda, in 1613. Matelieff states that this sharing of power was due to the fact that Alauddin, the elder brother, was incapable of governing on account of being a drunkard with loose morals, as were two of his brothers, the sultan of Siak and a third brother, Raja Laut.[32] Only the youngest brother, Raja Sabrang, allegedly had the necessary qualities to be sultan.[33] They also differed in their preferences, the sultan being favourably inclined towards the Portuguese and Raja Bongsu towards the Dutch.

This duality of power is something that has not been explained clearly: was it only a lack of interest on the part of Alauddin, who left

---

[30] Letter from the bishop of Melaka to the king, 15-12-1588. AGS, *Secr. Prov.*, book 1551, fl. 400v.

[31] *Bongsu*, 'youngest'; *seberang*, *sebrang* or *sabrang*, 'other side', 'opposite side'. The latter is due to the fact that he established his palace on the other side of the Johor River, opposite the fortress of his brother, the sultan. *See* the excerpt of a report from Cornelis de Matelieff in Borschberg, 'Description of Batu Sawar'.

[32] *Laut*, 'sea'. *See* Borschberg, 'A description by Admiral Cornelis de Matelieff de Jonge of the four Johor Rulers'.

[33] Valentijn, 'Description of Melaka', Pt 2, p. 134, follows Matelieff. Gibson-Hill deals with this issue in detail in 'On the alleged death…'. The 'History of the Ming Dynasty' also confusingly mentions both brothers (published by W. P. Groeneveldt, 'Notes on the Malay Archipelago…', p. 255). The identity of the character mentioned by Diogo do Couto and in the letter quoted in note 29, referring to a son of Ali Jalla called 'Raia Itão' (Raja Hitam, 'Black King'), is unknown.

affairs of state in the hands of his brother, as European sources mention?[34] The fact that Raja Bongsu established his residence on the other side of the river, in a fortress that was similar, albeit on a smaller scale, to the fortress of Batu Sawar,[35] possibly constituting his own court, could be an indication of a sharing or even absorption of power on the part of the younger brother. One only needs to observe the ease with which Raja Bongsu handled affairs of state, namely, at the time in which he managed to sign agreements with the Dutch against Melaka, between 1603 and 1607. His political, as well as military, influence was on the rise, even internally.[36]

Alauddin seemed to be dragged to take radical decisions, such as the hostility declared against the Portuguese, towards which he was perhaps not inclined. Even Erédia states that his acts were due to the 'bad advice' of his brother.[37] Balthasar Bort, the governor of Melaka in the second half of the 17th century, transcribes the treaty between Matelieff and Johor in his report, which was signed thus at the end: 'We, Jan de Patuan and Rajah Sabrangh, Kings of Johor, do hereby promise to maintain the above agreement'.[38] Thus there appears to have been two powers in the sultanate during some years, a situation that the sultan of Aceh took advantage of to strike a decisive blow in 1613.

---

[34] The *Silsilah Melayu dan Bugis* (p. 348) presents a similar version. Also *see* the royal letter to the viceroy, 24-12-1610, *DRI*, I, p. 414, where it is mentioned that Raja Bongsu 'is in charge of matters of war' in Johor.

[35] According to Valentijn, it was 1,300 paces 'in circumference' and that of Kota Sabrang, about 400 or 500 ('Description of Melaka', Pt 3, p. 293). John de Mandelslo says almost the same ('The Remaining Voyages of...' in Harris, *Navigatium atque Itinerantium Bibliotheca*, vol. I, p. 783). Both had certainly followed the first-hand information by Cornelis de Matelieff; *see* note 31, above.

[36] When Johor went to war against Melaka in 1606, the *orang kaya* of Johor refused to place their men under the command of anyone but Raja Bongsu; Andaya, *The Kingdom of Johor*, p. 34, note 37. Bocarro says this character was 'the most important warrior among the Malays' (*Década 13*, I, xliv, p. 165); *see* letter quoted in note 34, above.

[37] Erédia, 'Declaraçam de Malaca...', fl. 44v.

[38] Bort, 'Report of Governor Balthasar Bort...', p. 12. 'Jan de Patuan' is an obvious corruption of 'Yang di Pertuan', a title of the Malay royalty.

Several sources describe the attack on Batu Sawar and the capture of Raja Bongsu, who was taken as a prisoner to Aceh along with other members of the royal family.[39] At this point Raja Bongsu already eclipsed and superimposed himself over his brother to such an extent that various sources state that the latter was the one who had been captured by Aceh, not making any distinction between the two characters.[40] As for Alauddin, everything points towards the fact that he fled to Bentan, in Riau. An Acehnese general was punished for not having managed to capture him.[41] Subsequently, Raja Bongsu married one of Iskandar Muda's sisters and was sent back to Johor with a large number of Acehnese to reconstruct the razed city.[42] In any case, the pact between Iskandar Muda and Raja Bongsu allowed the latter to assume power in Johor, where he immediately tried to assert his legitimacy in Riau, one of the key centres of the sultanate.[43]

The events of 1615 are tinged with a certain degree of confusion. The generally accepted version claims that Alauddin was removed from power after 1613 and that he subsequently wandered around the archipelago for an unknown period of time, perhaps being assassinated by Iskandar Muda.[44] The sources once again mention the 'king' of Johor, but it is

---

[39] Amongst others, his brother, the sultan of Siak. 'The Standish-Croft Journal' in Best, *The Voyage of Thomas Best*, pp. 169–170; Floris, *Peter Floris*, p. 81; Bocarro, *Década 13*, xxxix, p. 165; ch. XCIV, p. 417.

[40] For instance, the letter of T. Best, 12-7-1613, *LREIC*, I, p. 270; Bocarro, *Década*, p. 417, says Raja Bongsu 'is the same as the King'. Gibson-Hill, 'On the Alleged Death of Sultan Ala'u'd-din II of Johor', defines and clarifies the confusion for the first time; Lombard quotes him, but his conclusions are quite different (*Le Sultanat d'Atjéh...*, p. 92, note 3); Andaya still holds that they were both captured and that Alauddin died in Aceh and Raja Bongsu was sent back to Johor (*The Kingdom of Johor*, pp. 24, 40, 53, note 15).

[41] 'Standish-Croft Journal' in Best, *The Voyage of Thomas Best*, p. 171.

[42] In October or November 1613, according to Floris, *Peter Floris*, p. 102.

[43] Floris, ibid., says (on 8 November) that, about 14 days earlier, Raja Bongsu had left for Riau while trying to depose his brother and seize the throne (information provided by a *selete*). If one accepts that the 'Shellabear version' of the *Sejarah Melayu* was composed during his reign, it is therefore possible that it could have been written during this period of 1613–14, when he was attempting to overthrow his brother.

[44] Gibson-Hill, 'On the Alleged Death of Sultan Ala'u'd-din II of Johor', p. 135.

generally accepted that they are referring to Raja Bongsu, now known as Sultan Abdullah Maayat Syah. This question is associated with Iskandar Muda's attack on Melaka in 1615, but a more careful analysis of the sources enables one to suggest some interesting hypotheses.

Iskandar Muda's expansionist policy came up against Melaka and Johor. In the case of the latter—and even though the sultanate did not have the power it had attained during the reign of Ali Jalla, especially prior to 1587—Johor still wielded sufficient prestige to constitute an obstacle for the ambitious Acehnese sultan. Thus the strike of 1613 served his objectives, not from the point of view of eliminating a military threat, as Johor was a weakened power, but in the sense of controlling the young and undoubtedly dissatisfied Raja Bongsu, taking him prisoner and marrying him to one of his sisters, thus guaranteeing a fusion of bloodlines. Thus, we can see how this manoeuvre was far more advantageous than an order to simply assassinate Raja Bongsu. We could even consider that he would have preferred Alauddin, who managed to escape.

For Raja Bongsu, this manoeuvre was far from unfavourable, for it would finally enable him to remove his brother and seize power in Johor. However, in 1614, having rebuilt his capital in Batu Sawar, it seems that the new Abdullah Maayat Syah, as Raja Bongsu was now known, attempted to shake off his brother-in-law's tutelage. He tried to back away from the alliance against Melaka, from where he received an embassy.[45] A skilled diplomat,[46] he probably tried to avoid a direct confrontation with his Portuguese neighbours without arousing the hostility of the delicate sensibilities of his brother-in-law. The subsequent events indicate that Iskandar Muda did not give him any room for manoeuvre for these intentions, keeping him on his side for some time still.

In September 1615 the Portuguese detected and managed to deter a powerful Acehnese armada, commanded by the sultan himself,[47] bound for Melaka. We can state with some degree of certainty that the sultan

---

[45] Bocarro, *Década*, xciv, pp. 418–419. However, this author clearly exaggerates the sultan's receptivity to the pressure exerted by the Portuguese ambassador, Fernão da Costa.

[46] According to Winstedt, *A History of Johore*, p. 39.

[47] Anonymous letter [1615], BN, *Res*, cod. 1975, fls. 193–194v.; it also mentions the date of the Acehnese attack (Document Appendix, No. 19); Bocarro, *Década*, xciii, p. 413, also states that the sultan himself was in command of the fleet.

who was to be found in Johor at this point was Alauddin, who certainly took advantage of his brother's absence, testified by various sources: in April, Bongsu/Abdullah was, without doubt, in Pedir with Iskandar Muda, preparing the offensive against Melaka.[48] At the end of June he was in Aceh,[49] and stayed with his brother-in-law during the following months.[50] This appears sufficient to allow one to conclude that Abdullah accompanied Iskandar Muda during the preparations for the armada and the attack on Melaka carried out in September.[51] Diverse sources affirm that, at the time, a 'king' who was friendly to the Portuguese was to be found in Johor; therefore it could only be Alauddin.[52]

As has already been analysed in another chapter, Iskandar Muda made peace with the Portuguese after the naval defeat he suffered en route to Melaka, communicating his intentions of attacking Johor.[53] He does seem to have done so immediately, at the end of October or in early November, running into a Dutch armada on the Johor River.[54] The

---

[48] Letter from A. Spaight to N. Downton, 4-7-1615, *LREIC*, III, p.127. He would have left Johor in late 1614. In August of the same year he was still in Batu Sawar, where he received a Dutch ambassador, having refused permission to build a fortress (Winstedt, *A History of Johore*, p. 39). A letter from Philip II to the viceroy, dated 6-2-1616, states that, 'When these events occurred, he and his brother the King of Siak had both gone to Aceh because that King had summoned them' (*DRI*, III, p. 380).

[49] Letter from John Millward to the EIC, 13-11-1615, *LREIC*, IV, p. 225.

[50] The letter from J. Sandcroft and E. Aspinall to the EIC, 12-10-1615, *LREIC*, III, p. 190, referring to Iskandar Muda, says: 'The King of Johor, who is now there, having married his sister, although he be his prisoner do often drink drunk together.'

[51] In a letter to R. Wickman, William Eaton says: 'The King of Aceh and Johor are gone to take Melaka with an infinite number of people and galleys' (22-6-1616, *LREIC*, IV, p. 121).

[52] A. Botelho de Sousa, despite his knowledge of English, Dutch and Portuguese sources, was not aware of this fact, having considered Alauddin to have died in 1613 and assuming all these events to involve Abdullah (*Subsídios para a História...*, II, pp. 368–369). The same opinion might be expressed about Andaya, *The Kingdom of Johor*, pp. 24–25.

[53] Letter quoted in note 47, fl. 193v.

[54] Winstedt, *A History of Johore*, p. 38, quotes a letter from the Dutch captain, Steven van der Hagen, who stated that he had found an Acehnese fleet in

urgency with which he attacked Johor, having hastily made peace with the Portuguese, suggests that Alauddin would have triumphantly returned to power, taking advantage of the fact that his brother was, really or hypothetically, a captive. He had set in motion another manoeuvre that represented a potential threat for Aceh: he had placed his son Raja Bujang, under Portuguese escort, on the throne of Pahang—a fact that Gibson-Hill dates to August 1615[55]—taking advantage of a dynastic crisis in that sultanate.[56] This version does not, however, enjoy unanimous support from historians.[57] The agreement between the Portuguese and Alauddin

---

the Johor River in October. The Acehnese vessels had destroyed the city and the sultan had fled to Bentan (Riau), despite the help he received from the Portuguese. However, Botelho de Sousa says the Dutch left Banten on 24 October and arrived at Johor only in late November (*Subsídios* ..., II, pp. 469–470). This Dutch fleet was detected by the ships of Gonçalo Rodrigues de Sousa on their way from Manila to Melaka, in the Straits of Singapore. The Portuguese vessels were awaiting the arrival of the carrack from Macao but, when they received the news about the Acehnese strike on Melaka, they decided to go up the Johor River, where they noticed the presence of 'the local king, who is our friend' (Bocarro, *Década*, xciii, p. 416). After the Acehnese strike on Melaka, the Dutch fleet was also detected by Alauddin, who rapidly informed the Portuguese that it was moving towards Melaka (letter mentioned in note 47, fl. 193v.). Shortly thereafter, the English on board the *Solomon*, who wanted to pass through the Straits on their way from Patani but were anchored near one of the Karimun islands, blocked by both the Portuguese and the Acehnese, saw the Dutch fleet pass through (*see* letters quoted in note 58, below). The Dutch did eventually make a strike on Melaka (Bocarro, *Década*, xcv, pp. 422–424).

[55] Gibson-Hill, 'Johor Lama ...', p. 158, note 85; 'On the alleged death...', p. 133, note 28.

[56] Gibson-Hill says that this Raja Bujang had married the daughter of Raja Ahmad, son of Abdul Kadir, sultan of Pahang, and that Alauddin claimed the throne for his son when a dynastic crisis took place in Pahang at this time.

[57] Andaya, *The Kingdom of Johor*, p. 25, confirms this version, but imputed this action to Abdullah (whom he designates 'Hammat Syah') and accepting Alauddin's death in 1613. However, Linehan says the daughter of Raja Ahmad of Pahang married Abdullah of Johor (and not his nephew) whose son, Raja Bajau, would inherit the throne of both sultanates (*A History of Pahang*, pp. 34–44). This author also refers to a deal between Alauddin and Melaka but does not mention any source (Ibid., p. 35).

is possible, but one wonders how the Portuguese could pay attention to Alauddin and make resources available to escort a prince to Pahang in August 1615 when Melaka had already received news of the proximity of Aceh's armada, just as it is also difficult to explain the total silence in Portuguese sources in this regard.

Alauddin definitively placed Pahang in Johor's orbit, probably preparing himself to regain the sultanate's erstwhile power. The attack he suffered in 1615 thus served the interests of Iskandar Muda and those of Abdullah. Once again, Alauddin was obliged to flee,[58] and all trace of him is lost from this point onwards.[59] This second attack by Aceh on Batu Sawar marked the end of Alauddin's pretensions to power, and he was definitively replaced by his brother, who thus skilfully utilised the military might of his brother-in-law to assert his political power once and for all. The armada's other objectives are unknown; it is possible that it stayed in Johor for some time in an attempt to capture the fugitive sultan. In any case, at the end of November Iskandar Muda had not yet returned to Aceh.[60] As for Abdullah, as was seen in a previous chapter, he founded a new capital in Lingga, and reigned until 1623, managing to reconstitute an important part of Johor's erstwhile empire. However, he permanently came into conflict with the sultan of Aceh, and even rejected the sultan's sister, whom he had married in 1613.

---

[58] The English on board the *Solomon* made contact with him at the mouth of the Straits of Sabang, stating that 'the King of Johor ... came aboard our ship, who flying from the King of Aceh durst not remain in his own country but lived on the water like a fugitive.' Alauddin informed them about the situation in Melaka and the presence of the Dutch and the Acehnese in the neighbourhood, but the English did not believe his words due to his well-known friendship with the Portuguese (Report from the factors of the 'Solomon', 9-11-1615, *LREIC*, III, pp. 212–213; also *see* the letter from L. Antheunis to Sir Thomas Roe, 15-2-1616, ibid., IV, pp. 30–31).

[59] Gibson-Hill says he was probably murdered by the command of Iskandar Muda. 'On the alleged death...', p.135.

[60] Letter from W. Nicholls to J. Millward and J. Yates, 24-11-1615, *LREIC*, III, p. 236.

Genealogy of the Sultans of Johor

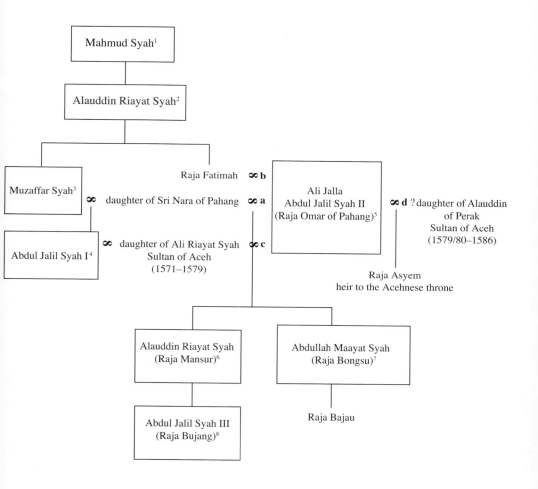

1. Mahmud Syah I   1511–1528
2. Alauddin Riayat Syah II   1528–1564
3. Muzaffar Syah   1564–1568/69
4. Abdul Jalil Syah I   1569–1579/80
5. Ali Jalla Abdul Jalil Syah II (Raja Omar) 1579/80–1597 (ruled 1569–1579/80 as regent)
6. Alauddin Riayat Syah III (Raja Mansur) 1597–1613/1615
7. Abdullah Maayat Syah (Raja Bongsu)   1613/15–1623
8. Abdul Jalil Syah III (Raja Bujang)   1623–1677

The Sultanate of Aceh: Genealogical Questions and Problems

The genealogy of the sultans of Aceh is less confused than that of Johor during the period under study. Also, another advantage is the greater attention that this sultanate and its political history have received from scholars. However, some doubts remain, especially with regard to the dynastic crisis of the years between 1586 and 1589. Anyway, the chronology is far easier to reconstruct. The most important Malay sources for this period consist, essentially, of two works: the *Bustan us–Salatin* and the *Hikayat Aceh*. Both pose the same problem for the historian: although they are chronologically close to the events that they relate (they were produced in the early 17th century), their preparation conformed to a well-defined political objective: to exalt the figures of the sultans who commissioned them, Iskandar Thani and his predecessor Iskandar Muda, respectively. The second work is especially significant as it entailed the preparation of a suitable genealogy for the sultan, attributing to him royal origins that he clearly did not possess.

The chronology of the sultans of Aceh up until the crisis of 1579 has already been prepared in detail, by cross-referencing European and

Malay sources.[1] Denys Lombard also presents a chronology covering the 16th century and part of the 17th century.[2] In this way, although it is unlikely that significant new information will be presented, one must gather the available data about dynastic questions in the sultanate during the 16th and 17th centuries, suggesting some ideas for the crisis of 1586–89.

The dynastic history of Aceh during this period can be divided into three phases: until 1579, the year in which a grave internal crisis took place and a royal lineage came to an end; 1579–89, the period of the so-called 'foreign sultans' in which the throne was occupied by characters from other sultanates who did not, however, manage to achieve a continuity of the lineage; and from 1589, when Sultan Alauddin Riayat Syah al-Mukammil took power and founded a new dynasty. Until 1579 the genealogical history of Aceh does not present great difficulties. The most important name is, without doubt, that of Alauddin Riayat Syah al-Kahar, although it was his father, Ali Mughayat Syah, who was, in Lombard's words, 'The true founder of Acehnese power'.[3] However, it was only under Alauddin that Aceh projected itself as a great regional power, champion of Islam and privileged agent of the anti-Portuguese structures throughout the Indian Ocean. It was during his rule that Acehnese contacts with the Ottoman Empire became consistent and it was also the period when the sultanate's expansion along the eastern coast of Sumatra led to closer ties between Johor and the Portuguese.

He was succeeded by his son Ali Riayat Syah,[4] who continued his father's course of action, proceeding with the policy of exerting growing pressure on Melaka during the great sieges of the 1570s. This succession was contested by his brother Mughal, the prince of Priaman, who conspired against him but was discovered and executed. There is some

---

1   Alves, *O Domínio do Norte de Sumatra*, p. 190.
2   Lombard, *Le Sultanat d'Atjéh* ..., Ap. I, pp. 185–186.
3   Ibid., p. 37.
4   Jorge de Lemos was not very far from the truth when he affirmed that Alauddin Riayat Syah al-Kahar had left his sons 'as tetrarchs of certain districts of cities and towns of the coast, subordinated to the oldest one', for this rivalry would cause instability in the subsequent years (Lemos, 'Hystoria dos Cercos ...', fl. 62v.).

information in Portuguese sources that can help to explain the difficulties that this sultan experienced in imposing his authority: the fact that he was a second son, his brother, the first-born son and original heir to the throne having perished during the attack on Melaka in 1568.[5] Thus his reign was afflicted by a climate of conspiracy that proved to be his greatest concern.[6] As has already been explained, he married one of his daughters to the young Abdul Jalil, heir to the throne of Johor, under the tutelage of his uncle Raja Omar/Ali Jalla.

In 1579 Ali Riayat Syah died, paving the way for a period of instability and civil war that would only cease in 1589. He left as his successor his son Muda, who was very young and was unable to withstand the climate of political instability and the struggle for the throne headed by diverse belligerent groups. He was assassinated after a few months and his uncle, Sri Alam, prince of Priaman, was placed on the throne.[7] This character was assassinated, too, and was replaced by another nephew, the prince of Aru, Zainal Abidin, who also suffered the same fate after an extremely brief reign.[8] The throne was eventually handed over to a personage from Perak, who came to power as Alauddin or Mansur Syah,[9] in 1579 or 1580.

The Portuguese became aware of the situation in 1580 itself when the first news of the civil wars in Aceh and tidings of the sultanate's momentary weakness reached Melaka, a rather important issue for the

---

[5]   Pereira, *História da Índia* ..., pp. [234]–[237]); Pinto, *Peregrinação*, ch. XXXII.
[6]   Alves, *O Domínio do Norte de Sumatra*, pp. 169–170.
[7]   According to the genealogy in Lombard, *Le Sultanat d'Atjéh* ..., pp. 186–187; Alves refers to him as the prince of Priaman but he says he was a nephew (and not brother) of Ali Riayat Syah and son of Sultan Mughal of Priaman (*O Domínio do Norte de Sumatra*, p. 172).
[8]   Kathirithamby-Wells does not accept this chronology, presenting one that is rather different, which is, however, to all appearances only supported by data provided by the *Bustan* ('Royal Authority ...', p. 263, note 35). About the general backdrop of this crisis, *see* Alves, *O Domínio do Norte de Sumatra*, pp. 170–172.
[9]   Lemos says this choice was the only way to put an end to the climate of conspiracy and insubordination that existed in some circles of the Acehnese court, for which purpose the 'ruler of Perak' was summoned ('Hystoria dos Cercos ...', fls. 62v.–63).

city due to the recent sieges it had suffered.[10] The new sultan was undoubtedly faced with the problem of the stability of his power, which he never managed to resolve during his reign. One must consider that he would have tried to offset his weak internal authority with a solid foreign policy, reinforcing the anti-Portuguese role of his sultanate and promoting ties with Johor, whose sultan, Ali Jalla, had emerged strengthened by the crisis and weakness of his most direct rival. Likewise, as has been analysed, the sultan of Johor also took advantage of Ali Riayat Syah's death to seize power, eliminating his nephew Abdul Jalil.

At this point, the questions involving dynastic ties with Johor still raise some doubts as the sources are not devoid of contradictions in this regard. First, it seems to be certain that Mansur Syah sent, on an unknown date, one of his daughters to Johor to marry Ali Jalla, thus sealing a mutually beneficial alliance.[11] From this union was born a son, a future heir for both sultanates, named Raja Asyem, who was sent to Aceh to be educated with the intention of his succeeding his grandfather.[12] He would later be killed on the orders of Sultan Alauddin Riayat Syah al-Mukammil, who thus eliminated a potential risk for himself, an event that would revive the long-lasting animosity of Johor.[13] In 1587, against a

---

[10]   *See* several Jesuit letters in *DI*, vol. XII: Rui Vicente, 20-10-1580, p. 101; Gomes Vaz, 3-12-1580, p. 159; Pedro Gomez, 26-3-1581, p. 267; P. R. Vicente, 2-12-1581, p. 482; bishop of Melaka, 7-1-1582, p. 564.

[11]   Erédia, in his 'História de Serviços ...', BN, *Res*, cod. 414, fl. 8, refers to 1578, but Mansur Syah was not yet sultan in that year. There are two possibilities: either in 1580, immediately after Mansur seized the throne, and in this case the strike on Johor in 1582 would therefore have involved a quarrel with Ali Jalla or, most probably, after the attack of 1582, when the sultan of Aceh would establish a long-lasting peace between the two sultanates trying to ensure, at the same time, that the amicable relationship between Johor and the Portuguese would not be a threat to himself.

[12]   Information by John Davis, 'A briefe Relation ...' in Purchas, *His Pilgrimes*, II, p. 319.

[13]   Several authors accept this version, for example, Reid, 'Trade and the Problem of Royal Power in Aceh', p. 48; Winstedt, *A History of Johore*, p. 29 and Gibson-Hill, 'On the alleged death ...', p. 135. The hostility between Aceh and Johor is well documented in Portuguese sources. Erédia refers to the fact in two works: 'Declaraçam de Malaca ...', fl. 44v. and *Informação da Aurea Chersoneso*, pp. 76 and 85.

backdrop of crisis between Melaka and Johor, the death of Mansur Syah resulted in the cancellation of the armada that he had been preparing to help his son-in-law against the Portuguese. Thus, Ali Jalla hastened to immediately contact the new sultan, preparing a new alliance, sending an embassy and, according to some sources, one of his daughters to seal the agreement; she was captured by Dom Paulo de Lima Pereira when, having come from Goa, he headed the efforts to come to Melaka's aid.[14] Diogo do Couto presents a different version: the young girl who was found on board one of the ships captured by Mateus Pereira, which also transported Johor's ambassador to Aceh, was merely going to visit the queen of that sultanate, by whom she had been raised.[15] Thus there is some uncertainty about the actual realisation of the alliance sealed by a marriage.[16]

For a better understanding of this issue one must touch upon the problem of Mansur Syah's reign and the crisis unleashed by his assassination in 1586. At the time, power was seized by a personage who a

---

[14] Letter from Luís Góis de Lacerda to the king, 10-1-1588, AGS, *Secr. Prov.*, book 1551, fl. 314 (*see* Document Appendix, No. 4). The 'Relação' by D. Paulo de Lima Pereira only mentions the presence of an ambassador from Johor (*DUP*, I, p. 10); the anonymous report 'De las Victorias que don Paulo de Lima Pereira tuvo en la India ...' says the ambassador's guards were Acehnese soldiers (BNM, cod. 1750, fl. 181).

[15] Couto, *Da Ásia*, X, IX, vi, p. 443; *Vida de D. Paulo ...*, p. 90. It is interesting to note how the story of the bride captured by the Portuguese spread in different versions; Linschoten tells the tale in reverse, describing how the sultan of Aceh sent his daughter to Johor; she was taken prisoner with a large quantity of artillery (*The Voyage of ... to the East Indies*, I, pp. 109–110). Argensola reports an identical story but presents 1581 as the exact date (*Conquista de las Islas Malucas*, p. 144). The confusion is undoubtedly due to a combination of three distinct events: the wedding of the young Abdul Jalil of Johor and the daughter of Ali Riayat Syah, most probably in the mid-1570s; the marriage of Ali Jalla of Johor to a daughter of Mansur Syah, in the early 1580s; and the events of 1587.

[16] A letter written in Melaka, dated 17-12-1588, states that the sultan of Aceh provided help to Johor because he was 'his relative' (letter from the *ouvidor* of Melaka to the king, AGS, *Secr. Prov.*, book 1551, fl. 470).

local source[17] identifies as being a prince from Indrapura,[18] which was then part of Aceh's dominions. This individual came to power under the name of Ali Riayat Syah, or Raja Buyung.[19] His reign was characterised by great instability, and even anarchy, within the sultanate. The most serious events of this period concern the wars in the Minangkabau region, which was his original homeland. Unfortunately, the circumstances concerning these events are unknown. This sultan would, likewise, be assassinated in 1589[20] and the throne was seized by another figure, called Alauddin Riayat Syah Sayid al-Mukammil, who would found a new dynasty in the sultanate. This is the version that is generally accepted by historians. However, we are faced with the problem of identifying each one of these personages and with the task of elaborating the most plausible scenario for this turbulent period.

Two successive crises, two assassinations, in 1586 and 1589. This distinction is of fundamental importance, as some sources confuse the two events. With regard to the former, some Portuguese sources claim that it was orchestrated by the sultan's wife. The closest information that we have is the data contained in a letter from Viceroy Dom Duarte de Meneses to the king, dated 23 November 1587, that refers to the news from Melaka that had arrived in Goa on 7 February, and stated:

---

[17] Lombard, *Le Sultanat d'Atjéh* ..., p. 38, does not identify the source, which is undoubtedly the *Bustan us-Salatin*, as the *Hikayat Aceh* only mentions Mansur Syah in an excerpt. Lombard contradicts his own statement on p. 167, note 2. Reid seems to have a poor knowledge of the work, since he states that it does not mention either of the two foreign sultans ('Trade and the Problem of Royal Power in Aceh', p. 47). The chronicle published by Dulaurier in the late 18th century refers to both: with regard to the former, it says he was from Perak, but gives no further information about the latter, only stating that both met with a violent death (*Chronique du Royaume d'Atcheh dans l'Ile de Sumatra*), pp. 19–20.

[18] Son of Munawar Syah, sultan of Indrapura, a sultanate on the west coast of Sumatra, in the region known as Minangkabau which was in permanent tension with Aceh. *See* Kathirithamby-Wells, 'Achehnese Control over West Sumatra ...', p. 458.

[19] *Buyung*, 'youngest'.

[20] Mentioned by Lombard, *Le Sultanat d'Atjéh* ..., who provides the exact date: 28 June 1589, according to the tombstone of the sultan.

'I have understood from some sources that the Sultan of Aceh is dead, and on the orders of his wife, who soon married another King, about which there were some differences.'[21]

This information, which circulated in Portuguese sources for some time,[22] allows us to confirm the idea transmitted in the *Bustan* with regard to the royal blood of the usurper. At this time, the bishop of Melaka, Dom João Ribeiro Gaio, said that the new sultan, with whom the queen was discontented, was from Minangkabau.[23] Diogo do Couto calls him 'Mora Ratissa', 'captain-general of Aceh', former slave of the sultan, and poses the question as to whether the queen was involved in the conspiracy.[24] Denys Lombard presents an interesting hypothesis: that the usurper was, in fact, a prisoner of war from the royal family of Indrapura, and he thus appears as a former 'slave'.[25] The designation of 'slave' does not necessarily denote a prisoner of war[26] and could, in the present case, simply refer to a prince of Minangkabau who was a dependant of the sultan of Aceh so as to ensure his vassal's fidelity. One must also mention a Chinese source that notes the rise to power of 'one of the great dignitaries of the kingdom'.[27] In any case, Ali Riayat Syah ascended to the throne amidst great turbulence, providing tutelage to the son of Mansur Syah.[28]

His reign was brief. In 1589, Alauddin Riayat Syah al-Mukammil rose to power. This figure still remains shrouded in some controversy. Historians generally cite the two most important sources of information: John Davis,

---

[21] AGS, *Secr. Prov.*, book 1551, fl. 71.
[22] Letter from Viceroy D. Duarte de Meneses to the king, 15-4-1588, AGS, *Secr. Prov.*, book 1551, fl. 553 (copy of the same letter in fls. 295–302); letter from Governor Manuel de Sousa Coutinho to the king, 12-12-1589, AGS, *Secr. Prov.*, book 1551, fl. 747.
[23] Letter of 15-12-1588 included at the end of his 'Roteiro' (Gaio, *O Roteiro*, p. 102).
[24] Couto, *Da Ásia*, X, VIII, xiii, p. 362.
[25] Op. cit., p. 38.
[26] About slavery and dependency in Southeast Asia, *see* the works mentioned in chapter 4, note 16.
[27] *The History of the Ming Dynasty*, with a few excerpts published by W. P. Groeneveldt in 'Notes on the Malay Archipelago ...', pp. 213–214.
[28] 'The Sultan of Aceh is dead; he left a young son in the care of one of his captains, who is now the regent of the Kingdom'; letter by Luís Góis de Lacerda quoted in note 14, above.

who was in the sultanate as a member of the first Dutch expedition to anchor there, in June 1599, when this sultan still ruled, and Augustin de Beaulieu, who arrived there in 1621 during the reign of Iskandar Muda, his grandson who continued his policies. The first source attributes a humble origin to Alauddin (fisherman),[29] stating that he achieved some prominence as a warrior, attaining an important place in the court as a military chief, and managed to marry a woman of the royal family. After the death of the 'old king', he seized power as tutor to the heir to the throne, an act that prompted great opposition on the part of the 'nobility'. He assassinated the legitimate heir (which would provoke the wrath of Johor) and also destroyed the sultanate's aristocracy.[30] Twenty years later, the story told by Beaulieu was already substantially different: once the ancient line of the sultans of Aceh petered out, the *orang kaya* chose a *kadi* greatly respected by all who, after a series of refusals, accepted the post and then proceeded to eliminate, in one strike, this class of *orang kaya*.[31]

The efforts to legitimate the sultan are clearly evident. In 1599 the events that had taken place ten years previously were obviously still fresh in the minds of many people; in 1621, 32 years after, the scenario had already changed, even more so because Iskandar Muda now ruled the sultanate with an iron grip, and legitimised his power, just like his grandfather's. It is curious to observe how in Beaulieu's version, which would be very close to the 'official' version of events, the massacre of the *orang kaya* is justified by attributing to them a series of defects and excesses, and they are also deemed to be the cause of the anarchy in the kingdom and the weakness of royal power before the arrival of Alauddin.

These efforts to legitimise Iskandar Muda's ancestry would not have been limited to merely attributing to him respectable origins; it was necessary to provide him with a royal origin, so that the *daulat* could be unequivocally claimed. The *Hikayat Aceh*, written on his orders, provides him with a royal ancestry on both his maternal and paternal

---

[29] Information confirmed by the report of the Frenchman François Martin who was in Aceh in 1601, quoted in Lombard, *Le Sultanat d'Atjéh* ..., p. 68, note 3.

[30] Davis, 'A briefe Relation ...', in Purchas, *His Pilgrimes*, II, pp. 318–319.

[31] Beaulieu, 'Memoires du Voyage aux Indes Orientales du General Beaulieu', pp. 110–111.

sides.[32] One needs to keep these designs in mind when approaching these problems.

Alauddin's very ascension to power must be questioned: the idea of the *orang kaya* handing over the throne does not seem plausible. Davis affirms that Alauddin's rise as protector of the heir to the throne aroused opposition in various sectors of the court. Once again, one may observe the division of the sultanate's elite classes into parties and factions, and not the solidarity of a supposedly all-powerful nobility. Alauddin, a military chief and skilled and powerful adventurer probably supported by military sectors, did not seem inclined to support any faction. On the contrary, the strike he launched as soon as he obtained the throne was aimed at eliminating, once and for all, these factions and at reconstituting the political elite based on his own power. Upon ascending the throne he immediately proceeded to decapitate the nobility, confiscated their properties and started a process of centralisation of power, based on a military elite, which would reach its zenith with Iskandar Muda. None of this matches the version according to which the *orang kaya* calmly called a respected elder who suddenly turned against his protectors. In any case, it was clearly an act of force, whether or not we accept the version that indicates that Alauddin assassinated his predecessor.[33] However, opposition to his power did not cease, contrary to what these accounts could seem to indicate. Some echoes of this reached the ears of the Portuguese at the end of the century,[34] and would continue until Iskandar Muda definitively managed to impose his rule.

---

[32] Lombard, *Le Sultanat d'Atjéh* ..., pp. 165–166. This author presents both versions (Davies' and Beaulieu's) on p. 38, as does Marsden (*The History of Sumatra*, pp. 433–435). However, in the genealogy (pp. 186–187) and while describing the origins of Iskandar Muda (p. 166) he accepts that this sultan descended from the dynasty of Dar ul-Kamal, as does Reid ('Trade and the Problem of Royal Power ...', p. 48).

[33] Erédia, *Informação da Aurea Chersoneso*, p. 85; the Chinese source mentioned in note 27, above, states that Alauddin was 'a slave' of his predecessor, having murdered Mansur Syah in order to procure the throne for his master. He subsequently also killed him and seized the crown for himself.

[34] 'His Majesty is informed that, as the King of Aceh is not the legitimate lord of that kingdom, he is hated by the local people, and seeks all means to secure his position'; letter to Viceroy D. Francisco da Gama, 30-3-1598, BN, *Res.*, cod. 1975, fl. 331 (*see* Document Appendix, No. 9).

Alauddin reigned until around 1604. He had two sons, who soon disputed the throne. The elder son remained in Aceh to succeed his father, while the younger son went to Pedir. The old sultan would end up being imprisoned by his elder son, who seized power under the name Ali Riayat Syah, and came into open conflict with his brother.[35] Even before the expedition by Dom Martim Afonso de Castro in 1606 which would indirectly and involuntarily change the course of the sultanate's history, the Portuguese exerted pressure upon Aceh at this time, undoubtedly taking advantage of the climate of instability. They intended to construct a fortress in the sultanate, intensifying their contacts (begun in 1592) with a view to accelerating the negotiations before the Dutch or the English could steal a march on them. A Portuguese source records the situation of civil war that prevailed in the sultanate in 1603 while describing an embassy headed by the Augustinian friar Amaro de Jesus.[36]

For the rest of the story we have to turn to Beaulieu: Iskandar Muda, despite his mother's influence, was obliged to seek refuge in Pedir, placing himself on the side of his uncle in the dispute. He would end up commanding an army that marched upon Aceh, was defeated and taken prisoner. It was at this point that news was received of the Portuguese disembarkation in the sultanate in June 1606. Iskandar Muda asked for permission to repel the intruders, an endeavour in which he was successful. In the meantime, the sultan died and Iskandar Muda was crowned sultan,

---

[35] Lombard, *Le Sultanat d'Atjéh* ..., p. 70. This author quotes two sources, Pyrard de Laval and Beaulieu; he assumes that the version of the latter—who says that the dynastic struggle took place only after the death of the old sultan in 1603—must have been based upon an 'official' source. Another account, the report of the second voyage of John Davis, clearly says (while mentioning the events of 1605) that the old sultan was a prisoner and that his two sons were fighting each other ('The Second Voyage of ..., with Sir Edward Michelborne, into the East Indies' in Purchas *His Pilgrimes*, II, p. 355).

[36] Fr. Félix de Jesus, 'Primeira parte da Chronica e Relação do principio que teue a congregação da ordem de S. Augusto nas Indias Orientais ...', AN/TT, *MssLiv.*, No. 731, fl. 66v. (*see* Document Appendix, No. 22). The general instability in the sultanate is echoed in the Portuguese report about the conquest of Aceh (BA, Liv. 51-VI-54$\frac{18}{}$, fls. 36–37 v. (Document Appendix, No. 17).

in large measure due to the actions of his mother, who seduced the *orang kaya* with generous promises. The new sultan rapidly rid himself of his uncle in Pedir and assumed absolute power.[37] Iskandar Muda ruled until 1636 and his reign marked the golden age of Aceh's history.

---

[37] Beaulieu, 'Memoires du Voyage aux Indes Orientales', pp. 113–114. It is doubtful that the military command, and thus the subsequent victory over the Portuguese, was attributed to Iskandar Muda himself. It was probably a modification *a posteriori* with a view to praising this figure after he ascended the throne. Portuguese sources are silent on this issue. The only reference one is aware of is a royal letter to Viceroy Rui Lourenço de Távora, dated 24-12-1610. It refers to the construction of a fortress in the sultanate, which 'had been offered by the King of that Kingdom who is now dead as are his brothers and sons, and his nephew is now the ruler but he is so weak that we can easily manage to achieve this' (*DRI*, I, p. 416).

Genealogy of the Sultans of Aceh

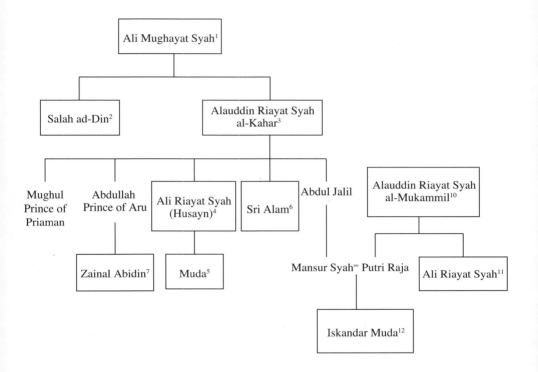

1.	Ali Mughayat Syah	?–1530
2.	Salah ad-Din	1530–1539
3.	Alauddin Riayat Syah al-Kahar	1539–1571
4.	Ali Riayat Syah	1571–1579
5.	Sultan Muda	1579
6.	Sultan Sri Alam	1579
7.	Zainal Abidin	1579/80
8.	Alauddin of Perak (Mansur Syah)	1579/80–1586
9.	Ali Riayat Syah (Raja Buyung)	1586–1589
10.	Alauddin Riayat Syah al-Mukammil	1589–1604
11.	Ali Riayat Syah	1604–1607
12.	Iskandar Muda	1607–1636

Captains of Melaka (1567–1620)

Leonis Pereira (1567–70)

Francisco da Costa (1570–73)

Francisco Henriques de Meneses (1573–74)

Tristão Vaz da Veiga (1574–75)

Miguel de Castro (1575)

Aires de Saldanha (1576–79)

João da Gama (1579–82)

Roque de Melo (1582–85)

João da Silva Pereira (1585–May 1587)

João Ribeiro Gaio, Bishop of Melaka (May 1587–February 1588)

João da Silva Pereira (February–September 1588)

Diogo Lobo (1588–90)

Pero Lopes de Sousa (1590–93?)

Francisco da Silva de Meneses (1594?–97)

Martim Afonso de Melo (1597–1600)

Fernão de Albuquerque (1600–03)

André Furtado de Mendonça (1603–06)

António de Meneses (1606–07)

Sebastião de Távora (1607–09)

Francisco Miranda Henriques (1609–13?)

Gaspar Afonso de Melo (1613–15)

João Caiado de Gamboa (1615–16)

António Pinto da Fonseca and João da Silva (1616)

João da Silveira (1616–18)

Fradique Lopes de Sousa (1618–20)

Viceroys and Governors of India (1564–1622)

Antão de Noronha (1564–68)

Luís de Ataíde (1568–71)

António de Noronha (1571–73)

António Moniz Barreto (1573–76)

Diogo de Meneses (1576–78)

Luís de Ataíde (1578–81)

Fernão Teles de Meneses (1581)

Francisco de Mascarenhas (1581–84)

Duarte de Meneses (1584–88)

Manuel de Sousa Coutinho (1588–91)

Matias de Albuquerque (1591–97)

Francisco da Gama (1597–1600)

Aires de Saldanha (1600–05)

Martim Afonso de Castro (1605–07)

Friar Aleixo de Meneses (1607–09)

João Pereira Forjaz (died on his way to India)

André Furtado de Mendonça (1609)

Rui Lourenço de Távora (1609–12)

Jerónimo de Azevedo (1612–17)

João Coutinho (1617–19)

Fernão de Albuquerque (1619–22)

Maps

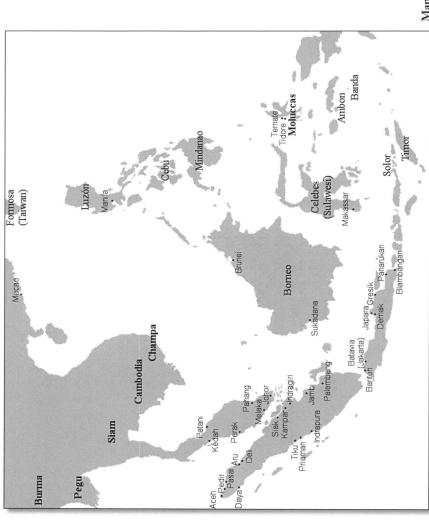

Map 1. Southeast Asia

Map 2. Melaka and its Neighboring Countries

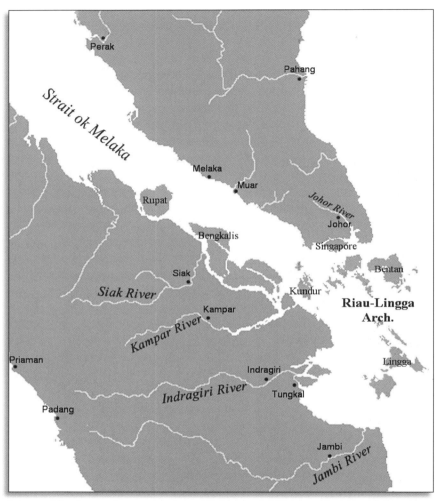

Map 3. The Straits Region

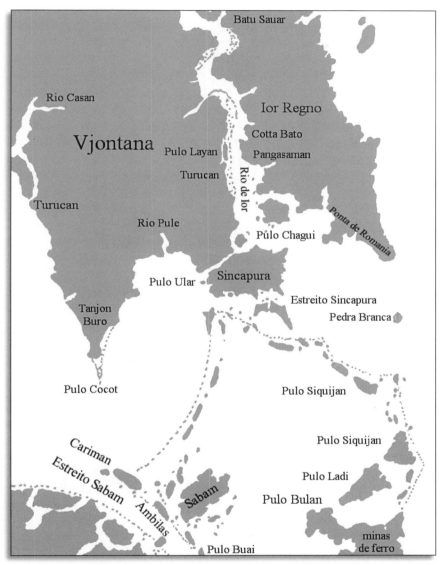

Map 4. The Straits according to Manuel Godinho de Erédia (adapted) "Declaraçam de Malaca e India Meridional com o Cathay", published as *Malaca, l'Inde Orientale et le Cathay* by L. Janssen, Brussels, 1881.

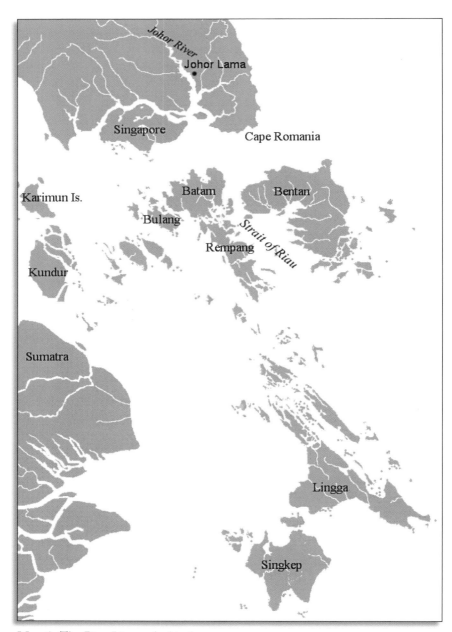

Map 5. The Riau-Lingga Archipelago

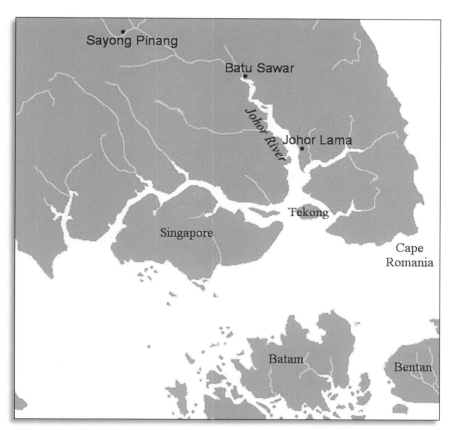

Map 6. The Johor River

Document Appendix

Document 1

'The life and actions of Mathias de Albuquerque, Captain and Viceroy of the Estado da Índia. First and Second part, in which are described all his actions, and the actions of his celebrated feats that took place in the memorable capture of the Hillock of Chaul. Copied in the year 1749' (excerpts). BN, *Res.*, cod. 482[1].

(fl. 14) 'As Matias de Albuquerque had given such ample proof of himself that one could rightly trust him with any great enterprise as the King, Dom Sebastian, was sending an armada that would defend the fortress and protect the seas of Melaka, that the King of Aceh had overrun with a large number of ships and soldiers, as well as due to the old and natural

---

[1] Published by A. Vignatti in *Mare Liberum*, No. 15, June 1998, pp. 139–245; No. 17, June 1999, pp. 269–360. There are some minor differences between the transcription presented there and this one.

enmity that he always had with us, and his own interests that he hoped to obtain from this, as by having a daughter married to Recalale, nephew and heir of the King of Jor, descended from the ancient line of the Kings of Melaka, who when evicted from the city went to establish their settlements alongside this river of Jor, preserving the title and empire over those few Malays who withdrew with them, and the souls and hearts of all those who stayed in Melaka, hoping for just what the dispossessed wished, and with the renewed help of Aceh, they sought to strike us, a rather arduous and difficult business for our men, which saw them placed in a position of great care and pressure. To this end, the eyes of the King fell upon Matias de Albuquerque, whom he called in January 1576 and entrusted him with the Captaincy-General of the said armada, exhorting him with many honourable words to go and defend that fortress, which his uncle Afonso de Albuquerque had won with such renowned efforts. The order that (fl. 15) he gave him was, that he accompany Dom Diogo de Meneses, to whom he had initially entrusted that enterprise, and in the event that Dom Diogo did not go, as he already suspected and as came to pass, he would remain as Captain-General of that entire sea, with the powers, jurisdiction and instructions that had been given to Dom Diogo. He set sail from this kingdom on 2 March, aboard the carrack *Santa Catarina*, accompanied by Baltasar Pessanha, Captain of the galleon *São Jorge*, because the rest of the armada had to be formed from the ships, soldiers and captains who were to be found in those parts, according to the instructions that he had received. ... (fl. 15v.) He finally arrived at that fortress, which he found lacked almost all the things necessary to prepare an armada and soldiers and captains who were anxious to return to India ....

(fl. 16) Arriving with this armada [consisting of twelve vessels] at the Straits [of Singapore], he placed himself at the watering spot that exists on the other bank, where he also gathered a junk and a carrack that was coming from China, and sent Luís de Carvalho to go to the Johor River in his galley, along with a brigantine, to capture some sentry, from whom they would be able to get accurate news about their enemies. Luís Carvalho returned shortly thereafter, saying that the armada of the King of Aceh was approaching them. This armada consisted of one hundred and fifteen sailing vessels, which included thirty-six royal galleys, fifty galliots, pinnaces and launches, and twenty-nine light brigantines. It was headed by Ciri Marcalela with ten thousand fighting men, men of great daring and tenacity in the feats they had realised, a lot of heavy artillery and munitions, and Recalale, the nephew and heir of the King of Johor, with whom we say that the King of Aceh had married a daughter and to whom he wished to restore the sceptre of Melaka, which had formerly belonged to his ancestors, was also on board.

The enemy did not take long in coming in search of our armada, as they had the monsoon and winds behind them, with the intention, to all appearances, of seeing if they could evict them from the watering spot and take the carrack and junk from China, on whose trail they had come, because they had appeared along the coast for this reason. This was observed by Matias de Albuquerque with his galley and a brigantine, who, as a decoy, went to invite them to weigh anchor from the land, so that the artillery of the large ships could destroy them. However, they contented themselves with merely using a few pieces (fl. 16v.) of his artillery, without wishing to change the port. On the following day, 1 January 1577, at daybreak, as the wind had calmed, and as our enemies were so much better placed, they came in search of our armada with their galleys at the forefront, in rows of six, and the battery lasted more than three hours. (…) As the resistance of our men was so great, and they showed their habitual courage, the enemy began to withdraw to re-supply their artillery, and the Captain-General was relieved of them, but not of the care and vigilance of his armada. …

Having received news that there were four galleys and a launch from Aceh in the river of Kedah, he sent Dom Henrique Bandarra with two galleys and nine brigantines to go and engage in battle with them, which our men did with great valour, killing many of the enemy soldiers and setting fire to a galley and a launch, and the other three they brought to Melaka loaded with a lot of pepper and other merchandise, and they found twenty-three pieces of artillery, of which three had the royal coat of arms of Portugal. …

(fl. 23) In the year 1580, as the Sultan of Aceh was dead and his kingdom racked by discord, and this situation afforded Matias de Albuquerque a great opportunity to conquer and destroy Aceh, from which would be obtained not merely fitting revenge for past insults, but also security so that in future they would fear us. With the approval of the people and city council of Melaka, he came to (fl. 23v.) India in a galleon to give to the Viceroy, Dom Luís de Ataíde, an account of the opportunity, exhorting him to personally assist this venture that was so dear to the King, or if he could not do so himself, to give him at least a thousand men, because with them he hoped to be able to put an end to this expedition ... and thus preparations for this expedition were begun, which continued till May of the following year, in which they realised that it would not be possible due to the siege in Sri Lanka. ...

(fl. 55v.) On 16 April [1592], he sent Dom Bernardo Coutinho as Captain-General of Melaka, with a galleon and four galleys, and orders that, if it were necessary, he equip the galleon of the Moluccas and the galliots that were in Melaka with arms. He ran into Sirima Laguilela, the nephew of the Sultan of Aceh, with whom he engaged in battle and killed him along with many of his men, seizing his galley and eleven launches that were accompanying him, and after this he went in search of more of the enemy's men in Gori, where he had received news they were to be found, and set fire to one of their galleys and thirty small boats, and restored possession of his state to the King of Johor, who had been deprived of it by the violence of that tyrant.'

Document 2

> Royal instructions to the Viceroy Dom Duarte de Meneses (excerpt). Lisbon, 10-3-1584. AN/TT — *Fundo Português da Biblioteca Nacional de Paris*, No. 48 (copy), 28 fls.

(fl. 8) 'I am informed that every year some vessels come to the city of Macao [sic] that bring gold from the island of Sumatra, which is brought by the people of Minangkabau who live on the other coast of the same island in the direction of Sunda, that there are fifteen or twenty vessels that come every year, and that they are small boats as they come from peripheral kingdoms, avoiding the port of Aceh that is at the tip of the said island; and that this people who bring goods to Melaka pay a sum per head and that no one knows how much is brought and what is brought every year, and that before Aceh became so powerful, many more vessels used to come to Melaka and that only a small portion of this gold goes to India, and the greater part of it goes to the Coromandel coast or to the kingdoms of Sumatra, enriching them, and that there is no other trade in gold other than this that they do via Melaka on the ship (fl. 8v.) of the Coromandel voyage and they have some trade with Aceh itself. For this reason, it seemed to me that the quantity of gold that comes to Melaka on these boats must be rather large and that there must be sizeable reserves of gold on this island of Sumatra, and that these individuals who bring this gold to Melaka do not reveal it except to local merchants who habitually buy it and conceal it from the Portuguese; it is said that most of this gold comes in the form of gold dust and is very fine, and that until now one does not know the source of it. And I have already written about this matter in 1582 to the Count Viceroy and to the Captain of Melaka, and now I am once again writing to the present Captain of the said city, in order to save time by means of the ship that goes directly to Melaka.

I order you to be informed about this business and to find out if anything has been done in this regard, and to give orders (if nothing has been done) to do so immediately and to find out for sure from where this gold originates and its appearance and if it goes to other parts and what can be done to ensure (fl. 9) that all of it comes to Melaka; and according to the messages and intelligence that you receive in this regard from the said Captain to whom I am writing, you will proceed; you shall deal with this matter in the manner that you feel is in the best interests of my service and will keep me informed of everything you receive in this regard.

I am informed that it would be very beneficial for my service and for the security of navigation in the South to establish a fortress in the Straits of Singapore, in the place and site that is most suitable for the purposes that are intended for it, and that one must hasten to do so before our enemies are on their guard and build this fortress for themselves first, because I am also informed that Aceh and the King of Johor had this in mind and wish to begin work on it. For this reason I entrust you with closely overseeing when and how one must deal with this fortress so that time is not lost and the opportunity is seized, and whether you wait for the enterprise of Aceh to then be able to handle the situation better and more easily (fl. 9v.) without any impediments for the fortress, or whether it is more suitable and can be done immediately, and in this I trust that you will see what is better for my service, according to the state in which you find all these matters; and I am writing to the Captain of Melaka to apprise you of all the information he obtains in this regard.

Dom João da Gama, who was Captain of Melaka, wrote to me saying that he had slowly been proceeding with the fortification of that city which is so important to the Estado da Índia and so coveted by many, and that neither the revenue of one per cent nor the voyage of China that was earmarked for this purpose is sufficient and that one could not get any assistance from the customs revenues as these funds were all spent on everyday expenses. I order you to look into the state of this fortification and what has been done in this regard and what still needs to be done, and what money is employed for this and how much it pays each year (keeping in mind what has been mentioned before in the first chapter of these instructions with regard to the duties and taxes of the fortresses of India), and how much will still be necessary in order to finish (fl. 10) fortifying everything and one shall see from where these funds can be found and the way they are employed, and that as soon as you can assist without inconvenience, you will do so according to the importance of that city and its needs, and you will inform me of everything that you shall see fit with your reports and attend to this matter according to my service.

Dom João da Gama also wrote that he had not handed over one of my letters that I had sent him for the King of Jantana [Johor], as he was one of the enemies who most favoured the Acehnese during the sieges upon Melaka, and that he received them in his lands and allowed them to kill two Portuguese there, and that, as a result, he, Dom João, had hastened to assist and sent certain boats that did a lot of damage to his ports and destroyed them and his boats and killed many people. When the King saw this destruction he offered apologies as he had already been chastised, Dom João accepted the apologies and declared a truce. You will keep yourself informed as to how this situation is currently and if this king has been behaving well in my service, to whom I am once again writing this year (fl. 10v.); one of the copies is being sent in the ship that is going to Melaka, addressed to the Captain so that according to how the situation seems to him and to you who does this in my service, will either give it to him or not and you shall have the same orders with regard to the other copies that are being sent in this armada, proceeding, in all matters, as you believe is in my best interests.

The officials of the city council of Melaka have asked me to request the following: that all the residents of the city, both Christians as well as heathens, be they of any class or rank, be allowed to load and unload their merchandise freely, without them being hindered nor seized at the customs house, nor outside it, and that they be able to take these goods to their houses and sell them freely, and that in addition no person be allowed to buy nor obstruct the ships nor take goods that are not theirs.

And that the *casados* and residents of that city hold official posts, both offices of Justice as well as of my Exchequer, and not the Captains' men while their mentors serve as Captains, and that the (fl. 11) officials of the city council be able to elect and appoint these said *casados* to these offices.

And that the said residents and *casados* be exempted from paying any duties on their goods at the customs house, as well as the ground rents, and that they receive their wages to be paid normally while war prevails and the fortress remains unfinished, and that the sea and navigation not be prohibited to them and that they be able to come and go where they wish in order to earn their livelihood, as long as it is not to enemy lands nor forbidden places; that the ships of that city which would come to this Kingdom not pay more duties nor freight here than those paid by the ships that come from India; that the weight *dachém* not be used in the customs house of Melaka, as are currently used, as much deception takes place by this, and that the Portuguese weights be used, as are used as the norm in all the fortresses of India, and that the judges for the orphans do not marry the orphans until they have at least attained the age of twelve years. I greatly rely upon you to inform yourself about all these matters and to listen to their grievances, and the causes and reasons they have for this and if some of this is harmful for my interests and causes considerable damage and loss to my Exchequer, hearing what the procurators and people of the said city have to say in this regard, and the causes and reasons that they give, and in the things in which it seems to you that they are right and it is just and that you can immediately resolve without being inconvenient you shall do so, writing to me about what you have done (fl. 11v.) in this regard and also about what must be resolved, along with your opinion, to do so in the manner in which you see is most suitable for my service.

They also wrote to me to say that the Captains of the said fortress of Melaka take goods from the city's customs house against the wishes of the owners and at whatever price they wish, to earn a profit from them, and that for this reason and the vexation that this causes to the city's residents they have stopped running goods and that the city's habitual trade no longer exists. You shall keep yourself informed about this and attend to the situation so that henceforth this does not happen. And you shall do the same with regard to the money of the orphans that I have been informed that the said Captains take for their contracts and own uses, which is greatly against my service and even against the service of this Kingdom, giving orders in this matter so that henceforth they do not do so themselves or by means of third parties, on pain of the penalties that you see fit to impose that shall be strictly carried out against those who behave to the contrary.

The Kelings and heathen people of the city of Melaka sent me a letter complaining of some vexations that they face in the said city by my officials and magistrates, both ecclesiastical as well as secular, about which I have written to the Captain of that city, to assist them in all matters in which they are right and to help keeping in mind the services that they render in that city and fortress (fl. 12). You shall keep yourself informed of this matter and of their services and according to your findings shall deal with the matter as you feel is most suitable for my service and the peace of this Kingdom.

They have written to me to request that in recompense for their services that it be ordered that those of their slaves who converted and became Christians may be sold in public auctions according to the price set by their owners, despite the provisions in this regard by the provincial synod because the foreigners present in the said city set the price of their slaves that convert to Christianity, and the heathens say they deserve the same rights.

And that the heathens vary in their rites and customs, and that neither the judge for the orphans nor the purveyors of the deceased seize their goods nor make an inventory of them nor interfere with their children, nor take them away, or trouble them in any other way. And that they be exempted from all requisitions and loans, and that if it be necessary to request a loan for things of my service, that this be made equally to everyone, without there being any exceptions.

That they be free and at liberty to freely and without any contradiction, navigate (fl. 12v.), deal in and send their boats and goods to all the ports of Java and Sunda, and to the most frequented ones. I entrust you to inform yourself about all these things, listening to the procurators of the said port about the way in which they proceed in these matters and the obstacles that there are in each and every thing to grant or refuse it, and the information that you find, you shall write to me of each thing in particular very openly, with your opinion, so that according to what you write to me about these petitions I will order responses according to my interests and in those matters that you can resolve, you shall do so as you see fit. ...

(fl. 28) Written in Lisbon on 10 March 1584 – consists of 19 half sheets – King – Dom Duarte de Meneses, I say – second set of instructions for Viceroy Dom Duarte de Meneses – third copy – Miguel de Moura.'

Document 3

Letter from the Viceroy, Dom Duarte de Meneses, to the King. Goa, 6-12-1587, AGS, *Secr. Prov.*, Book 1551, fls. 69–69v., 80–81v.

'Sir

I have received great favour from Your Majesty in having thought of me for new tasks and services, and even though I am so unworthy of them, this particular regard that Your Majesty has shown me will give me strength and courage for everything, for which reason I kiss your hand many times for having entrusted me with the enterprise of Aceh, which I hope with God's favour can be realised, and is the greatest favour that I could receive from Your Majesty, and to be in your service is the greatest prize of all. Your Majesty writes to me saying that in Your opinion the opportunities of this enterprise are not yet over, as the Captain and Bishop of Melaka have written thus to You. I do not know if they are well informed in this regard, or if they have understood it in the way they have written, because all these days past they were waiting each day expecting the armada from Aceh, and with news of it being a very powerful one, and that it would not be possible to resist without great assistance from India; which seems to contradict the information received about it being a good occasion, and until now I have not been able to obtain any other tidings, despite the great efforts I ordered be done in this regard, except for the news that the Sultan of Aceh was killed on the orders of his wife, and she is now married to another king, as I have written to Your Majesty in another letter and this is all so confused that nothing can be confirmed, nor held to be true. (fl. 69v.) Dom Paulo de Lima was repeatedly alerted about this matter.

I believe he will find out the truth about it, despite the fact that the ports and sites of that coast are always so well guarded and closed, and have such little trade and friendship with those of the Estado, that one does not know anything of what goes on there and even less about the manners of fortification and the state of their defences, that is one of the main things about which it is particularly convenient to have information. And as I hold so dear the affairs and people of India, not only have the promptness and desire with which I offered myself to the service of the Kingdom for this task not diminished, but to the contrary, as Your Majesty has shown, and the great desire that I have to serve you has always spurred me on, on top of finding so many failings and timely occasions, which Your Majesty did not mention in last year's letters, nor sent in all these affairs any money nor the most necessary things, I became aware that the undertaking was being delayed for another year, as it is an enterprise that requires a great deal of continuity and resources in all aspects, which did not happen during these years, as nothing came even for the ordinary armadas, despite my having asked all of these years.

And every time one dealt with this enterprise, apart from what I have said, every year there came an abundance of money to prepare and buy whatever was necessary here. And this at a time in which the Estado was flush with funds and did not have so many shortages as in present times. I speak of this so particularly, because in addition to the duties of my office, my responsibilities have now been doubled by Your Majesty (fl. 80) assigning me this enterprise, and I am endeavouring to ensure that the mission has the desired effect and that everything is arranged so that not only does it finish well, and with honour, but that the peace and security of the Estado is assured.

Your Majesty writes to me that in this following year you will send three hundred thousand *cruzados* in money for this task, and four thousand men; this number of people should always be sufficient for the purpose, especially if half of them are good soldiers, but I am not aware of these men being here in India, and the arrivals from Portugal this year are even less. Some will be suitable to engage in battle with the armada of the Turk, but not to march on land obediently in an orderly fashion, and to knock down and scale fortresses, as they do not have any experience of this, but in the absence of men who are experienced one must use what one has. I do not know if this sum of money, even though it is fine for the needs of the moment, will be enough to cover all the expenses of the enterprise, as just the wages of soldiers and officials, and purchases of supplies, munitions and so many other things will probably consume all of it, and furthermore, as one must take into account the delays and events of war that in such far-off and arduous missions are numerous and uncertain, and always prove to entail far greater costs and delays than one imagines. Which must all be prevented, because where one seeks the honour and betterment of states (fl. 80v.) one does not risk one thing or the other, due to which I am of the opinion that a greater amount of money should be sent, because it is necessary that our fortresses here be well provisioned, and with greater garrisons and better salaries, because although we are now at peace with these neighbours, events can happen that could change this situation, and disasters take place, God forbid, by which we would put everything we have earned at risk, due to which this precaution should be taken, so that one can aspire to do great work, so that everything is well arranged for this enterprise. And on account of the dearth in India of men of government, I have often thought of Matias de Albuquerque having gone to Portugal, who Your Majesty had appointed to be here, and today I do not see anyone of his calibre and experience for this office and who I could leave in it without taking the greatest care for the same undertaking, because apart from the known reasons, there is now talk of many Turkish galleys. And these neighbouring kingdoms are once again allied by peace and marriages, and just like they are against Akbar now, given an occasion, they could easily turn against the Estado. I have reminded Your Majesty of all these things because as I have said I have redoubled obligations, and greatly desire to carry them all out completely in Your Service, and I am prepared and ready in every way for the task, with the same desire and enthusiasm with which I came to serve. And Your Majesty knows (fl. 81) that I have done so until now, what I have to ask in all this is that if this enterprise is to be realised during my tenure, Your Majesty order it to be speeded up, because I am getting old and am increasingly indisposed, and just like it would be a great dishonour to die on the streets of Goa, I shall consider it a great honour from God and Your Majesty to die on the beaches of Aceh, and I shall esteem this more than any other request, and can hope for. By the grace of Our [Lord] may the life and Royal state of Your Majesty prosper for many years.

From Goa, 6 December 15 […]
I kiss the Royal hands of Your Majesty
Dom Duarte de Meneses'

Document 4

Letter from Luís de Góis de Lacerda to the King, Cochin, 10-1-1588. AGS, *Secr. Prov.*, Book 1551, fl. 314.

'Sir

After having written to Your Majesty, it so happened that a letter arrived by means of Pegu with news of the events in Melaka, where the Viceroy of India had sent Dom Paulo de Lima to assist them in their hour of need, who, like a practical captain did not go directly to Melaka with the armada but sailed along the shores of Aceh, and sent a part of the armada, consisting of oared boats, which caused great damage along the coast, and came to know of the news that the Sultan of Aceh was dead, and that one of his sons, a young boy, was entrusted to one of his captains, who is now the regent of Aceh, and the King of Johor has contracted to marry one of his daughters to him, who came in a ship to Aceh to hand herself over to the regent as his wife. Dom Paulo came across this ship and captured it and the princess, passing through the Straits and proceeded, and the King of Johor had constructed a fort at the mouth of the Straits to impede the passage of the ships from China, and Dom Paulo took this fort in great style, and demolished it, and after it had been demolished, established himself in the harbour and fortress of Johor, and at the time that the letter was received he was at the fortress, with these prior victories, and one understands that he had taken the fortress. I thus thought it fit that these ships shouldn't leave without taking these tidings to Your Majesty, because the Viceroy would not have mentioned this information in his letter as the news did not arrive in time; God willing, more progress will follow, and great victories, as such a good captain is involved in this mission. And in this manner, Portuguese glory shall be revived and Your Majesty's dominions shall expand. And the experts say that this is the juncture in which things could be decided for once and for all with Aceh.

From Cochin, on 10 January 1588.

Luís de Góis de Lacerda'

Document 5

Letter from Dom Henrique Bendara to the King, Melaka, 16-12-1588. AGS, *Secr. Prov.* Book 1551, fls. 524–524v.

'Sir

As vassals have a special obligation in the letters they write to their Kings and lords to weigh their words and evaluate their services in accordance with the services rendered, in this letter I shall do no more than relate how, once the fortress of Johor had been destroyed by Dom Paulo de Lima, the Rezalle [Raja Ali] once again built another, of such solid and strong wood, and at a site that is so fortified and invincible, that without doubt it surpassed the first fortress. And as there was no doubt that if he were allowed to finish, it would be impossible to capture it except by means of an organised long term siege, as the captain Dom

Diogo Lobo was keenly aware of this, as a zealous servant of Your Majesty, seeing how imperative it was for the peace of this Estado not to allow them to establish roots, he impressed upon me how important it was that it not be realised, and asked me to accept the mission of destroying it and razing it to the ground. As it was such an honourable task, and as I have sacrificed my life for so long for any service to Your Majesty, I gladly accepted without paying heed to the difficulties involved in the task, that was very dangerous in everyone's opinion, and that it seemed impossible to manage to carry out, as this city lacked the armada and men necessary to realise a task of such importance. However, putting aside all the objections that many people pointed out, with thirty light vessels, of which I prepared five at my own expense and cost, I set sail and landed, and attacked the said fortress that had many men stationed there, where, after firing the artillery that they had, it seemed that the enemy, seeing me so resolute upon a firm conclusion, terrified, fled from there, and I entered the fortress without any bloodshed, and I set fire to it and razed it to the ground. And I took the remnants of the artillery that was left from the first defeat, that consisted of twenty-five pieces, and going four leagues upriver, I burnt and destroyed all the places and cities that I found, that were many. And I sank more than one hundred large vessels that were loaded with wares, and fifty of which were loaded with provisions, which were in acute short supply due to past shortages, and as there was nothing else to be done, I withdrew to safety.

And because Dom Diogo Lobo will write in further detail to Your Majesty, I shall not hold forth any longer, except to say that this victory left the enemy so broken that he will raise his head again only after a long time or never, for which reason it was considered all round to be a more important victory than the first one.

I have been granted two voyages of the Moluccas by Your Majesty, which, as they shall be delayed and I shall be old, I think that I shall not be able to realise them, and because of this I am once again obliged to mention my great poverty and many services, and request that Your Majesty remember to grant me (fl. 524v.) greater favours. Seeing as how I will have to withdraw from the post of *bendara*, an office that I served and from which I met my needs this year, as it shall go to the son of Dom João Leal, whose office it is, for which I ask that, as I have described to Your Majesty the misery in which I live, that I be granted a suitable favour to enable me to sustain myself, until the said voyages take place, and that I can also bequeath them and leave them in my will to my sons, as I see fit. I pray to Our Lord that the life and Royal state of Your Majesty prospers and grows for the peace of your vassals and the expansion of all of Christendom.

From Melaka, on 16 December 1588.

Humble vassal of Your Majesty, who kisses your Royal hands.

Dom Henriques'

Document 6

Letter from the Bishop of Melaka, Dom João Ribeiro Gaio, to the King (excerpts). Melaka, 31-12-1588. AGS, *Secr. Prov.*, Book 1551, fls. 403–414v.

'(fl. 403v.) … The Viceroy, Dom Duarte de Meneses, after being given four victories in this Estado by Our Lord, that is, that of Johor, that Your Majesty will see in another letter that goes with this one, the victory of Sri Lanka, the victory of the coast of Malindi, about which you will have been informed by India, and the victory of the fortress of Solor against the King of Demak, that is also described here below, Our Lord saw fit to call him to his service, a very good Christian, and he left no estate. At present, Manuel de Sousa Coutinho governs, who succeeded to the post in the second succession; Our Lord will be served if he discharges the post as necessary. The Viceroy that Your Majesty sends, may he be a friend of God and a person who is suitable for this governance as much needs to be done, and may this choice be as judicious as Your Majesty is judicious in all his choices.

The Viceroys do many and great disgraces, and have stopped paying the expenses, in which the Estado is greatly in debt, about which I remind Your Majesty below to provide for, to serve your interests.

The Captain of this fortress, who is serving now, who took up the post this past 10 September, is Dom Diogo Lobo. God will be served if he can fulfil his obligations, he is very sick, and it happens very often that they die in that fortress that is separated, and far away from Goa, that very often it happens that neither a ship nor word arrives from Goa within a year (fl. 404) and it happens that the captain dies, or is not in a state to govern, and there is disquietude. For this reason, Your Majesty must give orders about the succession of this fortress, and for those of the Moluccas, of Hormuz and Mozambique, and for all the others that are in far-flung areas, until the Viceroy makes appointments.

Also, the heathens in these areas, during these past three years, have had many wars, namely, the King of Pegu, with three hundred thousand men besieged the King of Siam, and has not done anything due to the hard winters. And the emperor of Java, with the King of Demak, over whom he will be emperor. And the lands of Java are all lost. And in Japan there are many wars, so that the ship from Macao has not come for the past two years because of them. Likewise, the regions of Hormuz and the lands of the Adil Khan are witnessing wars, which Your Majesty will know of via India. And similarly, Aceh has much war with deaths and famines, and from the Minangkabau people, that it is in a state in which Our Lord can give Your Majesty great victories here. ...

(fl. 404v.) The Captains of Melaka seize and buy at an unfair price all the spices and wares of tin, gold and other things that come to this fortress by means of the heathens who are not vassals of Your Majesty, and pay them in cloth and other inferior goods, by which they greatly coerce the said infidels and cause great losses to Your Majesty and to the merchants, because as I have written at length to Your Majesty in past years about the *terços* of these spices from the Moluccas, namely, mace, nutmeg and cloves, that are due to you as the islands of the Moluccas are mines, and not only the faithful, but the heathens who go to these islands to procure the said spices owe these *terços*, to which Your Majesty has responded in your letters that you felt it was a good idea to warn the Viceroy, which I did, and he has not taken measures. Your Majesty must take measures from Portugal, as this year only six hundred *bares* of spices entered this fortress and, of this, two hundred *bares* were on account of the *terços*, that are worth twenty thousand *cruzados*, and apart from this, the greater part of the duties, that are set at seven per cent, and your vassals neither sell nor buy nor do they have a livelihood, and the infidels, on account of the harassment, no longer return to the fortress. The said captains say they have provisions from the Viceroys.

(fl. 405) The captains, mainly those of Melaka, do not allow anyone to navigate, and they sell the voyages, on account of which much disservice is done to Our Lord and losses to your treasury, and to your vassals who, if they were able to sail freely, as God and Your Majesty order, would bring to this fortress many wares upon which duties would be paid, and your vassals would be able to live. For everything they say they have provisions from the Viceroys, and the China voyages are enough for the captains of Melaka, from whence they take thirty-six thousand *cruzados* during their three-year tenure, and three from Bengal, fifteen thousand,

and furthermore they now have the habit of having carracks, and do not let anyone load unless their own, and there are no merchants who wish to come to this fortress any longer. And the captains of the Moluccas, and the captains of the voyages do not let the merchants load cloth, and the captains of the voyages of Banda do the same, so that they alone can buy, by which your treasury suffers losses, and your vassals do not have a livelihood, and they say they have provisions from the Viceroys for everything.

The captains of Melaka buy many papers and old debt bonds of other fortresses and benefits that the Viceroys issue so that, at present, there are more than fifty thousand *cruzados* in this fortress, and the fortress expenses are not paid, which is done in all fortresses. For your affairs to be in order, Your Majesty must order that a register and books be made and a list of everything that the revenues of each fortress yields and is worth, namely, a general record of the entire Estado be kept in Goa, and other particulars in each fortress, and once the said lists are done, that each fortress shall have its own, that no provision of the Viceroy shall be paid, nor any other from outside, until the common expenses and needs of the said fortress have been paid and met, and this with penalties, and with what is left over, whatever the Viceroy orders shall be done, that the Viceroy can easily know from the general list that will be in Goa, and that the Viceroy should not grant favours nor prepare (fl. 405v.) papers for the said fortresses, unless it is in the sum that is left over, which Your Majesty must ensure because, as things are not working in this way, the debts for expenses are great, and your interests are not served.

The captains of the Moluccas take the *terços* in the fortresses of Tidore and Ambon because they are not properly provided, by which your treasury suffers great losses, as six hundred *bares* of cloves, which are worth sixty thousand *cruzados* and should come to this fortress, are instead sold in the Moluccas for less than eight thousand, and the needful must be done in the provisions for these fortresses, and no less, and it has to be done from Goa, and not from this fortress, because the greatest enemy of the fortresses of the Moluccas is the Captain of Melaka who, as he intends for the spices to come to Melaka by means of the infidels for the reasons mentioned above, hinders every kind of good for the Moluccas; and that the captains of the fortress, chiefly those of Melaka, not obstruct supplies, nor their wives, nor their mothers-in-law, nor their retainers, and that the Captain of Melaka oblige the factor to buy the rice necessary for the armadas every year, and more for reserves in times of siege, and that the city council of Melaka do the same, and that there not be a Treasury inspector, nor Treasury administrator, nor any other Treasury official, nor a purveyor, but only a factor, nor must there be a *xabandar*, nor a bailiff of the Captain, nor guards nor a *sobrerrol*, nor a *tomungão*, and other unnecessary officials, as the auditor and *alcaide do mar* are sufficient, and the *alcaide da terra*, and factor, and captain.

In the fortress, three hundred soldiers are paid for duty here, that soldiers not be paid except for those that go registered in the armada, and that the said three hundred soldiers not be paid if they are *casados* on land, nor bachelors (fl. 406), because the retainers of the captains receive the pay and salaries of the said three hundred soldiers that they take from the *casados* and from other people that come from outside, and that the retainers that the captain, bishop, auditor and factor have, that they be paid in cash, because the interests of Your Majesty will be served by this order, and there will be soldiers.

The learned magistrate that Your Majesty sent to this fortress got married the other day, and is very well-connected, and a great merchant; Your Majesty must appoint another one, which is a great service of God, and the list of instructions for Justice that Your Majesty sent is very holy and Catholic, and is clearly instituted by the orders of Your Majesty. However, I do not see it being upheld in this fortress, chiefly by the retainers of the captains, who are all Justice and Treasury officials.

The officials of the Melaka city council make many by-laws and many proclamations and do not uphold anything; that Your Majesty order them to make by-laws according to the dispositions and privileges that they have, and that they carry them out, principally for the things of the processions, and that the money from the one per cent, that they spend it well, and that they cannot spend it on anything except for the fortifications, and that when they take money for war it will be with the advice of the captain and prelate.

This year of 1588, at the end of the month of May, an English galleon, a ship with three decks, came to Blambangan, that is an island that is in Java, and on this island there is the port of Panarukan, where the Capuchin fathers are, which had a lot of artillery on board, and almost two hundred men, and as it seemed to the Portuguese that this galleon, being anchored in the sea in front of Blambangan, that is on the side of the opposite coast of the said island, was one of our ships, they asked for permission from the King of Malambuam, who is a great friend of ours, to go to the said ship along with a negro of the said king, and they went and found the said ship to be of the said English. These Englishmen did not do any harm to the said Portuguese; rather, they gave them some pieces, and the said negro, and also sent pieces to the said king, and the said king in return sent them supplies of chickens and victuals from the land, and furthermore the captain of the said Englishmen wrote a letter to Dom Diogo, captain of this fortress, and another letter to me. ...

(fl. 407v.) And thus they assure me that the Englishman asked a lot about Aceh and about navigation from Aceh to the Straits of Mecca and about the Strait of Sunda, and that he said that his intention was to set upon this shipping in order to reach an agreement with the Turk and to gain control of Aceh and the Sunda Strait, to take the spices to the said Straits of Mecca and thus to England, that Our Lord will be served if Your Majesty has already attained a victory over England, so that both here and over there your interests are served.

Thus, for the aforementioned reasons, in this next chapter as also because Aceh is currently very weak as Our Lord has given them many famines and diseases, and a foreign king who is very unpopular all around, and also has wars with his neighbours the Minangkabau people. It is important that Your Majesty quickly order the conquest of Aceh, that once victory over Aceh, that Our Lord will give to Your Majesty, is attained, everything will calm down, as will some disturbances that the King Raialle of Johor, who remained alive still gives us, as does Sunda (fl. 408), and this State, and your Treasury, will be very rich, with which one will conquer these parts. ...

(fl. 409) This customs house of Melaka, before the capture of Johor, was leased for fifty thousand *cruzados*, and sometimes for less; this year, after the capture of Johor, it was leased for seventy-three thousand *cruzados* because there is not enough to pay the ordinary expenses due to the many papers purchased that the captains and other officials bring, and due to the many favours that the Viceroys grant by their provisions, and the order that has been described above seems a service of God and Your Majesty.

The ship from Portugal did not come this year, which was a great loss for this fortress that, in great measure, is sustained by it, by which Your Majesty would do a great service to God, and for the welfare of these people to send a ship every year to this fortress, and if the city does not respond, both in terms of pepper as well as the wintering, it is the fault of the factors and contractors because the factor of the pepper contractors takes the money in *reales* and sends it to China, and they do not buy any pepper other than what the infidels bring to Melaka, and they do not undertake any diligences, nor efforts, nor risks to go and procure pepper, that if they took due diligence there would be enough pepper cargoes for two ships, because Kedah has pepper, and a lot of it, and Jambi, and Indragiri, and Patani and Sunda have pepper, from (fl. 409v.) where the king has written that he will give it but no efforts are made to procure it, and as for the factor of the contractors of the ship, he also takes the money and sends the *reales* to China, and when the ship comes to trade, there is no money, and there are quarrels about everything with the officials of the ship, and if they die, some sell the offices to people who do not deserve it, nor know how to sail, and those who merit it, the factor does not give them the offices, so that the ships stay in the port and are sailed badly, so that Your Majesty must take steps to order that a ship come to these parts.

The missionaries who come and are sent to these lands for the Christian communities must be virtuous and able to endure hardships and hunger, that they come to die in the said Christian communities, excepting those that are old and sick, that cannot withstand the hardships of this work, and hunger, or any other impediment that may intervene, it is better that they not be in the Christian communities, and that the ambassadors and other people who come to this fortress be assisted by the captains, especially the ambassadors of kings who consent conversions in their Kingdoms, because due to our sins the captains favour the ambassadors who send their ships to Your Majesty's mines in the Moluccas to procure spices, and bring them to Melaka in the manner described above, and the ambassadors of the kings that consent Christian communities in their kingdoms do not receive any protection from them. It will be a service to God if Your Majesty orders that no duties be taken up to a certain quantity of goods that the said ambassadors may bring, and given that their kings consent that Christians be converted in the kingdoms, and it is also necessary that Your Majesty protect the missionaries who go to the Christian communities by giving them the necessary wherewithal and paying them very well, because the money that is given to the ministers of the Church is very badly paid. ...

(fl. 411) The armadas that are assembled in these parts are already functioning better, for which Your Majesty must thank the Viceroys because the armada that Dom Duarte de Meneses, Viceroy of India, mustered and sent to this fortress, that joined up with another that was mustered here, under the command of Dom Paulo de Lima, took Johor, and another that the said Dom Duarte de Meneses assembled, that he sent to the coast of Malindi, under the command of Martim Afonso de Melo also fulfilled (fl. 411v.) its obligations, and another that was also assembled for the siege of Sri Lanka, under the command of Manuel de Sousa Coutinho, who is now Governor, fulfilled its obligations; also the armada that was mustered in Melaka, whose Captain-General was Dom António de Noronha, both before and after it joined the said armada under the command of Dom Paulo de Lima, fulfilled its obligations, and another armada that was assembled in Solor, governed by the fathers of the Dominican Order and by the captain, António Viegas, against the king of Demak, fulfilled its obligations. Your Majesty must praise Our Lord for the blessing of these victories that have caused great fear and awe amongst the negroes in these parts, and it is certain that if one now targets Aceh, with the spirits of the Portuguese in great form with these victories and those of the infidels greatly dejected, Our Lord will bless Your Majesty, that everyone thinks that victory is certain.

In Solor there is an enemy of negligible power who lives as a bandit, and only fifty soldiers along with a captain are enough to destroy him; Your Majesty must order the captain of this fortress by a provision, that will be given to the missionaries of the Dominican Order to carry it out, that the said captain give the said soldiers and captain, paid in this fortress from your Treasury.

The Moluccas are neither at peace nor at war, those who come from there affirm that the islands are now in greater danger, due to which one must provide help and quickly and it would be wise to stop Aceh, that with this victory everything will be peaceful, both Johor as well as the Moluccas and one can make provisions about the armada itself in the manner in which I have described in my reminders to Your Majesty over past years with regard to Aceh. And the Moluccas, as I have mentioned above, one must send the necessary appointments from Goa and not from this fortress. Likewise, the galleons that go to the Moluccas run up great expenses and show little profits; as I have written to you in the past, Your Majesty must make these voyages freely accessible, so that everyone can go to the Moluccas and Banda, and that everyone shall pay the *terços* and duties at Melaka. (fl. 412) China and all these parts that I have not mentioned are peaceful, and our friends, and we are awaiting four ships from China this year. ...

(fl. 412v.) I, during the time I served as captain, took in this city, as I have written at length in another letter that goes with this one, up to a sum of forty thousand *cruzados*, to equip the armadas, chiefly the armada that took Johor, where it was necessary, as there was no other money to be found, about seven thousand *cruzados* was taken from the pepper money for the factor of this fortress to pay them. Dom Diogo Lobo took over as captain with a provision from the Viceroy as Treasury inspector, and he takes all the money and pays his obligations and debts that he brought from Goa. Thus, Your Majesty must provide by your provision that the money that this customs house yields be paid, in order to be able to make payments. And that Your Majesty know that this pepper money was only taken due to great necessity, and only after no one was found who had money to lend, and after all the silver of the churches was pawned. Our Lord will be served if this fortress never finds itself in dire straits, because if this should happen there is no one who can lend any money to Your Majesty nor to the person who holds the post of captain.

(fl. 413) The *casados* of this fortress are leaving the city on account of the many vexations on the part of the captains, so that Your Majesty must take measures so that they are not harassed, so that they do not leave, and that the captains not deprive the city of any privilege, for which provisions must also be made; and one should not refer to the Viceroys, that they should not make provisions in matters of the captains, and this city is very poor, and does not have revenues for her needs such as for streets, bridges and fountains, so that Your Majesty must order that these works be handed over to the magistrates of the auditorship, that each year yields more than a thousand *cruzados*, and after the expenses of the magistrates are paid, more than five hundred *cruzados* are left over.

The pinnaces and *bantins*, and other armada ships, the captains give them as favours, and others go to wrack and ruin as no one looks after them and nor is there a harbour to keep them, there being many places in which one could make a fine harbour; Your Majesty must order that the said harbour be made and that the captains not bestow any ships of the armada as favours.

Our Lord will be served and will give Your Majesty victory over Aceh, for which orders and powers must be given to the *conquistador* who will come, because it has many rivers and large settlements to be given as *encomiendas*, in the manner of the Philippines, that thus a great increase in Christianity shall take place and in your Treasury, and it will provide livelihoods for your vassals. For everything that has been presented to

Your Majesty in the reminders that I write in this letter, and what you think suitable for this fortress, it is not enough to charge and entrust the Viceroys, nor to write to the captains, because nothing will be done. Your Majesty must provide by your Instructions in the manner in which provisions have been made for the affairs of Justice, and one must verify that they are fulfilled, and punish transgressors and those who disobey, and grant favours to those who obey and fulfil them; those who do the most harm in these parts, we do not see anyone of them punished, and those who do good are very badly treated, not by Your Majesty, but by the Viceroys and captains, that even (fl. 413v.) those who write the truth are treated very badly, and because I have done so with your Viceroys, I have received some letters with wicked words, and the captains who are in Goa to enter in this fortress may be warned by the information that I give them of the fortress, as Your Majesty has ordered me to, and also by Your Majesty's letters to them, but they say that I wrote such warnings to Your Majesty. ...

May Our Lord guard the Royal person of Your Majesty for many years for the expansion of his Holy Catholic Faith; three other letters are going with this one, one about the capture of Johor and another about the journey of Father Custódio, and another about a fort that was now taken from the Rajalle.

From Melaka, on the last day of December 1588.

Chaplain of Your Majesty

The Bishop of Melaka'

Document 7

Letter from the King to António Fernandes de Ilher. Lisbon, 12-1-1591. AHU, *Cons. Ultr.*, cod. 281, fl. 164v. (Reply to the letter dated 5-12-1589)

'António Fernandes de Ilher. I, the King, greet you. I saw your letter from Melaka, dated 5 December 1589, where you tell me that you have not had word for the past two years about the pepper that is arranged in that fortress for the cargo of the ship that visits it every year, that was not able to go in these two years past (as it is going now), and I have ordered that it go every year, and with the necessary money for the pepper that it must bring, for which reason I order you to do everything possible on your part to ensure that this ship, and all the others that shall henceforth go there each year, come loaded with a good cargo of pepper, as I trust you shall do. And you did well to send to India the pepper that was bought to come in the ships to Lisbon, as well as to buy from the Chinese all the pepper that they brought to that fortress, so that in future they rejoice coming there. And you remind me that it would be better for my interests to impede these Chinese so that they do not go to source this pepper in Sunda, Patani and the other places that you have mentioned, you will also make a similar reminder to the Viceroy, who I am ordering to write about this matter, to act in this matter in the way which is most suitable for my interests.

Written in Lisbon on 12 January 1591.'

Document 8

> Charter by the Viceroy, Matias de Albuquerque. Goa, 25-9-1596.
> HAG, *Regimentos e Instruções*, Vol. 2, fl. 54.

'Francisco de Bulhões, contractor of the Melaka customs house

Matias de Albuquerque etc. I make known to all those who see this charter that as I am aware that the lease contract for the customs house of Melaka that was made with Gonçalo de Sousa de Freitas [?], for a period of four years, will terminate at the end of December of this year, I think it fit and it pleases me that Francisco de Bulhões, who succeeded the said Gonçalo de Sousa in the said contract after having settled payments for himself and his predecessor with the treasury of His Majesty and his factors the sum of the said lease, accordingly, can receive and shall receive freely all the profits of the said customs house, without anyone impeding him, until the end of the said month of December, under pain of whosoever shall act to the contrary, paying to the said Francisco de Bulhões all the money and merchandise that was taken from him with all the damages and interest. To him [?] Francisco, as well as to the Captain of Melaka, the factor and other magistrates, officials and people, all concerned in this matter, and I order them to carry this charter out and keep it and ensure that it is carried out and kept so that its contents are free from doubt or impediment. Prepared by João de Freitas; in Goa, on 25 September 1596.

Written by Luís da Gama.

The Viceroy'

Document 9

Letter to Viceroy Dom Francisco da Gama. (excerpt). Lisbon, 30-3-1598. BN, *Res.* cod. 1975, fls. 331–332v. (1st copy)

'His Majesty is informed that, as the King of Aceh is not the legitimate lord of that kingdom, he is hated by the local people, and seeks all means to secure and keep his position, and as it seemed to him that a friendship with this Estado would give him that, and would greatly check his vassals, he began to interact with Pero Lopes de Sousa, who was then Captain of Melaka, making on his part demonstrations of good friendship, contrary to that of past times, offering a site where one could establish a fortress, and assurances of help with the construction, and he then sent his ambassadors to the Viceroy, Matias de Albuquerque, to whom it did not seem a good idea to enter into an obligation with Aceh with a peace treaty; and he thus bid his ambassadors farewell with words of greetings and signs of friendship, and with letters and a present for the King, and he sent an order to the Captain of Melaka that he continue his relations with him by means of good correspondence, and send to his main port, every so often, some ships owned by merchants, and visits so that they could acquire information about the land, and the place and its maritime sites, and that all the Acehnese who went to Melaka with their wares to sell and buy, especially those who took pepper, be treated well so as to thus better preserve this new friendship.

His Majesty is also informed that presuming that the said King of Aceh be content with His Majesty establishing a fortress in his main port, where the bulk of the commerce and trade in pepper is carried out, one should not accept his offer in this regard, due to the great inconveniences and damage that could result from the establishment of the said fortress.

And it is for these reasons that one must not do anything more at present, than to have this (fl. 331v.) door open by means of continuous communication, until there is sufficient power in India for the conquest of that kingdom, and in the meanwhile one can pursue a contract for pepper with Aceh, in which one obliges him to send it in his ships to Melaka, for the price that the Javanese sell pepper at the same fortress, that would be very important, because it would reduce in some measure the trade in this spice to the Red Sea, apart from appreciating thirty per cent until Cochin, where one has to bring it to load the cargoes of the ships. In this matter it seems that the said ruler of Aceh will acquiesce easily when he understands that it is to his advantage or for any other purpose that the friendship of the Estado serves him, that can only be preserved with him if there are some benefits to be obtained.'

(2nd copy of the document in AN/TT, *Misc. Mss. do Conv. da Graça de Lisboa*, box 2, Tome III, pp. 553–556; 3rd copy pp. 573–576).

Document 10

'Notes that the City of Melaka sent to the City of Goa, which they present to Your Excellency in the name of the city', 1599. BN, *Res*, cod. 1973, fls. 57–58v.

To the Viceroy, Dom Francisco da Gama, Count of Vidigueira.

'In the first place we request Your Excellency to grant us the favour of a provision which enables us to buy spices freely as we consented to the fourteen per cent with this condition, or order the Captains to release half the spices that are brought to this land by the Javanese, which their factors, especially the one who presently serves this Captain, completely monopolise and resell them to the men of India, as one who knows these tricks, and thus he is the only one who profits, and all the *casados* of this land, and Portuguese merchants who come here from India, suffer losses, due to buying them at very high prices. And it seems fair that we should have a livelihood, and not be prevented from realising the commerce and trade that is free in all parts of the world, and that these goods not pass through only a single channel, which causes no slight damage to the residents of the city of Goa, and even more so to the service of His Majesty in the revenues of his customs houses, on account of which in this particular, and in the others mentioned below, that Your Excellency will grant us the favours that we are awaiting with great hopes, as we merit it from His Majesty and Your Excellency, as a descendent of Dom Vasco da Gama, patron of this Estado. And we thus ask Your Excellency to forbid the Captains who come to the Captaincy of this fortress to bring with them New Christian factors because with their network of contacts and large volumes of business nobody manages to live and they are prejudicial to all of India.

[in the margin:] S. prepare a provision so that everyone who wishes can freely buy spices in Melaka, as has already been ordered by another provision by Viceroy Matias de Albuquerque, and if the Captain or his factor impedes these said purchases, he will be considered guilty during the inquiry and will pay three thousand *cruzados* for each purchase that is proved to have been hindered by him, applied for the Treasury of His Majesty and for the fortification of the city of Melaka. And, in the said provision, it is not necessary to give the justification that is given in the second rule of this chapter, in this regard, on 21 April 1599.

May Your Excellency please also favour us with another provision, by which it is ordered that the Javanese should not enter the city walls, not even to deal with the Captain's factor or other people, and that there be guards at the doors of the city, paid by the Treasury of His Majesty, and that the factors of the Captain have houses outside the limits of the walls outside Melaka, where they can deal with the Moors, because more than twenty thousand of them gather here every year, and freely enter within the walls, for which reason we obstructed them to our best abilities by placing guards and with tones of friendship and really we would do well to take precautions, keeping in mind the examples of the betrayals that we experience every day from these people that we dread an untoward event, God protect us, and we request that this be provided for presently, due to the arrogance with which they are flaunting the success of their galleys, that well demonstrates their bad intent being equipped for other occasions and one can expect anything from such a wicked people (fl. 57v.) and our own notable negligence.

[in the margin:] Two decrees were prepared to make provisions about the two matters of this chapter, in which adequate measures were taken.

And thus may Your Excellency grant us another provision, by which let it be ordered, under pain of serious penalties, that all the residents who have houses covered with palm leaves roof them with tiles, as many are produced in this land, and tell the Captain that he order that the tower of the fortress in which the gunpowder is stored and the bulwarks be covered, and we thus also request Your Excellency to order that this fortress be provided with artillery and bombardiers, which are sorely lacking.

[in the margin:] S. prepare this provision and the officials of the city council establish a time limit within which the houses be covered with tiles, and whosoever does not do so shall pay for each one [?], if they do not obey, ten *cruzados* for the fortification of the city. In this regard, on [?] April 1599.

The King of Cambodia is in possession of his kingdom, and received our fathers and Portuguese well there, and gave an island measuring six leagues to His Majesty so that a fortress can be built on it, which he did not wish to grant the Castillians who went there. He sent an ambassador and ships with provisions here, and asks that he be paid the money that Francisco da Silva took from him here. In a ship that came to this city from Japan, due to the fact that its captain died on the voyage, we request Your Excellency to order Francisco da Silva, to pay this money, and likewise an additional nine hundred *xerafins* that he owes this city from the one per cent, which he should have sent but did not do, as can be seen from the papers we are sending.

We also remind Your Excellency that the English have been gaining a lot of knowledge about these regions on account of our sins, so that Your Excellency take care of this particular with the necessary remedy, before they firmly establish themselves in one of these lands, where it will be very difficult to later uproot them.

And thus we ask Your Excellency to grant us the favour of a provision by which this city is granted, in the name of His Majesty, the ball game that it made, which is in possession due to the Captains Francisco da Silva and Martim Afonso having passed us a provision in this regard.

[in the margin:] It was ordered that this provision be prepared with the declarations done.

We also sent, three years ago, instruments to His Majesty and Your Excellency in which we certified how much of a disservice it was to pay the duties on exits as stipulated by the provision that came here, due to the damage that results from this; we have not had a response from His Majesty. About this particular, we request Your Excellency to grant a favour by ordering that the execution of the said provision be halted until we receive a response from His Majesty.

[in the margin:] what His Majesty has ordered has to be carried out.

The pharmacist that we had here died, and we have entrusted the post to an Italian master with great experience, and he sends for remedies for the pharmacy at his own expense; we request Your Excellency to kindly grant that a provision be passed in favour of this Italian, and not to anyone else.

(fl. 58v.) Notes from the city of Melaka that the city of Goa presented to me in the monsoon of April 1599.'

Document 11

> Letter from the King to the Sultan of Aceh. Lisbon, 4-3-1600. AHU, *Cons. Ultr.*, cod. 282, fls. 8–8v.

'Mighty King of Aceh. I, King Philip, King of Portugal by the grace of God, etc., inform you that I have just sent Aires de Saldanha, of my council, as Viceroy of my Estado da Índia. And I have ordered him to punish the Dutch for their daring to go trade in those parts of the South, in Sunda and Java, as well as those who received them in their ports, for which reason (fl. 8v.) I request you very earnestly to favour the said Viceroy with whatever you can offer to be better able to carry this out, as I trust you will do. I understand how important the friendship of this Estado is to you, and I shall always remember to rejoice with you in your affairs as much as possible, and demonstrate the goodwill that I have for you; mighty King of Aceh: may Our Lord illuminate you with his Grace, and with him may your person and state be in His Holy safekeeping. Written in Lisbon on 4 March 1600.

Similar letters written to:

> Very Noble King of Johor. I, the King
> Noble and honoured King of Pasai. I, the King
> Noble and honoured King of Indragiri. I, the King
> Noble and honoured Queen of Japara. I, the King
> Noble and honoured King of Perak. I, King Phi
> Noble and honoured King of Pahang. I, King Phi
> Noble and honoured King of Blambangan. I, the

The Viceroy took these 8 letters to send to these rulers, only a single copy was made of them, and all were made essentially in the mould of the letter to Aceh. Made on 4 March 1600.'

Document 12

> Letter from the King to Viceroy Aires de Saldanha. Valladolid, 12-2-1602. AHU, *Cons. Ultr.*, cod. 282, fl. 66.

'Aires de Saldanha, Viceroy and friend. I, the King, greet you. In the ships last year I sent you a particular instruction that you should keep in the expedition that I ordered you to carry out to Melaka and Sunda against the Dutch rebels who navigate those seas. And that you be sent sixty thousand *cruzados* in money, and a provision for you to borrow in the manner described in these instructions, another hundred and fifty thousand *cruzados*. And with this money or with the part of it that you can obtain, I am sure that you will have already commenced the said enterprise in person, and that it will have the intended good results and that it will conform with the confidence that I had in you when I sent you as my Viceroy to the Estado, entrusting you above all with this matter as the most important and principal one of this office. And seeing that you wrote to me after your arrival, requesting that you be sent three hundred thousand *cruzados*, it seemed to me that I should order you and entrust you, as I do, to realise the said expedition with the said money that has already been sent to you last year, and with any other funds you can obtain from the revenues of the Estado, because I am informed that being the said revenues as well administered as I hope they are, in your time they will be sufficient for everything. And I trust you to serve me in this matter, and that you shall overcome all the difficulties that may arise with your good industry and care, and that the love and zeal that you have for my interests will help you to overcome all obstacles. Written in Valladolid on 12 February 1602.'

Document 13

Letter from the Archbishop of Goa to the King (excerpt). Goa, 6-4-1603. AN/TT - *Col. S. Vicente*, Vol. 12, pp. 115–118.

(p. 116) 'The Dutch and English ships are so numerous this year that all these seas are besprinkled with them .... In the lands with which the fortress of Melaka trades, this year there were thirty ships between Dutch, English and some French ones; they appear to have their main port of call in Aceh, where nine vessels went; and on 13 June four English ships from the State arrived and a brigantine that left from London and were captained by Jacques Delestes [James Lancaster], heavily equipped with artillery and people, which went to lie in wait for the ship loaded with cloth from S. Tomé and captured it as a large prize, with which they trade for pepper, and the Javanese, because of this, did not go to buy cloth in Melaka; another two Dutch ships captured a *nau* that was coming from Solor, and killed some Portuguese, and took others prisoner; they have made agreements with all the Kings of Java and they all receive them well, and with all this our position has been so weakened it does not even defer our things. In Aceh they are hand in glove with the King, and have a factory built of stone and lime, almost like a fort, and are established there, and General Jacques intends to capture the *naus* from China, due to which the Captain of Melaka helped with three *naus* and two galliots under the Captain-General Francisco da Silva de Meneses, who had arrived with the armada of André Furtado; may God grant him success, because from China we have not yet had any word if any Dutch went there. It is important that Your Majesty assist the affairs of the South, because in India there is no capacity to continue with the ordinary wars and to contract such a large number of ships, and this apart from helping the city from so far away, as is Goa.

Seven ships went to Patani, of which four left loaded with pepper; in Banda three were loaded; seven went to Sunda; to Priaman (p. 117) and Makassar four and to Aceh, the said nine, which make up the thirty I have mentioned; we do not yet know if any went to China, besides the Moluccas, Ambon, Sri Lanka and the Moluccas, due to which the customs house of Melaka has no profits and embassies did not come to the city as they used to; on the contrary, it seems that the neighbouring kings have hostile intentions towards us, judging by the delegations they have been exchanging amongst themselves; in September one awaits a response to the ambassadors that went to Holland from the King of Aceh, inviting them to bring many people to build a base, and in the next year word from the Queen of England, in response to the information that Jacques sent her.

André Furtado, with his armada, went to Sunda, where he found seven Dutch ships, but in such a way that he could not cause damage although he followed them and as a result overshot the harbour of Sunda and could not take it, which seems to have been divine providence, because there were thirty thousand men inside who had come from all over Java to help upon hearing news of the armada, and the King of Palembang, who helped André Furtado to help the Moluccas and Ambon, where it seems that if he had not gone, these two fortresses would have been lost because the Dutch were in collusion with the Kings of Hitu and Ternate, awaiting ten ships, all of them subjected to Duke Maurice [of Nassau], with a galleon of cloves as a tribute and other things at the price of the Portuguese and determined to take the fortress of Ambon, where three Dutch ships arrived, and turned back upon seeing our armada. Those who were in Hitu came to lie in wait for our ships at a place that is called Nau Forte, where André Furtado, upon disembarking, captured the King of Hitu and some Englishmen died, and amongst them the Captain, with which André Furtado subjected all the neighbouring places, taking the heads to Ambon, and for now has helped the Moluccas and Ambon, and hoped to come to Melaka to take Aceh from there, help from here going to assist him. The assistance that is going now does not have the capacity for this, and I do not have anything more to say to Your Majesty in this regard except that the South is lost, and with it all the good [?] of India, and I do not feel there is any remedy except for what God and Your Majesty give it from there, about which I write to you every year via the ships and only a distinct government in Melaka, ships and men sent from Portugal could give the city some help if it could receive it right away; in all the courts of the Kings who have seaports one can find ambassadors of these men ....'

Document 14

Letter from the King to the Viceroy of Portugal. Valladolid, 27-12-1604. AN/TT, *Núcleo Antigo*, No. 870, fls. 1–4v.

'Reverend Bishop, Inquisitor-General and my friend the Viceroy. I, the King, send you many greetings. As experience has shown the little effect that has resulted until now from the armadas that were sent in past years from India to the lands of the South to wage war against the rebels from Holland and other enemies that sail those seas, and from the one that went there under the command of André Furtado de Mendonça, the most important is to assist the South with the greatest force, the Viceroy of India going in person on this undertaking. Complying myself in this regard with what has been discussed here at length about this issue by people of great skill and experience, and with what seemed recently to be best in the opinion of the Council of India, I have decided that the Viceroy, Dom Martim Afonso de Castro, go from Goa to Melaka with the greatest and most powerful armada of oared ships and large ships that it is possible to assemble, and take as many men of war, munitions, provisions and other necessary things that can be obtained from that Estado, and that they leave without fail throughout the month of April 1606, being possible for it (fl. 1v.) to proceed with the war against the said rebels, providing (?) their customary assistance in the city of Melaka, and sending the armada divided into fleets from there to the Straits of Singapore, and of Sabang and Sunda, and to wherever else it be necessary to secure those seas, and to cleanse them of the said rebels that ply those seas because with him helping in that city, for the time that is suitable and necessary for this purpose, is to believe that one can manage the positive effects that are intended, and with his name and authority one will undoubtedly find help there with more men of war and abundant provisions, and the heathen Kings of those lands will restrain themselves and will assist with goods and supplies, and will refrain from trade with the rebels.

And from Melaka he will be able to govern everything like from Goa, where due to his absence he will leave the government of the Estado entrusted to and committed to the same people to whom I ordered and instructed Aires de Saldanha to leave it entrusted, he having to go to Melaka in person. All of whom must be subordinated to him, for which purpose by this letter of mine I wished to inform you so that you will understand, and so that you give an account of this resolution of mine to the Council of India, ordering it that it should quickly see to the number of ships, both (fl. 2) oared as well as *naus*, of men of war, munitions, provisions and other things that should be taken, and the most suitable time when the armada can leave, and the Instructions that must be kept, both for the expedition as well as for the government of the affairs of the Estado, that must be left settled and in order, and a draft of this should be sent to me very soon so as to send it with the letters that will be written about this matter.

And so that there is no delay in going to provide succour to Melaka, that going by the warnings could be greatly in need of help, in case the Viceroy cannot go there as quickly as is necessary, and so that when he arrives there, he finds more forces with which to wage war, and for other considerations with regard to this matter, I have also decided that the armada that will be sent from that Kingdom to those regions go directly to Melaka and not to Goa, nor to any other halt in India, as the reasons that were proposed to me in this regard are of greater force and convenience, and the damages and difficulties will be far greater than if it were otherwise, and that five galleons go, and in them the greatest number of men of war that can be raised, which are the three that are ready in Lisbon, and the two ships of the bailiff Luís Álvares de Távora that are presenting themselves at Oporto. And all (fl. 2v.) of them will be forewarned and prepared for everything that is necessary, the time in which, without fail, they can leave is throughout the month of January, or at the very latest at the beginning of February, without there being any failure in this, because if it is not thus they will risk not being able to go on to Melaka, that in case the ships of the bailiff do not arrive there in time to be able to depart along with the three other ships, that under no circumstances should they wait for them, because they can do their voyage later, and that Álvaro de Carvalho goes as General of this armada, and Manuel Mascarenhas in his company to also be General of one of the fleets that will be divided in Melaka, and that from Lisbon to there the said Manuel Mascarenhas will go under the command of the said Álvaro de Carvalho.

And in the same way he shall be so in Melaka until the Viceroy arrives there, and that each of them has as salary in each year, for the time that they serve in the said armada, two thousand *xerafins* and a thousand *xerafins* more as allowances for ordinary expenses, also in each year, and one thousand five hundred *cruzados* each one of them as allowances for expenses for their vessels, paid in that city, and one thousand *cruzados* advanced on account of their salaries, and that in the said galleons shall go eighty thousand *cruzados* in money and the greatest amount of munitions, supplies and other necessary things that is possible, and eight fathers (fl. 3) of the Society, with ten thousand *cruzados* for them to rent, upon their arrival in Melaka, some houses in which to establish a hospital to cure the sick (in case that city does not have one), which will always be under their charge. And that in the armada they take at their own cost the pharmacy and necessary things for the sick and their medical treatment, which will be bought according to the orders of the fathers, in accordance with what I have already ordered be written in this regard.

And that the revenues of the customs house of that fortress not be spent on any other thing other than in the running expenses of it and the upkeep of the said armada, for the time in which it shall be in that region. And for the inspector of the Treasury of Melaka and purveyor of the same armada, I have appointed Pero Mexia, and I grant him the favour of ordering him to be awarded the habit of the Order of Christ, with an annuity of thirty thousand *reis*, and the promise of the privileges of a nobleman of my house, with two thousand *reis* of residence should he serve well and to my satisfaction. And with the office of inspector of the Treasury of Melaka he shall have the same salary as the inspector of the Treasury of Goa.

And so that there are men of the sea who wish to go on these galleons they shall be given some wages in advance, and be promised on my behalf that on the ships that shall go to Melaka in the next year they shall be given passage and permission to return on them and their pay and the (fl. 3v.) tons that the Council of India (with whom you shall communicate) deems fit that they shall be given exempt from freight, so that they can bring their merchandise, or that of other people at a profit, and that apart from this that the same Council of India and the Estado see what else can be conveniently done with these people so that they are not lacking in number for the needs of this armada, and that what is fixed is carried out and executed, and that one proceeds with rigour and punish in the way that seems fit in the opinion of the said Council of India, those who do not wish to go, so that in these two ways one facilitates and eliminates all the difficulties that could arise in this matter.

And that in these galleons, two thousand *quintais* of rice should be sent for this, from the reserves, which you shall seek to buy in that city in any way possible, or should it be possible, one shall order it to be brought from other areas to sustain the men of war of the said armada, after having arrived in Melaka, and that the forty thousand *cruzados* which I have ordered be handed over to the bailiff Luís Álvares de Távora for the preparation of the said two galleons be remitted to the port with due diligence, in accordance with which I most particularly order and charge Dom Estevão de Faro, of my Council of State. And that the Viceroy in India be informed by my letters of this assistance that I am sending directly (fl. 4) to Melaka, and the fleets that will be divided to go to the Straits of Singapore and Sunda must always go under the command of the said Álvaro de Carvalho and Manuel Mascarenhas, whom I have appointed as the generals of these fleets, and that apart from all this I have decided that Melaka should have its own forces with which henceforth one can assist against the incursions of the enemies that come back to the lands of the South, without having to wait for help from India, that very often cannot go nor reach in time. From the year 1606 onwards, every year, two ships shall go directly to that city, that take people and whatever else is needed from Portugal, which shall return with loads of pepper and other spices, that are available there at a better price than in India, advising the Viceroy that, upon arrival in Melaka, he shall begin to take care of the cargo that the ships that shall leave in the said year of 1606 will bring. And that the Council of India be informed of this, so that they can immediately order all the official documents that are necessary, and that they be sent to me for my signature.

All of this you shall carry out and execute in the way that has been specified, and thus I greatly entrust and charge you with this, and you shall attend to all these (fl. 4v.) things and to the preparation of this armada with the greatest possible care and diligence, this matter being of the greatest importance and consideration and a pressing need of the day because of its nature, and being the first since you have begun to serve me in the government of that Kingdom I trust that you will proceed in a manner by which one shall effectively realise my intentions in this matter and wherever you may be when this Council reaches you, you shall take care of affairs in Lisbon with due diligence so that the said Dom Estevão de Faro is given the documents for him to take (of which a copy shall go to you with this). And you shall also write to him whatever else you feel is necessary until your arrival in Lisbon, from where you shall continuously inform me with great punctuality and particular detail of everything you do, because I shall rejoice to know of this, and as time is already racing and no more should be lost, you shall order that one shall work night and day so that this armada can leave as has been described.

Written in Valladolid on 27 December 1604.'

Document 15

Letter from the King to Viceroy Dom Martim Afonso de Castro (excerpts). Valladolid, 5-3-1605. HAG, *Monções do Reino*, 6B, fls. 9–16.

'Dom Martim Afonso de Castro, my friend the Viceroy. I, the King, send you many greetings. … I see fit and order that you personally do the said expedition to the South and the enterprise against the said enemy rebels, in which matter you shall proceed according to these instructions of mine, not letting yourself be swayed (fl. 9v.) by difficulties of any kind that may arise, no matter how great they be, to delay the execution of this order of mine, and I shall not accept any excuse from you that is not of such a quality, that one can see that you gave priority to another greater service to me. And on account of having understood by the information that came from those lands last year of the great number of enemy vessels that passed through those areas, and that they could have occasion to need assistance more urgently than what you can provide to them from that land of India, I have decided to send from this Kingdom, directly to Melaka, an armada of three galleons with the people, arms and munitions that they can carry for the said assistance, and to provide a guard for the ships of my vassals and confederates who navigate the waters of the said region, and you shall find greater forces and power when you arrive there.

And I have appointed Álvaro de Carvalho, from my Council, as General of this armada, who will serve as Captain-General of the armada, and armadas that shall sail in those regions, subordinate in everything to you, and according to the orders that you shall give him (as the Captains-General of the Estado do) and after you have arrived in Melaka, you shall order that the armada be divided into two fleets. ...

(fl. 11v.) And due to the shortage of provisions that I understand there is in the city of Melaka, and because it is certain that the Javanese will not take supplies to the city, knowing of your trip, you shall immediately seek in the monsoon of September of this year to send an order to Bengal, with sufficient money to procure the necessary provisions, and to send them from there to Melaka, so that you find everything provided for when you arrive and, apart from this, you shall take your armada well provisioned with the necessary supplies and other items in this regard, and reserve supplies. And the provisions that you make for gunpowder, and other munitions, arms and artillery, shall be in such a manner so that you do not find yourself later lacking in any of the things that you could need for the realisation of the said enterprise.

As soon as you arrive in Melaka you shall inform yourself about the state of affairs of the South, and any news that there may be of the rebels and other enemies, if they have gone there, and of the effects of the armada that is now going from this Kingdom directly to Melaka, and of the other particulars that seem necessary in your opinion for the realisation of this enterprise, and once you have all this information you shall convene a council of the captains of the said armadas, and the captain of the fortress of Melaka, and other people with experience who you find in your company, and seem to you to be so, and will apprise them of the state of affairs and of my order that you shall take, so that once all the individuals are well informed in this matter (fl. 12) they can counsel you better.

And in the first monsoon after having arrived in the said city of Melaka, you shall leave with all the might of the armada of the South, sailing throughout that archipelago, and you shall seek to severely castigate the King of Sunda and the other Kings that receive the Dutch rebels and give them cargoes of spices, destroying them and wreaking upon them the greatest damage possible, so that it is an example to the others not to receive or help them.

And once this is done, you can return to Melaka, leaving two fleets, or the number that you think fit in those seas, to impede the navigation and trade of the enemy if they return there, and the ships that normally take the spices from Banda to Java, and other regions, to capture the cargoes of the Dutch rebels, or to come to the port of Melaka, and thus you shall leave any other orders that seem necessary in your opinion for the prosecution of the said enterprise, and to achieve the intended objectives of eliminating the enemies from that navigation and impeding them from indulging in all the said commerce.

And should it be the case that the enemies have fortified themselves on land, you shall seek to dislodge them and fight them in the places where they may be, and you shall always occupy their place in the ports and places that they frequent most until you have completely uprooted them from the said regions. And you shall seek to inquire from practical people, and those with experience, whether it is convenient to make a fortress in Sunda, or in another area that is suitable to restrain the locals and impede the enemy from loading cargoes, and for my armadas to shelter, when they go to the said regions, as has already been indicated to me on other occasions, and in a place that can be assisted and sustained in case of sieges. And should it be found advisable to do so, you shall immediately put the fortress in a defensible state, and you will place a very trustworthy captain there, of such a conduct that one can trust him, who will be more interested in serving me and meriting other honours (fl. 12v.), than in the interests and profits that he hopes to gain from the post. ...

And while you are still awaiting the monsoon with which you shall leave with the entire said armada to the region of Sunda, as has been mentioned above, I feel you should send the part of the armada that you feel necessary against the King of Johor, to give him a severe punishment for the help that he gave to the said rebels to enable them to capture the ship from China. And because the experience of the case of Lourenço de Brito and other similar losses and disasters have shown how much damage and losses result from the goods that are captured if they are loaded in oared vessels, because with them they are unable to defend themselves and attack the enemy, I entrust you that you shall strictly forbid that the said captured goods be placed in the vessels of the armadas, principally in the oared ones, and for this purpose you shall order that all those wares that are captured be burnt.

And so that the locals do not be offended with the force and grievances that be done to them, you shall forbid with great severity that no ship be seized that does not plainly belong to the enemy and adversaries that must be punished, in every matter adhering entirely to the order and form of my instructions. And to the vessels belonging to the *chinchéus*, with whom this Estado is not at war, nor there being any occasion for it, no harm shall be done and (fl. 13) instead, you shall order that they all be treated well, in order to bring them to my service, being however warned of the betrayals and deceit that the Javanese customarily commit in everything.

And because I have been informed these past years that the King of Aceh had offered to my Viceroy, Aires de Saldanha, a place in his kingdom to built a fortress, and that he later made the same offer to the Dutch who went there, and with them sent his ambassadors to Holland, and it was understood that the King was inclined to give the place for the said fortress to whosoever arrived first, I order that as soon as you arrive in Melaka, and while the monsoon with which you shall go to the South sea does not arrive, you shall seek to find out the intentions of that King, and induce him to carry out what he offered about the said fortress, even if it be necessary to send a part of your armada for this purpose, because I understand that it will be of great importance to my interests to build the said fortress there, for the security of navigation and commerce in those areas, and to prevent the said rebels from establishing roots there, because of how difficult a task it will be to later uproot them, and to avoid the damages that they could do from there, and once he gives the said place, you shall endeavour with great haste to get the construction work of the said fortress underway, and you shall provide it with a captain, a person of suitable qualities and experience, to keep it in a well-guarded state of defence, and with men, munitions, artillery and supplies besides, so that it be defensible in all ways. And in case the Dutch have occupied the said place, you will propose in a council with the said captains and other people that I have mentioned above if it would be better for my interests, before proceeding, to try and dislodge them and fight them in the said place, and what you decide in this matter, you shall execute with the diligence and care that I trust in you. ...

(fl. 13v.) And because I have ordered that the revenues of the Melaka customs house that are left after its running expenses have been met shall be employed for the expenses of this armada, as you shall see from the provision that I have ordered be prepared about this, I trust that you will not spend the said revenues on other things, so that the course of the said enterprise is not hindered due to a lack of essentials.

And so that the said revenue continues to grow, I order and trust that you shall take particular care to put in order the good government and administration of the said customs house, endeavouring that the customs officials wholly fulfil their obligations, and that the merchants who come here are treated well as is just, their navigation not being impeded nor putting a spoke in their interests to give them reason to leave, and you shall order that the weights and measures are equal as it should be between Christians, Moors and Gentiles, so that the irregularities that there exist in this regard cease, and that they rejoice to come to the said customs house, and continue the trade from which there will surely follow great gains in the said revenues of the customs house. And you shall not allow (fl. 14) anyone to hinder the provisions, nor other wares that the Javanese, or any other merchants bring to the said city, nor permit that my factors and officials trade in provisions and munitions to resell them, on pain of losing their posts, to which you shall immediately appoint other people, without their being appointed by me, and you shall thus order this to be divulged so that this information is brought to everyone's notice. ...

Valladolid, on 5 March 1605.'

(Another copy of the document on fls. 1–8)

Document 16

'Account of the events of the armada of the Viceroy, Dom Martim Afonso', undated, AN/TT, *Mss. da Livraria*, No. 1113, fls. 192–193v.

'The armada of oared boats that left first went to make for land on the island of Nicobar, and here some vessels were lost in the sand-banks due to the water currents, and two were lost in the large gulf; the Viceroy arrived with the bulk of the armada, with the exception of Dom António de Meneses' ship that was going to Melaka, that was lost in Tuticorin, as also the galleon of Dom Luís Lobo that reached the coast and arrived in Manar, where he ordered it to be burnt without having seen enemies, and the entire armada went together to make for land in Aceh, where they appeared on the eve of St. Peter, and the Viceroy immediately sent António de Vilhegas as an ambassador, requesting the fortress and artillery for it, so that the pepper was contracted only to Our King for the price that was to be fixed. They say that the King of Aceh responded that he would give a fortress and pepper, but that it was not fair to ask him for the artillery as he needed it and it had cost him money; finally, he detained the ambassador for three days, and in them he finished fortifying five bulwarks that he had made in the port and sent his secretary as ambassador, committing himself to what he decided, who bid farewell to the Viceroy binding himself to persuade the king to grant everything that he had requested, who, as soon as he reached land, responded with many cannon-shots that he immediately fired upon our armada, and with this the Viceroy decided to disembark and did not wish to attack the harbour as five bulwarks and seven stockades had been built there; instead he did so on the open coast, with great risk and delays, and there two other ships were lost.

The Viceroy gave the lead to Álvaro de Carvalho, Dom António de Meneses and Dom Nun'Álvares, so that all three were to be in the lead, which Dom Nun'Álvares did not accept, saying that any one of those nobles was sufficient, and that he would not be missed where they were, due to which the Viceroy grew weary and immediately deprived him of his armada of oared vessels, and gave it to Dom António de Meneses, and the lead was formed by those two. But Dom Nun'Álvares did his job with valour; thus the Viceroy sought to compensate him and took him with him in his ship when he returned to Melaka. An attack was immediately made on an enemy defence, where there was great resistance and loss of men on our part, but the stronghold was taken with some artillery, but as the Viceroy saw the great efforts that would be necessary to conquer the other bulwarks, and having received word at the same time from a Moor of how Melaka was under siege, he set sail at night and captured three or four ships from Mecca and Surat that were in the port, and left for Melaka, leaving some skiffs from his ships that the enemy took from him with sailors; the captains that took these ships (fl. 192v.) burnt three of them; Dom Fernando Mascarenhas, to whom the other ship was entrusted, intended to take it to Melaka, and for this he stationed on board the vessel twenty of his soldiers who, finding themselves without sailors, ran aground, where they were captured and killed.

The Viceroy put Mateus [?] Dias in the Straits, and arriving at Cape Rachado, five leagues away from Melaka, found the Dutch armada that was waiting for him, who had been besieging Melaka for four months, with one thousand four hundred Dutchmen, apart from those that remained on board the *naus*, which were eleven in number, bigger than ours from Portugal, according to what the Viceroy wrote, as well as six additional light brigantines, and there were also sixteen thousand Javanese in the siege and seven neighbouring kings, and as soon as they heard that the Viceroy had come, they lifted the siege and the negros embarked on three hundred galleys and vessels in which they had come, and the Dutch burnt five of their brigantines and were left with eleven ships and a brigantine, and they came to lie in wait for the Viceroy in this condition, and the negros put themselves on an island, seeing the success of the battle, which began with twelve galleons on our part, although the others did not fight for fear, citing the wind as an excuse, due to which Guterres de Monroio, Dom Fernando Mascarenhas and João Pinto de Morais did not arrive, either due to a lack of wind or because they remained behind to take on water, fighting six or seven days, because the enemy had gained the windward advantage, until the wind turned in our favour, and with it our galleons attacked and engaged in battle with some enemy ships.

Álvaro de Carvalho came alongside the ship that had been under Sebastião Serrão, that the enemy had taken, and set fire to it after a long battle, and Duarte da Gama came alongside with another, and our men were stuck, in such a way that all were burnt with those of the enemy, and Duarte da Gama was very badly injured, and lost his arms, which were blasted off by a cannonball, and because there was no one to tow these ships, they were burnt, and as Duarte da Gama did not perish in the fire, he ordered one of his negros, who was the only one on the ship, to throw him into the sea, and both of them flung themselves into the sea and died. Álvaro de Carvalho, who had already been mortally wounded and whose galleon had been burnt, got into a small boat with some soldiers, and because they did not have oars they ran into an enemy ship, who asked them to surrender their arms and, because they would not give them up, killed them all with lance thrusts, and thus in this first battle two of our ships were burnt, and two other Dutch ships. Dom Henrique de Noronha engaged in battle with the enemy lead ship, and they fought for a whole day until they were both destroyed, without either power winning. The enemy suggested that they separate, as they were both completely devastated, and he accepted the request and let the ship be as he did not have any back-up; they say that the Viceroy took this the wrong way and deprived him of his galleon, and others say that he entrusted it (?) to come in the first thing, because the Viceroy had promised it to him thus with regard to the entrance of that fortress.

The Viceroy's ship was in constant battle with four enemy ships, who killed many of his men and even his pages, of which he was only left with two; Vilhegas escaped and they say that Dom Nun'Álvares did marvels, it was an intense battle and they say it was the most dangerous that had ever been fought in India to date, until the enemies turned tail and fled. But there was weakness on our part, and an aristocratic captain (fl. 193) who got into his gunboat and set out to sea and arrived in Melaka without his galleon. The Viceroy went after the enemy until Melaka and from then on the misfortunes or bad advice began; here André Furtado came aboard the Viceroy's galleon and told him to pursue victory, that he should not allow the enemies to regroup, as they had been devastated. The Viceroy sought counsel in this matter, despite André Furtado telling him that this was enough to obtain victory, and thus he let the enemy go and came and installed himself in Melaka; they say that it was because the captains had brought many bales of rice to sell in Melaka.

The Dutch went to regroup in Johor and the Viceroy ordered that a *bantim* be sent to see what they were up to, which returned saying that the enemy had left and were out of the Straits, some to one bank, and others to the other bank, on the basis of this news alone the Viceroy divided his armada and sent Dom Álvaro de Meneses with seven galleons to the Aceh bank to protect what he hoped was on its way from India and Portugal, and he left five galleons with the armada of oared vessels in Melaka to send it to Johor and to the Straits, and as soon as the enemy came to know of this division, as they had all been reinforced in Johor, they came back and set upon Melaka once more, and as soon as the Viceroy came to know of this he ordered five galleons to await the enemy, anchored in front of the fortress and alongside one another, and as soon as the enemies appeared, Dom Fernando Mascarenhas, who was one of these five and had been dismayed at not having been in the last battle, released his mooring cables and let himself go, falling upon the enemy, who had nine ships that were much larger than ours. Seeing this, Dom Pero Mascarenhas, who was on land with the Viceroy, went to tell him to order his brother to withdraw or to deprive him of the galleon; the Viceroy ordered him to get on board and make his brother go back, which could not be done due to the wind and the waters and, soon after, four enemy ships drew alongside, and in this way dawn broke to find them fighting, and as Dom Nun'Álvares was the Captain-General of this fleet, on the ship of the Viceroy who gave it to him for this purpose, and he saw Mascarenhas in this state, he also released his moorings and all four fell upon the enemy, who immediately destroyed Dom Fernando's galleon without them being able to help him, and both died in this battle with all their people, and the galleon was burnt.

Dom Francisco de Noronha, who was the captain of another galleon, was soon killed by a cannon-shot; he was succeeded by a certain João Machado Boto who, with his father, had found himself in the battle against the Dutch in the Moluccas and soon the gunpowder store-house caught fire and our galleon was burnt. Sebastião Soares, who was another captain, and André Pessoa, a *casado* from Melaka, to whom the Viceroy had given one of the galleons that he had taken from Dom Henrique, and Dom Francisco de Sotomaior was rammed and all his people died, and they were invaded and taken captive, and the galleons taken. Sebastião Soares would die on land of his wounds, because he and André Pessoa were ransomed for two thousand *cruzados*, but they say that they all fought like lions in this battle, and that it was the most horrendous thing that had ever been seen.

Dom Nun'Álvares escaped with his galleon, but it was completely devastated and destroyed; the Viceroy immediately ordered him to evacuate it and he burnt it along with Dom Paulo Portugal's ship that was going to China. The enemy stationed themselves (fl. 193v.) within sight of the fortress with two of our galleons; the Viceroy immediately despatched the caravel to come with the news and go to Portugal, and for this entrusted it to Manuel Mascarenhas, who ran aground and came back and anchored in Melaka, and thus the Viceroy did not let him go, and put Francisco Rebelo Carvalho in his place, who arrived in Cochin with this news, and from there immediately left for Portugal in the same caravel. The Viceroy writes that he has sent orders to the six galleons not to return to Melaka and that they were to return to India to seek help, because there were six Dutch ships in Sunda, and the enemy were awaiting thirteen from Europe without fail, but had not decided who was the person he should send aboard them to seek this assistance, but it would probably be André Furtado, and better opinion has it that it is the Viceroy himself; until now there has been no news of the galleons, nor is there anything in this Estado that they can take back with them. The enemy is still in plain sight in Melaka, God forbid that there should be another disaster; if the Viceroy had not passed there, the fortress would certainly have been taken due to hunger. Dom Manuel Mascarenhas died on Dom Henrique's galleon, and while he was alive he did not consent to an agreement.

André Furtado braved this siege with a hundred and eighty men; more than five thousand people died of plague and hunger because they even reached the stage of eating dogs and rats. André Furtado made some sorties in which he killed many men, and they say that during the course of the siege he would have killed four hundred Dutchmen. João Rodrigues Camelo, who had gone to the Moluccas to help with two galliots, went to Manila as he found that everything had been taken by the Dutch; from there the Governor came with six hundred Spaniards, and after taking Tidore made this king, who had always been our friend, emperor of those islands, and then immediately went to Ternate and besieged it, and gave the lead to João Rodrigues Camelo, with fifty or sixty Portuguese, and it was decided to scale the fortress at a certain hour of the night, and he informed João Rodrigues about when it should be done, who sought the advice of the Portuguese and decided to attack for two hours, as they did, and they entered the fortress until they conquered it, so that the Moors should be aware of all the might of the army, and when the Governor gave the signal to begin combat he was already in possession of everything. The Governor captured the King of Ternate and his children, and took them with him to Manila, and left Captain Galinato and the Spanish in the fortress. João Rodrigues and the Portuguese went to two entrances twenty leagues below, and went on, making their way through the bush, and twenty-five of their men died of hunger, and along with the ones who remained they went to the Melaka River and, travelling downstream, went to the fortress, and André Furtado greatly appreciated this, and with them later did the sorties that have been mentioned above.

The Dutch took André Furtado's ship that left from this fortress, and another small ship that went from Nagapattam with supplies, which was carrying Fernão de Mercado, the factor of Dom António de Meneses, Captain of Melaka, who was ransomed from the Dutch for three hundred *cruzados*.'

Document 17

Opinion about the conquest of Aceh, undated [1st decade of the 17th century]. BA, book 51-VI-54[18], fls. 36–37v.

'I did not see the settlement in which the King of Aceh resides, but it must be large as it always was and is the head of that kingdom where the inhabitants of that great island reside.

Its port is on the southern side, about twelve leagues from the tip of Gomispola, that is the first land of the said island of Aceh, commonly called Sumatra, on the northern bank at six degrees and two-thirds.

It has a good port but is not defensible due to the great sand-banks that appear slightly away from the land; they are safe from storms as in those lands there are no tempests that do damage as it is at the entrance to the Malay Sea, calm, and there are only thunderstorms that, despite being the greatest that one can experience in the open, do not change the sea and last only a short while.

The port and settlement on the opposite coast of Sumatra is called Daya; as far as I can recall, our men do not deal with and have not dealt with it because it is very far off from our normal route when we sail from India to Melaka. And thus it is difficult to ascertain the truth about this port, except from anyone who has been held captive on the island and went there; one has only understood that in this port are loaded the ships that leave from here for the Straits of Mecca, and that via the opposite coast of Sumatra great quantities of cloves and other spices come here that the Javanese bring there to sell, and that the Sultan of Aceh has a fortress in it and a customs house that provides him with much revenue.

There are more or less sixty leagues to be sailed from Gomispola to Melaka, from Melaka to the Straits of Singapore there are about thirty, and to the Straits of Sabang, close to forty; I mean its mouth from the northern bank, as the southern one is more than sixty (fl. 36v.), because that strait is very long.

The splendours of the island of Sumatra are many and far greater than the other islands that there are in all the discovered world of the Orient because it contains numerous and rich mines of gold, and of a good quality, because those of Minangkabau alone are astonishing from what one hears about them. There is as much or even more pepper as there is on the Malabar coast, and much better in quality; there is a lot of benzoin and camphor, great copper mines, a lot of wood for the building of ships of all dimensions that one wishes to construct, iron and everything else that is necessary for the building of vessels, from masts, spars, great quantities of pitch and that too of the best quality in the world; the only thing lacking is material to make sails of cotton, that comes from India in large quantities.

It is very fertile in foodstuffs and, especially, is far more wholesome than the land on the side of Melaka; the locals are very weak people who would be easy to conquer as soon as they see the King routed; his entire power and might lies in the foreigners that he has in his kingdom, acquired to keep the locals in subjection to him, as he fears that they will rebel against him on account of the many tyrannies that he perpetrates upon them, and they say that this kingdom and island are currently in the most miserable state in terms of power and force.

From the things I have mentioned one can easily understand the advantages that can be obtained from the conquest of this island, and that on it one can make a greater state and monarchy than that of India because, once it is conquered, all the rest of that archipelago of the South will be easily subjected, and by the customs houses and other revenues of the said island one can in the future sustain the war with the other neighbouring kings (fl. 37), when they wage war, or when it be necessary to make the armadas that are necessary in the South sea and there will still be revenues left over for all these and other expenses that arise, and from there more ships loaded with pepper and spices can come to this kingdom than come from India, and will not go astray as they have until now, sent to the Straits of Mecca, nor to other areas, due to which the spices in this Kingdom will be worth much more and the customs revenues will rise along with this, with the duties of the goods that will inevitably be produced from what they will go and bring from there.

It is better to conquer this island of Sumatra than any other in that region, apart from what has already been mentioned, because as this king was and is the most powerful of them (although today his power has been greatly weakened), when the neighbouring Kings, who are much inferior to him, see that we have conquered him, they will all be fearful of the same fate, and with this fear they will stop at the frontier and as this is, as has been said, a land fertile and wholesome in provisions, situated in the middle of that archipelago, because should His Majesty at any time wish to have a separate government for the lands of the South, no other place could be more suitable to assist the Governor than that island, in the site and port that he will see is the most suited for this.

The island of Sumatra and the port and city of Aceh will measure some hundred and sixty leagues across, more or less; one can navigate the whole year around, where one can help in the things of Siriam with great ease and swiftness, so that one can obtain what one aspires from here, and there is no doubt that the advantages that could result for this Crown by conquering this island and separating this governance from that of India are many, as well as the many others that the island itself promises, such as emerging as the greatest and being the means of (fl. 37v.) obstructing the trade with the foreigners from Europe, as this island is the main land where they load pepper, and with the armadas that will sail that sea, they shall be prevented from trading in any other region.'

Document 18

>List of the services of Agostinho de Almeida (excerpt), undated. HAG,
>*Consulta do Serviço de Partes*, Vol. 3, fls. 32–35.

(fl. 32v.) 'And that in 1613 he embarked in Bengal on the *sanguicel* of
Cristóvão Ferreira that was on its way to meet with the armada that left
Goa that year for Melaka, whose Captain-General was Diogo de Mendonça
Furtado, he went with the said armada to the fortress of Melaka, where
he assisted as a soldier there till 20 April 1614, finding himself in the
battle that the said Cristóvão Ferreira had with the Moors on the coast of
Pahang, serving on this and on other occasions that occurred in the said
period; and while he was on land, he assisted in one of the companies of
the fortress that was captained by Jerónimo de Mendonça, entering and
leaving guard shifts and keeping a watch over his quarter; and in Melaka
he set sail in November 1615 as a soldier, aboard the galliot of the said
Captain-General Diogo de Mendonça and accompanied him all the time
that he went abroad battling with the Moors, setting fire to them and
sinking many of their boats and galleys, until the arrival of the galleons
of the armada of the Captain-General Francisco de Miranda Henriques,
in whose galleon the said Agostinho de Almeida was stationed, and he
found himself aboard this vessel during the battle that it fought with
the armada from Aceh, that consisted of more than three hundred sails,
which included many galleys, fighting fourteen hours continuously with the
enemies who had put great pressure upon the said galleon, always assisting
with his weapons on the stern, where he received five wounds, namely, two
arrow shots to the head, and the foot and right hand scorched by fire, and
a spear wound under his left armpit, on account of which he was on the
brink of death, healing and curing himself of them in Melaka.

And even before he was fully recovered he once again joined the
said galleon of the Captain because of seven ships and a brigantine of
the Dutch, who attacked the armada of the said Francisco de Miranda
and assaulted it with a lot of power and force, where he also emerged
with a gaping wound on his right foot, due to which he was on the brink
of death; and that in the same year of 1615 he set sail from Melaka
aboard one of the four *jáleas* commanded by Diogo de Mendonça da
Silva that, on the orders of the said Captain-General Diogo de Mendonça
Furtado, went to reconnoitre the power of Aceh, that had passed through
the Straits, and found himself in the battle that was fought with a fleet
(fl. 33) of three galleys, five ships and seven *panchalões*, which resulted in

the surrender of one of the said ships, killing and capturing many of the enemy, always fighting bravely, and they forced a ship of the same enemy armada to run aground.'

Document 19

Anonymous letter, Melaka [1615]. BN, *Res.*, cod. 1975, fls. 193–194v.

'Copied from a letter by a secular

After my arrival in Melaka a month later, that was at the end of September, more or less, three hundred and fifty vessels from Aceh passed along this port, the king himself sailing with them, which included a hundred and eighty galleys, eighty with topsails, and each of them carried at least six hundred men, and that of the king carried a thousand or so fighting men with more than 25 pieces of artillery, and such large ones, that most of them would fire sixty *arráteis* of pig iron; these were present on almost all the galleys, and I can tell you that they were so large that they loomed over our galleons, with which they fought, Francisco de Miranda Henriques being the Captain-General, who had not gone to the Moluccas as he took four months to reach Melaka from Goa, as he was wintering in the city he set sail with his four galleons to meet the enemy, and with him Diogo de Mendonça, Captain-General of the Sea of Melaka, with six galliots that were taken from the merchants of this coast, and five or so more, and a further seven or eight *bantins*.

And all of them leaving thus, they went to meet the enemy along the Formoso River, where they immediately had a skirmish with the enemy armada, with that of Diogo de Mendonça, but being unable to bear the enemy onslaught, as they were so many in number, they retreated to where our galleons were, that were already arriving by this time, and when the enemy saw them they were left alone, and after a consultation between Diogo de Mendonça and his captains, which included Fernão da Costa, who had already burnt an enemy galley, they were of the opinion that they should put all the people aboard the galleons, and it was a pitiful sight to see due to the dearth of people they carried, that only Afonso Vaz took sixty men, and most of them did not have more than twenty-five, and with regard to the soldiers, some of them disappeared into the jungles and did not want to go and fight with the enemy; well, with the galleons thus, with the people of the armada inside, they went to meet the enemy, where they began to do damage to them, and Dom João, captain of a galleon, due to a good wind was able to penetrate the heart of the armada, where, on account of his sins, the wind suddenly calmed, which was seen by the enemy who attacked him and burnt him along with another galliot, which was captained by António Rodrigues, his brother-in-law and son of João Caiado, who had boarded the galleon with his people, and in this way everything was burnt and sixty (fl. 193v.) Portuguese were captured from it, including Dom João da Silveira himself along with his brother-in-law, and there were some dead.

And coming back to Francisco de Miranda, I say that he did nothing that day because he was unable to reach there on account of there being no wind, but the following day, which was Saturday, Our Lord gave him a good wind, and penetrating the enemy armada he sank twenty-eight galleys, killing fifteen or twenty thousand enemy men, and did so much damage that it was amazing; he was assisted in all this by his brother-in-law Afonso Vaz Coutinho and João Pinto, captain of another galleon, and all three of them fought bravely for two continuous days, and the Captain-General ran a great risk, and also his galleon, because they set fire to it four times, and Francisco de Miranda rose to each occasion with dauntless courage, and Fernão da Costa, whose presence was very effective in the said enterprise. And when the enemy saw his devastation, he immediately sent an embassy to Melaka, whose Captain was João Caiado, who received the embassy with great joy, lavishly entertaining the ambassadors, who said they would send for the captives who were in the power of the king, and that he had not come to fight with the Portuguese, but with the King of Johor as he deserved it, and that the Portuguese armada had wreaked havoc upon them, and that he would like to make permanent peace with the King of Portugal, which was all seen by João Caiado, who immediately consulted with his council who decided to promptly send at once a *bantim* to Francisco de Miranda, so that he ceased to fight with the King of Aceh due to the embassy Melaka had received.

And in this way this enemy escaped in a dark night, rowing away from our armada, and thus escaped with this trick, that was done for this sole purpose. And after all this, João Caiado bid farewell to the ambassadors, and with them Manuel de Matos, a *casado* from Goa who took four thousand *cruzados* to the King to send back his son-in-law and son and the other Portuguese who were there; to date we have not had more news of what happened there. Francisco de Miranda having turned back as soon as it was morning, and he saw that the enemies had moved a fair distance away, he could not take any action because of João Caiado, and the city having ordered him to not touch the enemy as I have already mentioned, and setting sail for Melaka, he arrived in the city. And at the end of five days, more or less, the King of Johor, who is a great friend of ours, sent a message to Miranda and to the city, as seven Dutch ships and a brigantine were on their way to battle with him, and the nobleman wished to wait for them on the high seas, but the city ordered him not to, and that he station himself at the Ilha das Naus, at a spring there (fl. 194), which he immediately did.

As the enemy were already upon him, and establishing themselves on land, he left with his three galleons, which were seen by the enemy, who ceased to be anchored in front of the coast until another day, and immediately began to fight with our galleons, entering by another channel that was unknown to our forces, which they had discovered that night with their launches on the sea flank; well, they spent three days battling with our men on the coast, everyone fighting very bravely, these poor galleons receiving no assistance from Diogo de Mendonça, who could have helped with his armada, nor did any *casados* from Melaka reach him, unless it was to fetch the dead, and bring them to land, nor did João Caiado wish to put two pieces of heavy artillery on the Ilha to defend the galleons. The most he did, after two days, was to put the pieces with many thefts by the people of the said Ilha with eight large river rafts, and there was such sloth that only one of them worked, with which they fired some shots at the Dutch nearby, but it was already of such little relevance because our galleons were already almost destroyed, and Afonso Vaz Coutinho had died due to a cannon-shot that took his jawbone off, and he fell dead without uttering another word, and four others of this same shot, being substituted by Pero Gomes, 'the villager', where he fought an entire day with his companions.

And in the end the galleons were all destroyed, and with them a little less than two hundred men were dead, and many wounded, which included many foreigners. Miranda, as soon as he saw he had only three or four men with him on board his galleon, had it set on fire by an Agostinho Lobato, a *casado* from Chaul, and thus the galleon exploded and he came to the Ilha with two friars, injured in one leg with a gaping wound, crying a thousand tears for the disastrous events and the death of his brother-in-law, who fought very bravely, and thus Pero Gomes also set fire to the flagship galleon, and came to the Ilha with 14 men in a skiff, and thus the two galleons burned, and while it was on fire a Dutchman climbed up onto the topmast on the stern, and took the flag of Christ and brought it over to the stern of his ship. And in another galleon, captained by João Pinto, they entered it and took all the artillery, and all the needful that was on board, and then set it on fire, and they also killed the Captain of this galleon; in short, I inform Your Excellency that our entire armada was destroyed, and the enemies did not escape unscathed as they lost three hundred men, more or less, dead, besides the injured, with their Captain-General and the (fl. 194v.) admiral, and of the seven ships they could not sail three of them; this was news we received from a Portuguese captive who came from their ships.

After everything was over, Diogo de Mendonça went to the said Ilha to commiserate with Miranda about his armada, but he sent a page to say that he did not wish them to come and that he leave, as he did not wish to be seen by weak men, and that his desires had already been fulfilled in how this man undoubtedly rejoiced in seeing all of this with poor Miranda, for the victory that he had achieved over the armada from Aceh, and on top of all this they had never got along well, and thus Francisco de Miranda already has three or four galliots to go to Manila and take paid soldiers on them, for which he already has the money, which was sent to him by the Governor of Manila to outfit the armada he had before, and from the Philippines to go to New Spain, and from there to Madrid, and he takes many good documents to present to His Majesty.

News from the Philippines has it that the Governor is readying ten very well-equipped galleons, and another ten galleys, which include four from the Estado to go upon the Moluccas and sent word to Miranda to wait for him in the Straits of Makassar, for them to go together to set upon twenty ships that were there, even though they knew more than the Governor because knowing of the wintering of the galleons in Melaka; they sent these seven ships and a brigantine to wreak destruction, as they did, and four more to China, to take the ship and the galleon that were there, God forbid such an event, even though the Governor sent a message to the city of Macao, that that year's ship should not set sail for India, and that the galleon wait for him in Makassar; I don't know who was the captain of this vessel, because its former Captain—who was called João Teixeira de Macedo, a *casado* from Goa—was killed by Pero Ferreira, a retainer of Dom Francisco Roxo, slashed with a cutlass on account of certain dealings. And all these events caused us great vexation in Melaka and an extra burden upon the poor merchants, who did not have any earnings except for a loss of profits; one per cent was taken from them for provisioning the armada, which had already been destroyed, and all this by the Auditor-General who passed through the city, but this will be enough for the men to not return any more, and I will not give more news because news of everything that took place will slowly reach there.'

(Another copy of this document in cod. 11410, fls. 61–64v.)

Document 20

Letter from the Viceroy to the Captain of Melaka. Goa, 1-4-1620. HAG, *Reis Vizinhos*, 1, fl. 101–102v. (In bad condition, with parts illegible.)

Chapter about relations with Aceh.

(fl. 102) 'Your Excellency must be aware how important it is to preserve [?] the friendship of the King of Johor with [?] favouring him [?] and that we help against the King of Aceh, that should not ... on account of being a neighbouring king; if it should happen that he be an enemy it will be necessary to be careful ... if the Malay armada unites with that of Aceh in the Straits ... each [?] hill; and apart from this, for military reasons, it suits one's purposes to favour this king [?] ... against Aceh, as he is less powerful, to give him something to do that ... and he does not have the opportunity to cause problems for Melaka.

And as for the friendship of the King of Aceh, it would be better if the city of Melaka regards him as a secret enemy as he is a tyrant king, from whom one cannot expect any truth; and that they outwardly show themselves to be peaceful, in conformance with the peace that João Caiado de Gamboa made. But Melaka should not have trade with Aceh, nor should Portuguese merchants go there, and one should make it clear that they should stop trading there and while this show of peace with Aceh on our part lasts, we should not give Aceh occasion for war because as this fortress of Melaka is so encircled by powerful enemies, one should not give occasion to place it in difficulties, for it to be necessary to send it help from India: which could only be sent with great difficulty, on account of the tight situation in which the Estado finds itself in terms of the Royal Exchequer, which is what wars are fought with ....'

Document 21

'Warning that Constantino de Sá de Noronha gave to the Viceroy',
undated. Annexe to the letter from the Viceroy to the Melaka city
council, dated 21-5-1620. HAG, *Reis Vizinhos*, 1, fl. 114. (In bad
condition, with parts illegible.)

'... at the end of February arrived on this island João Álvares, a *casado*
from Nagapattam who had been held captive in Aceh, who came in some
boats of a Malay who did him this favour for an extremely small [?], fled
from within the King's house [?] and [?] gives the following news.

The King of Aceh has gathered together seventy galleys, each one
of which is equipped with twenty-five pieces of artillery, and two ships,
one of which is of two thousand five hundred *candis* and the other of one
thousand, and thirty junks ranging from three hundred to eight hundred
each, which [?] makes six hundred sails altogether, in which he says one
hundred thousand men, ninety elephants, two hundred pieces of artillery,
three thousand ladders of thirty-two of up to 10 *côvados*, three thousand
pots of oil and all the other tools of war that are necessary for important
sieges will be taken.

In Deli he has fifteen thousand *gantas* of rice, apart from a lot more
that he has scattered around; the Dutch have promised him twelve ships
to accompany him, and he says that even without them he will set sail in
August because he wants to know in ... what comes from India, where
he knows of everything and of Melaka, by means of Johor, because he
sends his negros, and from the ambassadors of Johor, who promises help
against Melaka, on account of the fact that his son, the King of Pahang,
is being held captive by Aceh.'

Document 22

Friar Félix de Jesus, 'First part of the Chronicle and Account of the
beginnings of the congregation of the Order of St. Augustine in the
East Indies, and of the honour and glory that the first founders of the
Order earned with their hard work for Our Lord God in the conversion
of souls in those lands ...' (excerpts). AN/TT, *Mss. da Livraria*, No.
731, fls. 1–92.

(fl. 23) 'This missionary, Friar Domingos dos Santos, Prior of China,
left with two companions, Friar Amaro de Jesus and Friar Salvador da
Assunção; these fathers embarked in Goa on a ship aboard which a

nobleman called Dom Francisco de Sá was going as Captain-General of China and Japan. He was taking his wife, Dona Joana de Meneses, and two brothers, Dom Pedro and Dom Jorge, with him. And the ship was so beautiful that it invited all those who were going to those parts to embark upon her, and for this reason the Bishop of China, Dom Leonardo de Sá, embarked on this ship, which was going to his bishopric, and two Dominican friars, and many other people of quality and importance. (I describe the success of this ship and the journey because I hope it will be the occasion for God to grant us many blessings with regard to the conversion of souls which is the reason why we were sent to these regions.) Thus, they left from Goa with a favourable voyage but were a bit fearful because they did not have on board a pilot with suitable experience. After their departure, seeing the danger in which they were, they wished to go to Cochin to take supplies on board, but it was not possible. After a few days of travel, near the great island of Sumatra that is the kingdom of Aceh, they ran into rough weather, and as it seemed to the pilot that the ship was entering the openings of Nicobar and Gomispola, which is from where one enters for Melaka, and the ship found itself very close to land on the opposite coast of Sumatra, without any remedy as he did not know the depths nor the land that came into view. And later one cable and then another broke, without hope of remedy neither on sea nor on land they ran aground, and fleeing the furious sea and tempestuous weather, they handed themselves over to the terrible and cruel tyrant, lord of that land, placing themselves with a great effort in the hands of Our Lord God, not doubting that they would all soon die with cruel torments for the faith of Jesus Christ, as that was the custom of that tyrant, lord of that kingdom that was such an enemy of the Christian faith, that apart (fl. 24) from martyring all the people who professed the Law of Christ, when he did not have any against which to execute this ancient hatred he would pay money to buy Christians to fatten them up in their blood, and sacrifice them to their Muhammad, so much so that, until now, no one had escaped the ire and fury of these perfidious people.

As they were shipwrecked in this enemy land, one can well imagine the spirit of those who found themselves here; some jumped off the ship that had been smashed to pieces and swam away, and clinging onto pieces of planks went on land, preferring to be sacrificed to God than die by drowning; some clung to the broken ship fearing the fury of the sea, all of them wishing and trying in their own way to cling to life, something that is so natural to human nature. Young boys embraced their mothers, the mothers their husbands; there was great confusion all around, the air was filled with shouts and moans; the missionaries did not lose heart, instead, with a crucifix of Christ advised them of what was best, and provided comfort in the midst of that great hardship and struggle. In short, many drowned in this shipwreck, amongst whom Our Lord was served with the drowning and death of this religious father who was going as Prior; and two other companions managed to save themselves and reached land, Friar Amaro and Friar Salvador, and likewise, the Bishop, too, along with the Captain, and his wife with many other people. When all of them were together on a beach, the Bishop and missionaries took care of comforting everyone and instilling them with patience and courage for the martyrdom that all of them expected for the faith of Our Lord Jesus Christ.

Once the king of the land came to know of the ship's loss, and of the people who were on land, he sent one of his grandees to secure the entire group with great promises of setting them free, something that was so new and foreign to the condition of those barbarians that this immediately seemed to be *mutatio dexterae coeli*, a change by the hand of God. This individual, with allurements and promises, took them by means of safe routes, each of whom strove to do (fl. 24v.) their best to walk, seeking strength from the weakness in which they were with the travails through which they had passed, and as they had not eaten for three days, some carried others, others foraged for any food that the coast could provide, others took care of their young children, of tender years and weak; in short, everyone had for themselves, thus burdened they were representing, the figure of the innocent Isaac, walking towards the sacrifice that they expected would be made of them to God. Thus they all arrived as captives in the court of the king, who came out onto a courtyard to see them, and told them not to fret, that these things happened, and that he wanted peace and friendship with the Christians, and that for this purpose he wished to send an ambassador to the Captain of Melaka (that is the closest fortress to this kingdom), and because this said father Friar Amaro de Jesus, a missionary of our order, spoke the Malay language very well, the king set eyes upon him, and by common consensus he was elected to be the ambassador of the king, and later called him, and arranged the visit to Melaka with him and said: to tell the Captain on his behalf how he desired peace and friendship with the Portuguese, and that he gave his royal word that he would completely set free the captives that he had in his power if the Portuguese of Melaka would grant him free access to the sea, from there until the Kingdom of Johor, where he wished to go with four hundred sailing vessels, and the father soon left, in disguise.

And in secular dress, he arrived in Melaka on board an enemy ship, gave his embassy, informing everyone of the loss of the ship about which no news had been received, and gave an account of those who had died in the shipwreck and those who were held captive, everyone being most amazed that they were alive. Pero Lopes de Sousa, a great nobleman who was the Captain of Melaka, gave him the suitable order, thanking and (fl. 25) satisfying the King of Aceh with excellent demonstrations of friendship about what the king had requested of him, because apart from giving him free access to the sea, informed him of what suited his designs with a present of thanks. He sent back the father, who arrived in Aceh after running substantial risks to his person, and the king immediately set sail with this entire fleet against the kingdom of Johor, taking Friar Amaro in his royal galley, striking up such a great friendship with him that he trusted his royal person more with the father than with his own men because he understood the truth with which he spoke to him, and because he was able to talk to him in his own language.

In short, by this means this peace which was so important to the service of His Majesty, and the quietude of the Estado da Índia, was made in such a way that on his way back from the siege of Johor he set our people completely free, as he had promised to the Captain, Dom Francisco de Sá and his wife and his entire household, the Bishop and other people of great importance, all through the good works of this missionary, the king remaining, above all, such a good friend of his that he would go to wherever he was, and would send him presents, which seems that this is an indication of greater benefits, as we hope, and may the Lord God open their eyes so that, by means of the doctrine and our missionaries they convert to his holy faith. It is no small sign of this or the beginning of this happy situation that our missionaries are the first that until now, in that cruel and barbarous land, offered to God the true and propitiatory sacrifice, publicly raising an altar and saying Mass with complete freedom, and preaching in their captivity the word of the Lord God to all those who wished to listen, without any opposition; indeed, the King himself, prompted by his example, revealed himself to be inclined towards the things of Christianity, and intended to attend Mass one day and see the holy ceremonies of the Church, with which he revealed himself to be greatly edified. ...

(fl. 27) The city of Melaka and the Captain of the fortress needed to send an ambassador to Aceh in order to confirm the peace and other matters concerning the common good; Friar Jerónimo da Madre de Deus, the Prior from our convent in Melaka, was elected and sent for this task, accompanied by Tomás Pinto, with equal authority in the (fl. 27v.) embassy. They arrived in Aceh, and the king received them and heard them with great pleasure, confirming the peace and responding to the city in much the same vein. And due to the kindness with which this said father was treated by the King, he was emboldened to ask him for a proper and safe place where he could say Mass in that great island that was an enemy of the Christian faith, and thus he said Mass with the same freedom as the first fathers had done, by means of which we hope to remind the lord of those people that up until these years he had done nothing but torment and martyr Christians in his hatred of the Catholic faith. At this Mass the King and his children were present with great enthusiasm, granting for the Mass a decent, suitable and safe site and protecting the many Portuguese who were with the father. ...

(fl. 47v.) During that same time and year [1600], the Viceroy of India, the Count Admiral, asked the Provincial Vicar for one of our missionaries, called Friar Amaro de Jesus, to go to Aceh as ambassador to thus realise the service of God and His Majesty for the good of the Estado da Índia, since that missionary was known to and was a friend of that king, and that from the time he had been held there as a captive had been very favourably inclined towards him. This missionary was at the convent of Melaka, where he received the messages from the Viceroy and the Provincial Vicar. He was advised in Melaka by the Captain and city, on the orders of the Viceroy, and with a very important present that the Viceroy sent him in the name of His Majesty (fl. 48), the said father was publically appointed ambassador. They realised the public ceremonies for him that are customarily done for the ambassadors so that those kings recognise them as such; in a ship bought at His Majesty's expense, and with paid soldiers he embarked with his embassy for Aceh in the month of September.

Father Amaro de Jesus arrived in the kingdom of Aceh, being very well received by the king, and by his children; because they knew him they received him as ambassador with great pomp. He carried out his embassy and dealt with the King of Aceh about the matters in which he had been entrusted by the instructions of the Viceroy. The king favoured this missionary to such an extent that he conferred a title upon him (of

Bintara Orang Kaya Maharaja Lela Putih), that is the second highest title of great merit from the king in his kingdom, that is the title of grandee, and was continuously with him, entering wherever he was with great freedom, even if he was in his bath, which is a place that is very intimate for them. He honoured him with costly things, and money, without the father wanting more than whatever was necessary to sustain himself and his people.

It so happened that shortly thereafter two large and powerful Dutch ships arrived at that port of Aceh, which had come to the said port and kingdom to load pepper, as there was much to be had there, and of a very good quality; they sent their gifts ashore to the King, and informed him of their arrival, attending to their business dealings. The father went to the King and told him how those people were enemies of His Majesty, and being his true and proper vassals they were mutineers and had become (fl. 48v.) pirates, and came to these regions against his will, oppressing his vassals, that in no way should he receive them in his kingdom, nor allow them to buy pepper, because His Majesty would be greatly offended by this, and instead should detain them with words until he was able to advise Melaka and the armada that was there, under André Furtado de Mendonça, to come and set upon them. The king immediately carried out his request, and delayed them, setting an excessively high price for the pepper. As they were thus distracted, the father warned Melaka. At that time, as the Dutch were growing weary of the King's tardiness, seeing that he was not reaching an agreement with them, got suspicious, and one day they made up their minds and in the port found some ships of Gujaratis that had been loaded there with pepper, and other spices and merchandise, and they captured them and maliciously robbed them, which was seen by the king on land, who ordered his people to take arms, and thus sent many people to the harbour fortress, for if they bombarded the shores they would be able to disembark, and immediately called the father and sent him to the harbour fortress, and gave him the title of Captain-General, and proclaimed that all should obey his Bintara (which was what he called him), on pain of death.

The said Friar Amaro did all this with great prudence, and stationed himself in the fortress with the king's people, as it served His Majesty. However, Sebastião Cipriano, which was what the Dutch general was called, unfurled his ship's sails, and they went away without any more pepper other than what they had stolen. And then the said father was present in the court of the King of Aceh, having advised India and Melaka about the events. The next year, four English ships, two large ships and two brigantines, came to the same port in the same way to procure pepper. The father immediately went to the king, and told him the same thing he had said about the others. The king did not listen to the Englishmen and ordered that (fl. 49) they be told that he had no pepper, preparing himself in the same way and readying himself to battle with them and defend his lands, the father once again returning to the harbour fortress, and when the English saw this turn of affairs, and that time was running out, they went away without procuring what they sought.

And as things were in this state with the King of Aceh, and the father had this close relation with him, he requested permission to be able to baptise whoever wished to be a Christian in his kingdom, due to the inclination that he saw in some Acehnese, to which the King responded to him that he was content, but that he first wished to qualify the peace with the Viceroy of India, and be a brother to His Majesty, and give him a fortress in his kingdom to defend against the Dutch and English who went to his lands. And for this reason asked him if he would like to go to India with his ambassadors to the Viceroy, and indicate to him his desire. The father accepted carrying out this service for the King, on account of the many things for which he was obliged to him, and because he saw the limited might that existed in that kingdom, and the ease with which it could be conquered, and the risk that the Estado da Índia ran if the Dutch or English were to take possession of Aceh. In order to inform the Viceroy of these particulars, he left from Aceh with two ambassadors of the King, and because it was winter and the monsoon had finished, he reached the other coast with great effort and risk to his person, and with the frights that habitually happen on these routes, passing the lands of many kings who were enemies of our holy faith; he went walking with the ambassadors on land, and having passed through all these difficulties, God be praised he arrived in India, at Goa. The Viceroy received the father and the ambassadors with great pomp and sumptuous celebrations; they realised their embassies, and the father clearly showed the opportunity that existed to take that kingdom, that was with a candle in its hands, about which he informed His Majesty about everything, who with great care helped as one shall shortly see. We trust in the Lord God that in that land where the first sacrifice of our missionaries to (fl. 49v.) God was made, that he may choose ministers that can do him great services in the capitulation of that kingdom that with his help shall soon convert to our holy faith. ...

(fl. 66v.) The year of 1603 arrived, at the end of it the Viceroy of India, Aires de Saldanha, ordered that the missionary Friar Amaro de Jesus, who had come from Aceh with the ambassadors, as has been described, return with them to Melaka, and seeing the good opportunity that there was to conquer and take the kingdom of Aceh with ease, on account of the discord that existed between the old king and his sons, ordered that five ships go with people, and that the father go aboard them, writing to André Furtado de Mendonça, Captain of Melaka and General in the South Sea, that he not lose this opportunity, and ordered him to undertake that enterprise with the armada and the people who were on board. The father arrived in Melaka after passing through endless difficulties on the journey, gave the Viceroy's messages to the General, who immediately prepared himself and made arrangements for the expedition, mustering together his entire armada and all the forces that he was able, and because he was not fully informed about what was happening in Aceh, and the forces that he would face there, and Friar Amaro had such great influence in that kingdom, the General ordered that the missionary go to Aceh in a *bantim* (a light boat of that region) to see what was going on there, and with his information would decide how the enterprise should be carried out.

The father went and arrived on the coast of Aceh, taking the fortress that is called Pedir, where he found a son of the King in revolt against his father, who received the father with great demonstrations of love as he knew him, and gave him free access to the field, and gave him his word that if the General arrived there, that he would give him the fortress, and likewise that of the Aceh harbour, on the condition that he help and favour him in his claims to the kingdom against another brother. With this answer and news (fl. 67) the father returned at the time that the General was ready with the largest armada and greatest number of people that he was able to muster. However, with a different intent, because the Rajale, King of Johor, our old enemy, had allied with the Dutch, and with their help and protection had taken a ship that was coming from China full of costly wares, and was resolutely bent on taking many others and impeding the trade and passage to China (something that is so important for the service of God and His Majesty), it was necessary for the General to go and assist in this matter and not leave this enemy behind our backs, and so close. And thus, at that moment, he turned his forces on Johor, taking the father and the missionary Friar Francisco da Presentação, a religious preacher and man of letters, with him who, on this expedition, rendered great services to Our Lord at sea, confessing and preaching to everyone in the armada, and on land in the skirmishes and sorties that the soldiers carried out, stirring them on and encouraging them with great efforts; this expedition did not produce the desired result for the General as the Moors were very well fortified and helped by the Dutch, and thus he came back without them having been suitably punished ....'[2]

[2] Published by A. Hartmann in *Analecta Augustiniana*, XXX, 1967, pp. 5–174, under the title 'The Augustinians in Golden Goa: According to a Manuscript by Félix de Jesus, OSA'. There are some minor differences between the AN/TT manuscript presented here and the text published by this author, which follows the later manuscript of Biblioteca Pública de Évora (Public Library of Évora, Portugal).

Glossary

adiá	Gift or present (from the Arabic *hadyia*).
alcaide	General name for a responsible of a fortress or castle; specifically in Melaka, it refers to a particular office, in charge of the port affairs (*alcaide do mar*) or the security of the city (*alcaide da terra*).
arrátel	Portuguese measure of weight, of 459.5 g.
balão (pl. *balões*)	Portuguese general form to designate a small oared boat, in all Maritime Asia; its origin is obscure (possibly from the Malay *balang*).
bangaçal	Warehouse, probably of Indian origin (from the Sanskrit *bhandaçala*).
bantim	Light ship, generally with oars (from the Malay *banting*).
bar (pl. *bares*)	Measure of weight, with different values depending on the region of Asia; in Melaka the *bar pequeno* ['small bahar'] *dachém* (183.6 kg) was used to weigh tin, silk, ivory, opium and other products and the *bar grande* ['big bahar'] *dachém* (210 kg) was used

mostly for spices. *See* chapter 1, note 56 and chapter 5, note 61 (from the Arabic *bahar*).

bendara   Portuguese form of the high Malay office and title *bendahara*, sort of a prime minister during the times of the sultanate of Melaka and incorporated into the Portuguese administrative system. *See* chapter 5, *The Bendara and the Tomungão*.

candil   Measure of capacity, equivalent to 245 l; it also had a weight value of aprox. 240 kg. *See* chapter 5, note 33 (from the Malayalam *kandi*).

captain   General name for a military commander of Portuguese forces or settlements; in Estado da Índia, the 'captain' of a fortress or a city was a three-year commanding officer, with military and supervising functions, also the highest authority under the orders of the viceroy of Goa only.

cartaz   Safe-conduct pass (from the Arabic *qirtas*).

cate   Measure of weight, with different values; in Melaka a *cate* of 803 g, of 20 *taéis* each, was commonly used to weigh gold and other commodities. See chapter 4, note 91 (from the Malay *kati*).

chinchéus   Portuguese form to designate the people from Fujian. *See* chapter 5, note 40.

choquel (pl. *choquéis*)   Tax on freight imposed in Melaka on clove cargoes from the Moluccas. *See* chapter 1, note 28 (from the Malay *chukai*).

côvado   Portuguese measure of length, equivalent to 0.66 m.

cruzado   Golden or silver currency of general use in Portugal and in Portuguese Asia, with a general value of 400 *reis*, equivalent to a *ducado*; however, in Melaka, silver *cruzados* were the most commonly used, their standard value being 360 *reis*. *See* chapter 5, note 27.

dachém   Technical specification of the *bar* in Melaka (from the Malay *dashin*). *See bar*.

Estado da Índia   Official structure of Portuguese Asia, composed of a network of cities, ports, factories or other official settlements, ranging from the Cape of Good Hope to the Moluccas.

ganta	Measure of capacity, equivalent to 1.75 l (from the Malay *gantang*).
governor	*See* viceroy.
jálea	Light ship, smaller than a galliot, similar to a *bantim*.
Kelings	Caste of Hindu merchants from the Coromandel coast in southern India, very important in Melaka, both before and after the Portuguese conquest.
menancabos	Portuguese general form to designate the people from Minangkabau, in Sumatra; more specifically, the word referred to those who inhabited some villages located in the hinterland of Melaka, namely Naning.
panchalão	Large Malay ship (from the Malay *panchalang*).
pardau	Golden or silver currency of Estado da Índia (from the Hindu kingdom of Vijayanagara) worth 360 or 300 *reis* (from the Sanskrit *pratapa*).
quintal (pl. *quintais*)	Measure of weight; the Portuguese *quintal* most commonly used in the 16th and 17th centuries was equivalent to 4 *arrobas* or 128 *arráteis* (about 58.8 kg). *See* chapter 1, note 56.
real (pl. *reis*)	Portuguese unit of currency; from 1433 onwards it became the unit of account in Portugal. A $ symbol was used to express the thousands, i.e. 5$000 meaning 'five thousand *reis*'.
real (pl. *reales*)	Spanish silver unit of currency of 3,35 g, worth 34 *maravedis*, but sometimes it is used to mean the famous coin of 8 *reales* or 1 *peso* (called *real de a ocho* or *peso de a ocho*).
regimento	List or organized corpus of orders and instructions, sometimes detailed, issued by the king or a high authority to a viceroy or a governor, concerning a specific mission or office.
sanguicel	Small and fast ship of war, smaller than a galliot; it probably originated from the west coast of India.
sobrerrol	Old form of the office of *sobrerronda*, meaning a watchman.
tael (pl. *taéis*)	Measure of weight, with different values according to each region of Asia, used to weigh precious

metals and other products; in Melaka it was 1/20 of a *cate* of 803 g, but in other places it was 1/16 or 1/12 of a *cate*. *See* chapter 4, note 91 (from the Malay *tahil*).

terços Tax imposed on private traders on the spice cargoes sailing from the Moluccas and Banda to Melaka, created by Viceroy D. Garcia de Noronha in 1539. It was an obligation to sell one-third of the load at cost price to the Royal Treasury in Melaka.

tomungão Portuguese form of the Malay minister *tumenggung*, responsible for the security, the prison and the customs house during the time of the sultanate of Melaka and incorporated into the Portuguese administrative system. *See The Bendara and the Tomungão.*

viagem (pl. *viagens*) Meaning 'voyage' in Portuguese, it referred in the 16th and 17th centuries to specific lines of commerce linking two ports; in the Southeast Asian context, they generally had Melaka as the final destination or port of departure.

xabandar Captain of the port; in Malay Melaka, each mercantile community had its own, appointed by the local authorities (from the Persian *shahbandar*).

xerafim (pl. *xerafins*) Golden or silver currency of Estado da Índia with variable value; it was commonly used as unit of account of 300 *reis* (from the Persian *ashrafi*).

viceroy The highest civil and military authority in Estado da Índia, whose power was exerted over all Portuguese possessions and resources east of the Cape of Good Hope; a governor had similar functions but was a less prestigious rank.

Bibliography

Archival Sources

Arquivo Histórico Ultramarino (Overseas Historical Archives) (Lisbon)
Conselho Ultramarino – Cods. 281, 282, 500.
Índia – Box 1, docs. 10, 20, 76, 86; Box 3, docs. 21, 23, 36, 64, 114, 140; Box 20, doc. 106.

Arquivos Nacionais (National Archives)/ Torre Do Tombo (Lisbon)
Cartas dos Vice-reis – Nos. 41, 181.
Chancelaria de Filipe I, Doações – book 18.
Colecção de S. Vicente – Vols. 12, 14, 17, 18, 26.
Corpo Cronológico – Part 1, packs 111, 112, 114.
Manuscritos da Livraria – Nos. 699, 731, 805, 1107, 1112, 1113, 1116, 1699.
Miscelâneas Manuscritas do Convento da Graça de Lisboa – Box 2, tome III; Box 3, tome VI L; Box 4, tome III F; Box 6, tome II E; Box 16, tome VI F.
Fundo Português da Biblioteca Nacional de Paris – No. 48.
Núcleo Antigo – Nos. 870, 871.

Biblioteca da Ajuda (Ajuda Library) (Lisbon)
Book 51-VI-54[18].

341

Biblioteca Nacional (National Library) (Lisbon)
Reservados – Cods. 206, 414, 482, 638, 1540, 1973, 1975, 1976, 1979, 1980, 2298,
    2702, 9861, 11410.

Archivo General de Indias (General Archives of Indies) (Seville)
Patronato – *legajo* 53, R. 1.

Archivo General de Simancas (General Archives of Simancas) (Spain)
Secretarias Provinciales – Books 1550, 1551.

Biblioteca Nacional de Madrid (National Library of Madrid)
Cod. 1750

British Museum
Add. 9852, 9853, 28432, 28433.

Historical Archives of Goa
Provisões dos vice-reis – Vols. 1, 2.
Cartas Patentes, Provisões e Alvarás – Vol. 1.
Consulta do Serviço de Partes – Vol. 3.
Mercês Gerais – Vol. 2.
Regimentos e Instruções – Vol. 2.
Reis Vizinhos – Vol. 1.
Cartas Patentes e Provisões – Vol. 3.
Monções do Reino – Vols. 2A, 6A, 6B, 7, 8, 9, 11, 12.
Livro Morato.
Livro Verde.
Provisões e Regimentos – Vol. 1.
Assentos do Conselho da Fazenda – Vol. 2.

Published Sources

Aduarte, Fr. Diego, *Historia de la Provincia del Santo Rosario en la Orden de
    Predicatores en Filipinas, Japon y China*, Madrid: Consejo Superior de
    Investigaciones Científicas, 1962, 2 vols.
Alatas, Syed Hussein, 'On the Need for an Historical Study of Malaysian
    Islamization', *JSEAH*, 4/1 (1963): 62–74.
Albuquerque, Brás de, *Comentários do Grande Afonso de Albuquerque*, Lisbon:
    Imprensa Nacional-Casa da Moeda, 1978, 2 vols.
Albuquerque, Luís de (ed.), *Dicionário de História dos Descobrimentos*, Lisbon:
    Círculo de Leitores, 1994, 2 vols.
———— *Portugal no Mundo*, Lisbon: Alfa, 1990, vol. V.

Além-Mar: Códice Casanatense 1889/ Os Portugueses na Índia: Viagens, Aventuras, Conquista, Milan: F. Maria Ricci/Liv. Bertrand, 1987.

Ali Haji Ibn Ahmad, Raja, *The Precious Gift: Tuhfat al-Nafis*, ed. Virginia Matheson and Barbara Watson Andaya, East Asian Historical Monographs, Kuala Lumpur: Oxford University Press, 1982.

Almeida, M. Lopes de (ed.), *Breve Discurso em que se conta a Conquista do Reino do Pegu*, Barcelos: Portucalense Ed., 1936.

Alves, Jorge M. dos Santos, *A Hegemonia no Norte de Samatra; Os Sultanatos de Pacém, Achém e os Portugueses (1509–1579)*, Masters thesis, New University of Lisbon, 1991, 2 vols.

―――― 'Dois Sonhos Portugueses de Negócio e Evangelização na Insulíndia em finais do século XVII', in Artur Teodoro de Matos and Luís Filipe F. R. Thomaz (eds.), *As Relações entre a Índia Portuguesa, a Ásia do Sueste e o Extremo Oriente*, Lisbon/Macao, 1993, pp. 235–254.

―――― *O Domínio do Norte de Samatra: A história dos sultanatos de Samudera-Pacém e de Achém, e das suas relações com os Portugueses (1500–1580)*, Lisbon: Sociedade Histórica da Independência de Portugal, 1999.

―――― 'Os Mártires do Achém nos séculos XVI e XVII: Islão versus Cristianismo?', in *Missionação Portuguesa e Encontro de Culturas (Actas)*, Braga: U.C.P, 1993, vol. II, pp. 391–406.

―――― (ed.), *Portugal e a China: Conferências nos Encontros de História Luso-Chinesa*, Lisbon: Fundação Oriente, s.d. [2002].

―――― 'Une Ville Inquiéte et un Sultan Barricadé: Aceh vers 1588', *Archipel*, 39 (1990): 93–112.

Andaya, Barbara Watson, 'Cash Cropping and Upstream–Downstream Tensions: The Case of Jambi in the Seventeenth and Eighteenth centuries', in A. Reid (ed.), *Southeast Asia in the Early Modern Era: Trade, Power, and Belief*, Asia East by South, Ithaca, NY: Cornell University Press, 1993, pp. 91–122.

―――― 'Malacca', in *Encyclopédie de l'Islam*, vol. 6, Leiden: E. J. Brill, 1991, pp. 191–198.

―――― 'Melaka under the Dutch, 1641–1795', in K. S. Sandhu and P. Wheatley (eds.), *Melaka: The Transformation of a Malay Capital c.1400–1980*, Kuala Lumpur: Oxford University Press, 1983, vol. 1, pp. 195–241.

―――― 'The Nature of the State in 18th century Perak', in A. Reid and L. Castles (eds.), *Pre-colonial State Systems in Southeast Asia*, MBRAS Monograph No. 6, Kuala Lumpur: Malaysian Branch of the Royal Asiatic Society, 1975, pp. 22–35.

Andaya, Barbara W. and Leonard Y., *A History of Malaysia*, London: Macmillan, 1982.

Andaya, Leonard Y., *The Kingdom of Johor 1641–1728*, Kuala Lumpur: Oxford University Press, 1975.

—————— 'The Structure of Power in 17th century Johor', in A. Reid and L. Castles (eds.), *Pre-colonial State Systems in Southeast Asia*, MBRAS Monograph No. 6, Kuala Lumpur: Malaysian Branch of the Royal Asiatic Society, 1975, pp. 1–11.

Anderson, James N. and Walter T. Vorster, 'Diversity and Interdependence in the Trade Hinterlands of Melaka', in K. S. Sandhu and P. Wheatley (eds.), *Melaka: The Transformation of a Malay Capital c.1400–1980*, Kuala Lumpur: Oxford University Press, 1983, vol. 1, pp. 439–457.

Aparicio-López, Teófilo, 'La Orden de San Agustín en la India (1572–1622)', *Stvdia*, Nos. 38 (July 1974), 39 (Dec. 1974), 40 (Dec. 1978).

Arasaratnam, S., 'Monopoly and Free Trade in Dutch–Asian Commercial Policy: Debate and Controversy within the VOC', *JSEAS*, 4/1 (1973): 1–15.

—————— 'The Use of Dutch Material for Southeast Asian Historical Writing', *JSEAH*, 3/1 (1962): 95–105.

Archivo Ibero-Americano: Estudios Históricos sobre la Orden Franciscana en España y sus misiones, Madrid: Padres Franciscanos, 1914–.

Argensola, Bartolomé Leonardo de, *Conquista de las Islas Malucas*, Madrid, 1609.

Arquivo das Colónias, Lisbon, 1917, vol. I.

Aubin, Jean (ed.), 'Le Orçamento do Estado da India» de António de Abreu (1574)', *Studia*, 4 (1959): 169–281.

Baião, António (ed.), *A Inquisição de Goa/ Correspondência dos Inquisidores da Índia (1569–1630)*, ed. Academia das Ciências de Lisboa, Coimbra University Press, vol. II, 1930.

Barbosa, Duarte, 'Livro do Oriente de Duarte Barbosa'. Reproduction of the edition of the Academia Real de Ciências, Lisbon, 2nd edn, 1867, in *Além-Mar: Códice Casanatense 1889/ Os Portugueses na Índia: Viagens, Aventuras, Conquista*, Milan: F. Maria Ricci/Liv. Bertrand, 1987, pp. 35–115.

Barbuda, Luís Coelho de, *(Reyes de Portugal, y) Empresas Militares de Lvsitanos, escriptas por Lvys Coello de Barbuda criado de su Magestad, natural y vesino de la Ciudad de Lisboa*, Lisbon: Pedro Craesbeck, 1624.

Barreto, Luís Filipe, 'Em Torno da *Reformação da Milícia e Governo do Estado da Índia Oriental* de Francisco Rodrigues Silveira', in *Portuguese Voyages to Asia and Japan in the Renaissance Period (Proceedings of the International Conference, Sophia University, Tokyo, 1993)*, S.l.: Embassy of Portugal in Japan, s.d., pp. 177–207.

Barros, João de, *Ásia,* Lisbon: Liv. Sam Carlos, 1974–75 (reprint of the edition of 1788), 4 Decades, 9 vols.

Bassett, D. K., 'European Influence in Southeast Asia, *c.*1500–1630', *JSEAH*, 4 (1963): 173–209.

Bastin, John and R. W. Winks (eds.), *Malaysia: Selected Historical Readings*, 2nd edn, Nendeln: KTO Press, 1979.

Beaulieu, Augustin de, 'Memoires du Voyage aux Indes Orientales', in M. Melchisedec Thevenot (ed.), *Relations de Divers Voyages Curieux qui n'ont point este publiées ... augmentée de plusiers Relations curieuses*, Paris: T. Moette, 1696, vol. 1.

Best, Thomas, *The Voyage of Thomas Best to the East Indies 1612–1614*, ed. William Foster, London: Hakluyt Society, 1934.

Blair, Emma Helen and J. A. Robertson (eds.), *The Philippine Islands 1493–1803*, Cleveland: Arthur H. Clark, 1903, vols. I–XXXII.

Blussé, Leonard, 'Chinese Trade to Batavia during the days of the V.O.C.', *Archipel*, 18 (1979): 195–213.

Blussé, Leonard and George Winius, 'The Origin and Rhythm of Dutch Aggression against the Estado da India, 1601–1661', in Teotónio R. de Souza (ed.), *Indo-Portuguese History: Old Issues, New Questions*, New Delhi: Concept Publishing Company, 1985, pp. 73–83.

Bocarro, António, *Década 13 da História da Índia*, ed. R. J. Lima Felner, Monumentos Inéditos para a História das Conquistas dos Portuguezes, tome VI, Lisbon, Academia Real de Ciências, 1876, 2 vols.

———— 'Livro das Plantas de todas as Fortalezas, Cidades e Povoações do Estado da Índia Oriental', in *Arquivo Português Oriental*, ed. A. B. de Bragança Pereira, tome IV, vol. II, parts 1 and 2, 1938, 2 vols.

Boletim do Arquivo Histórico Colonial, Lisbon, 1950, vol. I.

Boletim Oficial do Governo do Estado da Índia, New Goa, Nos. 45–55, 113–119 (1880); Nos. 112, 138–143, 161–165, 166–171, 178, 183–189, 206–208, 228–231, 238 (1882); Nos. 50–54, 58–61, 61, 89–99, 100–106, 153–167, 170–199, 199–278, 284–285 (1883).

Borschberg, Peter (ed.), 'A Description by Cornelis Matelieff of the Four Johor Rulers: Alauddin Riayat Shah III, Raja Bongsu, Raja Siak and Raja Laut, 1606', in <http://www.borschberg.sg>.

———— 'Description of Batu Sawar, Kota Sabrang and the Surrounding Region, by Cornelis Matelieff de Jonge, 24 August, 1606', in <http://www.borschberg.sg>.

———— (ed.), *Iberians in the Singapore-Melaka Area (16th to 18th Century)*, Wiesbaden/Lisbon: Harrassowitz Verlag/Fundação Oriente, 2004.

———— 'The Johor-VOC Alliance and the Twelve Years' Truce: Factionalism, Intrigue and International Diplomacy 1606–13', *International Law and Justice Working Papers*, New York University School of Law, Working Paper 2009/8, 2009.

———— 'Portuguese, Spanish and Dutch Plans to Construct a Fort in the Straits of Singapore, ca. 1584–1625', *Archipel*, 65 (2003): 55–88.

———— 'Remapping the Straits of Singapore? New Insights from Old Sources', in P. Borschberg (ed.), *Iberians in the Singapore-Melaka Area (16th to 18th Century)*, Wiesbaden/ Lisbon: Harrassowitz Verlag/ Fundação Oriente, 2004, pp. 93–130.

_____ 'The *Santa Catarina* incident of 1603: Dutch Freebooting, the Portuguese *Estado da Índia* and Intra-Asian Trade at the Dawn of the 17th Century', *Review of Culture*, Macao, 11 (2004): 13–25.

_____ 'Security, VOC Penetration and Luso-Spanish Co-operation: the Armada of Philippine Governor Juan de Silva in the Straits of Singapore, 1616', in P. Borschberg (ed.), *Iberians in the Singapore-Melaka Area (16th to 18th Century)*, Wiesbaden/ Lisbon: Harrassowitz Verlag/ Fundação Oriente, 2004, pp. 35–62.

_____ 'The Seizure of the *Sta. Catarina* Revisited: The Portuguese Empire in Asia, VOC Politics and the Origins of the Dutch-Johor Alliance (1602–c.1616)', *JSEAS*, 33/1 (2002): 31–62.

_____ 'VOC Blockade of the Singapore and Malacca Straits: Diplomacy, Trade and Survival', in J. P. Costa and V. L. Rodrigues (eds.), *O Estado da Índia e os Desafios Europeus/ Actas do VI Seminário Internacional de História Indo-Portuguesa*, Lisbon: Centro de História de Além-Mar/ Centro de Estudos dos Povos e Cultura de Expressão Portuguesa, 2010, pp. 163–186.

Bort, Balthasar, 'Report of Governor Balthasar Bort on Malacca, 1678', *JMBRAS*, 5(1) (1927): 1–46.

Botelho, Simão, 'Tombo do Estado da Índia', in Rodrigo J. Lima Felner (ed.), *Subsídios para a História da Índia Portuguesa*, Monumentos inéditos para a História das Conquistas dos Portugueses ', tome V of the 1st series, Lisbon: Academia Real de Ciências, 1868.

Bottoms, J. C., 'Malay Historical Works', in K. G. Tregonning (ed.), *Malaysian Historical Sources*, 2nd edn, Singapore: University of Singapore, 1965, pp. 36–57.

Bouza-Álvarez, Fernando, *Portugal no Tempo dos Filipes: Política, Cultura, Representações (1580–1668)*, Lisbon: Ed. Cosmos, 2000.

Bowen, John R., 'Cultural Models for Historical Genealogies: The Case of the Melaka Sultanate', in K. S. Sandhu and P. Wheatley (eds.), *Melaka: The Transformation of a Malay Capital c.1400–1980*, Kuala Lumpur: Oxford University Press, 1983, vol. 1, pp. 162–179.

Boxer, Charles Ralph, 'Asian Potentates and European Artillery in the 16th–18th Centuries: A Footnote to Gibson-Hill', *JMBRAS*, 38/2 (1965): 156–172.

_____ *The Dutch Seaborne Empire*, London: Hutchinson, 1977.

_____ 'A Note on Portuguese Reactions to the Revival of the Red Sea Spice Trade and the Rise of Atjeh in 1540–1600', in C. R. Boxer, *Commerce in Southern Asia 1500–1750*, London: Variorum Reprints, 1985.

_____ 'Portuguese and Spanish Projects for the Conquest of Southeast Asia, 1580–1600', in C. R. Boxer, *Portuguese Conquest and Commerce in Southern Asia 1500–1750*, London: Variorum Reprints, 1985.

_____ *Portuguese Conquest and Commerce in Southern Asia 1500–1750*, London: Variorum Reprints, 1985.

Boxer, Charles Ralph and Frazão de Vasconcelos, *André Furtado de Mendonça*, Lisbon/Macao: Fundação Oriente/ Centro de Estudos Marítimos de Macau, 1989.

Boxer, Charles Ralph and Pierre-Yves Manguin, 'Miguel Roxo de Brito's Narrative of his Voyage to the Raja Empat, May 1581–November 1582', *Archipel*, 18 (1979): 175–194.

Braginsky, V. I., 'Hikayat Hang Tuah: Malay Epic and Muslim Mirror: Some Considerations on its Date, Meaning and Structure', *Bijdragen tot de Taal-, Land- en Volkenkunde*, 14/4 (1990): 399–412.

Brakel, L. F., 'State and Statecraft in 17th century Aceh', in A. Reid and L. Castles, *Pre-colonial State Systems in Southeast Asia*, MBRAS Monograph No. 6, Kuala Lumpur: Malaysian Branch of the Royal Asiatic Society, 1975, pp. 56–66.

Burridge, Kenelm O. L., 'The Malay Composition of a Village in Johore', *JMBRAS*, 29/3 (1956): 60–77.

Buyong Adil, *Sejarah Johor*, Kuala Lumpur: Dewan Bahasa dan Pustaka, 1980.

Cácegas, Fr. Luís de and Fr. Luís de Sousa, *História de S. Domingos*, Tesouros da Literatura e da História, vol. II, Porto: Lello & Irmão, 1974.

Caetano, Marcello, *Portugal e a Internacionalização dos Problemas Africanos*, 4th edn, Lisbon: Ed. Ática, 1971.

Carletti, Francesco, *Voyage autour du Monde de Francesco Carletti (1594–1606)*, ed. Paolo Carile, Paris: Ed. Chandeigne, 1999.

Casale, Giancarlo, 'His Majesty's Servant Lufti: The career of a previously unknown sixteenth-century Ottoman envoy to Sumatra based on an account of his travels from the Topkapi Palace Archives', *Turcica*, 37 (2005): 43–81.

———— *The Ottoman Age of Exploration*, New York: Oxford University Press, 2010.

Castanheda, Fernão Lopes de, *História do Descobrimento e Conquista da Índia pelos Portugueses*, ed. M. Lopes de Almeida, Tesouros da Literatura e da História, Porto: Lello & Irmãos, 1979, 2 vols.

Catálogo dos Manuscritos Ultramarinos da Biblioteca Pública Municipal do Porto, Lisbon, 1935.

Chang Tien-Tse, 'The Spanish–Dutch Naval Battle of 1617 outside Manila Bay', *JSEAH*, 7/1 (1966): 111–121.

Costa, João Paulo Oliveira and Vítor Luís Gaspar Rodrigues (eds.), *O Estado da Índia e os Desafios Europeus/ Actas do VI Seminário Internacional de História Indo-Portuguesa*, Lisbon: Centro de História de Além-Mar/ Centro de Estudos dos Povos e Cultura de Expressão Portuguesa, 2010.

———— *Portugal y Oriente: El Proyecto Indiano del Rey Juan*, Portugal y el Mundo. Madrid: Editorial Mapfre, 1992.

Couto, Diogo do, *Da Ásia*, Lisbon: Liv. Sam Carlos, 1974–75 (reprint of the edition of 1788), 9 Decades, 15 vols.

_____ *O Primeiro Soldado Prático*, ed. António Coimbra Martins, Outras Margens, Lisbon: Comissão Nacional para as Comemorações dos Descobrimentos Portugueses, 2001.

_____ *O Soldado Prático*, 3rd edn, Lisbon: Liv. Sá da Costa, 1980.

_____ *Vida de D. Paulo de Lima Pereira*, Lisbon: Biblioteca de Clássicos Portugueses vol. XXXV, 1903.

Coutre, Jacques de, 'Vida de Jacques de Coutre', published with the title *Andanzas Asiaticas* by E. Stols, B. Teensma and J. Werberckmoes, Cronicas de America 61, Madrid: Ed. Historia 16, 1991.

Cowan, C. D., 'Continuity and Change in the International History of Maritime Southeast Asia', *JSEAH*, 9/1 (1968): 1–11.

Cowan, C. D. and O. W. Wolters (eds.), *Southeast Asia History and Historiography: Essays presented to D. G. E. Hall*, Ithaca, N.Y.: Cornell University Press, 1976.

Cruz, Maria Augusta Lima, 'Degredados e arrenegados portugueses no espaço Índico nos primórdios do século XVI', *Povos e Culturas*, 5 (1996): 41–61.

_____ 'Exiles and Renegades in Early 16th century Portuguese India', *The India Economic and Social History Review*, 23/3 (1986): 248–262.

Curto, Diogo Ramada, *O Discurso Político em Portugal (1600–1650)*, Lisbon: Universidade Aberta, 1988.

Dalgado, Sebastião Rudolfo, *Glossário Luso-Asiático*, Coimbra: Imprensa da Universidade, 1919.

Damais, Louis-Charles, 'L'Épigraphie Musulmane dans le Sud-Est Asiatique', *Bulletin de l'École Française d'Extrême Orient*, 54 (1968): 584–587.

Danvers, F. C. and W. Foster (ed.), *Letters Received by the East India Company from Its Servants in the East*, London: Sampson Law & Co., 1896–1900, 6 vols.

Das Gupta, Arun, 'The Maritime Trade of Indonesia: 1500–1800', in Ashin Das Gupta and M. N. Pearson (eds.), *India and the Indian Ocean 1500–1800*, Calcutta: Oxford University Press, 1987, pp. 240–275.

Das Gupta, Ashin and M. N. Pearson (eds.), *India and the Indian Ocean 1500–1800*, Calcutta: Oxford University Press, 1987.

Daus, Ronald, *Portuguese Eurasian Communities in Southeast Asia*, Singapore: Institute of Southeast Asian Studies, 1989.

Dias, Luís Fernando de Carvalho, *O Ultramar Português e a Expansão na África e no Oriente*, Off-print of *Garcia de Orta*, vol. III, no. 2 and following.

Diffie, Bailey W. and George D. Winius, *A Fundação do Império Português, 1415–1580*, Documenta Historica, Lisbon: Vega, 1993, vol. 2.

Disney, A. R., *A Decadência do Império da Pimenta*, Lugar da História 16, Lisbon: Ed. 70, 1981.

Documentação Ultramarina Portuguesa, Lisbon: Centro de Estudos Históricos Ultramarinos, 1960–6, vols. I–IV.

Domingues, Francisco Contente and Luís Filipe Barreto (eds.), *A Abertura do Mundo/ Estudos de História dos Descobrimentos Europeus*, Métodos Nos. 23–24, Lisbon: Ed. Presença, 1987, 2 vols.

Downton, Nicholas, *The Voyage of Nicholas Downton to the East Indies 1614–1615*, ed. William Foster, London: Hakluyt Society, 1939.

Dulaurier, E. (ed.), *Chronique du Royaume d'Atcheh dans l'Ile de Sumatra*, Paris: Imprimerie Royale, 1839.

East (The) and West Indian Mirror: Being an Account of Joris van Speilbergen's Voyage around the World (1614–1617), ed. J. A. J. Villiers, London: Hakluyt Society, 1906.

Encyclopédie de l'Islam, new edn, Leiden: E. J. Brill, 1960–2004, 12 vols.

Erédia, Manuel Godinho de, *Declaraçam de Malaca e India Meridional com o Cathay*, published with the title *Malaca, l'Inde Orientale et le Cathay* by L. Janssen, Bruxelas, 1881.

———— *Informação da Aurea Chersoneso, ou Península, e das Ilhas Auríferas, Carbúnculas e Aromáticas*, ed. Rui Manuel Loureiro, Lisbon, 2008.

———— 'Lista das principais Minas aurífares alcançadas pela curiosidade de Manoel Gedinho [sic] de Heredea Cosmografo Indiano', in *Leis que existem no fim do Manuscrito original das Ordenações da Índia (...) copiadas fielmente de hum original autografo (...)*, Lisbon, 1807, pp. 81–86.

Falcão, Luís de Figueiredo, *Livro em que se Contém toda a Fazenda e Real Património dos Reinos de Portugal, India e Ilhas Adjacentes e outras particularidades ordenado* [1607], Lisbon: Imprensa Nacional, 1859.

Fitzler, M. A. Hedwig and Ernesto Ennes, *A Secção Ultramarina da Biblioteca Nacional/ Inventários*, Lisbon: Biblioteca Nacional, 1928.

Flores, Jorge Manuel (ed.), 'Os Mares da Ásia 1500–1800: Sociedades Locais, Portugueses e Expansão Europeia', *Revista de Cultura*, 13–14 (1991).

Flores, Maria da Conceição, *Os Portugueses e o Sião no século XVI*, Mare Liberum, Lisbon: Comissão Nacional para as Comemorações dos Descobrimentos Portugueses, 1994.

Floris, Peter, *Peter Floris: His Voyage to the East Indies in the Globe 1611–1615*, ed. W. Moreland, London, Hakluyt Society, 1934.

Fontes para a História do Antigo Ultramar Português, Lisbon: Academia Portuguesa de História, vol. I, tome I, 1978.

Foster, William (ed.), *Early Travels in India 1583–1619*, Oxford: Oxford University Press, 1921.

———— *The Voyages of Sir James Lancaster to Brazil and the East Indies 1591–1603*, London: Hakluyt Society, 1940.

Freire, P. António (ed.), *Primor e Honra da vida soldadesca no Estado da Índia*, Lisbon: Tipografia de Jorge Rodrigues, 1630.

Frutuoso, Eduardo, 'Macau e Manila no Arbitrismo Ibérico', *Review of Culture*, 23 (2007): 117–144.

Furber, Holden, *Rival Empires of Trade in the Orient, 1600–1800,* Minneapolis: University of Minnesota Press, 1976.

Gaio, João Ribeiro, *O Roteiro das Cousas do Achem de D. João Ribeiro Gaio: Um Olhar Português sobre o Norte de Samatra em finais do século XVI,* ed. Jorge M. dos Santos Alves and Pierre-Yves Manguin, Outras Margens, Lisbon: Comissão Nacional para as Comemorações dos Descobrimentos Portugueses, 1997.

Gibson-Hill, C. A., 'Johore Lama and other ancient sites on the Johore River', *JMBRAS,* 28/2 (1955): 127–197.

_____ 'On the Alleged Death of Sultan Ala'u'd-din of Johore at Acheh, in 1613', *JMBRAS,* 29/1 (1956): 125–145.

Godinho, Vitorino Magalhães, *Les Finances de l'État Portugais des Indes Orientales (1517–1635),* Paris: Calouste Gulbenkian Foundation, 1982.

_____ *Os Descobrimentos e a Economia Mundial,* 2nd edn, Métodos vols. 7–10, Lisbon: Ed. Presença, 1983, 4 vols.

Goor, J. van (ed.), 'Empires: Strategies and Trade. The Origin of the Ideas of Jan Pieterszoon Coen', in J. P. Costa and V. L. Rodrigues (eds.), *O Estado da Índia e os Desafios Europeus/ Actas do VI Seminário Internacional de História Indo-Portuguesa,* Lisbon: Centro de História de Além-Mar/ Centro de Estudos dos Povos e Cultura de Expressão Portuguesa, 2010, pp. 419–442.

_____ *Trading Companies in Asia, 1600–1830,* Utrecht: HES Uitgevers, 1986.

Groeneveldt, W. P., 'Notes on the Malay Archipelago and Malacca', in *Miscellaneous Papers Relating to Indo-China and the Indian Archipelago* ... 2nd series, vol. I, London: Trubner & Co, 1887, pp. 126–262.

Guedes, M. Ana de Barros Serra Marques, *Interferência e Integração dos Portugueses na Birmânia, c.1580–1630,* Lisbon: Fundação Oriente, 1994.

Guerreiro, Fernão, *Relação Anual das Coisas que fizeram os Padres da Companhia de Jesus nas suas Missões nos anos de 1600 a 1609,* ed. Artur Viegas, Lisbon: Imprensa Nacional, 1930–1942, 3 vols.

Guillot, Claude, 'Les Portugais et Banten, 1511–1682', in Jorge Manuel Flores, 'Os Mares da Ásia', *Revista de Cultura,* 13–14 (1991): 80–95.

_____ 'Libre entreprise contre économie dirigée: guerres civiles à Banten, 1580–1609', *Archipel,* 43 (1992): 57–72.

Gune, V. T. (ed.), *Assentos do Conselho da Fazenda 1613–1621,* Goa, Directorate of Historical Archives & Archaeology (Museum), 1979, vol. I, part 1.

Hair, P. E. H., 'Dutch Voyage Accounts in English Translation 1580–1625: A Checklist', *Itinerario,* 14/2 (1990): 95–106.

Hall, D. G. E., *A History of South-East Asia,* 3rd edn, London: Macmillan Student Editions, 1970.

Harris, John (ed.), *Navigatium atque Itinerantium Bibliotheca or a Complete Collection of Voyages and Travels,* London, 1744, 2 vols.

Hartmann, Arnulf (ed.), 'The Augustinians in Golden Goa. A Manuscript by Felix de Jesus, O.S.A.', *Analecta Augustiniana,* XXX (1967): 5–167.

Hikayat Negeri Johor, ed. Ismail Hussein, MBRAS Reprint 6, Kuala Lumpur: Malaysian Branch of the Royal Asiatic Society, 1992, pp. 227–284.

Hikayat Patani: The Story of Patani, ed. A. Teeuw and D. K. Wyatt, Bibliotheca Indonesica 5, The Hague: Martinus Nijhoff, 1970.

Hill, Ronald D., 'The History of Rice Cultivation in Melaka', in K. S. Sandhu and P. Wheatley (eds.), *Melaka: The Transformation of a Malay Capital c.1400–1980*, Kuala Lumpur: Oxford University Press, 1983, vol. 1, pp. 536–567.

Inventario General de Manuscritos de la Biblioteca Nacional, Madrid, 1970, vol. IX.

Iovrnal du Voyage de l'Inde Orientale, faict per les Navires Hollandoises: Leur Courses & Rhombes, certaines Marques, & Decouvrements de Terres ..., Paris: Adrien Perier, 1598.

Iria, Alberto, *Elementos de Estudo da possível contribuição portuguesa para a organização do Museu Histórico de Malaca*. Off-prints of *Studia*, Nos. 5–8, 1960/61.

Irwin, Graham, 'Melaka Fort', in K. S. Sandhu and P. Wheatley (eds.), *Melaka: The Transformation of a Malay Capital c.1400–1980*, Kuala Lumpur: Oxford University Press, 1983, vol. 1, pp. 782–805.

Israel, Jonathan I., *Dutch Primacy in World Trade 1585–1740*, New York: Oxford University Press, 1992.

Ittersum, Martine Julia van, *Profit and Principle: Hugo Grotius, Natural Rights Theories and the Rise of Dutch Power in the East Indies (1595–1615)*, Leiden: Brill, 2006.

Jacobs, Hubert (ed.), *Documenta Malucensia*, Monumenta Historica Societatis Iesu' vols. II–III, Rome: Jesuit Historical Institute, 1980.

————— 'Un Réglement de Comptes entre Portugais et Javanais dans les Mers de l'Indonésie en 1580', *Archipel*, 18 (1979): 159–173.

Johns, A. H., 'Islam in Southeast Asia: Problems of Perspective', in C. D. Cowan and O. W. Wolters (eds.), *Southeast Asia History and Historiography: Essays presented to D. G. E. Hall*, Ithaca, N.Y.: Cornell University Press, 1976, pp. 304–320.

Josselin de Jong, P. E., 'Who's Who in the Malay Annals', *JMBRAS*, 34(2) (1961): 1–89.

Jourdain, John, *The Journal of John Jourdain 1608–1617*, ed. William Foster, London: Hakluyt Society, 1905 (Reprinted by Klaus Reprint Limited, 1967).

Juynboll, Th. W. and P. Voorhoeve, 'Atjéh', in *Encyclopédie de l'Islam*, Leiden: E. J. Brill, 1960, vol. I, pp. 761–770.

Kartodirdjo, Sartoro, 'Religous and Economic Aspects of Portuguese–Indonesian Relations', *Studia*, 40 (1978): 251–272.

Kathirithamby-Wells, Jeyamalar, 'Achehnese Control over West Sumatra up to the Treaty of Painan, 1663', *JSEAH*, 10/3 (1969): 453–479.

————— 'Banten: A West Indonesian Port and Polity During the Sixteenth and Seventeenth Centuries', in J. Kathirithamby-Wells and J. Villiers (eds.),

The Southeast Asian Port and Polity: Rise and Demise, Singapore: Singapore University Press, 1990, pp. 106–125.

_____ 'The Dutch in the Straits of Malacca', in Zainal Abidin Wahid (ed.), *Glimpses of Malaysian History*, Kuala Lumpur: Dewan Bahasa dan Pustaka, 1980, pp. 48–53.

_____ 'Forces of Regional and State Integration in the Western Archipelago, c.1500–1700', *JSEAS*, 18/1 (1987): 24–44.

_____ 'Restraints on the Development of Merchant Capitalism in Southeast Asia before c.1800', in A. Reid (ed.), *Southeast Asia in the Early Modern Era: Trade, Power, and Belief*, Asia East by South, Ithaca, NY: Cornell University Press, 1993, pp. 123–148.

_____ 'Royal Authority and the *Orang Kaya* in the Western Archipelago, c.1500–1800', *JSEAS*, 17/2 (1986): 256–267.

Kathirithamby-Wells, Jeyamalar and John Villiers (eds.), *The Southeast Asian Port and Polity: Rise and Demise*, Singapore: Singapore University Press, 1990.

Khasnor binti Johan, 'The Johor-Riau Empire in the 18th century', in Zainal Abidin Wahid (ed.), *Glimpses of Malaysian History*, Kuala Lumpur: Dewan Bahasa dan Pustaka, 1980, pp. 42–47.

Lapian, A. B., 'Le Rôle des Orang Laut dans l'Histoire de Riau', *Archipel*, 18 (1979): 215–222.

Laval, Pyrard de, *Voyage de Pyrard de Laval aux Indes Orientales (1601–1611)*, Paris: Ed. Chandeigne, 1998, 2 vols.

Lee Kam Hing, 'Acheh and the Malay Peninsula in the 16th and 17th centuries', in Zainal Abidin Wahid (ed.), *Glimpses of Malaysian History*, Kuala Lumpur: Dewan Bahasa dan Pustaka, 1980, pp. 34–41.

Lemos, Jorge de, 'Hystoria dos Cercos qve em Tempo de Antonio Monis Barreto Governador que foi dos estados da India, os Achens, & Iaos puserão â fortaleza de Malaca, sendo Tristão Vaz da Veiga capitão della', published with the title *História dos Cercos de Malaca*, Lisbon: Biblioteca Nacional, 1982 (facsimile of the edition of 1585).

León-Pinello, D. Antonio, *Epitome de la Biblioteca Oriental y Occidental, Nautica y Geografica*, Madrid, 1737, 3 vols.

Leupe, P. A. 'The Siege and Capture of Malacca from the Portuguese in 1640–1641: Extracts from the Archives of the Dutch East India Company', *JMBRAS*, 14/1 (1936): 1–178.

Liaw Yock Fang, 'The *Undang-Undang* Melaka', in K. S. Sandhu and P. Wheatley (eds.), *Melaka: The Transformation of a Malay Capital c.1400–1980*, Kuala Lumpur: Oxford University Press, 1983, vol. 1, pp. 180–194.

Linehan, W., *A History of Pahang*, MBRAS Reprints No. 2, Kuala Lumpur: Malaysian Branch of the Royal Asiatic Society, 1973.

Linschoten, Jan Huygen van, *The Voyage of Jan Huygen van Linschoten to the East Indies*, London: Hakluyt Society, 1885 (following the English edition of 1598), 2 vols.

Lobato, Manuel Leão Marques, 'A Carreira da Índia e a variante de Malaca', in Artur Teodoro de Matos and Luís Filipe F. R. Thomaz (eds.), *A Carreira da Índia e as Rotas dos Estreitos*, Lisbon/Macao, 1993, pp. 343–376.

———— *Fortificações Portuguesas e Espanholas na Indonésia Oriental*, Lisbon: Prefácio, 2009.

———— 'Notas e correcções para uma edição crítica do Ms. da Livraria No. 805 (IAN/TT), a propósito da publicação de um tratado do Pe. Manuel de Carvalho, S.J.', *Anais de História de Além-Mar*, 3 (2002): 389–408.

———— *Política e Comércio dos Portugueses na Insulíndia: Malaca e as Molucas de 1575 a 1605*, Macao: Instituto Português do Oriente, 1999.

———— *Política e Comércio dos Portugueses no Mundo Malaio-Indonésio (1575–1605)*, Masters thesis, New University of Lisbon, 1993.

Lobo, A. de S. S. Costa (ed.), *Memórias de um Soldado da Índia compiladas de um manuscrito do Museu Britânico*, Biblioteca de Autores Portugueses, Lisbon: Imprensa Nacional-Casa da Moeda, 1987 (reprint of the 1877 edition).

Lombard, Denys, *Le Carrefour Javanais: Essai d'Histoire Globale*, Civilizations et Sociétés, 79, Paris: École des Hautes Études en Sciences Sociales, 1990, 3 vols.

———— *Le Sultanat d'Atjéh au Temps d'Iskandar Muda 1607–1636*, Paris: École Française d'Extreme Orient, 1967.

———— 'Le Sultanat Malais comme Modèle Socio-économique', in D. Lombard and J. Aubin (eds.), *Marchands et Hommes d'Affaires Asiatiques dans l'Océan Indien et le Mer de Chine 13e.–20e. siécles*, Ports, Routes, Trafics, 29, Paris: École des Hautes Études en Sciences Sociales, 1988, pp. 117–124.

———— 'Martin de Vitré, premier breton à Aceh (1601–1603)', *Archipel*, 54 (1997): 3–12.

———— 'Pour une Histoire des Villes du Sud-Est Asiatique', *Annales. Économies. Sociétés. Civilisations*, 4 (1970): 842–856.

Lombard, Denys and Jean Aubin (eds.), *Marchands et Hommes d'Affaires Asiatiques dans l'Océan Indien et le Mer de Chine 13e.–20e. siécles*, Ports, Routes, Trafics, 29, Paris: École des Hautes Études en Sciences Sociales, 1988.

Lombard-Jourdain, Anne, 'Augustin de Beaulieu et son dessein touchant les Indes Orientales (1631–1632)', *Archipel*, 54 (1997): 13–26.

Loureiro, Rui and Serge Gruzinski (eds.), *Passar as Fronteiras: Actas do II Colóquio Internacional sobre Mediadores Culturais, séculos XV a XVIII*, Lagos: Centro de Estudos Gil Eanes, 1999.

Loyola, Martin Ignacio de, *Viaje alrededor del Mundo*, ed. J. Ignacio Tellechea Idígoras, Cronicas de America 54, Madrid: Historia 16, 1989.

Luz, Francisco P. Mendes da (ed.), *Livro das Cidades e Fortalezas que a Coroa de Portugal tem nas partes da Índia*, 2nd edn, off-print of 'Studia', 6, Lisbon, Centro de Estudos Históricos Ultramarinos, 1960 (facsimile edition).

———— *O Conselho da Índia*, Lisbon: Agência Geral do Ultramar, 1952.

Macgregor, Ian A., 'Johore Lama in the sixteenth century', *JMBRAS*, 28/2 (1955): 48–125.

———— 'Notes on the Portuguese in Malaya', *JMBRAS*, 28/2 (1955): 5–47.

———— 'A Sea Fight near Singapore in the 1570s', *JMBRAS*, 29/3 (1956): 5–21.

Machado, Diogo Barbosa, *Bibliotheca Lusitana*, Coimbra: Atlântida, 1976 (reprint of the 1747 edition), 4 vols.

Mandelsloe, John Albert de, 'The Remaining Voyages of John Albert de Mandelsloe through the Indies', in Harris, John (ed.), *Navigatium atque Itinerantium Bibliotheca or a Complete Collection of Voyages and Travels*, London, 1744.

Manguin, Pierre-Yves, 'Manpower and Labour Categories in Early Sixteenth Century Malacca', in A. Reid (ed.), *Slavery, Bondage and Dependency in Southeast Asia*, St Lucia, Qld: University of Queensland Press, 1983, pp. 209–215.

———— 'Of Fortresses and Galleys', *Modern Asian Studies*, 22/3 (1988): 607–628.

———— 'The Vanishing *Jong*: Insular Southeast Asian Fleets in Trade and War (Fifteenth to Seventeenth Centuries)', in A. Reid (ed.), *Southeast Asia in the Early Modern Era: Trade, Power, and Belief*, Asia East by South, Ithaca, NY: Cornell University Press, 1993, pp.197–213.

Marsden, William, *The History of Sumatra*. Reprint of the 3rd edn, London: Oxford University Press, 1986.

Matheson, Virginia, 'Concepts of State in the *Tuhfat Al-Nafis*', in A. Reid and L. Castles (eds.), *Pre-colonial State Systems in Southeast Asia*, MBRAS Monograph No. 6, Kuala Lumpur: Malaysian Branch of the Royal Asiatic Society, 1975, pp. 12–21.

———— 'Strategies of Survival: The Malay Royal Line of Lingga-Riau', *JSEAS*, 17/1 (1986): 5–36.

Matheson, Virginia and M. B. Hooker, 'Slavery in the Malay Texts: Categories of Dependency and Compensation', in A. Reid (ed.), *Slavery, Bondage and Dependency in Southeast Asia*, St. Lucia, Qld: University of Queensland Press, 1983, pp. 182–208.

Mathew, K. S. (ed.), *Studies in Maritime History*, Pondicherry: Pondicherry University, 1990.

Matos, Artur Teodoro de, 'The Financial Situation of the State of India during the Philippine Period (1581–1635)', in Teotónio de Souza (ed.), *Indo–Portuguese History: Old Issues, New Questions*, New Delhi: Concept Publishing Company, 1985, pp. 90–101.

———— *Na Rota das Especiarias: De Malaca à Austrália*, Lisbon: Imprensa Nacional-Casa da Moeda, 1995.

———— *O Estado da Índia nos anos de 1581–1588/ Estrutura Administrativa e Económica: Alguns elementos para o seu estudo*, Ponta Delgada: Azores University, 1983.

Matos, Artur Teodoro de and Luís Filipe F. R. Thomaz (eds.), *A Carreira da Índia e as Rotas dos Estreitos: Actas do VIII Seminário Internacional de História Indo-Portuguesa*. Angra do Heroísmo, 1998.

———— *As Relações entre a Índia Portuguesa, a Ásia do Sueste e o Extremo Oriente/ Actas do VI Seminário Internacional de História Indo-Portuguesa*, Lisbon/Macao, 1993.

———— *Vinte Anos de Historigrafia Ultramarina Portuguesa, 1972–1992*, Lisbon: Comissão Nacional para as Comemorações dos Descobrimentos Portugueses, 1993.

Meilink-Roelofsz, M. A. Petronella, *Asian Trade and European Influence in the Indonesian Archipelago between 1500 and about 1630*, The Hague: Martinus Nijhoff, 1962.

———— 'European Influence in Southeast Asia 1500–1630: A Reply', *JSEAH*, 5/2 (1964): 184–197.

———— 'The Structures of Trade in Asia in the 16th and 17th centuries', *Mare Luso-Indicum*, 4 (1980): 1–43.

Middleton, Henry, *The Voyage of Henry Middleton to the Moluccas, 1604–1606*, ed. William Foster, London: Hakluyt Society, 1943; Millwood, New York: Klaus Reprint, 1990.

Mills, J. V., 'Two Dutch–Portuguese Sea-Fights', *JMBRAS*, 16/1 (1938): 139–149.

Missionação Portuguesa e Encontro de Culturas (Actas): Congresso Internacional de História, Memorabilia Christiana 4, Braga: Universidade Católica Portuguesa, 1993, vol. II.

Monteiro, Saturnino, *Batalhas e Combates da Marinha Portuguesa*, Lisbon: Liv. Sá da Costa, 1990–1993, vols. III–IV.

Morga, Antonio de, *Sucesos de las Islas Filipinas (1609)*, ed. J. S. Cummins, Hakluyt Society, Cambridge University Press, 1971.

Muhammad Abu Bakar, Amarjit Kaur and Abdullah Zakaria Ghazali (eds.), *Historia* (Essays commemorating the 25th Anniversary of the Department of History of the University of Kuala Lumpur), Kuala Lumpur: Malaysian Historical Society, 1984.

Muhammad Haji Salleh, 'Didactism and Conflict Resolution in the *Sejarah Melayu*', paper presented at the 8th European Colloquium on Indonesian and Malay Studies, Kungälv, May 1991.

Mullins, E. L. C., 'Works Published by the Hakluyt Society 1846–1973', in D. B. Quinn, *The Hakluyt Handbook*, II. London, Hakluyt Society, Hakluyt Society Second Series, No. 145, pp. 611–648.

Murteira, André, 'A Carreira da Índia e as Incursões Neerlandesas no Índico Ocidental e em Águas Ibéricas de 1604–1608', in J. P. Costa and V. L.

Rodrigues (eds.), *O Estado da Índia e os Desafios Europeus/Actas do VI Seminário Internacional de História Indo-Portuguesa*, Lisbon: Centro de História de Além-Mar/Centro de Estudos dos Povos e Cultura de Expressão Portuguesa, 2010, pp. 503–513.

Noonan, Laurence A., 'The Portuguese in Malacca', *Studia*, 23 (1968): 33–104.

Nunes, António, 'Livro dos pesos da Índia, e assy medidas e mohedas', in Rodrigo J. Lima Felner (ed.), *Subsídios para a História da Índia Portuguesa*, Monumentos Inéditos para a História das Conquistas dos Portugueses, tome V of the 1st series, Lisbon: Academia Real de Ciências, 1868.

Ollé, Manel, *La Empresa de China: De la Armada Invencible al Galeón de Manila*, Barcelona: Quaderns Crema, 2002.

Owen, Norman G. (ed.), *Death and Disease in Southeast Asia: Explorations in Social, Medical and Demographic History*, Singapore: Oxford University Press, 1987.

Pato, Bulhão and A. Silva Rego (eds.), *Documentos Remetidos da Índia ou Livros das Monções*, Lisbon: Academia de Ciências, 2 series, 10 vols.

Pato, Raimundo António de Bulhão (ed.), *Cartas de Afonso de Albuquerque, Seguidas de Documentos que as Elucidam*, Lisbon: Academia Real das Ciências de Lisboa, 1884–1903, 3 vols.

Pereira, António Pinto, *História da Índia no tempo em que a governou o Visorei Dom Luís de Ataíde*, Lisbon: Imprensa Nacional-Casa da Moeda, 1987.

Pereira, Nicolau, 'Lista de moedas, pesos e embarcações do Oriente, composta por Nicolau Pereira S.J. por 1582', ed. José Wicki, *Studia*, 33 (1971): 137–148.

Pigeaud, Theodore G. and H. J. de Graaf, *Islamic States in Java 1500–1700*, Verhandelingen van het Koninklijt Instituut voor Taal-, Land- en Volkenkunde, 70, The Hague: Martinus Nijhoff, 1976.

Pina, Gregório de, *'Relação de todo o Dinheiro que se fez na Venda dos Cargos e Fortalezas que se Uenderão por ordem de Sua Magestade neste Estado da Índia' (1639), feita*, ed. Maria Manuela Sobral Blanco, PhD dissertation in the History of the Portuguese Expansion, Lisbon University, 1992.

Pinto, Paulo Jorge de Sousa, 'Captains, Sultans and *liaisions dangereuses:* Melaka and Johor in the Late Sixteenth Century', in P. Borschberg (ed.), *Iberians in the Singapore-Melaka Area (16th to 18th Century)*, Wiesbaden/ Lisbon: Harrassowitz Verlag/Fundação Oriente, 2004, pp. 131–146.

———— *Melaka, Johor and Aceh: A bird's eye view over a Portuguese-Malay Triangular Balance (1575–1619)*. Off-print of the Archives of the Calouste Gulbenkian Cultural Centre, Paris, vol. XXXV (proceedings of the conference on 'Nouvelles Orientations de la Recherche sur l'Histoire de l'Asie Portugaise', Paris, 3–4 June 1994), 1996.

———— *No Extremo da Redonda Esfera: Relações Luso-Castelhanas na Ásia, 1565–1640: Um Ensaio sobre os Impérios Ibéricos*, PhD thesis, Catholic University of Portugal, 2011.

――― 'Purse and Sword: D. Henrique *Bendahara* and Portuguese Melaka in the late 16th Century', *Santa Barbara Portuguese Studies*, 2 (1995): 75–93.

――― 'Traços da Presença Chinesa em Malaca (século XVI-primeira metade do século XVII)', in J. M. S. Alves (ed.), *Portugal e a China: Conferências nos Encontros de História Luso-Chinesa*, Lisbon: Fundação Oriente, s.d. [2002], pp. 133–145.

Pires, Tomé, *A Suma Oriental de Tomé Pires e o Livro de Francisco Rodrigues*, ed. Armando Cortesão, Coimbra University, 1978.

Pissurlencar, Panduronga S. S. (ed.), *Assentos do Conselho de Estado*, Bastorá-Goa: Arquivo Histórico do Estado da Índia, Tipografia Rangel, 1953, vol. I.

――― *Regimentos das Fortalezas da Índia*, Bastorá-Goa: Arquivo Histórico do Estado da Índia, Tipografia Rangel, 1951.

Purcell, Victor. 'Chinese Settlement in Malacca', *JMBRAS*, 20/1 (1947): 115–125.

Purchas, Samuel (ed.), *Hakluytus Posthumus or Purchas His Pilgrimes: Contayning a History of the World in Sea Voyages and Lande Travells by Englishmen and Others*, Glasgow: James MacLehose & Sons, 1905, 20 vols.

Queirós, Fernão de, *História da Vida do Venerável Irmão Pedro de Basto*, Lisbon: Miguel Deslandes, 1699.

Quiros, Pedro Fernandez de, *The Voyages of Pedro Fernandez de Quiros 1595–1606*. London: Hakluyt Society, Kraus reprint, 1967, pp. 453–466.

Rego, A. da Silva (ed.), *Boletim da Filmoteca Ultramarina Portuguesa*. Lisbon, Centro de Estudos Históricos Ultramarinos, 1954–.

――― *Documentação para a História das Missões do Padroado Português do Oriente/ Índia*, Lisbon: Agência Geral do Ultramar, 1958, vols. XI–XII.

Reid, Anthony, 'An "Age of Commerce" in Southeast Asian History', *Modern Asian Studies*, 24/1 (1990): 1–30.

――― '"Closed" and "Open" Slave Systems in Pre-Colonial Southeast Asia', in A. Reid (ed.), *Slavery, Bondage and Dependency in Southeast Asia*, St. Lucia, Qld: University of Queensland Press, 1983, pp. 156–181.

――― 'Elephants and Water in the Feasting of Seventeenth Century Aceh', *JMBRAS*, 62/2 (1989): 25–44.

――― 'Islamization and Christianization in Southeast Asia: The Critical Phase, 1550–1650', in A. Reid (ed.), *Southeast Asia in the Early Modern Era: Trade, Power, and Belief*, Asia East by South, Ithaca, NY: Cornell University Press, 1993, pp. 151–179.

――― 'The Islamization of Southeast Asia', in Muhammad Abu Bakar, Amarjit Kaur and Abdullah Zakaria Ghazali (eds.), *Historia* (Essays commemorating the 25th Anniversary of the Department of History of the University of Kuala Lumpur), Kuala Lumpur: Malaysian Historical Society, 1984, pp. 13–33.

――― 'Low Population Growth and Its Causes in Pre-colonial Southeast Asia', in Norman Owen (ed.), *Death and Disease in Southeast Asia: Explorations in*

Social, Medical and Demographic History, Singapore: Oxford University Press, 1987, pp. 33–47.

———— 'Sixteenth Century Turkish Influence in Western Indonesia', *JSEAH*, 10/3 (1969): 395–414.

———— 'Slavery and Bondage in Southeast Asian History', in A. Reid (ed.), *Slavery, Bondage and Dependency in Southeast Asia*, St Lucia, Qld: University of Queensland Press, 1983, pp. 1–43.

———— (ed.), *Slavery, Bondage and Dependency in Southeast Asia*, St Lucia, Qld: University of Queensland Press, 1983.

———— *Southeast Asia in the Age of Commerce, 1450–1680*, London, New Haven, Yale University Press, 1988–93, 2 vols.

———— (ed.), *Southeast Asia in the Early Modern Era: Trade, Power, and Belief*, Asia East by South, Ithaca, NY: Cornell University Press, 1993.

———— 'The Structure of Cities in Southeast Asia, 15th to 18th centuries', *JSEAS*, 11/2 (1980): 235–250.

———— 'Trade and the Problem of Royal Power in Aceh, Three Stages: *c.*1550–1700', in A. Reid and L. Castles (eds.), *Pre-colonial State Systems in Southeast Asia*, MBRAS Monograph No. 6, Kuala Lumpur: Malaysian Branch of the Royal Asiatic Society, 1975, pp. 44–55.

Reid, Anthony and Lance Castles (eds.), *Pre-colonial State Systems in Southeast Asia*, MBRAS Monograph No. 6, Kuala Lumpur: Malaysian Branch of the Royal Asiatic Society, 1975.

Relação das Plantas, & dezcripções de todas as Fortalezas, Cidades & Povoações que os Portuguezes tem no Estado da India Oriental, Lisbon: Biblioteca Nacional, 1936.

Ribeiro, João, *Fatalidade Histórica da Ilha de Celão*, Biblioteca da Expansão Portuguesa 3, Lisbon: Alfa, 1989.

Rivara, J. H. da Cunha (ed.), *Archivo Portuguez Oriental*, New Goa: Imprensa Nacional, 1857–1876, 6 vols (10 tomes).

———— *Catálogo dos Manuscritos da Biblioteca Pública Eborense*, Lisbon, 1850, 3 vols.

Rodríguez Rodríguez, Isacio (ed.), *Historia de la Provincia Agustiniana del Santísimo Nombre de Jesús de Filipinas*, Manila: Arnoldus Press/ Valladolid, Ed. Estudio Agustiniano, 1978–1988, vols. XIII–XX.

Sá, Artur Basílio de (ed.), *Documentação para a História das Missões do Padroado Português do Oriente/Insulíndia*, Lisbon: Agência Geral do Ultramar/Instituto de Investigação Científica Tropical, 1958–1988, vols. IV–VI.

Saldanha, António Vasconcelos de, *Iustum Imperium: Dos Tratados como fundamento do Império dos Portugueses no Oriente*, S.l.: Fundação Oriente/ Instituto Português do Oriente, 1997.

San Agustín, Gaspar de, *Conquistas de las Islas Filipinas (1565–1615)*, ed. Manuel Marinero, Madrid: Consejo Superior de Investigaciones Científicas, 1975.

San Antonio, Gabriel de, 'Breve y Verdadera Relacion de los Sucesos del Reino de Camboxa', in Roberto Ferrando (ed.), *Relaciones de la Camboya y el Japón*, Cronicas de America 46, Madrid: Historia 16, 1988.

Sandhu, Kernial Singh and Paul Wheatley (eds.), *Melaka: The Transformation of a Malay Capital c.1400–1980*, Kuala Lumpur: Oxford University Press, 1983, 2 vols.

Santos, Catarina Madeira, *Goa é a Chave de toda a Índia: Perfil político da capital do Estado da Índia (1505–1570)*, Outras Margens, Lisbon: Comissão Nacional para as Comemorações dos Descobrimentos Portugueses, 1999.

Santos, Fr. João dos, *Etiópia Oriental e Vária História de Cousas Notáveis do Oriente*, ed. Manuel Lobato, Outras Margens, Lisbon: Comissão Nacional para as Comemorações dos Descobrimentos Portugueses, 1999.

São José, Fr. Gonçalo de, 'Jornada que Francisco de Souza de Castro Fidalgo da Casa de sua Magestade (...) fez ao Achem com huã importante embaixada inviado pelo V. Rey da India Pero da Sylva no Anno de 1638', published by C. R. Boxer with the title 'Uma Obra Raríssima impressa em Goa no século XVII', *Boletim Internacional de Bibliografia Luso-Brasileira*, VII(3) (1967): 431–528.

Sassetti, Fillipo, *Lettere da Vari Paesi (1570–1588)*, ed. Vanni Bramanti, Milan: Longanesi & Cª, 1970.

Scammell, G. V., 'The Patterns of European Trade in the Indian Ocean c.1500–1700', in K. S. Mathew (ed.), *Studies in Maritime History*, Pondicherry: Pondicherry University, 1990, pp. 1–12.

Schrieke, Bertram, *Indonesian Sociological Studies*, Selected Studies on Indonesia, The Hague: W. van Hoeve, 1959, 2 vols.

Sejarah Melayu or Malay Annals, A Translation of Raffles Ms. 18, ed. C. C. Brown, *JMBRAS*, 25(2/3) (1952): 1–276.

Sen, S. P., 'The Role of Indian Textiles in SE Asian Trade in the 17th century', *JSEAH*, 3/2 (1962): 92–110.

Sieveking, G. de G., Paul Wheatley and C. A. Gibson-Hill, 'Recent Archaeological Discoveries in Malaya (1952–53): The Investigations at Johore Lama', *JMBRAS*, 27/1 (1954): 225–233.

Silsilah Melayu dan Bugis dan Sakalian Raja-raja-nya, ed. Hans Overbeck, *JMBRAS*, 4 (1926): 339–381.

Silva, António Barreto da, António Simões and Francisco de Sousa, 'Lista de todas as capitanias, e cargos que ha na India, e sua estimação, e rendimento' (1616), *Revista Portugueza Colonial e Marítima*, Lisbon: Liv. Ferin, 1899–1900, 2nd sem., pp. 173–181, 237–245, 300–308; 1900–1901, 1st sem., pp. 12–19, 231–242, 278–286, 344–353.

Silva, Beatriz Basto da, 'Between Goa and Macau: Portuguese and Dutch Rivalry in the Seventeenth Century', in *Portuguese Voyages to Asia and Japan in the Renaissance Period (Proceedings of the International Conference,*

Sophia University, Tokyo, 1993), S.l.: Embassy of Portugal in Japan, s.d., pp. 116–133.

Silveira, Francisco Rodrigues, *Reformação da Milícia e Governo do Estado da Índia Oriental*, ed. Luís Filipe Barreto et al., Lisbon: Fundação Oriente, 1996.

Sousa, Alfredo Botelho de, *Subsídios para a História Militar Marítima da Índia (1585–1669)*, Lisbon: Ministério da Marinha, 1930–53, 3 vols.

Sousa, Francisco de, *Oriente Conquistado a Jesus Cristo*, Tesouros da Literatura e da História, Porto: Lello & Irmão, 1978.

Sousa, Manuel de Faria e, *Ásia Portuguesa*, Biblioteca Histórica: Serie Ultramarina vols. V–VI, Lisbon: Liv. Civilização, 1947.

Souza, George Bryan, *A Sobrevivência do Império: Os Portugueses na China (1630–1754)*, Anais 16, Lisbon: Pub. D. Quixote, 1991.

Souza, Teotónio R. de (ed.), *Indo-Portuguese History: Old Issues, New Questions*, New Delhi, Concept Publishing Company, 1985.

Subrahmanyam, Sanjay, *A Presença Portuguesa e o Comércio do Coromandel*, Lisbon: Academia da Marinha, 1990.

⸺ *Comércio e Conflito: A Presença Portuguesa no Golfo de Bengala, 1500–1700*, Lisbon: Ed. 70, 1994.

⸺ 'Commerce and Conflict: Two Views of Portuguese Melaka in the 1620s', *JSEAS*, 19/1 (1988): 62–79.

⸺ 'Notas sobre um rei congelado: O caso de Ali bin Yusuf Adil Khan, chamado Mealecão', in Rui Loureiro and Serge Gruzinski (eds.), *Passar as Fronteiras: Actas do II Colóquio Internacional sobre Mediadores Culturais, séculos XV a XVIII*, Lagos: Centro de Estudos Gil Eanes, 1999, pp. 265–289.

⸺ *O Império Asiático Português, 1500–1700: Uma História Política e Económica*, Memória e Sociedade, Lisbon: Difel, 1996.

⸺ 'Os Holandeses na Insulíndia e no Ceilão', in Luís de Albuquerque (ed.), *Portugal no Mundo*, Lisbon: Alfa, 1990, vol. V, pp. 51–64.

⸺ 'Persians, Pilgrims and Portuguese: The Travails of Masulipatnam Shipping in the Western Indian Ocean, 1590–1665', *Modern Asian Studies*, 22/3 (1988): 503–530.

⸺ 'Portugal no jogo das lutas interimperialistas (finais do século XVI – primeira metade do século XVII)', in Luís de Albuquerque (ed.), *Portugal no Mundo*, Lisbon: Alfa, 1990, V, pp. 65–76.

⸺ 'Pulverized in Aceh: On Luís Monteiro Coutinho and his "Martyrdom"', *Archipel*, 78 (2009): 19–60.

⸺ 'The Tail Wags the Dog or Some Aspects of the External Relations of the Estado da Índia, 1570–1600', *Moyen Orient & Océan Indien*, 5 (1988): 131–160.

⸺ 'Through the Looking Glass: Some Comments on Asian Views of the Portuguese in Asia, 1500–1700', in Artur Teodoro de Matos and Luís Filipe

F. R. Thomaz (ed.), *As Relações entre a Índia Portuguesa, a Ásia do Sueste e o Extremo Oriente*, Lisbon/Macao, 1993, pp. 377–403.

Teensma, B. N. (ed.), 'An Unknown Portuguese text on Sumatra from 1582', *Bijdragen tot de Taal-, Land- en Volkenkunde*, 145(II–III) (1989): 308–323.

Teixeira, Manuel, *The Portuguese Missions in Malacca and Singapore (1511–1958)*, Lisbon: Agência Geral do Ultramar, 1961, 3 vols.

Thevenot, M. Melchisedec (ed.), *Relations de Divers Voyages Curieux qui n'ont point este publiées ... augmentée de plusiers Relations curieuses*, Paris: T. Moette, 1696, 2 vols.

Thomaz, Luís Filipe F. R., 'A Crise de 1565–1575 na História do Estado da Índia', *Mare Liberum*, 9 (1995): 481–519).

———— 'A Escravatura em Malaca no Século XVI', *Stvdia*, 53 (1994): 253–315.

———— *A Questão da Pimenta em meados do século XVI: Um debate político do governo de D. João de Castro*, Estudos e Documentos 7, Lisbon: Centro de Estudos dos Povos e Culturas de Expressão Portuguesa, 1998.

———— (ed.), *Aquém e Além da Taprobana: Estudos Luso-Orientais à memória de Jean Aubin e Denys Lombard*, Lisbon: Centro de História de Além-Mar, 2002.

———— *De Ceuta a Timor*, Memória e Sociedade, Lisbon: Difel, 1994.

———— 'Do Cabo Espichel a Macau: vicissitudes do corso português', in Artur Teodoro de Matos and Luís Filipe F. R. Thomaz (eds.), *As Relações entre a Índia Portuguesa, a Ásia do Sueste e o Extremo Oriente*, Lisbon/Macao, 1993, pp. 537–568.

———— 'The Indian Merchant Communities in Malacca under the Portuguese Rule', in Souza, Teotónio de (ed.), *Indo-Portuguese History, Old Issues, New Questions*, New Delhi: Concept Publishing Company, 1985, pp. 56–72.

———— 'Java', in Luís de Albuquerque (ed.), *Dicionário de História dos Descobrimentos*, Lisbon: Círculo de Leitores, 1994, vol. 1, pp. 541–554.

———— 'Les Portugais dans les Mers de l'Archipel au XVIe siécle', *Archipel*, 18 (1979): 105–125.

———— 'Malacca: The Town and the Society during the first Century of Portuguese Rule', in Jorge M. Flores, 'Os Mares da Ásia 1500–1800: Sociedades Locais, Portugueses e Expansão Europeia', *Revista de Cultura*, 13–14 (1991): 68–79.

———— 'The Malay Sultanate of Melaka', in A. Reid (ed.), *Southeast Asia in the Early Modern Era: Trade, Power, and Belief*, Asia East by South, Ithaca, NY: Cornell University Press, 1993, pp. 69–90.

———— 'O malogrado estabelecimento oficial dos Portugueses em Sunda e a Islamização da Java', in Luís Filipe Thomaz (ed.), *Aquém e Além da Taprobana: Estudos Luso-Orientais à memória de Jean Aubin e Denys Lombard*, Lisbon: Centro de História de Além-Mar, 2002, pp. 381–607.

———— 'Os Frangues na terra de Malaca', in Francisco Contente Domingues and Luís Filipe Barreto (eds.), *A Abertura do Mundo/ Estudos de História dos*

Descobrimentos Europeus, Métodos Nos. 23–24, Lisbon: Ed. Presença, 1987, vol. II, pp. 209–217.

―――― *Os Portugueses em Malaca (1511–1580)*, graduate thesis, University of Lisbon, 1964, 2 vols.

―――― 'Sumatra's Westcoast in Portuguese Sources of the Mid 16th Century', in Bernhard Dahm (ed.), *Regions and Regional Developments in the Malay-Indonesian World [6. European Colloquium on Indonesian and Malay Studies (ECIMS)]*, Wiesbaden: Otto Harrassowitz, 1992, pp. 23–32.

Tregonning, K. G. (ed.), *Malaysian Historical Sources*, 2nd edn, Singapore: University of Singapore, 1965.

Trindade, Fr. Paulo da, *Conquista Espiritual do Oriente*, Lisbon: Centro de Estudos Históricos Ultramarinos, 1962–67, 3 vols.

Undang-Undang Melaka: The Laws of Melaka, ed. Liaw Yock Fang, Bibliotheca Indonesica 13, The Hague: Martinus Nijhoff/ Koninklijk Instituut voor Taal-, Land- en Volkenkunde, 1976.

Valentijn, François, 'Valentyn's Description of Malacca', *JSBRAS*, 13 (1884): 49–74B; 15 (1885): 119–138; 16 (1885): 289–301.

Valladares, Rafael, *Castilla y Portugal en Asia (1580–1680): Declive imperial y adaptación*, Leuven University Press, 2001.

Van Leur, J. C., *Indonesian Trade and Society*, Selected Studies on Indonesia, The Hague/Bandung: W. Van Hoeve, Royal Tropical Institute, 1955.

Veen, Ernst van, 'Dutch Strategies and the *Estado da Índia*', in J. P. Costa and V. L. Rodrigues (eds.), *O Estado da Índia e os Desafios Europeus/ Actas do VI Seminário Internacional de História Indo-Portuguesa*, Lisbon: Centro de História de Além-Mar/ Centro de Estudos dos Povos e Cultura de Expressão Portuguesa, 2010, pp. 401–418.

Vicks, Robert Sigfrid, *A Survey of Native Southeast Asian Coinage, circa 450–1850: Documentation and Typology*, PhD thesis, Cornell University, 1983.

Vignatti, Antonella (ed.), 'Vida e Acções de Mathias de Albuquerque', *Mare Liberum*, 15 (1998): 139–245; 17 (1999): 269–360.

Villiers, John, 'Makassar: The Rise and Fall of an East Indonesian Maritime Trading State, 1512–1669', in J. Kathirithamby-Wells and J. Villiers (eds.), *The Southeast Asian Port and Polity: Rise and Demise*, Singapore: Singapore University Press, 1990, pp. 143–159.

Vink, Mark, '*Mare Liberum* and *Dominium Maris*: Legal Arguments and Implications of the Luso–Dutch Struggle for the Control over Asian Waters ca. 1600–1663', in K. S. Mathew (ed.), *Studies in Maritime History*, Pondicherry: Pondicherry University, 1990, pp. 38–68.

Vlekke, Bernard H. M., *Nusantara: A History of the East Indian Archipelago*, Harvard University Press, 1943.

Wake, C. H., 'Melaka in the Fifteenth Century: Malay Historical Traditions and the Politics of Islamization', in K. S. Sandhu and P. Wheatley (eds.), *Melaka:*

The Transformation of a Malay Capital c.1400–1980, Kuala Lumpur: Oxford University Press, 1983, vol. 1, pp. 128–161.

Wang Gungwu, 'Southeast Asia between the 13th & 18th centuries: Some Reflections on Political Fragmentation & Cultural Change', in Muhammad Abu Bakar, Amarjit Kaur and Abdullah Zakaria Ghazali (eds.), *Historia* (Essays commemorating the 25th Anniversary of the Department of History of the University of Kuala Lumpur), Kuala Lumpur: Malaysian Historical Society, 1984, pp. 1–12.

Wicki, J. (ed.), *Documenta Indica*, Monumenta Historica Societatis Iesu vols. XII–XVIII, Rome: Instituto Histórico Societatis Jesu, 1988.

_____ (ed.), 'Duas cartas oficiais de Vice-Reis da Índia, escritas em 1561 e 1564', *Studia*, 3 (1959): 36–89.

_____ (ed.), 'Duas relações sobre a situação da Índia portuguesa nos anos 1568 e 1569', *Studia*, 8 (1961): 133–220.

_____ 'Matias de Albuquerque, 16º vice-rei da Índia, 1591–1597', *Studia*, 48 (1989): 77–100.

Winius, George D., *The Black Legend of Portuguese India*, New Delhi: Concept Publishing Company, 1985.

_____ 'Jacques de Couttre e o ambiente de Malaca', *Povos e Culturas*, 5, Lisbon, Centro de Estudos de Povos e Culturas de Expressão Portuguesa, 1996, pp. 99–113.

Winstedt, R. O., 'The Genealogy of Malacca's Kings from a copy of the Bustanu's-Salatin', *JSBRAS*, 81 (1920): 39–47.

_____ *A History of Johore*, MBRAS Reprint No. 6, Kuala Lumpur: Malaysian Branch of the Royal Asiatic Society, 1992, pp. 1–226.

_____ (ed.), 'A Malay History of Riau and Johore', *JMBRAS*, 10(2) (1932): 302–320.

_____ 'Outline of a Malay History of Riau', *JMBRAS*, 11(2) (1933): 157–160.

_____ 'Taju's Salatin, The Crown of Kings', *JSBRAS*, 81 (1920): 37–38.

Winstedt, R. O. and P. E. de Josselin de Jong (eds.), 'The Maritime Laws of Malacca', *JMBRAS*, 29(3) (1956): 22–59.

Zainal Abidin Wahid (ed.), *Glimpses of Malaysian History*, Kuala Lumpur: Dewan Bahasa dan Pustaka, 1980.

_____ 'Glimpses of the Malacca Empire' (I and II), in Zainal Abidin Wahid (ed.), *Glimpses of Malaysian History*, Kuala Lumpur: Dewan Bahasa dan Pustaka, 1980, pp.19–23, 24–33.

_____ 'Power and Authority in the Melaka Sultanate: The Traditional View', in K. S. Sandhu and P. Wheatley (eds.), *Melaka: The Transformation of a Malay Capital c.1400–1980*, Kuala Lumpur: Oxford University Press, 1983, vol. 1, pp. 101–112.

Index